THE
EARLY ENGLISH
TRADE UNIONS

THE
EARLY ENGLISH
TRADE UNIONS

Documents from
the Home Office Papers
in the Public Record Office

by

A. ASPINALL

M.A., D.LITT.

Professor of Modern History
in the University of Reading

LONDON
THE BATCHWORTH PRESS

PUBLISHED IN 1949 BY
BATCHWORTH PRESS LTD
20 TUDOR STREET, EC4

PRINTED IN GREAT BRITAIN BY
JAMES UPTON LTD
LONDON AND BIRMINGHAM

CONTENTS

CONTENTS

THE LAST YEARS OF THE COMBINATION ACTS *(contd.)*

1825. The Lancashire cotton spinners and weavers. The colliers in Lancashire and in the Potteries. The Manchester dyers, farriers and shoemakers. The seamen of Sunderland and Scarborough. The cotton spinners of Glasgow. The shipwrights of London. The drafting of the amending Act of 1825

INTRODUCTION

COMPARATIVELY little is known about the history of the English trade unions previously to the repeal of the Combination Laws in 1824. Being illegal, they were necessarily underground organisations. The Home Office papers in the Public Record Office contain extraordinarily few references to them before 1790, but that does not, of course, mean that trade unions were then only just emerging. The fact that, at the end of the eighteenth century there were more than forty[1] Acts of Parliament to prevent workmen from combining, is suggestive both of the widespread existence of trade unions over a long period of years, and of the willingness of the Legislature to support the labour policy of the employers. That policy was, in brief, to suppress combination and to keep down wages — low wages being inevitable because of foreign competition. The workers were quite prepared to accept the regulation of wages by the local Justices of the Peace acting under statutory authorisation, in lieu of the right to raise wages by their own efforts. But *laisser faire* doctrines were gaining popularity both inside and outside Parliament during the last quarter of the century, and were epitomised in the *Report of the House of Commons Committee on the State of the Woollen Manufacture in England* (4 July, 1806), which declared that 'the right of every man to employ the capital he inherits or has acquired, according to his own discretion, without molestation or obstruction, so long as he does not infringe on the rights or property of others, is one of those privileges which the free and happy Constitution of this country has long accustomed every Briton to consider as his birthright.' Parliament was less ready to acknowledge the rights of the workers than to safeguard the interests of the employers, and Adam Smith's view that liberty of combination ought to be recognised by law was not the view of the Legislature before 1824. The various Acts which directed the Justices at the Quarter Sessions to fix wages were repealed in 1813. Lord Sidmouth, the Home Secretary, remarked that, until lately, their very

---

[1] This was Whitbread's estimate (*Parliamentary Register*, lv. 469 [11 February, 1800]).

existence had been unknown 'even to high authorities in the law, as well as to the Committee of the House of Commons which had the subject of wages under their consideration last Session.' He added that if the Act of Queen Elizabeth had remained a dead letter there would have been no necessity to repeal it, but in some instances recently vexatious attempts had been made to use its provisions. He was probably referring to the cotton weavers of Glasgow, who had struck work because their employers had refused to pay the rates of wages fixed by the Justices, and it was this unfortunate incident which apparently caused the Government to get these forgotten Statutes repealed. 'He was satisfied there was no necessity for him to point out to the enlightened minds of their Lordships the pernicious consequences which must result from the operations of Acts of this description.'[1]

The working-class movement for social and political reform which was inspired by the 'Ideas of 1789' and the progress of events in France after the summoning of the States-General, was, perhaps, a more important factor in bringing the existence of trade unions to the notice of the authorities, than the rapid progress of industry and of the factory system of production. The Home Office papers, then, are the most important single source of information about English trade unions during and after the Revolutionary and Napoleonic Wars. Nowhere else can the policy of the Government, the administration of the laws against combination, and the activities of these illegal societies, be conveniently studied in detail.

The most cursory examination of the Statute Book will be sufficient to disprove the statement that the Combination Acts of 1799 and 1800 were the first legal enactments against the right of working men to combine for an increase of wages or a reduction of hours of labour. They were indeed the first Acts to prohibit all combinations whatsoever, but even so, they represented no change of policy on the part of the Government. Combination 'in restraint of trade' had always been an offence indictable as a conspiracy at common law and liable to severe punishment. Various Statutes had made illegal combinations of workmen in specified trades, the maximum penalty for a breach of the law being three months' imprisonment. These Acts were passed at the request of the employers in the trade concerned, and that of 1799 had a similar origin, the master millwrights of London having petitioned Parliament to make illegal the combinations

---

[1] *Parl. Deb.*, xxv. 595 (6 April, 1813.)

of their own journeymen.[1] On 9 April, 1799, Sir John William Anderson, M.P. for the City of London, asked the House of Commons for leave to bring in a Bill, but Wilberforce suggested that, since combinations were 'a general disease in our society' the Bill should be widened in scope so as to make all combinations illegal. The Speaker, however, ruled that a Bill of general application could not be founded on the limited motion before the House. Leave was given to bring in a Bill 'to prevent unlawful combination of workmen employed in the millwright business, and to enable the magistrates to regulate their wages within certain limits.' It was read a first time on 6 May, and a second time four days later.[2] The workmen presented two petitions against it, but on 10 June, the Bill passed the Commons without a division.[3] Sir Francis Burdett opposed the principle of the Bill. 'He thought the existing laws sufficient for every fair and reasonable purpose the framers of the Bill could have in view, and believed that there was seldom a combination of the kind complained of, without a great grievance to provoke it.' He quoted Adam Smith in support of his opinions, and said that 'it was the wise policy of every well regulated State to leave trade of every kind to find its own level.[3] Replying to these observations Anderson suggested that the Baronet would have formed different opinions as to the nature and extent of the combinations had he attended the meetings of the House of Commons' Committee to which the employers' Petition had been referred. Benjamin Hobhouse[4] was the only member to support Burdett.[5]

Wilberforce's suggestion was adopted, and on 17 June the Prime Minister himself asked for and obtained leave to bring in a Bill 'to prevent unlawful combinations of workmen.' Whether Wilberforce, as a highly respected independent member, was put up by Pitt to make the suggestion, we do not know. Nor is it certain whether the existence of a powerful combination of Lancashire cotton weavers, of which the Home Office had been apprised,[6] was the factor which caused the Government to introduce this general measure. The

---

[1] *House of Commons Journals*, liv. 405-6 (5 April, 1799); *Parl. Register*, liii. 323 (9 April, 1799).

[2] *H. of C. J.*, liv. 532.

[3] *Parl. Register*, liii. 687 (10 June, 1799.)

[4] He was the father of Byron's friend John Cam Hobhouse. The Prince Regent made him a Baronet in 1812.

[5] *Parliamentary Register*, liii. 687.

[6] Nos. 23 to 29.

Home Office papers give no alternative clue. Pitt certainly made a special reference in his speech on 17 June to the combinations in the north.[1] The disturbed state of the country at this time may help to account for the Government's attitude : Ministers were clearly afraid of the workmen combining for political purposes too. It is also worth noting that on 6 May, when the millwrights' Bill was read a first time, another Bill to prevent combinations among the Scottish miners was read a second time in the Commons.[2]

The phrase 'to prevent unlawful combinations of workmen' is significant. The Bill did not make illegal what had before been legal ; it was to be a measure of administrative reform, designed to check a growing and illegal practice. Pitt said that he could not 'state particularly the nature of the Bill which he intended to move for leave to bring in, but it would be modelled in some respect on that of the Bill for regulating the conduct of the paper manufacturers.'[3] The more limited measure against the journeymen millwrights was dropped in the House of Lords on 11 July before it has got as far as the second reading.[4]

The new Bill was prepared by the Prime Minister, the Law Officers of the Crown, the Joint Secretary of the Treasury (George Rose), and Charles Bragge (Henry Addington's brother-in-law). It was read a first time in the Commons on 18 June, 1799, and a second time the following day.[5] Opposing the Solicitor-General's motion to go into a Committee of the Whole House (26 June), Hobhouse referred to his earlier speech against the Millwrights' Combination Bill. 'He had at that time, also, observed, that combinations among workmen were more easily broken than combinations among masters, because it could not be long before their finances were exhausted, and then they must apply for employ.' No one who opposed either the Bill of 1799 or that of 1800 did so on the ground that it was wrong to make combinations illegal. Hobhouse, for example, said that the existing law — by which he clearly meant the

---

[1] *The Times*, 18 June 1799. 'These combinations, he observed, existed to a very great degree in the northern parts of the kingdom.' This remark is not to be found in the *Parliamentary Register*.

[2] *House of Commons Journals*, liv. 513 (6 May, 1799). Leave was given to introduce this Bill on 19 April; it passed the Commons on 10 May, and received the royal assent on 21 June.

[3] *Parliamentary Register*, liv. 22 (17 June, 1799).

[4] *House of Lords Journals*, xlii 329.

[5] (*H. of C.J.*, liv. 653). The Bill was presented by George Rose (*Ibid.*, liv. 662).

common law of conspiracy — would have been fully adequate had the Attorney-General 'carried into effect the intention he had announced of bringing in a Bill to render trials for misdemeanours more speedy. Workmen charged with conspiring to raise their wages might put off their trials for six months, or longer.'[1] It was not until 1819, when the Attorney-General, Sir John Scott, had been transformed into Lord Chancellor Eldon, that this useful and practically non-controversial measure of administrative reform was carried : it was one of the much-maligned 'Six Acts.'

Hobhouse failed to arrest the Bill's progress, and the House went into Committee.[2] His chief criticisms of the Bill on points of detail were these : it virtually deprived an accused person of the right of trial by jury ; although 'there was scarcely a single manufacture in the country in which the masters were not guilty of combination,' the journeymen alone were to be imprisoned for breaking the law ; and if the right of trial by jury was to be taken away, two magistrates, not one, should constitute a court of summary jurisdiction. In the Lords the London calico printers were allowed to state a case at the Bar, Mr. Gurney acting for them. Lord Holland was apparently the only peer who opposed the Bill in a set speech, and it was passed on 9 July. It had, therefore, been rushed through Parliament during the last four weeks of the session, and the newspaper reports of the debates were even scantier than usual. The result was that the labourers, mechanics and artificers of Liverpool heard of it only after it had become law, and Petitions to Parliament praying for its repeal had to be deferred until the following year.

These Petitions[3] were discussed by the Commons on 30 June, 1800.[4] Expressing his regret at not having attended to oppose the Bill, Sheridan made a slashing attack on it as 'pregnant with the foulest injustice,' 'replete with the grossest aggressions against the principles of the law of the land and against the rights of the subject,' 'a disgrace to the Statute Book.'[5] But even he expressed no desire to make combinations of workmen legal : he would have been content to see the Act of 1799 repealed, leaving intact earlier Acts 'which experience had proved to be perfectly adequate to the purposes for

---

[1] *Parliamentary Register*, liv. 65 (26 June, 1799).

[2] Several amendments were made in Committee. (*H. of C.J.*, liv. 698 [26 June, 1799].)

[3] *Parliamentary Register*, lvii. 110–12 ; *H. of C. Journals*, iv. 645.

[4] *Parliamentary Register*, lvii. 218–24.

[5] *Ibid.*, p. 219.

which they were intended.' Neither Sheridan nor any of his Whig friends made the slightest attempt to repeal the amending Act of 1800 when they came into office again six years later, nor did they subsequently raise the matter in Parliament during their long period in opposition.

By 30 June, 1800, Pitt had forgotten what were the provisions of the Act of 1799. He would not oppose the introduction of an explanatory and amending Bill, but he would fight tenaciously against absolute repeal.[1] Five members, Sheridan being one, were appointed to prepare an amending Bill,[2] which was hurried through Parliament with the same speed as its predecessor. It was read a second time in the Lords on 28 July, passed through all its remaining stages that day, and received the royal assent on the 29th, when Parliament was prorogued.

To what extent did the amending Act of 1800 (39 and 40 George III, c. 106) meet the criticisms brought against the Combination Act of 1799 (39 George III, c. 81) ? The complaint that the law of the land had been altered by the clause declaring that an accused person might be convicted upon his own confession, was ignored — Pitt pointing out that persons charged with any other offence might be similarly convicted.[3] The Act of 1799 said that one or more Justices were to try offenders. It was very wrong, declared General Tarleton, that a single magistrate should have power to tyrannise over all the workmen in his neighbourhood. In 1800, a concession was made : two or more Justices were to constitute a court of summary jurisdiction. The Petition from the London journeymen asserted that the Act of 1799 'by the use of . . . uncertain terms' had 'created new crimes of boundless extent' — for it was illegal for any person directly or indirectly to attempt to prevail upon any workman to quit his work. Under the Bill, Lord Holland had alleged, 'a person might be prosecuted as concerned in a combination, for merely giving his friendly and well-intended advice' to seek an

---

[1] *Ibid.*, p. 220.

[2] Gascoyne, General Tarleton and the Lord Mayor of London, two of whom had opposed the 1799 Bill, were among the five members. (*Ibid.*, p. 224.) The Bill, therefore, was not a Government Bill. Moreover, on the motion for the third reading of the new Bill in the House of Commons on 22 July, 1800, the Attorney-General spoke strongly in opposition to the clause providing for arbitration by a magistrate between an employer and his workpeople. (*Ibid.*, p. 459.)

[3] *Parliamentary Register*, lvii. 222.

increase in wages.[1] The journeymen of London and Westminster declared, 'It will hereafter be dangerous for the petitioners to converse with one another, or even with their own families.'[2] The third section of the amending Act, however, made only slight changes in the phraseology. Any workman entering into a combination for obtaining higher wages, reducing hours of labour, or decreasing the quantity of his work, should, upon conviction, be imprisoned in the common gaol for a period not exceeding three calendar months, or be committed to a House of Correction, with hard labour, for a maximum period of two months. Any workman who should, by persuasion, solicitation or intimidation *wilfully and maliciously*[3] try to prevent any unemployed person from accepting work, or who should *wilfully and maliciously* attempt to persuade, by influence or intimidation, any person already in employment to quit his work, who should *wilfully and maliciously* prevent any employer from employing such workmen as he thought proper, or anyone who should, *without any just or reasonable cause*, refuse to work with any other employed person, should be similarly punished.

The fourth section of the Act of 1800 meted out the same punishment to persons who should (1) attend a meeting for carrying on any combination ; (2) try to persuade any employed person to attend such meeting ; (3) collect, demand, ask for or receive money in support of a combination ; (4) endeavour, by persuasion or by intimidation, to induce a workman to enter into or be concerned in any combination ; and (5) pay money for the support or encouragement of any illegal meeting or combination.

Section five said that no person, whether employed or not, should *wilfully* pay any money for the support or maintenance of strikers.[4] The penalty was a fine not exceeding £10. Anyone collecting or receiving money for such purpose was to be fined a sum not exceeding £5. To extort money by threats was, of course, a felony. Half the fine was to be given to the informer. By the sixth clause, money already collected for such unlawful purpose before the passing of

---

[1] *Ibid.*, liv. 564.

[2] *Ibid.*, lvii, 111 ; *H. of C. Journals*, lv. 646.

[3] These, and subsequent words in italics were not in the Act of 1799.

[4] This section of the Act was printed and circulated as a handbill headed 'Caution to the Public' by the Manchester magistrates in September, 1818, in reply to the handbill (see illustration opposite page 294) in which the weavers appealed to the public for financial assistance during their strike. See Nos. 294 and 298.

the Act, and remaining undivided for three months, and also money collected after the Bill had received the royal assent, was to be forfeited. The person holding such money should if necessary be sued for it, and half the sum confiscated was to go to the informer. Colonel Gascoyne had suggested in Parliament that the whole of a Friendly Society's funds might be seized in this way if it were proved that a single shilling thereof had ever been given for an unlawful purpose.[1] Pitt, however, declared that this was a misrepresentation : only such money was liable to be forfeited which had been expressly contributed for an unlawful purpose ;[2] and this clause of the 1799 Act remained unaltered.

An appeal from the sentence passed by the Justices to the Court of Quarter Sessions, was allowed by clause 13. The Petition to the House of Commons from Lancashire had complained that the Act of 1799 had allowed no *certiorari* whereby proceedings might be transferred to the Courts at Westminster. This was remedied in 1800. Section 14 of the Act of 1799 had said that any person wishing to appeal against the magistrate's sentence should be required to enter into recognisance with two sufficient sureties in the sum of £20[3] to prosecute the appeal ; and he should be required to pay such costs as the court of appeal might award against him. If such costs were not paid he should be detained in prison until they were. How could poor workmen, asked Lord Holland, ever appeal under these circumstances ? 'It was impossible to suppose they could ever give sureties to that extent, without pre-supposing the existence of a combination for such purpose ?[4]

Sections 16 to 22 of the Act of 1800 were new. No magistrate should function who was also an employer in the trade in which the accused was employed. The seventeenth clause made it illegal for masters to combine for the purpose of reducing wages, increasing or altering the usual hours of labour, or increasing the quantity of work to be done. Employers, however, were not to be imprisoned, but merely fined £20. Should the fine not be paid forthwith, it should be levied by distress and sale of the offender's goods ; only in the unlikely event of the proceeds of the sale proving insufficient was the master to be committed to prison for not more than three

---

[1] *Parliamentary Register*, lvii. 221 (30 June, 1800).

[2] *Ibid.*, p. 222.

[3] This was amended in 1800 in clause 23. The appelant was to find £10, and his two sureties £5 each.

[4] *Parliamentary Register*, liv. 565 (9 July, 1799).

months nor less than two. An employer, unlike a workman, could not be cross-examined on oath.

'And whereas it will be a great convenience and advantage to masters and workmen engaged in manufactures, that a cheap and summary mode be established for settling all disputes that may arise between them respecting wages and work,' clause 18 provided that in cases where masters and men failed to agree about wages or work done, disputes might be settled by arbitration. One arbitrator was to be appointed by the employer, the other by the men, and their award was to be binding on both parties. If the arbitrators failed to agree, or failed to make an award within three days of the dispute being submitted to them, either party to the dispute might require the arbitrators to go before a magistrate forthwith, and the magistrate should himself make the award.

The Act of 1800, though it cannot be compared in point of severity with the 'Gagging Acts' which followed the outbreak of war with Revolutionary France, and of which it really formed part, was, nevertheless, an odious piece of class legislation. The clause prohibiting combinations of employers was very difficult to enforce, and masters hardly made a pretence to obey the law. It was obviously unjust that workmen alone could be cross-examined on oath and sent to prison.

Since men could be prosecuted by indictment at the Quarter Sessions or the Assizes for entering into a combination, and punished much more severely than the Act of 1800 prescribed, why was this Act passed ? In their Petition to Parliament in 1799, the master millwrights had emphasised the point that the existing law was ineffective in suppressing trade unionism. They said that under the existing law workmen could be punished only 'by preferring an indictment at the Sessions or Assizes after the commission of the offence ; but, before that time arrives, the offenders frequently remove into different parts of the country, so that, even if their places of residence should be discovered, it would be a long time before they could be brought to trial, and the expense of apprehending and bringing them back, by *habeas*, to the place where the offence was committed, is so heavy to the masters whose businesses have been stopped by the desertion of the journeymen, that (aware of these difficulties) the journeymen carry on their combinations with boldness and impunity.'[1]

This statement explains too, why the Government did not deal

[1] *H. of C. Journals*, liv. 406 (5 April, 1799).

B

with the situation simply by speeding up the administration of justice at the Assizes as was actually done by the Misdeameanours Act of 1819 — by depriving the accused of his ancient right of traversing, or postponing his trial to the next Assizes.

There was, of course, nothing unprecedented about the procedure actually adopted in 1799 — to extend the summary jurisdiction of the magistrates. As Pitt declared, the Act of 1799 was largely modelled on that of 1796 (36 George III, c. 111)[1] for suppressing combinations among the paper makers. The Act of 1796 had authorised a single magistrate to try offences in a summary way, and to pass sentences of imprisonment with hard labour for a period not exceeding two calendar months.[2] Even in Blackstone's time, when the power of the Justices was less extensive than at the end of the century, it had been enlarged beyond what was considered either politic or just.[3] The right of trial by jury was one of the most cherished privileges of Englishmen, and this right was being invaded. Trial by magistrates, said General Tarleton, was alien to the laws of England.[4]

The purpose of the Act of 1799, then, was not merely to suppress combination, but also, in the words of the Preamble, to bring offenders 'to more speedy and exemplary justice.' Since the maximum sentence which the magistrates could impose was one of three months' imprisonment, and since under the existing law offenders could be transported for seven years,[5] it cannot be maintained that

---

[1] The Preamble to this Act reads : 'Whereas great numbers of journeymen paper makers, in various parts of this kingdom, have lately entered into unlawful meetings and combinations to obtain an unreasonable advance of their wages, and for other illegal purposes, and the laws at present in force against such unlawful conduct have been found to be inadequate to the suppression thereof, whereby it is become necessary that more effectual provision should be made against such unlawful combinations, and for preventing such unlawful practices for the future, and for bringing all offenders . . . to more speedy and exemplary justice . . . '

[2] Similarly, by section 8 of the Treasonable and Seditious Practices Act of 1799 (39 George III, c. 79), one Justice only might summarily try persons accused of unlawful combination and confederacy 'as is in this Act described', and pass a sentence of up to three months' imprisonment or impose a fine of £20.

[3] This was Lord Holland's view (*Parliamentary Register*, liv. 565.)

[4] *Ibid.*, lvii. 223.

[5] Under the Treasonable and Seditious Practices Act of 1799, persons found guilty of unlawful combination, upon indictment, could be sentenced either to seven years' transportation or two years' imprisonment.

the Acts of 1799 and 1800 were unprecedented for their severity.

Pitt's Gagging Acts succeeded in driving underground the working class movement for political reform which the French Revolution had inspired, and the popular Clubs such as the London Corresponding Society, the Constitutional Society, and the Scottish Society of the Friends of the People, as well as the avowedly revolutionary Societies like the United Irishmen and the United Scotchmen, had practically disappeared by the dawn of the new century. Why, then, was the Act of 1800 less successful in putting an end to trade unions ? Why were the employers so mistaken in assuming that only a speeding up in the administration of justice was needed to coerce their workmen into abandoning such nefarious practices ? Why did the employers, in their efforts to suppress combination, often enough have recourse, not to the Act of 1800, but to the common law and the pre-1800 Statute Law which they had so recently declared to be inadequate to deal with a thoroughly menacing situation ?

As early as 1802, the employers in the woollen branch of the textile industry in Yorkshire were thinking of asking Parliament for new laws, and one was actually passed a year later which, applicable to Ireland only, increased the maximum sentence from three to six months' imprisonment, or from two to three months with hard labour.[1] Strikes sometimes went on for months without any attempt at suppression by legal action on the part either of the employers or of the magistrates. The Under-Secretary of State remarked in 1818 that the Act of 1800 seemed to be 'almost a dead letter, while conspiracy is increasing on every side.' The masters, according to Lord Fitzwilliam, had yielded so often that they had lost all authority. 'The journeymen are now masters.'[2] The employers were inclined to maintain that the maximum sentence of three months' imprisonment which a court of summary jurisdiction was empowered to impose, was altogether ineffectual,[3] but in view of the criticism that a cherished privilege was already being disregarded,

---

[1] 43 George III, c. 86. See No. 141n. Because of its backwardness in civilisation and the disaffection of its people, Ireland was always considered to be a special case. The magistrates of Dublin ordered men suspected of having met to form a combination, to be publicly whipped through the streets. This was under the Act 3 George III, c. 34, section 24. (*Fifth Report from Select Committee on Artizans and Machinery*, 1824, p. 467 ; *Parl. Deb.*, New Series, xii, 1310. [29 March, 1825]).

[2] No. 65, p. 64.

[3] A Nottingham magistrate thought so too, in 1814 (No. 153).

Parliament was most unlikely to increase the magistrates' powers. Mr. Norris, the Manchester magistrate, thought that the right of appeal to Quarter Sessions should be abolished : the Combination Act was of very little use.[1] Often enough, employers were afraid to prosecute : to do so would be to incur the certain displeasure of their workmen, and to run a serious risk of injury to their persons and property. Had not one employer's corpse been found floating in a canal ? And were not others assassinated or murderously attacked ? We hear of another who not only had to capitulate to his workmen but also to pay the expenses of their combination.[2] It was believed that the mine-owners at Kingswood connived at the existence of the miners' union, knowing that the additional cost of higher wages could be passed on to the consumer.[3]

The old laws against combination would not have been resorted to had the Act of 1800 succeeded in its aim. Being illegal organisations, trade unions had to try to ensure the loyalty of their officials by the administration of an oath of fidelity and secrecy. This in itself was illegal, and one prosecution of trade unionists in 1803 was under the Act 37 George III, c. 123 'for more effectually preventing the administering or taking of unlawful oaths.'[4] This Act declared unlawful : (1) Societies (except the Masons) whose members took an oath not authorised by law ; (2) Societies any of whose members' names were kept secret from the rest of the members ; and (3) Societies composed of different divisions or branches, with separate officials for each. Prosecutions under this Act, however, were rare because of the difficulty of getting evidence. Other proceedings were started under the Treason and Sedition Act of 1799 (39 George III, c. 79), and in 1811 some of the Nottinghamshire magistrates inquired whether this Act could be invoked against the frame-work knitters.[5]

Most prosecutions, however, were instituted either under the Combination Act of 1800 or the common law, and Joseph Hume said in 1825, that those which flowed from the common law were ten times as oppressive as those which sprang from the statute law.[6] The securing of speedy convictions seems to have been the main object

[1] No. 253.
[2] Nos. 75, 102, 150.
[3] No. 7.
[4] No. 55, pp. 50–1.
[5] Nos. 75, 112.
[6] *Parl. Deb.*, New Series, xii. 1302 (29 March, 1825).

when proceedings were started under the Act of 1800. When work-men were committed for trial, either they were the leading members of the Union, or they were charged with more serious offences arising out of combination. Crimes of violence were the inevitable result of the action taken by employers to break a strike by using blackleg labour, and of the failure of strikers to get united action in support of their claims. But severe punishments were not invariably imposed even when prosecution by indictment was resorted to. Baron Richards, for example, took a lenient view in March, 1819, when several cotton spinners were tried at Lancaster Assizes for con-spiracy : they were merely bound over in the sum of £20 each.[1]

Although the magistrates naturally tended to take the side of the employers, they were not invariably hostile to the workers. Had they been so they would have shown a greater disposition to suppress trade unionism. They often enough did their best to stand aside from trade disputes, and consequently earned the reproaches of the masters. The strike of the Manchester cotton spinners in the summer of 1818 had lasted for several weeks before the magistrates men-tioned it to the Home Office.[2] Almost ostentatiously they ignored the dispute, leaving it to the employers to take what action they chose under the Combination Law.[3] Their sole object, they said, was to preserve the public peace.[4] Mr. Norris, the magistrate, re-gretted that the demands of the weavers were not conceded, said that the men had been very temperate in their manner of asking for a wage increase, and declared that public opinion was certainly in their favour.[5] Mr. Chippindale, Colonel Fletcher's agent who watched the Oldham district, strongly sympathised with the cotton weavers, and disapproved the conduct of the masters.[6] Similarly in Scotland, the Sheriff-substitute of Renfrewshire said that it was not customary for the Justices to take proceedings against trade unionists except when their actions endangered the public peace.[7] Sometimes, on the other hand, the magistrates would have taken action against strike leaders had the necessary evidence been avail-able. Rowland Burdon, who was a member of Parliament, planned

[1] *Macclesfield Courier*, 3 April, 1819.
[2] No. 233.
[3] No. 234.
[4] No. 236n (p. 259).
[5] No. 238.
[6] No. 232, p. 252.
[7] *Report of Select Committee on Combinations*, 1825, p. 318. And see p. 65.

to avoid further disputes between the Tyneside shipowners and the seamen by means of an Act of Parliament which would appoint a tribunal consisting of representatives of both sides, empowered to fix wages annually and settle all disputes.[1] His plan was doubtless impracticable, but it does reveal his synpathy for the workers.

And what of the attitude of the Government ? Living under the shadow of the French Revolution, the statesmen of the time held exaggerated fears of a revolution in England too, and in the circumstances it was inevitable that a policy of repression should be pursued. Trade unions, as illegal organisations, must be suppressed, and breaches of the law punished, but the Home Office was not indisposed to attend to the complaints of the workers when these complaints were believed to be reasonable. The official view was that the employers themselves must undertake prosecutions of their workmen, and assistance from London must not be looked for. 'Whatever may be the merits of the matter in dispute between the master and the workmen, the public peace must be preserved. Were the demands on either side just and reasonable, the law could not suffer them to be enforced by violence and outrage.' These words, actually written by Lord Melbourne in 1830, might have come from any Home Secretary of the period.[2] The Attorney-General found the problem of combination a baffling one. 'These combinations are mischievous and dangerous, but it is very difficult to know how to deal with them.'[3] By the autumn of 1814, Lord Sidmouth had come to the conclusion that the whole question would have to be reconsidered by Parliament,[4] but the Law Officers of the Crown were confident that Parliament would be disinclined to increase the punishment prescribed by the Act of 1800.[5] Nor could they accept the suggestion that the strict rules of evidence should be relaxed in order the more easily to secure convictions. 'We are of opinion that the law, as it stands at present, would be found sufficient, if duly enforced.'[6] It was precisely on this ground, too, that the Whig Opposition in Parliament criticised the Government's policy in

[1] No. 19.

[2] Melbourne to Major-General Sir H. Bouverie (at Manchester), 9 December, 1830 (H.O. 41/8/451–2).

[3] No. 135.

[4] No. 164.

[5] Nos. 184, 186.

[6] No. 186.   And see No. 340.

1817 and 1819 in asking for new laws to suppress the Radical agitation in the country.

Both the Government and the employers were all too conscious of
the fact that in seeking to suppress combination they were fighting
a losing battle : as they were, too, in seeking, by means of severe
laws and punitive taxation, to prevent political information from
reaching the masses through the medium of popular newspapers.
Propaganda through the Press, through public meetings and through
the various Radical Reformist Societies which re-emerged during the
last years of the Napoleonic War, was powerfully contributing to
increase the political consciousness of the working class. The great
improvement of the postal service after 1784, and the multiplication
of accelerated stage coaches, enabled the trade unions in time to
organise themselves on something wider than a merely local basis ;
and in an effort to destroy this new advantage the Home Secretary
sometimes instructed local postmasters to stop all letters addressed
to suspected members of these illegal organisations. The evidence
given before the Select Committee of 1825 on the Combination Laws
shows that Freemasonry, with its signs, passwords and oaths of
fidelity,[1] familiarised trade unionists with the idea of organising
themselves as a secret society[1]; and so did the Radical Societies like
the United Irishmen and the London Corresponding Society.[2] The
Methodist movement, together with these democratic Societies,
acquainted trade unionists with the ideas of representation, delegation and federation.[3] The street processions, with banners and

---

[1] *Report of Select Committee on Combinations*, 1825, p. 76.

[2] Just as to-day strikes are often attributed to communist activities, so a
hundred and fifty years ago they were believed to be the work of Radical
agitators. The democrats who infiltrated into the Lancashire textile unions
were active in denouncing the war, and the reactionary Government as the
cause of it. The arrest of some of these agitators in 1801 encouraged several
large-scale manufacturers in Lancashire 'to examine into the political opinions
of their workmen' and to dismiss such as were known to be Jacobins — just
as to-day the Government institutes inquiries into the political opinions of
civil servants in confidential positions with the view of weeding out avowed
Communists. Colonel Fletcher, himself an employer, suggested that this
procedure, if generally adopted, would be most efficacious in checking subversive political opinions (To the Duke of Portland, 6 June, 1801. [H.O.
42/62].) The secret agents whom he employed in his magisterial capacity, he
was apt to refer to as his 'missionaries' (e.g. to Beckett, 18 March, 1815. [H.O.
42/143]).

[3] The words of the Preamble to the Treasonable and Seditious Practices
[*Continued on p.* **xxiv**]

musical accompaniments, which were such striking features of the Radical demonstrations which shook the country in 1819, were ideas of which trade unionists themselves often made use during their turn-outs. To the public-house, too, they owed something. However much the temperance party might denounce the public-house as an agency of social degradation ; however much frightened Tories might dislike it as a place where the lower orders talked sedition and voiced their discontent, it was immensely useful as a meeting-place when trade unions were under the ban of the law. Exasperated employers were for ever calling upon the authorities to punish publicans extending their hospitality to trade union meetings by depriving them of their licenses,[4] just as reactionary Tories, fearful of the progress of Jacobinism demanded that inn-keepers should be similarly treated who took in 'seditious' news-papers and pamphlets for the benefit of their customers. But even Lord Sidmouth thought it inexpedient to ask Parliament for authority to abate this nuisance — pointing out that if new meas-ures drove trade union meetings away from the public-house to a private dwelling, it would be much more difficult to procure information about them.[5]

Finally, the trade unions owed something to the Benefit Clubs which, formed under the protection of the law to provide working men with a modest maintenance whilst in sickness, grew steadily in number until by 1816 they had about 700,000 members in England.[6] The Unions could easily shelter under the title of Friendly Societies, and hold their meetings under cover of the rules allowed to these Clubs in pursuance of the Friendly Societies Acts. There was,

[Continued from p. xxiii]
Act might appropriately have been applied to a trade union : 'Many of such Societies [i.e., the London Corresponding Society, the United Irishmen, &c.] are composed of different divisions, branches or parts, which communicate with each other by secretaries, delegates, or otherwise, and by means thereof maintain an influence over large bodies of men, and delude many ignorant and unwary persons into the commission of acts highly criminal.'

[4] Section 14 of the Treasonable and Seditious Practices Act of 1799 said that the magistrates might deprive a publican of his license who allowed his premises to be used by any Society declared by the Act to be an unlawful combination.

[5] No. 156. The landlord of a public-house in Yorkshire was once sent to prison for three months, and fined five pounds for allowing a trade union committee meeting to be held on his premises (*Fifth Report from Select Committee on Artizans and Machinery*, 1824, p. 406.)

[6] Smart, *Economic Annals of the Nineteenth Century*, i. 505.

too, reason to believe that even when a trade union was not disguised as a Benefit Club, it obtained financial assistance from this source during a turn-out.

In many ways Peel was an excellent reforming Home Secretary, an immense improvement on his predecessor. And Huskisson, his colleague at the Board of Trade, said in 1825 that he himself had always advocated the principle of allowing every man to dispose of his labour to the best advantage, and that he considered many of the combination laws oppressive and cruel.[1] Yet both these eminent statesmen left it to members of the Opposition to take the initiative in raising the question of repeal in Parliament. On the other hand, the debates which followed showed that it was no party question. By 1824, members on all sides had become convinced that the combination laws had not only failed in their object but had dangerously antagonised the working class. Many even of the employers now felt that the attempts at suppression had done more harm than good, and that wages should be regulated by the market price for labour. All the other great reforms of the period — the abolition of the slave trade, catholic emancipation, the repeal of the Test and Corporation Acts, the Reform Act of 1832, and the abolition of slavery itself — were preceded by periods of agitation outside Parliament conducted through the Press and public meetings. But the repeal of the combination laws was mainly the work of one man, the famous Radical tailor of Charing Cross,[2] though even Francis Place's efforts would have failed had not the *laisser faire* ideas embodied in the *Wealth of Nations* gradually found acceptance by the governing class. He helped to form public opinion by contributing articles on the subject to provincial newspapers, and by organising Petitions to Parliament. He prevailed on Joseph Hume to assume the parliamentary leadership of the cause, but 1819 was not a good year in which to raise questions of that kind, because the Government was alarmed at the Radical demonstrations in the country. In the House of Commons, Hume was supported, not by the old Whigs, but by new members such as Edward Ellice and William Williams. The question was dropped until 1823, when on 3 March, Peter Moore moved for leave to bring in a curiously assorted Bill which, among other things, would repeal the combination laws.[3] Huskisson asked him to postpone it so that the House could

[1] *Parl. Deb.*, New Series, xii. 1288. (29 March, 1825).
[2] Graham Wallas, *Life of Francis Place*, ch. viii.
[3] *Parl. Deb.*, New Series, viii. 366 (3 March, 1823.)

consider its contents at leisure.[1] The employers petitioned against it and it was abandoned. At the end of the session, Hume gave notice of his intention to bring the question forward, and on 12 February, 1824, he rose to fulfil his pledge. A Select Committee of the House was appointed to inquire into the combination laws, and also into the laws relating to the emigration of artisans and the exportation of machinery. Saying that they had greatly aggravated the evil they were intended to remove, the President of the Board of Trade supported the motion. 'It was no slight objection to those laws,' he added, 'that they created between the employer and the employed, relations diametrically opposite to those which ought to exist, for they created jealousy, ill-will and discontent, instead of that feeling of goodwill that was calculated to make each party stand by the other in any period of mutual distress.' 'To remove from the Statute Book some laws which were too oppressive to be executed, and others which it was impossible to execute — he thought that this inquiry ought to be instituted.'[2] It was a system, said Charles Grant, the Vice-President of the Board of Trade, 'of terror and compulsion.'[3]

For the customary Report to the House, the Select Committee substituted a series of Resolutions. They declared that the existing laws had been systematically violated and had resulted in serious breaches of the peace and acts of violence ; that employers too had often united for the purpose of reducing wages and regulating hours of labour ; that many workmen had suffered inprisonment, but that no instance had come to light of a master being punished for breaking the law, though several had been prosecuted, and that both employers and men considered that the Acts tended to produce mutual irritation and to make combination highly dangerous to the public peace.

The Committee make the following recommendations :

1. That the Statute Laws[4] which prohibited combination should be repealed, and that the common law, under which a peaceable meeting either of masters or of workmen might be prosecuted as a conspiracy, should be altered.

[1] *Parl. Deb.* New Series, viii, 366 (3 March 1823)

[2] *Ibid.*, x. 149 (12 February, 1824). For the extraordinary complexities of the law, so far as Scotland was concerned, see *Edinburgh Review*, January, 1824, pp. 336–40 ; also *Fifth Report of Select Committee on Combinations*, 1824, pp. 484–99.

[3] *Ibid.*, xii. 1312 (29 March, 1825).

[4] Thirty-five are specifically mentioned in clause 1 as being repealed.

2. That the practice of settling disputes by arbitration, since it had produced good results, should be continued, and that the laws regulating arbitration should be consolidated and made applicable to all trades.

3. That it was absolutely necessary to enact such a law as might, by summary process, punish either masters or workmen who by threats, intimidation or acts of violence, should interfere with that freedom which ought to be allowed to each party, of employing his labour or capital in the manner he might deem most advantageous.[1]

A Bill was brought in by Hume on 27 May which more or less embodied these Resolutions, and he hurried it through the Commons at top speed to avoid inconvenient discussion of its controversial clauses. It passed the Commons on 5 June, was read a first time in the Lords four days later, and received the royal assent on the 21st. So little was it noticed out-of-doors that, several weeks after it had become law, some Lancashire magistrates unwittingly sentenced certain cotton weavers for combination.[2] Later, the Prime Minister declared that he was unaware of its nature, and that he would certainly have opposed it had he known what it contained.[3]

The first clause repealed, either in whole or in part, 35 Acts of Parliament respecting combinations, 'together with all other laws . . . now in force . . . relative to combinations.' The next said that workmen should not be liable to indictment or prosecution for conspiracy or combination, or to any other punishment whatever, under the common law or the statute law, who entered into a combination : (1) to fix rates of wages and alter hours of labour ; (2) to induce workmen to quit or refuse work ; (3) 'to regulate the mode of carrying on any manufacture, trade or business, or the management thereof.' So not merely the statute law but the common law of conspiracy too, was repealed. The common law could no longer be applied except where a breach of the peace had acutally occurred.[4]

Section five said that persons should be sent to prison for two months if they employed violence, threats or intimidation : (1) to prevent a man from working or from accepting work ; (2) towards anyone who failed to obey the Rules of the Union ; (3) in order to force an employer to alter the methods of conducting his business. And section 6 said that persons should be similarly punished who

[1] *Parl. Deb.*, New Series, xi. 812–13.
[2] S. and B. Webb, *History of Trade Unionism*, p. 103 (1920).
[3] *Parl. Deb.*, New Series, xiii. 1478 (4 July, 1825).
[4] *Ibid.*, xiii, 368 (4 May, 1825).

combined to effect any of these objects — 'provided always that
nothing herein contained shall alter . . . any law now in force for the
prosecution and punishment of the said offences.'

Trade and industry were flourishing in 1824. The workers naturally tried to enforce their claim to a share of their employers' prosperity. In any case, as Francis Place said, they had convinced
themselves that the combination laws were chiefly responsible for
low wages, and believed that repeal would be followed suddenly by
a great rise.[1] Now that they were no longer under the ban of the
law, trade unions sprang up everywhere, thus confounding Place's
confident prediction that repeal would lead to their disappearance.[2]
There was an epidemic of strikes which quickly alarmed not only
the masters but the Government. It disquieted, too, the best friends
of the workers, and, at Place's instigation, Joseph Hume himself
sent the strikers several warning letters. 'I should be very un-
candid,' he told the Manchester cotton spinners in December, 'if I
did not inform you that, unless the operatives act in a manner more
moderate and prudent than they have done in some parts of the
country, I fear that many members of the House of Commons may
be disposed to re-enact the laws that they have repealed.' The trade
unionists were 'estranging their best friends, and generally raising
the community against them.' These warnings went unheeded, and
several months later (26 March, 1825), Hume wrote again, this time
to the shipwrights of Dundee : 'I am quite certain that if the operatives do not act with more temper, moderation and prudence than
they are now doing, the Legislature will be obliged to retrace its
steps, and to adopt measures to check unreasonable proceedings and
exorbitant demands, too often accompanied with violence.'[3]

There can be no question as to the gravity of the crimes that
were now being committed, the victims being workers who refused to
join the unions, blacklegs whom employers brought in to break a
strike. At least two such people were murdered in Dublin ; a Stirlingshire miner was almost beaten to death ; and between seventy and
eighty people in Ireland were wounded, over thirty of them having
their skulls fractured. Cases of vitriol throwing had started in Scotland
at least as early as 1820, and several people were dreadfully
burnt and blinded for life. No convictions followed, for it was

[1] Graham Wallas, *Life of Place*, p. 214.
[2] *Ibid.*, p. 217.
[3] *Parl. Deb.*, New Series, xiii. 1463 (30 June, 1825) ; Smart, *Economic Annals of the Nineteenth Century*, ii. 232–33.

impossible for the victims, assaulted as they were in the darkness, to identify their assailants.[1]

In other ways the workers were abusing their new freedom. One miners' union in Scotland had a rule that no one coming into their district should be allowed to work as a miner until he had paid five pounds to the union funds. The officials were required by the rules 'to point out the masters they dislike,' 'to warn such masters of the danger in which they are placed in consequence of this combination,' and 'to try everything which prudence might dictate to put them out of the trade.' The employers were not to be allowed to have stocks of coal on hand — otherwise they would be less dependent on their workmen. These employers were not allowed to employ non-unionists. One of the seamen's unions, too, said that their members working in the coasting trade might not put to sea unless every member of the crew was a member of the union. It was reported that a ship laden with coal had recently gone aground in the Thames estuary, but it was against the rules of the union for the men to save the boat by heaving the cargo overboard. Two other ships came to the assistance of the stranded vessel, and the owners had to pay £200 salvage money. The union committee of journeymen shipwrights on the Thames dictated to the employers how many men they should employ. When this committee sent four or five journeymen to a certain yard and ordered the employer to find them work, the foreman protested that there were no vacancies, and all the men in that yard immediately went on strike. The unions also tried to dictate to the employers whether they should take any apprentices or not. Even Joseph Hume condemned this practice as violating the principle of that freedom of action which the workers themselves had demanded and gained. Some coal miners would not allow their employer to take on anyone who had not been a miner from the age of sixteen. A foreman who was not agreeable to the men would have to be dismissed.[2]

These murders, attempted murders, the violation of the rights of non-unionists, and the unwarrantable interference with the employers in the conducting of their business, soon provoked the renewed interference of the Legislature, and on 29 March, 1825, Huskisson moved for the appointment of a Select Committee to

[1] *Ibid.*, xii. 1307 ; xiii. 360, 1401 ; *Report of Select Committee on Combinations*, 1825, pp. 20, 320, 323, and *passim*.

[2] *Parl. Deb.*, New Series, xii. 1294, 1297, 1307 ; xiii. 358, 372 ; *Report of Select Committee on Combinations*, 1825, pp. 16, 95, 327–28, and *passim*.

inquire into the working of the Act of 1824. He admitted that when the 1824 Bill was before the House, he had not examined it with sufficient care. The Committee was appointed ; it reported in June, and on the 16th leave was given to Peel, Huskisson and Wallace to introduce an amending Bill. It passed the Commons on the 30th, and, after a rapid passage through the Lords, it received the royal assent on 6 July. In the words of the Preamble, it made 'further provision, as well for the security and personal freedom of individual workmen in the disposal of their skill and labour, as for the security of the property and persons of masters and employers.' It said that persons should be sent to prison for a term not exceeding three months who, by violence, threats or intimidation, or by molesting or in any way obstructing another person, should : (1) force or endeavour to force that person to quit or refuse work ; (2) force or endeavour to force men to belong to a union, to contribute to its funds, or to pay any fine or penalty which the union might exact ; (3) force or endeavour to force an employer to alter the mode of carrying on his business, or to limit either the number of his apprentices or the number or description of his workmen. No persons should be subject to punishment who should meet together for the sole purpose of consulting upon and determining questions of wages and hours of labour. In cases of combination, where it was extraordinarily difficult to get evidence, it was now felt that one credible witness might be competent legal testimony : the Act of 1824 had permitted a conviction only upon the evidence of two. An appeal to Quarter Sessions against the magistrates' sentence was allowed.

It would be going too far to say that the Act of 1825 allowed the trade unions only a bare existence. The recognition for the first time of the right of collective bargaining and of the right to strike was an important concession. It was no longer illegal to levy or pay contributions on a voluntary basis to enable a trade union, and strike action, to be carried on. It was no longer illegal to solicit people for money so long as threats, intimidation and violence were avoided. Francis Place himself said that 'no fundamental alteration' was made in any clauses of the Act of 1824, 'and very few were altered at all.' 'The law is, however, less precise.'

Supporting the new restrictions imposed in 1825, with the view of protecting the rights of employers and non-unionists, Lord Lansdowne declared 'that no manufacture could be carried on if workmen could dictate to the masters who should be employed, and prevent men from exercising their right of labouring on whatever terms they might please.'[1] This, he added, was what never could be tolerated in a free country. Since 1825, that which Lansdowne thought to be incompatible with freedom has come to pass. 'The men are masters now.' Lord Fitzwilliam's remark was hardly true when he made it in 1802,[2] and it would hardly have been true to-day but for the Act of 1825, the starting-point of a great new development in the history of English trade unions.

It is my pleasant duty to thank Mr. C. Nowell, the Manchester City Librarian, and Mr. F. Worthington, the General Secretary of the Felt Hatters and Trimmers Unions of Great Britain, for their kindness in sending me explanations of a few trade union terms used locally in South-East Lancashire.[3] I should also like to thank the officials of the Public Record Office for their unvarying courtesy and helpfulness.

November, 1948.

---

[1] *Parl. Deb.*, New Series, xiii. 1479 (4 July, 1825).
[2] No. 65, p. 64.
[3] No. 103.

I. BEFORE THE COMBINATION LAWS (1791–1799).

1791. The spirit of combination in Lancashire.
1792. The Liverpool carpenters and the Lancashire miners. Combinations in Sheffield. The Gloucestershire miners. The seamen of Norfolk, Tynemouth and Aberdeen.
1793. The scythemakers and the shag weavers.
1799. The Lancashire cotton weavers.

(1). *Thomas B. Bayley, J.P., and Henry Norris, J.P., to Henry Dundas*[1]

Hope, near Manchester, Tuesday evening, 19 *July,* 1791.

. . . The trade of this County is wonderfully prosperous. It produces its attendant evils ; amongst those I include a very numerous and *foreign* population (especially from Ireland), estranged, unconnected, and in general composed of persons who are in a species of exile. These men are full of money from the high rate of wages, and are frequently filled with liquor, and engaged in very *desperate* affrays. We have also now a very general spirit of combination amongst all sorts of labourers and artisans, who are in a state of disaffection to all legal control. The introduction of machinery to abridge labour in weaving, is also a subject, at this time, of peculiar disgust and jealousy. And, I fear, the example of Birmingham,[2] and an unhappy party spirit about the Revolution in France, heightened by the meetings on the 14th instant[3] (which I believe none of the magistrates in this County *approved, countenanced* or *attended*) has added to the general ill-humour and may be a pretext for mischief and outrage . . . (H.O.42/19).

[1] Home Secretary, June 1791–July 1794.
[2] Attacks on the houses of Dr. Priestley, the famous scientist, and other leading Nonconformist reformers were organised on the night of the 14th by a ' Church and King ' mob.
[3] The anniversary of the fall of the Bastille, an event widely celebrated by the English reformers.

I

C

(2). *Henry Blundell (Mayor of Liverpool) to William Pitt*

Liverpool, 14 April, 1792.

I am well informed the journeymen carpenters of this town (and who are a very powerful body of men) had a meeting of some of the heads of them on Saturday evening last, and were heard to say that if the abolition of the slave trade takes place, some houses in the town (which they had marked) should be pulled down.[1] As Chief Magistrate of this great trading town, I conceive it my duty to apprise you of it, and though I do not (I confess) apprehend much danger myself (having the 30th Regiment of Foot here) yet with submission, Sir, to yourself (and his Majesty's service will admit of it) I should recommend three troops of horse to be quartered in the neighbourhood till the present ferment subsides a little . . . It is proper also to inform you that these men have it in agitation to leave their work for the purpose of advancing their wages, and it is daily expected, for it has been long threatened. (H.O.42/20).

(3). *Henry Blundell to Henry Dundas*

Liverpool, 27 May, 1792.

I was informed yesterday afternoon that the great body of carpenters intended to leave their work on Monday morning unless their wages were advanced. I immediately sent to three of them to call upon me, that I wished to speak to them. They came. And in a conversation of some length they told me it was their intention to ask an advance of 4d. per day, but that they should request it civilly and obtain it peaceably or relinquish it ; and I might depend upon it, they would give me no trouble : they would not disturb the peace of the town, and I verily believe they will not. Yet it may not be quite prudent to rely upon this assurance, and perhaps you will be so good, Sir, as to order one of the troops of Grays, which are now at Manchester, into Warrington . . .

There seems too general an appearance of discontent amongst all artificers and labourers, which must if possible be prevented spreading into tumult. Annexed is the copy of a note I have this moment received, which comes from a large body of men, and we

---

[1] The prosperity of Liverpool as well as of Bristol had been to a considerable extent based on the slave trade, which was not abolished until 1807.

must either comply with this demand or be guarded against the consequences. The other owners of collieries and flats[1] in this neighbourhood have received the like notice.

[Enclosure unsigned].

Liverpool, 26 May, 1792 (Copy).

The masters of the coal flats in your employ do hereby give notice that they will not proceed in the said flats after the 9th day of June next ensuing, under one shilling per ton per trip—which they hope you will agree and consent to give without any stop being put to the said business as we are determined not to proceed under that price from that date. (H.O.42/20).

(4). *Henry Dundas to Henry Blundell*

Whitehall, 30 May, 1792.

I have been favoured with your letter of the 27th inst., giving an account of the combinations which have taken place among the carpenters and masters of the coal flats at Liverpool for the purpose of obtaining an advance of wages, and of your proceedings in consequence.

Although there may not be any immediate disposition to riot among these people, it appears from your representation to be extremely necessary that you should be watchful over their conduct, and that you should pursue every legal and constitutional means of suppressing such combinations and of bringing the ringleaders to punishment. From the disposition which has recently been shown by a certain class of people at Manchester, it is not conceived to be advisable at this moment to remove any part of the troops now stationed there from thence unless in a case of absolute necessity, and if such necessity should hereafter exist, of which you must of course be the most competent judge, the Commanding Officer at that place will have instructions to comply with any requisition from you for a detachment from the forces under his orders. (H.O.43/4/21-2).

---

[1] Flat bottomed boats generally used in river navigation.

(5). *Henry Blundell to Henry Dundas*

Liverpool, 5 June, 1792.

. . . It gives me much pleasure to inform you that there has been no disturbance whatever, and not more than one day's interruption to business, the merchants having agreed in part to the requisition of the carpenters. The flatmen are still off, but I apprehend they will return to their labour before the end of the week . . . (H.O.42/20).

(6). *Colonel De Lancey[1] (Deputy Adjutant-General) to ? the Secretary at War*

Hertford Street, 13 June, 1792. (Private) (Copy).
[At Sheffield] . . . I found that the seditious doctrines of Paine[2] and the factious people who are endeavouring to disturb the peace of the country, had extended to a degree very much beyond my conception; and indeed they seem with great judgement to have chosen this as the centre of all their seditious machinations, for the manufactures of this town are of a nature to require so little capital to carry them on, that a man with a very small sum of money can employ two, three or four men ; and this being generally the case, there are not in this, as in other great towns, any number of persons of sufficient weight who could by their influence, or the number of their dependents, act with any effect in case of a disturbance. And as the wages given to the journeymen are very high, it is pretty generally the practice for them to work for three days, in which they earn sufficient to enable them to drink and riot for the rest of the week, consequently no place can be more fit for seditious purposes.

The mode they have adopted for spreading their licentious principles has been by forming Associations on terms suited to the circumstances of the lowest mechanics, of whom about 2,500 are enrolled in the principal Society, and that it may not be confined, they allow any man to be present who will pay 6d. for admission.

---

[1] He had been ordered by the Secretary at War to make a tour of inspection through the quarters of various Regiments in order to find out the real state and disposition of the troops, and how far they were to be depended upon in emergency.

[2] Thomas Paine (1737–1809), author of *The Rights of Man*.

4

Here they read the most violent publications, and comment on them, as well as on their correspondence not only with the dependent Societies in the towns and villages in the vicinity, but with those established in other parts of the kingdom . . .

In the town itself there is no civil power. An establishment called the Cutlers' Company, whose authority extends (at least as far as it used at present [*sic*]) to regulating some part of the manufactures, is the only thing that exists like a resident jurisdiction. Two Justices of the Peace have been in the habit of coming once a fortnight to settle any differences that may arise, one of whom has a house within a short distance, the other lives about fourteen miles from the town, but both of them are out of the country at present, and indeed the one who lives nearest the town, and whose situation might enable him to be of use, having made some efforts during the riots last year relative to some enclosures, the populace burned a part of his property, and since that time he has been very little in the country. The other magistrates to whom they look for assistance are none nearer than ten miles, and on them little reliance can be placed, so that in case of any emergency the town must suffer materially before any assistance from the civil power could be obtained . . .

As a proof of the little opposition given by the magistrates and others to the unreasonable demands of the populace, I beg leave to instance a circumstance which happened while I was at Sheffield. The colliers belonging to the Duke of Norfolk, on whom the town and its manufactures are dependent, refused to work unless their wages were raised, in consequence of which, application was made to a magistrate to interfere, but he did not choose to do it, saying he was under the necessity of leaving the country. Recourse was therefore had to the master cutler, as being most interested, but he also refused to act, in consequence of which their wages have been raised, and it must ultimately increase the price of coals and consequently the manufactures throughout the town.

I was curious to know whether these people had real cause for their discontent, and was told they could earn from 3s. to 4s. 6d. a day. It therefore shows the unruly spirit of the people, and the little check given to it by the civil power, and so frequent are those combinations on the part of the manufacturers, that ultimately they must very materially hurt the trade of the place by enabling other countries to undersell them, for even at present, while the peace of the Continent is so much disturbed, the manufactures of Sheffield are

5

sold there at the prices given to the manufacturer, the merchant confining his profits solely to what he gains on the raw materials . . . (H.O.42/20).

(7). *Captain George Monro to ? Henry Dundas*

Bristol, 9 August, 1792.

. . . On Monday morning a large body of colliers who work in the mines in the neighbourhood of this City, encouraged, as is supposed, by the success of the shoemakers and other tradesmen who in this place lately stood out for an increase of wages, assembled, and in a peremptory manner demanded of their employers an addition of 2s. per week (their former wages was equal to 13s. per week). This demand not being complied with, they proceeded to the different Works in Kingswood, and prevailed on all the miners to join their party so as to enable them to compel all the others within six or eight miles of this city to concur in the same unlawful combination, and their success has been equal to their most sanguine expectation. They have hitherto met with no opposition from the magistrates of the County of Gloucester, nor has the Corporation of this city apparently taken any measures to counteract this alarming combination, which in its consequence to the manufacturing part of the inhabitants may be very serious indeed. It is supposed that the proprietors of these mines connive at this combination in order to have a pretence to raise the price of coals ; whether this rumour is well founded or not is immaterial, but if the parties succeed, the consequence to this city will really be alarming. Very numerous and extensive glass houses, very large copper Works, lead Works, distilleries and other concerns that consume immense quantities of coal, must of course feel a serious inconvenience, and perhaps a total suspension of their business, as a speedy nor indeed an effectual supply cannot be expected from Swansea or the Forest of Dean, the inland duty of 5s. per chaldron amounting nearly to a prohibition. One glass house will stop work this morning, and as the colliers will suffer no coal to be brought into the city, three more will stop on Monday should this combination continue. The house that will stop this morning employs near 200 people, and the glass business is so managed in this city that at least one half of these people, whether employed or not, receive wages nearly equal to at least £100 per week. I am just now informed that the Gloucester colliers to the amount of about 2,000 passed through the city this morning on their way to the pits at Bedminster, Ashton and Nailsea in Somersetshire to persuade or if necessary to compel the miners at these pits to leave off working and join their confederacy. They behaved very orderly, but said they were determined to carry their point.

On further inquiry the advance is not so unreasonable as I at first thought it. I find the most they get, except they work extra hours, is only 10s. per week. The people of Bristol are in continual fear of their committing some excess in the city, but further than stopping the coals nothing of that kind has as yet happened . . . (H.O.42/22).

(8). *Henry Blundell to Henry Dundas*

Liverpool, 1 October, 1792.
The agents from the extensive collieries in the neighbourhood of Wigan (and on which the town depends for its fuel) came this evening with the news of the colliers having left their work and collected in a riotous manner to the number of near 500 ; and had been with them thus assembled to demand an extravagant advance of wages. They have given them only till tomorrow at 3 o'clock to consider of it, and if their demand is not complied with, they threaten to destroy the Works by pulling up the engines, throwing down the wheels and filling up the pits. The consequences to the coal proprietors would be very serious and to the country in general, if this combination is not immediately suppressed . . .

I am requested by the coalowners who are now with me, to entreat of you to give orders to Major Campbell and the Commanding Officer at Manchester to march part of their men to Wigan in aid of the magistrates . . . (H.O.42/22).

(9). *Henry Dundas to Henry Blundell*

Whitehall, 3 October, 1792.
1 have this moment been favoured with your letter of the 1st inst . . . I have desired that instructions may be immediately sent to Major Campbell to give every assistance in his power to the civil magistrates in preventing any mischief.

These combinations have of late become so frequent that it requires a more than ordinary exertion of the civil power to suppress them, and in order to effect it, they ought to enforce a rigid execution of the law against those on whom it can clearly attach. (H.O.43/4/106).

(10). *Henry Blundell to Henry Dundas*

Liverpool, 3 October, 1792.

I returned this morning from Wigan . . . Our grand object is to save our steam engines for drawing the water.

No material mischief had been done last night, but they threatened much for to-day if their terms were not complied with. A good collier and his drawer can at present earn from 5s. to 8s. per day between them, and if we were to comply with their demand, the advance would be near 2s. per day more . . .

P.S.—This moment Mr. Blackburn informs me that the people at his collieries have quitted their work . . . (H.O.42/22).

(11). *Henry Blundell to Henry Dundas*

Liverpool, 7 October, 1792.

. . . I returned from the collieries last night and have the pleasure to inform you, Sir, that the appearance of assistance from the military has had the very best effect ; the mob are dispersed, and the people began to return yesterday morning to their work, and I am in hopes to-morrow the principal part of the works will be going again.

Very fortunately no damage has been done to the engines ; they were prevented working for two days, but from which I expect we shall none of us sustain any material injury . . . Many colliers and cannelers[1] from distant works had come to observe the progress of our people, and had they succeeded it would certainly have spread far over this County . . . (H.O.42/20).

(12). *The Marquess Townshend[2] to the Home Secretary*

Rudham Grange, 31 October, 1792.

. . . At Lynn I have just heard that the sailors have refused to go to sea unless their wages were advanced, because they heard it was at London and Newcastle. A meeting was called by the Mayor, and their demand was complied with ; that [*sic*] the porters on the quays then assembled and demanded double price for unloading of corn. Everyone is at present satisfied in my neighbourhood, but what the effects of example may be I can't presume to foresee. Lynn is about

---

[1] 'Cannell' coal, mined extensively in Lancashire, was a fine quality bituminous coal.

[2] Lord Lieutenant of Norfolk.

14 miles from hence. The Mayor, Corporation and merchants [meet]
to-day to take the demands of the discontented and the opinion of
the farmers (who now pay double at that Port) under consideration ...

(13). *Edmund Lacon (Mayor) to the Marquess Townshend*[1]

Yarmouth, 30 October, 1792.

... The beginning of last week many hundred seamen collected
together in a very tumultuous manner, put a stop to all the trade by
compelling all the seamen on board ship, in this harbour, to join
them, and insisted on the merchants and shipowners raising their
wages ; and as this was *then* their only pretence, and as they were
too numerous to be suppressed by the peace officers, the magistrates,
merchants and shipowners and principal inhabitants assembled at
the Town Hall, and heard the complaints of a few of the rioters who
pretended to be delegates by the rest ; and many of their requests
appearing not unreasonable, were consented to immediately, but
the same evening they assembled in still greater numbers and insisted on the whole of their demands being complied with, which the
merchants and shipowners at length consented to, and the rioters
dispersed ...

Yesterday the ship carpenters talked of leaving off work and taking their tools with them. We therefore sent off an express to
Norwich for a troop of horse with an officer ... (H.O.42/22).

(14). *Rowland Burdon,*[2] *M.P., to Henry Dundas*

Castle Eden, 3 November, 1792.

... Having been eyewitness to the determined, systematic manner
in which the sailors proceed upon the river Tyne to take the officers
(that is, mates and carpenters) out of the ships in Shields harbour, I
think it my duty to acquaint you with the situation of the trade in
that river. It is now near three weeks that the sailors, conceiving
their pay to be too little, have insisted upon an augmentation, and
have not suffered any ships to put to sea unless their owners would
sign a promise of payment of four guineas per voyage during the
winter months. 50s. was heretofore the usual allowance. The shipowners met at the Trinity House, Newcastle, October 24th, when I

[1] Enclosed in No. 12.
[2] M.P. for Durham County.

was present, as well as the Mayor of Newcastle and Mr. Brandling.[1] They determined to allow three pounds per voyage for four winter months, which offer being made to the sailors, was treated with contempt . . . Every day as the lightships return from London, these men board them, and oblige the officers and sailors to join in their revolt. South Shields has risen so rapidly, from the spirit of commerce, as to contain at least 14,000 inhabitants without a single magistrate to control it. None of its inhabitants are of a description to qualify for that office, and few would be active or hardy enough to undertake so penible a situation. Not a single soldier is there to protect a great and increasing property, for the dockyards and other naval establishments have flourished to such a degree that the property in shipping of the two Shields has multiplied itself within 30 years from 30 sail of colliers to not less than 120. The magistrates of Newcastle are either diffident of their power, or unwilling to exert it . . .

(15). *Joseph Bulmer to R. Burdon*

South Shields, 1 November, 1792.[2]
. . . I failed in getting our vessel to sea on Tuesday owing to the sailors who belonged her, objecting to go for less wages than four guineas. I therefore unshipped them . . . Though I cannot help shuddering at the idea, yet I must inform you that yesterday three of the sailors who had not been quite punctual at their meetings, were stripped naked and made to walk in that situation up the street of South Shields and round the Market Place.

In South Shields we have about 160 or 170 public houses, and I think they are equal to take three soldiers on an average, but in regard to our future plans I think Government ought to be at the expense of barracks here . . .[3]

Pray, Sir, do write Ministry, for our situation is truly alarming. When they know the nature of the mob, they'll conceive what is a sufficient force to suppress it. [I] dare say a few days will increase the number to 3,000. (H.O.42/22).

[1] Charles Brandling, M.P. for Newcastle-on-Tyne.
[2] Enclosed in No. 14.
[3] As a result of the old jealousy of a standing army, dating back to Cromwellian times, troops were still generally quartered in public houses, barracks being used only in fortresses and garrison towns. As a police rather than a military measure, barracks were erected all over the country during the French War.

(16). *Thomas Powditch to William Pitt*

North Shields, 3 November, 1792.

The situation of this unfortunate place begins to be so extremely alarming that I cannot refrain from making you acquainted with it. A long continuance of easterly wind had detained the ships in this port until a large fleet (about 400 sail) had accumulated. On the appearance of a change of wind from the east to the west (which is a fair wind for ships to proceed to sea) the seamen discovered a disposition to riot, and assembled in great numbers in different parts of the towns of North and South Shields, and in boats upon the river Tyne, insisting that the masters of all ships should pay four guineas wages for the voyage, although most of the people of the loaded ships had signed their articles for the usual wages (viz. 50s. for the voyage). This unreasonable demand the owners were unwilling to comply with.

The crews of each ship, when separately applied to, acknowledged themselves satisfied with the wages they had agreed for, and in excuse for leaving the ships and becoming a part of the mob, said they were obliged to do so or they would be ill treated by the rest of the seamen. They proceed[ed] in boats from ship to ship and compelled the reluctant or willing seamen and officers of every ship in the harbour to leave their ships and join the mob. By this means a great number of seamen were collected ; they then divided themselves into parties (forming two or three watches) under chiefs, and took possession of the port by stationing a body of seamen under one of these chiefs at the entrance of the harbour on each side of the river where it is very narrow, to prevent any ships from proceeding to sea in the nights. The hazardous situation in which some ships lay at that time (the harbour being much crowded) was the reason why their owners complied with the demands of the rioters. Their crews were then permitted to come on board their ships and take care of them, but the rioters obliged them to distinguish their ships by wearing at the masthead a jack. On the owners who had not complied, this badge of distinction had a wonderful effect by pointing out both the persons and the property of the persons who were, as they pleased to call them, the seaman's enemy. A fair wind came, and the ships distinguished by the jack at the masthead proceeded to sea amidst great acclamations and huzzas of the mob. The fear from the mob, the temptation of a fair wind, the great demand for coals at London, and no support in view were the causes, and are still the causes why the owners of the load ships complied and still comply with their unreasonable demands. A meeting of shipowners was called at the Trinity House, Newcastle, on the 14th of October, present, Mr. Brandling, Mr. Burdon, M.P., the Mayor of Newcastle, and the Town Clerk, when the trembling shipowners were prevailed upon to issue the enclosed handbill,[1] which had no other effect than to cause them to assume a more daring appearance. It then appeared (but how it happened I cannot tell) that Captain Leakey of his Majesty's ship *Racehorse* had had some talk with the mob and became a kind of mediator between them and the shipowners. Captain Leakey's interference, in my opinion, was very improper, for it surely had a great effect in confirming an opinion which they have, that the Government is afraid of provoking the lower class of people ; yet I am persuaded Captain Leakey was actuated by the best of motives.

A meeting of a committee of shipowners was then held at the Trinity House (for they still continued to occupy the entrance of the harbour, permitting no ships to sail in the night and only those during the day which had complied with their demands). At this meeting nothing was determined but to call a general meeting of shipowners (for the seamen now on the arrival of every ship into the port were taken out by the rioters unless the owner or master would sign their agreement and pay their crews four guineas for the next voyage) which was held at Trinity House on Wednesday the 31st of October. (This was the first meeting I had attended, for at that time I had no ship in the harbour, now I have one.) At this meeting no magistrate, no person of authority attended, only shipowners. Whether that circumstance increased their apprehensions I cannot tell, but the experience of near thirty years had convinced them that no reliance could be placed on the magistrates of the river Tyne for the protection of their property, or on the County's magistrates for the protection of either persons or property. Deeply impressed with this truth, cast down and dejected by the insults they were daily suffering from an unrestrained mob, trembling for their little property, from which they drew the support of their families, it was determined by a small majority once again to meet and to offer them such terms as it was impossible for the trade to bear, but such as their present unprotected state induced them to submit to if it would but preserve the peace of the port. This measure

[1] Missing.

was not unresisted, as you will see by my remarks at the meeting which were warmly supported by a few spirited men, but the majority was against us.

The place appointed for the meeting to make this humiliating offer was on board his Majesty's ship *Racehorse*.

They were met on Thursday last at Shields by Captain Leaky, some shipowners and the Town Clerk of Newcastle, but their offers were rejected, and the concessions of the shipowners had no other effect on these men (now intoxicated with a power too long enjoyed) but to increase their insolence, and they still persevere in their measures, nay to some who have wished to lay their ships by, they have threatened to burn them if they do not send them to sea.

As to myself, being a person of more spirit than prudence, makes me in some degree obnoxious to the mob, and no favourite with magistrates. And although some fears for myself, family and property may cause me sincerely to wish for peace being re-established, I should not have troubled you on that account ; but when I look round and see this country covered with thousands of pitmen, keelmen, waggonmen and other labouring men, hardy fellows strongly impressed with the new doctrine of equality, and at present composed of such combustible matter that the least spark will set them in a blaze, I cannot help thinking the supineness of the magistrates very reprehensible. It is possible, however, that they may think the force in this country not sufficient to authorise threatening measures, and may wish them to be amused until they can be safely resisted. If it be so, they are possessed of more wisdom than I apprehended . . .

P.S. Shocking to relate, the mob at this moment are driving some seamen or officers that have discovered a reluctance to comply with their mode of proceedings naked through the town before them.

Thomas Powditch's address to the chairman of the meeting at the Trinity House, Newcastle-upon-Tyne, the 31st October 1792 :

Mr. Chairman—It is my opinion that tampering with a mob, treating with rioters, or offering terms to people illegally assembled and for the purpose of extorting high wages from their employers, are crimes little inferior in magnitude to rioting itself. And it is my opinion that the measures hitherto adopted by the shipowners, though sanctioned by the presence of members of Parliament, the magistrates of the Corporation, the Town Clerk and other persons of importance, are measures very reprehensible indeed, and can have no other tendency than to promote future riots, and that raising the wages will not lessen but increase the evil, as the high wages given at this Port above the wages given at the neighbouring Ports are the occasion of many seamen coming to this place at this season, who, finding all the berths occupied, have no other resource but in creating confusion, and the successful riots of 30 years are sufficient encouragement for them to continue the practice Thirty years have the inhabitants of the towns of North and South Shields been under the dominion of mobs. Thirty years has the river Tyne been the theatre of their depredations and the place of their security, and thirty years has the magistracy of that district been disgraced by their rapacity in collecting the revenue and their incapacity to preserve the peace of the Port. If this be true—and if it is not true let anyone contradict me—we have one alternative, and that is, to encourage future riots by making concessions to the present rioters, or to come forward like men conscious of living under a mild but effective government, and take such steps as deliberate wisdom shall point out to suppress the present and discourage future mobs.

Measures recommended by T. Powditch :

That the committee employ an able solicitor to draw up a full and fair statement of the situation of this Port, the nature of its trade, the frequency of riots, the incapacity or neglect of the present magistracy to preserve the peace of the port, the unprotected state of the towns of North and South Shields for want [of] magistrates. To lay the same before his Majesty in Council, humbly to request him to grant adequate protection to the Port by putting it under the jurisdiction of active and independent magistrates or otherwise as his Majesty, &c. may see proper. In the meantime offer rewards and take such other measures as may appear the most effectual for bringing delinquents to justice.

I write the latter part of this information in such agitation, occasioned by the noise and confusion of the mob, that I fear you will hardly make it out. (H.O.42/22).

(17). *Lord Grenville*[1] *to the Bishop of Durham*[2]

Whitehall, 7 November, 1792.

By a letter from Mr. Burdon to Mr. Dundas, which in his absence has been brought to me, I learn that a combination has taken place

---

[1] Foreign Secretary, June 1791–February 1801.
[2] Dr. Shute Barrington (1734–1826), Bishop of Durham, 1791–1826.

among the seamen at South Shields on the pretence of the insufficiency of their wages, and that in order to compel a compliance with their demands, they have not only put a stop to the trade of that place, but have proceeded to other acts of violence.

His Majesty's servants were entirely uninformed of these circumstances previous to the receipt of Mr. Burdon's letter, but in consequence of that information, immediate instructions were given to the officer commanding the troops at Tynemouth to send three companies of the regiment under his orders to South Shields ; and a sloop of war, in addition to the *Racehorse* which was before stationed in the Tyne, has been ordered to proceed thither.

I understand that there has been some difficulty in procuring the assistance of magistrates to act on this occasion. I trust, however, that tranquillity and good order has before this been restored, but if that should not have been the case, I must request your Lordship as Custos Rotulorum of the County of Durham to call upon the magistrates of the County, particularly those resident in the neighbourhood of Shields, to take all proper and legal methods for breaking the combination above-mentioned, and for bringing to punishment the persons who have been active in any proceedings of violence.

Major Thompson, the officer commanding the 57th Regiment, has been directed to take the command of the detachment ordered to Shields. He is authorised, if he shall judge it expedient, to draw further succours from Tynemouth Barracks. He will also in case of necessity be reinforced by two troops of dragoons from York, and a further naval force will immediately proceed to the Tyne. With such assistance I trust there can be no doubt but that by a proper exertion on the part of the magistracy, any further mischief may be prevented, and a stop put to the spirit of combination which appears to have prevailed. (H.O.43/4/123–24).

(18). *Rowland Burdon, M.P. to Evan Nepean.*[1]

South Shields, Tuesday evening, 13 *November,* 1792.
. . . We are in a fair way of terminating the riot at this place and North Shields. The sailors have submitted to the umpirage of the magistrates, who have ventured to recommend the terms to the shipowners, and I have little doubt but to-morrow will place

[1] Under-Secretary of State for Home Affairs. Created baronet, 1802. (1751–1822).

matters here in a state of security. In the interim the dragoons are stopped at Durham, the *Martin* sloop is in the harbour, and will, I hope, remain some time. Indeed it would be highly proper that a frigate should be constantly attached to this port, with mooring chains in cases of riot to prevent any possibility of cutting her adrift . . . (H.O.42/22).

(19). *Captain Alexander Cochrane[1] to Henry Dundas*

Newcastle, 20 *November*, 1792.

. . . The wages of the seamen of this port have not been increased for a considerable time back, since which the price of every article of living has increased very much. About six weeks ago the seamen demanded an increase from 50s. to £3 per voyage to London during the six winter months. This was in the first instance positively denied them. They of course entered into a general agreement not to ship themselves under the sum of *four guineas* until a permanent agreement was made with the owners both as to wages and articles of agreement, which last is very often infringed on by the owners whom I am sorry to say that the sailors have but too much reason to complain of [*sic*].

Upon my arrival at Shields I found everything on shore perfectly quiet, the seamen everywhere behaving with the utmost degree of civility and regularity except that they made a point to board all the ships that sailed, to satisfy themselves that the crew had not broke through the general agreement, viz., not to take less than four guineas per voyage until the wages is settled.

From what I have heard it is the interest of many of the ship masters to foment these disturbances, as they are allowed by custom to receive the same wages for their apprentices that is paid the seamen, consequently it is their interest that it should be as high as possible. The shipowners seem to be at variance with the magistrates and do not appear at all willing to come forward to aid the civil power in settling these disputes, in which they are so deeply concerned.

Mr. Burdon, member for Durham, has taken much pains to bring about a compromise, and has proposed that if the owners will agree to pay the seamen £3 per voyage until next May, that he will endeavour to get Parliament to appoint a power consisting of a jury

---

[1] Afterwards Admiral Sir Alexander Cochrane (1758–1832) ; a younger son of the 8th Earl of Dundonald.

of shipowners and seamen to fix annually the rate of wages, and settle every future dispute. It appears that the seamen are willing to adopt this plan : it will therefore rest with the owners to put a final stop to these disputes.

I yesterday attended a meeting of the magistrates of this town, when it was agreed that on Wednesday they would meet at Shields and protect all ships then ready to sail from being boarded or hindered to proceed on their voyage by the seamen . . . (P.R.O., H.O.42/22).

(20). *George Auldjo* (*Provost*) *to the Lord Advocate of Scotland*[1]

Aberdeen, 5 December, 1792.

I had the honour to write you by last post, stating the disagreeable situation this City was in from a tumultuous association of the sailors to obtain an extravagant and intolerable advance of wages. Since last night they have taken possession of every vessel in the harbour and prevent the landing or loading of goods, and for that purpose even set regular watches day and night. The magistrates have satisfied themselves that the advance offered by the ship-owners is in exact proportion to what has been lately agreed to at other ports, but we have not the same power to reduce them to quiet. Though they form a pretty numerous and resolute body, I entertain however no doubt that the small military force here, if exerted to its utmost, would bring them to order, but not without resistance and of course bloodshed, which I by all means, unless driven to it by the last necessity, wish to avoid. As they are in every other respect behaving properly enough, and their conduct is re-probated by their friends and neighbours, I have urged the traders to put up with a day's interruption of their trade, in expectation that they will divide among themselves, but chiefly that your Lordship will relieve us by one of his Majesty's ships of war, and as it is impossible to say to what extremities they may go, I beg of your Lordship that no time may be lost in despatching her. Upon her appearance I have every reason to think the association will be dissolved, and it would not be improper if instructions were given to the captain of the ship of war to impress into his Majesty's service a few of the ringleaders of this scheme whom I shall point

---

[1] Robert Dundas of Arniston (1758–1819). His wife was the daughter of Henry Dundas, the Home Secretary.

17

D

out, and who, from having seen what passed at Newcastle, and judging of the military strength here, have induced the others to proceed to the extremities they have done . . .[1] (H.O.102/6).

(21). *Henry Dundas to Captain William Harness Dronfield*

Whitehall, 26 *January,* 1793.

Lord Grenville has transmitted to me your letter to his Lordship of the 17th instant, and I have since received from Mr. Burke a letter which had been written to him by you on the same day.

If what you represent in your letters with respect to Mr. Rotherham, particularly the encouragement said to be given by him to the scythemakers to persist in an illegal combination with a view of extorting an increase of wages, and of his countenancing any riotous proceedings of the nature you mention, can be brought to proof, there can be but little doubt that steps ought immediately to be taken concerning him. I wish therefore that you would furnish me as soon as you can with any authenticated documents as to the particular acts of misconduct attributed to Mr. Rotherham, that I may consider how far it may be proper for me to represent the same to his Majesty and receive his pleasure thereupon. (H.O.43/4/176).

---

[1] Lord Dundonald's letter of the 16th to the Lord Advocate has an interesting reference to the development of the cotton industry in Scotland and to the spread of 'Jacobinism' amongst the workers : '[At Dunfermline]. . . the manufacturers, who consist of weavers, have with their *morning drams* of whisky imbibed a spirit harsh and inflammatory as the liquor they swallow, its effects, aided by the fumes of constipated feces [*sic*] caused by the *sedentary profession* of weaving, and the whole set a fermenting by the characteristic sourness and morosity of Scots Presbyterian sectaries. I do not, my Lord, heighten the picture of many of this class of men. They are enemies to subordination. So prevalent is the levelling spirit that few of the labourers or tradesmen will lift their *Scots* bonnet or shew any mark of respect to those of the higher class. A spirit like this is not soon altered. On the contrary, it increases with the increase of manufactures and advance of wages, and with the *weaving* and *cotton* trade, has of late been spreading very fast through Fife.' (H.O.102/6). John Dunlop, the Provost of Glasgow, wrote to the Duke of Portland on 14 March, 1796 : '. . . We are very quiet here at present, and our manufactures are flourishing in a wonderful manner. The wages of labourers and of artisans of all descriptions are high beyond any former example, which has hitherto kept the people from complaining of the extravagant rate of provisions.' (H.O.102/13).

(22). *Robert Spillman, J.P., to Henry Dundas*

Banbury, 25 August, 1793.

I beg leave to inform you that a very extensive manufactory of shags[1] is carried on in this place, in which many hundred men are employed. They have of late years associated, formed laws of their own, and set those of their country at defiance. Upon the least disagreement, or whenever they choose to raise the price of their wages, they with one voice leave their looms and subsist upon a fund they have raised for that purpose.

About three weeks ago, one of their Society trangressed their laws by taking an apprentice ; this was sufficient for the body to assemble and repair to the masters by whom this individual was employed, to demand of him a dismission of the pretended offender. This was not complied with. The consequence was, every man working for the same master, amounting to 300, left his work and as usual lived upon their stock until Friday last, when it was discovered, one of the men, contrary to their order, had betook himself to work, which was sufficient to reassemble the body. Yesterday they met in this place, and a body of about 200 paraded the streets with martial music, and then proceeded to a place two miles distant, the residence of the man so working, and violently took his piece of shag from the loom and triumphantly returned two and two, with each a green bough in his hat, one of them bearing the shag mounted on an ass, preceding the rest with fifes playing. They were met by me as a magistrate of the place, and several of the inhabitants, who expostulated upon such unwarrantable proceedings in vain. I then thought it best to read the Riot Act, but in spite of every endeavour to resist they marched, and in triumph laid the shag at the door of the master to whom it belonged. Several of the rioters were seized, but by numbers were rescued. However in an hour they all departed . . .

I could apprehend several for the offence of cutting the work from the loom, but in our present want of assistance the offenders would be again rescued, and much mischief might ensue . . . (H.O.42/26).

---

[1] Pieces of long-napped rough cloth.

(23). *The Rev. Thomas Bancroft to the Duke of Portland*

Vicarage, Bolton, 11 *April,* 1799.

. . . We have an Association in this town and neighbourhood which at present seems to threaten harm. It is ostensibly formed for the regulation of the wages of the weavers in the cotton trade, but their publications and the arrangement of the plan are able and great. Their aim is, as they phrase it, to *move the County* and ultimately to petition Parliament for a *redress of grievances.*[1] It is distributed into divisional committees and a central committee, and pains are taking to confederate the neighbouring towns, and so to proceed. We have forbidden the publicans to encourage the meetings.

The editor (or rather an agent) for the *Courier* newspaper (as I am informed) has lately been in this neighbourhood to collect subscriptions among the *Clubs* for the support of their paper.[2] (H.O.42/47).

(24). *John Singleton to* ? *John King*[3]

Wigan, 27 *May,* 1799.

I beg to enclose you an advertisement, numbers of which are circulated. It is from the same channel as the last I had the honour to send.

I believe the people as a body are very loyal, but their leaders, as far as I know them, the reverse, no doubt . . .

In this paper things are much misrepresented, and are calculated greatly to inflame and mislead the labouring class, who, I assure you, are fully employed and *well*, very well, paid for their labour, and before these arts were used to disturb their peace and make them discontented, was both happy and contented.

The demand for manufactured goods is great—and were it possible to make one weaver into two weavers, they might be employed. Although numbers of our people are gone for soldiers and sailors there is still an increase of looms, for if a man enlists, his wife turns weaver (for here the women are weavers as well as the men) and

---

[1] They demanded the regulation of their wages by Act of Parliament. Pitt's Government rejected the idea of a minimum wage, and passed an Arbitration Act, which proved unsatisfactory.

[2] The *Courier* was still, at this time, a Radical paper.

[3] Under-Secretary of State for Home Affairs.

instructs her children in the art of weaving ; and I have heard many declare that they lived better since their husband[s] enlisted than before.

I cannot speak with truth respecting the numbers this Society consists of. In Wigan alone they amount to about 700. Their first committee of 21 members is dissolved, and another committee of two members chosen, who meet in private to transact business.[1]

(25). The Association of Weavers, &c., &c.
To the Public. [printed][2]

The present existing laws that should protect weavers, &c. from imposition, being trampled under foot, for want of a union amongst them, they have come to a determination to support each other in their just and legal rights, and to apply to the Legislature of the country for such further regulations as it may in its wisdom deem fit to make, when the real state of the cotton manufactory shall have been laid before it. The members of this Association have no other object in view but the mutual interest of both employers and employed—well knowing that to combine their interest together is the only method to expect success ; being sensible that the fair trader is exposed to difficulties through injurious practices that have crept into the cotton manufactory, and to study his interest is to study their own, for if a fair chance is given to him, theirs of course will follow. These being their sentiments, they flatter themselves with the support of men of this description ; earnestly desiring them to give the situation of weavers, &c. their candid consideration, how every necessary of life has increased in price, whilst the price of labour has undergone a continual decrease ; this being the case, it becomes a duty incumbent on both parties to search out the cause, and, if possible, remove it, that the effects may cease. And ye who are our enemies, do you not blush to hear these facts repeated— Great Britain holding the reins of universal commerce, is it not

[1] The letter is endorsed by the Duke of Portland : 'Can anything more be done in this case than calling the attention of the magistrates to the facts by a letter to the Chairman of the Sessions or some intelligent magistrate in that part of the Connty, which is indeed all, or at least the principal part of the manufacturing district ?'
[2] Enclosed in No. 24.

shameful that her sons should be thus imposed on? Are you afraid
that we should approach the Government, and there tell the truth?—
that ye use the mean artifice of stigmatising us with the name of
Jacobins, that ye raise your rumours of plots, riots, &c.

We disdain your calumny, and look upon you with that contempt
you merit. To the public we address ourselves—rioting, or any
illegal behaviour, we detest, and are firmly attached to our King
and country, and to promote their prosperity shall ever be the
object most dear to our hearts. How unjustly do those calumniate
us who assert that our meetings are calculated to sacrifice the
independence of our country! It is the reverse, for should the
clarion ever sound 'To arms! England is in danger!'—we know
what is our duty, and what is our interest; and not only ours, but
the duty and interest of every individual, to rally round Government,
and strike the daring foe prostrate at our feet. These being our
genuine sentiments, is there anything to fear by us meeting together? We shall neither interfere with Church nor State, but
strictly confine ourselves to a private grievance, which we wish to
lay before Government, and it will remain to be determined by it,
whether or not our case merits redress; but having that confidence
in Government which ought to be universal, we believe that when
our real situation is laid before the Legislature, some method will be
devised to ameliorate our condition.

There are some as ignorant of the very laws they pretend to
administer, that they would willingly confound our meetings with
those which are only calculated to undermine Government: it is
wonderful that they are not ashamed to expose their ignorance to
the public view—but, that their ignorance may not infect you, we
will take the liberty to state that it never was the intention of
Government to infringe upon the right of meeting together to lay
any matter of this kind before them.

On the contrary, the late laws on meetings[1] appear to us to be
only intended as a bridle to that wild democratical fury that leads
nations into the vortex of anarchy, confusion and bloodshed; if,
then, the laws of your country guarantee to you the right of meeting

[1] The Seditious Meetings Act of 1795 (36 George III c. 8) prohibited public
meetings of more than fifty persons unless previous notice had been given in
the newspapers and to a justice of the peace, if required. It expired in 1799,
when an Act (39 George III, c. 79) was passed 'for the more effectual suppression of societies established for seditious and treasonable purposes; and
for better preventing treasonable and seditious practices'.

together to consider of a private grievance of this kind, are you so foolish to be deterred in your proceedings by the misrepresentations of ignorant and designing men, who do more hurt to the Government than good ? Government does not stand in need of a blind attachment, for the more it is considered the more it is admired ; and the friends who are attached to it from understanding are the only real ones to be found :

It is the interest of every occupation to step forward and support us ; even the landed property feels the want of regulations in the cotton manufactory ; and to convince the landed interest that this is the case, we will point out the situation of those employed in it. They are continually subject to reductions in their wages, which never find their level. Draw the analogy any distant time back, and what we assert will be found true : but to be more particular, we will suppose a man to be married in the year 1792 ; he at that period received 22s. for 44 yards of cloth. We will follow him year after year ; his family keeps increasing, together with the price of every necessary of life, whilst his wages for labour decreases. Let us look at him in the year 1799, and we shall perhaps find him surrounded with five or six small children, and, lo ! instead of 44 yards they have increased the length to 60, and give him only 11s. for it ; and, to make ill worse, he must work it with finer weft ! No wonder that poor rates increase, when people are situated in this manner. A little reflection will show how matters of this kind affect the landed interest.

It is in vain to talk of bad trade ; if goods are actually not wanted, they cannot be sold at any price ; if wanted, 2d. or 3d. per yard will not stop the buyer ; and whether does it appear more reasonable that 2d. or 3d. per yard should be laid on the consumer or taken from the labourer ? A single 2d. per yard would increase the wages from 11s. to 21s., 3d. to 26s. Consider how little it would affect the one, and how important to the other. How impressed with gratitude must that man be with five or six small children, when informed that Government had devised certain measures, that where he now received only 11s., he might receive above 20s. for his work.

Ye whose hardened hearts are dead to humane feelings which should always adorn the human mind, may say it is impracticable, and are we yet to continue suffering on your barely asserting this ? No : we are determined that those who are appointed by the Constitution of our country to redress our grievances, shall have our real state laid before them ; and it must be their wisdom that must determine this point ; and with this determination we shall always think it our duty to comply. A peaceful demeanour shall always guide all our actions, and we trust a candid public will give the subject a mature consideration, and afford us that support we merit.

It was resolved unanimously, that this Address should be printed and distributed in the different towns, in the name of the General Committee, assembled at Bolton, on Monday the 13th of May 1799.

John Seddon, President.[1] (HO.42/47).

---

[1] The names of the committee follow. There are six from Bolton and the neighbourhood, three from Manchester and Salford ; two each from Stockport, Oldham, Wigan, Blackburn, Chorley, Newton, Warrington and Bury ; one each from Whitefield, Chowbent, and New Chapel, near Leigh. The handbill concludes thus : 'This Committee earnestly desire that weavers in general will step forward and give their support, and others who are interested in the welfare of the cause are desired to come forward, as they have nothing to fear.—James Holcroft, Secretary.'

II. THE COMBINATION ACTS OF 1799 AND 1800.

1799. The Lancashire cotton weavers. The London journeymen bakers. The Tyneside sailors.
1800. Combinations amongst farmers. The journeymen tailors and paper makers.
1801. The Tyneside shipwrights.
1802. The journeymen boot-and-shoe-makers. The Wiltshire shearmen and their campaign against gig mills. The caulkers and shipwrights of Deptford. The West Riding cloth workers, and their connection with the West of England shearmen.
1803. The combination of the Yorkshire cloth croppers.

(26). *John King to the Rev. Thomas Bancroft, of Bolton le Moors*

Whitehall, 2 August, 1799.

I am directed by the Duke of Portland[1] to inform you that his Grace has received your letter enclosing the paper signed by persons styling themselves the Presidents [*sic*] and Secretary of the Association of Cotton Weavers, and that the same have been submitted to his Majesty's Attorney and Solicitor-General for their opinion whether such Association be lawful. His Grace will take an early opportunity of informing you of the result, and of communicating to you his sentiments respecting it. In the meantime he is of opinion that it will be highly proper that you should employ some confidential persons to attend in those parts from whence the delegates are sent to the monthly meetings, in order that it may be known whether any other subjects are discussed there than those connected with the Petition to Parliament, and that you should transmit an account to his Grace of anything material that may occur . . .[2] (H.O.43/11/216).

[1] Home Secretary, July 1794–July 1801.
[2] Dr. and Mrs. Hammond erroneously state *Skilled Labourer*, p. 67 [1919] that 'it is in the year 1801 that the first mention is made in the Home Office Papers of that unhallowed band of informers and spies, of whom the magistrates henceforth made continual use.'

(27). *John King to T. B. Bayley, J.P.*

Whitehall, 6 *August*, 1799.

I am directed by the Duke of Portland to inform you that his Grace has received information that many persons in Manchester, Stockport and Bury and the neighbouring country have formed themselves into Associations, under an idea that the late Act of Parliament[1] for preventing unlawful combinations of workmen is oppressive to them, and that meetings are held in which delegates are chosen to conduct the affairs of the Association. It is very probable that you may already be in possession of these circumstances, which his Grace is informed Mr. Leaf and Mr. Richardson have already been made acquainted with. His Grace has a thorough reliance on your activity and discretion in conjunction with these gentlemen in developing this business, for which purpose his Grace recommends that some confidential persons should be employed to attend not only the general meetings but those of the persons choosing delegates . . . (H.O.43/11/224-25).

(28). *The Duke of Portland to the Rev. Thomas Bancroft*

Whitehall, 8 *August*, 1799.

I return you many thanks for the favour of your letter of the 30th ult. inclosing the paper sent by certain persons calling themselves Presidents [*sic*] and Secretary of the Associated Weavers at Bolton and in the neighbouring County, and I particularly desire to acknowledge this communication, as a very acceptable testimony of your attention to my former request.

Although it should seem, from the representation contained in that paper, that the object of the persons styling themselves the Presidents and Secretary of the Associated Weavers is to petition Parliament on the subject of the manufacture in which they are engaged, and that, so far, it is not contrary to the Act of 39 George III, c. 81, or any other laws affecting the same subject, it is manifest that the manner in which this Association is conducted, viz. by delegates, monthly meetings, the election of a Secretary and Presidents, and particularly by the printing an Address to the Public must lead to a conclusion that, if nothing injurious to the safety of the Government is actually in contemplation, Associations so

[1] 39 George III, c. 81.

formed contain within themselves the means of being converted at any time into a most dangerous instrument to disturb the public tranquillity.

The observation in your letter, that the spirit of association has spread itself into many parts of Lancashire and the neighbouring Counties, has great weight with me ; and connecting that circumstance with this case, as it appears from the representation of the persons themselves, I must earnestly recommend it to you to take every measure in your power in order that the proceedings and progress of these Societies be carefully attended to and watched, for which purpose it will be advisable that persons should be employed by you in the manner mentioned in Mr. King's letter to you of the 2nd inst., not only to attend the general meetings of the Society, but those which may be held by persons who are entrusted with the choice of delegates to it, in order that it may be distinctly known whether any other topics are discussed than those which relate solely to the Petition to Parliament, and in that case that we may be acquainted with the nature and tendency of them— all which information you will transmit to me from time to time, as it may appear to you to be material.

Whatever the expense may amount to which may be incurred in employing persons for the purposes above-mentioned, you will draw for it upon Mr. King, who will take care to discharge the same with the most punctual regularity. (H.O.43/11/222-23).

(29). *The Duke of Portland to the Rev. Thomas Bancroft*

Whitehall, 26 *August*, 1799.

I am favoured with your letter of the 22nd inst., together with one enclosed in it addressed to you, purporting that the Association of Weavers which we have had reason to suspect was convened for improper purposes, will speedily be dissolved. I beg to return you many thanks for the communication, by which I am happy to find that this affair is likely to terminate without any bad consequences to the public. (H.O.43/11/234).

(30). *R. Glynn (Lord Mayor) to the Duke of Portland*

Mansion House, 1 *October*, 1799.

. . . I have received information that most of the journeymen bakers in London, Westminster and its neighbourhood have determined individually to strike work unless their wages are raised. Some of them have already given warning to their masters, others are likely to do so in the course of the week.

I have seen some of the master bakers and shall again see them this day. I shall use my endeavours to compromise between master and servant if I can do it properly ; at the same time I shall not lose sight of punishment to those journeymen against whom there may be evidence of unlawful combination. (H.O.42/48)

(31). *The Duke of Portland to the Lord Mayor of London*

Whitehall, 2 October, 1799.

. . Every means that a regard for the public interest can suggest will, I am confident, be employed by your Lordship for suppressing this illegal proceeding and bringing to justice those who shall be found to have taken a part in it, and I trust that your Lordship's exertions in this behalf will be very much facilitated by the provisions of the Act which was passed last Session for preventing unlawful combinations of workmen.[1] (H.O.43/11/261).

(32). *John King to T. B. Bayley*[2]

Whitehall, 11 *November,* 1799.
I have received your letter of the 7th inst., which I will communicate to the Duke of Portland as you desire.

I am sorry to find that the circumstances you mention have afforded the means of renewing the opposition of the weavers to the Act of last Session ' to prevent the unlawful combinations amongst workmen,' for although it is evident that the Act in question can

---

[1] At 7 p.m. on Thursday the 3rd, six journeymen bakers were brought before the Lord Mayor, charged with being active, with many others, in an unlawful combination. The Master and members of the Court of Assistants of the Bakers Company, with many other master bakers, attended, and gave evidence that all their journeymen had given notice to strike unless their wages were advanced according to a plan laid down by a Society of journeymen bakers which they had joined. The Lord Mayor declared that this was the worst combination he had ever heard of, as all classes of people would be the sufferers. Two of the defendants were sent to prison for three months ; the others were discharged with a warning to take no part in future in such illegal proceedings. (*The Times,* 5 October, 1799).

[2] Of Hope, Derbyshire.

have no connection whatever with the real cause of the temporary distress among the weavers in your neighbourhood, I mean the reduction of wages, yet the ill-intentioned will not fail to take advantage of it as the cause of the present or any other distress which the weavers may experience.

The Duke of Portland will, I conceive, direct the papers you have enclosed to me to be laid before the Attorney and Solicitor-General, but they do not as far as I can judge of them contain anything to warrant a legal prosecution. You will be the best judge, yourself, but it occurs to me that it would be a good way of proceeding (after in the first place consulting, and arranging the matter with the principal and most intelligent of your brother magistrates) to have without delay as general a meeting of the Bench as possible, with a view first of manifesting to the weavers the readiness of the magistracy to take into consideration the difficulties under which they at present labour, and to explain to them the temporary causes to which those difficulties are only to be attributed ; and secondly, to guard them against being led away by ill-disposed and seditious persons who, without any intentions of assisting them, and without either the wish or ability to do so, endeavour to inveigle them into illegal proceedings and breaches of the public peace ; and thirdly, to apprise them in the most decided terms of the determination of the magistracy to suppress and punish in the most effectual and exemplary manner every such proceeding or any breach of the peace, or any act having such a tendency. It would also, I conceive, be of great service, if the magistrates were at the same time to take such measures as they are empowered by law to take for the temporary extension of the allowance made out of the poors rates, to those weavers who have families, including therein such others as the present want of employment has rendered necessitous.

Some mode of proceeding of this sort, of the execution of which you are a much better judge than I can be, would be the means of rescuing the weavers from the snares which have been laid for them by their enemies, and would tend in a great measure to restore the influence of the magistrates over them by convincing them of the attention which that respectable body is at all times ready to pay to their wants under any circumstances.

You will also be so good as to consider and report to me whether in the present state of things your neighbourhood might not be relieved, and the King's service at the same time promoted, by carrying the recruiting service more particularly into your quarter, and what stations for recruiting parties might be the most favourable for this purpose.

Independent of the measures which I have taken the liberty of suggesting to you, you will, I am sure, be more than usually attentive to the emissaries from the Societies,[1] who will be constantly on the watch to take every advantage of the present situation of the weavers. The apprehending any one of these emissaries will, as you know, tend more effectually than any other circumstances, to prevent any serious or regulated plan of operations from growing out of the temporary difficulties you have stated. . . (H.O.43/11/284-87).

(33). *John King to T. B. Bayley.*[2]

Whitehall, 18 *November*, 1799.

I have received the favour of your letter of the 16th inst., enclosing the printed papers marked 1, 2, 3, which have been already transmitted by the Duke of Portland's directions to his Majesty's Law Officers for their opinion, the result of which shall be communicated to you by the earliest opportunity. Enclosed I now send you a copy of the opinion of those gentlemen on the papers which I received from you in yours of the 7th inst., on which subject his Grace directs me to inform you that the plan of proceedings suggested by me in my letter of the 11th, and which I am happy to find meets with your approbation in the material points, seems to be in every respect such as may be attended, in your hands and under your authority, and that of the magistrates of the Hundred of Salford, with the most beneficial effects, in counteracting this attempt to excite a spirit of dissatisfaction amongst the workmen in your neighbourhood. . . (H.O.43/11/295).

---

[1] The Radical Societies such as the London Corresponding Society and the Society of United Englishmen (which had been founded in Lancashire before 1797). For their activities see the *Report from the Committee of Secrecy relative to a Treasonable Conspiracy*, 1799. (*Parl. Hist.*, XXXIV, 579–656).

[2] Mr. Bayley was informed on the 25th that 'It is the opinion of his Majesty's Attorney and Solicitor-General that "no prosecution can be instituted against the authors, printers and publishers" of the papers transmitted by you in your letter of the 16th inst.' (H.O.43/11/305).

(34). [The following document is a printed Handbill].

New Bayley Court-House, Salford. Thursday, 28 *November,* 1799.
At a general meeting of the acting active magistrates, within the
hundred of Salford, in the County Palatine of Lancaster, held here
this day—

We, the undersigned, taking into consideration the various and
repeated attempts that have lately been made to excite a spirit of
dissatisfaction amongst the weavers, and others employed in the
manufactures of this County ; and by violent handbills and other
inflammatory publications, to encourage an illegal opposition to the
Act passed in the last Session of Parliament, 'To prevent unlawful
combinations amongst workmen,' do hereby signify our determined
resolution to maintain, as much as in us lies, due obedience to the
laws ; and strictly to watch over, and severely to punish all persons
who shall offend in any of the cases above-mentioned. And we do
further declare to all persons in the lower stations of life amongst us,
that we at all times possess a most compassionate feeling for their
wants and distresses arising from the various events which Divine
Providence may permit to chasten us, and more particularly at this
time, when a sudden check has been given to trade, and a most unfavourable season has not bestowed upon us the kindly fruits of the
earth in their usual abundance, we declare our fixed purpose, both
as public and private men, to employ every means in our power to
protect and relieve all those who are in distress, and who shall conduct themselves orderly, lawfully and peaceably.

'Every confederacy to injure individuals, or to do acts which are
unlawful or prejudicial to the community, is a conspiracy.' And, in
our opinion, by the common law of England, a conspiracy whether
by masters or workmen, whether to raise or to lower the price of
labour, ought to be indicted and punished as an unlawful act. It
requires little experience to know that at all times, the price of
labour ought and must be free and unshackled. It is governed by a
greater or less demand, which depends on circumstances beyond the
control of masters or servants. Let both these parties seriously consider that their interests are mutual, that one cannot subsist without
the other. Let the masters, when trade is dead, consider the times
when goods have been, and may again be, in great demand, and in
this season afford to their poor distressed weavers every practicable
assistance in employment and wages ; and many weavers, and others

employed in manufactures, be sober, careful, and use all diligence, in patient expectation of better days.

And we do most affectionately advise and entreat them not to give ear to the evil suggestions and writings of a set of emissaries who, we have reason to believe, are now employed by certain unlawful and *seditious* Societies, to poison their minds and excite them to disaffection and mischief. [The signatures follow.] (H.O.42/48).

(35). *The Duke of Portland to R. S. Hedley*[1]

Whitehall, 21 December, 1799.

It has been represented to me that some colliers, destined for the London market, have been detained at Shields in consequence of a combination among the sailors at that place.

I am therefore to desire that you will make a speedy and particular inquiry into this circumstance ; and as all such combinations are unlawful, and are now more particularly provided against by the Act of the last Session for preventing unlawful combinations of workmen, I am to desire that you will use your best endeavours in suppressing such proceedings without loss of time, and that you will take the most effectual means for bringing to justice the persons who shall be found to have been the promoters of them . . . (H.O. 43/11/318-19).

(36). *R. S. Hedley to the Duke of Portland*

Newcastle-on-Tyne, 13 January, 1800.

I was honoured with your Lordship's letter of the 21st ult. desiring me to make speedy and particular inquiry into the circumstances of some colliers, destined for the London market, having been detained at Shields in consequence of a combination of the sailors at that place.

Since the receipt of your Grace's letter, my attention has been directed to the object pointed out, but I have not been able to trace any combination or any detention of the coal vessels, beyond what arises from the owners and their seamen differing as to the quantum of wages. It is (unfortunately perhaps) the practice to postpone the treaty for the wages of each voyage till the ship is loaded and ready

---

[1] Mayor of Newcastle-upon-Tyne.

for sea ; and any material difference of opinion between the parties on the subject, of course, retards her sailing. The demands of the sailors are generally governed by the then price of coals at market, and they are in consequence pretty uniform with each other in their amount, and perhaps it is to be lamented that the late high prices have induced a too frequent compliance of the owners, as well as incited unreasonable claims from the sailors.

On the present occasion, my Lord, no information or charge has been brought before me of any illegal measure taken by the sailors, nor have I been able to discover that any of them has transgressed the law. (H.O 42/49).

(37). *The Marquess of Buckingham[1] to the Duke of Portland*

Gosfield, [Essex], 2 November, 1800.

... Above all, I wish for powers to check that combination amongst farmers on the subject of labourers' wages, that throws them all upon the parish rates : a system that, to my ideas, is destructive of every vital principle of government, and which is now (by abuse) so established that nothing short of law (and strong law to be administered by magistrates in a summary way) can check it . . .[2] H.O.42/53).

(38). *To his Grace the Duke of Portland, the Humble Memorial of the Committee of Master Tailors appointed to prosecute their journeymen for a combination to obtain an advance of wages.* [1800].

Sheweth, that the journeymen of the different masters in the above trade have, in order to compel an advance of wages, recently withdrew themselves from work and have entered into a combination of so serious and dangerous a description that it threatens destruction to their trade if not suppressed by every legal means on the part of the masters.

[1] Second son of George Grenville, the Prime Minister, and brother of Lord Grenville, Foreign Secretary in Pitt's first Ministry.

[2] The Marquess wished for these powers in his private capacity. He was Lord Lieutenant of Ireland from 1787 to 1789, when he practically retired from active politics.

The year 1800 was a year of food scarcity, the harvest of 1799 having failed. The Duke of Portland wrote to Viscount Bulkeley on 17 November : ' I cannot refrain from observing to your Lordship how desirable it is, in times like the present, that wages should be paid, partly in provisions in all cases where the same is practicable.'

E

That this combination has been general throughout the trade, and the masters have convened meetings not only for the putting in force the existing laws against their men but also to ascertain how the evil will be best prevented in future.

That it appears to your memorialists that it will be impossible among so large a body of men as the journeymen tailors, amounting in number to 18,000 and upwards, ever to put it out of the power of them to enter into combinations against their masters, by carrying the laws into execution which cannot without great difficult[y] and expense be made to operate upon every offender, but that any means that can be devised for destroying the communication which the journeymen keep up through the medium of those public houses, in the language of their trade called houses of call, will be best calculated to effect the purpose.

That these houses of call are the very basis and foundation of such combinations is unquestionably the fact. In all parts of the metropolis these houses are established and every journeyman is compelled to belong and resort to a Society there formed.

That these houses of call keep up a correspondence with each other, and their object is by such correspondence to enable them to act in concert whenever they think proper to strike or withdraw themselves from work. Every journeyman contributes a certain portion of his wages towards raising a fund for the general purposes of the Society, the most obvious of which purposes is to maintain themselves when, as in the present case, they choose to absent themselves from work, and without such fund the necessity of resorting to legal means on this occasion would have been superseded by the men's return to their duty. One other very serious mischief attendant upon these houses of call and of which the present combination affords an alarming instance is their being enabled to act in unison with each other. The demand on the part of the men for advance of wages was no sooner signified to the masters and refused, than the whole body of journeymen to the number of 15,000 and upwards, in one morning withdrew themselves from work and are now in idleness, to the great surprise as well as injury of the masters who, the evening before, were total strangers to any such resolution of the men.

The Societies established at each of these houses of call may be considered as divisions of the Society at large, and consequently have delegates or representatives chosen from among them to communicate their resolutions to each other, and to manage their respective funds, and to enable them to act in a systematic manner, that there are now daily meetings of the men at those houses of call for the purpose of resisting any steps that the masters may take against them, and for consulting upon the means that may be most likely to injure and distress them.

That your memorialists are fully convinced that so long as these Societies or rather houses of call are kept up, it will be impossible for the masters ever to be secure from the combinations of their men, that the consequence of them is that the men are thereby enabled to control the masters, whose compliance with their demands is almost necessary to preserve their trade, that the abolition of them would not only be of the greatest benefit to the masters but also to the men themselves, many of whom, however industrious, are compelled by the terms of the Society to engage in every illegal object that the bulk of them think proper to pursue.

Your memorialists therefore on the part of themselves as well as the rest of the master tailors, humbly hope your Grace will, from this statement, take into your consideration the dangerous and alarming consequences of these Societies not only as they affect the trade in general which by their continuance is threatened with destruction, but also in a political point of view, the mischievous consequences that may result to society at large by so large a body of men as the journeymen tailors being enabled to withdraw themselves from work and support themselves in idleness and dissipation, and therefore humbly pray that your Grace will order and direct the magistrates in their respective divisions to summon before them the landlords of the different houses of call in such divisions, and admonish and forewarn them against suffering these Societies to be held any longer at their respective houses, upon pain of forfeiting their licenses, or that your Grace will adopt such other measures for their suppressing as to your Grace shall seem expedient.

Signed, by order of the Committee,
George Smith, Chairman.[1] (H.O.42/54).

[1] There is an accompanying note :—' H.R.H. the Prince of Wales sent to Mr. Ford yesterday and desired him to lay before the Duke of Portland the enclosed Memorial, with H.R.H.'s strong recommendation.' This is docketed by the Duke of Portland : 'I do not know that, as Secretary of State, I have any right to interfere that every magistrate does not possess equally with me.'

The *Annual Register*, 1801, Chronicle, p. 6, has the following paragraph : ' 26 January : The case of the journeymen tailors, who have so long stood out

[Continued on p. 36]

(39). *William Stephen Poyntz*[2] *to John King*

Cowdray Lodge, Midhurst, 8 *September,* 1801.

Enclosed I send copies of two letters which Mr Paine, the foreman of a paper mill at Sping, near Midhurst, has just delivered to me, as they throw some light on a serious combination throughout the kingdom, and which may not relate to paper-making alone. I am unwilling to take any steps, as a magistrate, by committing Midhurst the bearer of them, till I receive your Lordship's directions. Mr. Paine says Midhurst, who is a principal workman in Seikee Paper Mill near Haslemere, brought the letters to Spring Mill, and not finding Mullard, delivered them to another man in his presence, that he (Paine) opened and read them. That all the workmen at his mill immediately struck, and demanded 3s. a week more than they now receive, but that they returned to their work on the 5th and 9th articles of the Act relative to paper-makers being read to them[3] . . .

[*Continued from p. 35*]

for an increase of wages from 25 to 30s. per week, came on to be heard before Alderman Brook Watson (as *locum tenens* for the Lord Mayor), the Recorder, Sir William Anderson, and three other Aldermen. Mr. Gurney was heard on behalf of the journeymen, and the Common Serjeant for the masters. The court examined three of the principal tailors on behalf of the masters, and three of the principal workmen on behalf of the journeymen. The masters all swore that they considered 25s. a week a fair, just, and reasonable allowance, considering all the circumstances of the times, and that the trade had increased since 1795, as also the number of workmen. The three workmen, on the contrary, deposed that they could not live in comfort and support their families decently under 30s. a week ; they gave an account of their houses of call and their general system of proceeding. Every house of call had three books, on which the workmen were rated according to the length of their residence in London ; and those who were on the last or third book could not procure employment until all those of the preceding books were served. Each member paid 2d. a week at his particular house of call for this privilege : which sum went to create a fund for the support of the sick and infirm, and no others. Those who struck and would not work under 30s. were called *flints* : they were also called the *honourable men*, and would not work on the same board with those who should take less than 30s. and who were called *dungs*. The Recorder gave judgment : that the journeymen should be allowed 27s. a week, and double that sum, or 54s., in case of a general mourning.'

[2] M.P. for St. Albans. (1770–1840).

[3] 36 George III, c. 111. 'An Act to prevent unlawful combinations of workmen employed in the paper manufactory.' The penalty for breaking the law was imprisonment with hard labour for a period not exceeding two calendar months.

[*Enclosures.*]

To Mr. Mullard, Sping Mill.
Gents.—The enclosed was sent to Guilford, and forwarded to Hasle-mere, from thence to Sping.

Health and Fraternity,
Seikee Mill,

2 September, 1801.

Neckinger, 28 August, 1801.
Sir,—This is to acquaint you that we have now made our fifth sub-scription of 2s. 6d. each, which makes 12s. 6d. per man. Now our request is that your division will come forward now, as money is much wanted. We also desire you will forward this to the other divisions of Haslemere and Sping, &c. without delay. I have many things to acquaint you of, but for want of time I must defer till another opportunity. I shall mention to you that I have been to Maidstone by appointment, where I was met by a very respectable body of our trade, 44 in number, where I produced the sick, and secret articles of our trade, which were generally and universally approved and signed, and are to be printed ; also the cards of freedom. Everything bears a favourable aspect, and I hope will have a favourable issue. It would be a pity, after spending so many hundreds, to lose the cause at last for want of support. Manchester and Wells approve of our plan, and they say that they will establish it in every mill from Berwick to the Lands End. (*H.O.*42/62).

(40). *John King to W. S. Poyntz*

Whitehall, 14 *September*, 1801. (*Draft*).
Lord Pelham[1] not being in town, I take this opportunity of inform-ing you, in answer to your letter to his Lordship of yesterday's date,[2] that upon the receipt of yours of Tuesday last relative to the com-bination amongst the paper makers, it was immediately referred to the Attorney and Solicitor-General for their opinion as to what

---

[1] Home Secretary from July 1801 to August 1803.

[2] Poyntz's letter of the 13th inquired whether his earlier one had been received. He added, 'You will oblige me by communicating your wishes on the subject, as the paper makers in this part of the country have shown a disposition to riot, and their masters wish me to lay hold of the person who carried the letter from Haslemere to Sping Mill.'

steps it might be proper to take thereupon, and as soon as ever their report is received, not a moment will be lost in making you the necessary communications. (H.O.42/62. See also H.O.43/13/170).

(41). *William Blackburn to Rowland Burdon*

South Shields, 16 *December*, 1801.[1]

In consequence of a reduction of wages being signified to the shipwrights of this place, they chose to strike, as it is termed, and thereafter did assemble in large bodies, preventing any of their own fraternity working, and even attempting to decoy the foreman, but in consequence of Messrs. Bulmer acting spiritedly, as appears by the enclosed handbill No. 1, the tumult in the place subsided, but they still continue off work, and have since sent a threatening letter to Mr. Joseph Bulmer, a copy enclosed, No. 2—and Messrs. Bulmer have since issued the advertisement No. 3. In addition to which, they and the other gentlemen of this place, especially the shipbuilders and dockowners, have to request you will immediately apply to the Secretary of State to second such advertisement with his Majesty's pardon and reward, for such proceedings, unless speedily checked, may end in serious consequences.

[*Enclosures.*]

No. 1. [A printed handbill.]   *Town Hall, South Shields.*
We, the undernamed persons, shipwrights, resident in *South Shields*, do acknowledge that we have committed a great abuse in clandestinely entering the dockyard of Messrs. Bulmer in *South Shields*, and endeavouring to prevail on the foremen to quit their work ; and declare, in this public manner, our thanks to Messrs. Bulmer for their withdrawing the prosecution commenced against us, on the late Act of Parliament for preventing unlawful combinations of workmen : and promise that we will not invade the peace of the town or neighbourhood by a repetition of these acts.

---

[1] Enclosed in Roland Burdon's letter to J. King, Castle Eden, 7 December, 1801, in which he asks that his Majesty's pardon and reward should be offered, as proposed in Blackburn's letter.

We also consent that this declaration shall be published by a circulation of handbills.

> Peter Lawson, Thomas Hunter, James Hunter, Thomas Whiteman, William Newton, John Rutter.

Witnesses,
Charles Cockerill
Jonathan Cockerill
9 *December,* 1801.

No. 2. You Bulmer, if you do not give the carpenters a *guinea* a week as sure as Hell is hot O before winter is done you must be shot O . . .

No. 3.—[A printed handbill offering a reward of 100 guineas for information leading to the conviction of the writer of the threatening letter, which was put under the door of the Compting-house of Messrs. R. Bulmer & Co., and found on the 14th. The handbill is dated the 15th.]

(H.O.42/62).

(42) *Abstract of proposed Act of Parliament for abolishing and suppressing the Societies of Journeymen boot-and-shoe-makers, and for the more effectual preventing unlawful combinations of Journeymen.* (*Undated, Docketed, 'Found with March, 1802 Dom.'*)

Recites, That great numbers of journeymen boot-makers and shoe-makers within the United Kingdom of Great Britain and Ireland have for some time past formed themselves into Societies, and presumed, contrary to law, to enter into combinations for regulating the concerns of the trades and businesses of boot-and-shoe-making and have for that purpose adopted Bye-laws, subjecting the members of such Societies, under certain fines and penalties, to submit to the regulations of such Societies concerning their conduct in such trade and business, whereby the said Societies have obtained a controlling power over the masters in the said trade, to compel the said masters to submit to such rules and regulations as to such Societies seem meet, to the entire subversion and destruction of that subordination which should exist from a journeyman to his master, and to the great stagnation, interruption and obstruction of the said trade and business.

Enacts, That all such Societies, the members whereof are or shall be bound to submit to the Resolutions of such Societies touching their conduct in respect of their trade, shall be suppressed and prohibited, as being unlawful combinations and confederacies.

That every person who shall be guilty of any unlawful combination, as in this Act is described, and being convicted thereof by Indictment by due course of law, shall suffer such punishment as by law may be inflicted on persons convicted of combination.

That if any person shall knowingly permit any meeting of any such Society to be held in his house or apartment, such person shall be deemed guilty of an unlawful combination . . .

That it shall be lawful for any two Justices upon evidence on oath, that any meeting of any such Society hath been held at any house, &c. licensed for the sale of ale, beer, wine or spirituous liquors, to adjudge the license granted to the person keeping such house, &c. to be forfeited.

That on complaint on oath before any Justice, of any offence having been committed against this Act, such Justice is authorised to issue his warrant for apprehending the person charged, and to bind him in a recognisance to appear at the next Session to answer any complaint that may be exhibited against him.

That it shall not be lawful for any master boot- or shoe-maker after the expiration of [blank] days from the passing of this Act, knowingly to hire any person, being a member of any such Society, and that if any master shall hire any person being a member of any such Society, knowing him to be such, he shall forfeit [blank] £ for each and every day that he shall retain such member in his said trade . . . (H.O. 42/65).

(43). *Earl Fitzwilliam*[1] *to Lord Pelham*

Grosvenor Square, 7 June, 1802.

I have just now the honour of your Lordship's letter, enclosing one signed 'Fred. Flower' to Mr. Addington,[2] giving information of meetings in Dewsbury and Batley and other places in the manufacturing part of the West Riding.

---

[1] He was Lord Lieutenant of the West Riding of Yorkshire, 1798–1819. One of the 'Old Whigs,' he had joined Pitt's Government in 1794 as Lord President of the Council, and was Lord Lieutenant of Ireland for a short time in 1795.

[2] Prime Minister, 1801–4.

When I was at Leeds about the middle of April, a very active magistrate told me that he understood there had been meetings, or at least that he suspected it ; from that gentleman I have heard nothing since, so that I am confident that there have not been any to alarm him.

From another magistrate, who resides in Wakefield, I had a letter on other business, dated 27 May, which concludes with the following paragraph : 'Since my return from London (about a fortnight ago) I have been informed meetings of the lower orders continue frequently to be held. Their numbers and object may by some persons possibly be magnified, but as far as I can learn I conceive it to be only the different classes of people for the purpose of raising their wages, and from which nothing is to be apprehended.' (H.O.42/65).

(44). *Matthew Davies to Lord Pelham.*

Warminster, Tuesday evening, 15 *June,* 1802.
In addition to the many outrages lately committed in this town, I am sorry to be under the necessity of informing your lordship that this morning between 12 and 1 o'clock a rick of oats worth about £20, belonging to Mr. Peter Warren, clothier of this town, was maliciously set on fire and entirely consumed. A dog kennel at some distance therefrom, the property of the said Mr. Warren and others, was at the same time also set on fire and partly consumed.

That there is no doubt but this daring outrage was committed by some of the workmen usually employed in the woollen manufactory, who now and have for many weeks past refused to work on account of some machines being introduced which they consider as obnoxious, although the same have been used for many years in other parts of the kingdom.

They have at present no visible means of any livelihood, and there is good reason to think they are supported and encouraged by contributions from many of the innkeepers and other inhabitants of the place. It is thought some strong declaration on the part of Government of the illegality of this practice, addressed to the neighbouring magistrates with orders that it may be printed and posted up in different places, would be of great service.

They have secret combinations to support each other, which [it] is impossible to get good proof of without an accomplice will discover it . . . (H.O.42/65).

(45). *John Jones,*[1] *junior, to Lord Pelham*

Woolley, nr. Bradford, Wilts., 20 July, 1802.

. . . I solicit your Lordship to inform me if I shall be justified in endeavouring to seize a committee of 13 persons, with the papers and books belonging to the shearmen of Trowbridge, of which I have this morning obtained some intelligence, and I expect more momentarily.

It is reported these men are now soliciting a subscription throughout the country to support those refusing to work but upon their own terms, and that many persons have in consequence countenanced them by giving money. I learn the Committee issue pass tickets to their members.

. . . I am compelled to inform your Lordship the threats which the workmen in my mill have received from these shearmen (or cloth workers) induce them daily to leave it, and I dread to be forced thereby to stop the whole works. (H.O.42/65).

(46). *John Jones, sen., to John King*

Frankley, nr. Bradford, Wilts., 26 July, 1802.

. . . This day a deputation of seven men from the Society of these people waited on my son at his house in Woolley, nr. Bradford, and he having previous notice of their intention, requested Mr. Bush, a magistrate living at Bradford, and Mr. Hobhouse, M.P., living in our neighbourhood, with two other gentlemen and myself to attend, and we were all there, the result of which, taken down in writing, I have the honour to transmit to you as well as a copy of an anonymous letter sent to Mr. Hobhouse, and also a pass ticket given by this Society to their members, which entitles them to a certain pecuniary donation when they are out of employ, and serves as a token of their being known to be one of their Society . . .

Mills are destroyed weekly all over the country, and ricks of hay almost nightly. A great number of these people reside in Leeds in Yorkshire, and carry on a regular correspondence with those here, and not only that, they have frequent deputations passing from the different Counties where they are employed . . .

---

[1] He was a Wiltshire J.P.

[Enclosures.]

26 July, 1802—A deputation of seven shearmen, viz. Samuel Jones, John Mead, James Mead, Henry King, Benjamin Pitman, William Sheppard and Thomas Tuck, came to Mr. Jones's house at Woolley. When he offered them to employ all the men at this time out of work belonging to the parish of Bradford (stated by him at thirty) and always to give a preference to the employment of men of the said parish rather than use the frames for the cutting or shearing of cloth whilst any such men should want work, and added that in future no gigging[1] or shearing shall be done for hire by him on account of other manufacturers, which offer they rejected in behalf of the body of shearmen who deputed them, and declared it was the resolution of the shearmen throughout England, Scotland and Ireland not to work after machinery, in the presence of the following gentlemen who were with Mr. Jones—Benjamin Hobhouse, Esq., M.P., Thomas Bush, Esq., Acting Magistrate in Bradford, John Jones, senior, Thomas Tugwell, and John Hunt.

Note. Samuel Jones declared he would rather be hanged than recommend the shearmen to accept Mr. Jones's offer, or to work after machinery.

Opinion of the Law Officers of the Crown,[2] *28 July,* 1802.

We are of opinion that the conduct of the individuals who came to Mr. Jones's house will support an indictment for a conspiracy, and we should recommend an indictment to be prepared and sent down to the Assizes for Wiltshire, charging these seven men with such conspiracy, and that Mr. Hobhouse and the other persons present with Mr. Jones should attend at the Assizes to go before the Grand Jury with the Bill. (H.O.42/65).

---

[1] Gig mills were machines for raising the fibres in a piece of woollen cloth in order to form a nap on the surface which was later shorn off so as to give the cloth a smooth and soft appearance. The latter process was done by the shearmen, whose shears might weigh up to 40 lbs. The introduction into Wiltshire of this labour-saving machinery in 1802 resulted in many outrages. In Yorkshire the shearmen were known as croppers. See No. 65.

[2] Spencer Perceval (Attorney-General), and Thomas Manners-Sutton (Solicitor-General).

(47). *John Jones, jun., to Lord Pelham*

Woolley, 27 July, 1802.

. . . The very atrocious outrages which have been committed about this vicinity are most disgraceful to a civilised country, but such is the secrecy observed by these nightly assassins, no information has hitherto been obtained, and I lament to say the general intimidation of the country appears so strong that coercive measures alone will produce any discovery, for which the seizure of the committees formed and forming, seems most desirable, as also an examination at the Post Office in London of letters from the manufacturing towns in Yorkshire to those in Wiltshire, Somersetshire and Gloucestershire . . .

Not being able to attend the approaching Assizes at Salisbury, in consequence of my duties here, and not having the honour of knowing the Judges, I beg leave to suggest how far your Lordship may deem it advisable to acquaint their Lordships of the dreadful destructions which have taken place, as also of the existing combinations which threaten an annihilation of the trade ; respecting which, I respectfully request your Lordship's attention as concerns myself and partners in particular, for we experience the most wicked attempts to ruin our manufacture by threats not only against our own persons but likewise against the lives of such persons who shall continue to work for us, whereby one whole branch of our business is wholly stopped ; and without the declared support of Government in our favour, and protection of our works, we may suffer the demolition of a most extensive establishment, which I have not any hesitation in saying I consider of national consideration, and for which reason I beg permission to solicit the appointment of some person by Government to report of my assertions, for the effects of such combinations are more to be dreaded than even open attacks. (H.O.42/65).

(48). *Earl Fitzwilliam to Lord Pelham*

Milton, 28 July, 1802.

[Referring to a letter from Mr. Cookson, Mayor of Leeds] . . . Your Lordship will observe that the whole object of this letter is not to represent danger from seditious, revolutionary conspiracies, and from numerous meetings for such general purposes, but inconvenience and mischief to the manufacturer and merchant from clubs and combinations of workmen, for the special purpose of raising wages and the price of work : objects certainly of very different concern. When I was at Leeds in the spring of the year I then heard of nightly meetings, but upon conversing with a very sensible magistrate, a man very jealous of popular spirit, I found it to be his opinion that the principal incentives to those meetings were of this partial nature more than of a public one. But though this opinion of my friend seems much strengthened by the tenor of Mr. Cookson's letter, still there appears from the different reports I have lately had occasion to transmit to your Lordship, but too much ground of apprehension that though partial considerations may increase the numbers of those who have formed the late meetings, the persons who manage these meetings have very different objects in view, and will use the private motives of their followers to furthering their own public purposes.

I have much respect for the character of Mr. Cookson individu- ally, and a very high one for the general one of the body of merchants and manufacturers. Great attention ought to be paid to them and to their interests. But your Lordship will pardon me if I am frank in making a general observation on this occasion, that the consider- ation of partial evils (if they are really evils) arising out of public occasions, is very apt to lead to partial decisions. To convert the subject of public meetings, held for a general change of Government or annihilation of taxes, which is the same thing, into an occasion for obtaining more restrictive laws against combinations of journey- men for increase of wages, may lead to the consideration of a very difficult and doubtful subject, under circumstances, when prejudice may perhaps keep under, sound reason and just principle. Trades that have exclusive privileges by the favour of the law, ought to submit their profits to the decision of the law : if they are at liberty to fix their own price on the article of their monopoly, it is a crying grievance on their fellow subjects who are obliged to purchase from them : but where trades are open to the industry of every man, where there is no force on the buyer to purchase the article, but its in- trinsic value, it is scarcely fair to put limitation upon the price. I am inclined to think that every man is at liberty to weave, to dress cloth, to perform any of the processes in the manufacture, without having gone through any apprenticeship ; it is a trade open to all. If it is so, others will come in and do the work the persons in question refuse to do, but upon advance of wages, unless the art is so great that it cannot be done by every one : in which case these men have a right to the value of their ingenuity and to make, as occasion arises, as much of it as it will yield : when the demands for it are great, that is the season of harvest for them, and it would be hard to preclude them from the benefit of that season ; in truth, it would not be a measure of justice on the part of Parliament. I am not sure that we should not afford them ground of complaint against the Constitution, that we should not drive them into the service of the true Jacobin, and by our own acts, furnish a justification for theirs : for if the Legislature does not deal out equal justice and equal protection, much is to be said in justification of the subjects who attempt to withdraw from it.

But though I am perhaps very unfittingly obtruding sentiments of my own, in consequence of what I look upon to be the ultimate and principal drift of Mr. Cookson's letter, still I must recommend to your Lordship's consideration his concluding request that, owing to the circumstances of the times, not less than two troops of Dragoons be continued at Leeds. I believe this to be necessary . . .

I shall . . . go down to the Assizes and take my chance of meeting there[1] some of the magistrates, who are the best informed upon the subject of these meetings ; and by their assistance enter upon such measures as shall seem best suited to put an end to the sort of conspiracy which, I fear, does exist, in a greater or a lesser degree, I mean, the true Jacobinical sort of conspiracy. I trust, the real secret is in *very few* hands, that the rest are dupes ; but I cannot help believing there is much mischief in the minds of the men who agitate that country. (H.O.42/65).

(49). *John Jones, Jun., to Lord Pelham*

Woolley, 30 July, 1802.

In consequence of Mr. King's letter of yesterday I hasten to acquaint your Lordship the seven men who came to my house last Monday were promised that no advantage should be taken of their attendance upon that occasion by the person who persuaded them to see me, and although it is most certainly desirable to make examples without delay, yet I am of opinion I shall personally become reprobated for an apparent deception towards these men, who surely must have considered themselves secure from all proceedings against them under engagement, and therefore I am to solicit your

[1] At York, the following week.

Lordship will direct at least a suspension of the proposed prosecution, for I really feel I shall be unjustified in such a measure being adopted . . . (H.O.42/65).

(50). *John King to John Jones, Jun.*

Whitehall, [? 31] *July* 1802. (*Draft*).

I lose no time in informing you by direction of Lord Pelham that his Majesty's law servants are of opinion that the conduct of the individuals who came to your house on the 26th inst., as stated in the paper transmitted in your father's letter to me of that date, will support an indictment for a conspiracy ; and that in pursuance of that opinion, an indictment will be immediately prepared here by the Crown Solicitor, ready to be sent to the Assizes, charging the seven persons mentioned in that paper with such conspiracy.

Your father, Mr. Hobhouse, and the other persons present on the 26th inst., when the deputation came to your house, will, of course, attend at the Assizes, to go before the Grand Jury with the Bill. (H.O.42/65).

(51). *John Wells to John King*

Deptford, 3 August, 1802.

I take the liberty of communicating to you the consequence of the attendance of the magistrates with the police at Messrs. Barnard's Yard this morning. The caulkers from the King's Yard, Deptford, having the assurance of protection, proceeded to Messrs. Barnard's & Co. yard notwithstanding a show of ill disposition in a mob collected round the gates who, awed by the presence and determined conduct of the magistrates, did not offer any violence. Indeed, two of the caulkers standing out from work came forward with a proposition which I hope may settle this unfortunate business, which I assure you gives us much pain in presuming to trouble you with, but I must add that we did not apply to your Office till we had in vain made every effort to gain assistance elsewhere, and when referred to you to direct that power and protection without which we could not have proceeded for a moment, but have given in to be entirely dictated to by an illegal combination of people who have completely stopped the fitting of every ship in the river for two months, and have eventually threatened our lives and property. (H.O.42/66).

(52). *William Henry and George Sheppard to Lord Pelham*

Frome, Somerset, 5 August, 1802.

. . . Our workpeople stood by us until intimidated by the harsh threats of the multitude. They are for the most part *now sworn* to secrecy and *dare* not return. The extent of this league cannot be fathomed, and we fear, from the sound of delegates and meetings in the most secret way, as well as the support obtained, that it is deeper rooted than we are aware of . . . (H.O.42/66).

(53). *John Harriott[1] to John King*

Thames Police Office, 6 August, 1802.

. . . Notwithstanding the assurances given on Tuesday last by the disaffected caulkers not to disturb or molest others, complaints have been made before us of violent assaults made by them on those who are disposed to work—some of which complaints are now in a train to bring the offending parties forward. At the same time we hear they have retracted altogether their promise to leave this dispute to be settled by arbitration.

Late last night Mr. Brent, while attending on these complaints said he had heard a report that the caulkers at the King's Yard, Deptford, had been driven from their work. Although I could not believe it true, I thought it right to go down there this morning and am happy to say all was quiet. But I was informed by the officers of the Yard that on Wednesday night a strong party of men (supposed to be caulkers) went down the river in three boats to meet some King's caulkers coming from Chatham in a vessel to work at the merchants yards,[2] and compelled them to return. From the general spirit that seems to pervade the whole (shipwrights, caulkers and sawyers) I fear that nothing short of strong coercive measures will bring them to any order. (H.O.42/66).

---

[1] The Thames Police Court magistrate, 1798–1816 (1745–1817).

[2] For the decay of shipbuilding in the private yards of the Thames, see the petition, signed by 2,000 artisan shipbuilders of the Port of London, presented to the House of Commons on 23 March, 1814. There were at that time 41 slips for building ships. (*Parl. Deb.*, XXVII. 341).

(54). *Earl Fitzwilliam to Lord Pelham*

Wentworth, 9 August, 1802.

... There may be combination of workmen : it is very probable that there is here, from the state of the workmen of the West of England, hints of which your Lordship in your last letter communicated to me as being reported to you by Lord Pembroke ; not unlikely there is communication kept up between the two—but I am more and more inclined to hope that should unfortunately any flame burst out here, it will be found to originate, not in any principle of a public nature, but in the partial cause of jarring interests of masters and workmen. None, however, I trust will : but should anything lead to acts of outrage and violence, I am confident the magistrates of the West Riding will always be found vigilant, alert and resolute in suppressing the first symptoms of such a disposition in maintaining the just authority of the laws ... (H.O.42/66).

(55). *James Read[1] to Lord Pelham*

Bradford (*Wilts.*), 9 *August,* 1802.

... Hilliker has been committed to the County gaol.[2] We have two or three other men in custody for further examination, one of whom is stated to have come to a manufacturer (his master) about ten days ago, with a message (as he said, from the committee of the shearmen's Club, desiring to know what he meant to do in the business, as to acceding or not to the shearmen's terms of working — and upon the manufacturer saying he should do as other employers did, he desired him to be cool and take care what he said, as he (the messenger) had taken an oath to tell the committee everything he said ... The prisoner ... says he is a member of the shearmen's Club, and that lately he has been called upon to take an oath ' to be true to the shearmen, and see that none of them are hurt, and not to divulge any of their secrets.' That the committee consists of 13 and meet on Wednesdays—that there is a chairman, a clerk and two stewards, that the oath was administered to him by the clerk, that he has a printed ticket which he states to be the same as is used by the shearmen Clubs in Yorkshire, and if he were to go into Yorkshire

---

[1] The Chief Magistrate at Bow Street. He was sent into Wiltshire by the Government to inquire into the outrages.

[2] Hilliker (or Elleker) was charged with burning the mill at Littleton. He was capitally convicted at the Salisbury Assizes in March 1803, and executed.

F

it would enable him to get work there. He says the ticket is changed once a year, and that the shearmen will not suffer any man to work who has not got a ticket—that there is a Club in every town in Yorkshire and in many parts of England.

Upon this information I have judged it right to advise the magistrates to take up all the committee and to search the habitations of the Chairman, Clerk and Stewards, and if we should be fortunate enough to find any material papers, it may meet the evil at once. I am informed that the committee have always met on the same night when any violence has been done. The shearmen's Club in this County is clearly connected with a Club of the same description in Yorkshire, and although I have not yet discovered that they have any other object in view than that of making better terms with their employers and of getting rid of the gig mills, yet it appears to me that the Club is likely to become a dangerous engine—upon the present extensive plan. I am informed that the principal bank is at Leeds in Yorkshire, and I expect to-morrow to know the person . . .

Ibid. to Ibid., Bradford, 10 August 1802 :—I am sorry to say that the measure I intended of apprehending the Trowbridge committee and of searching the premises of four of them did not succeed owing to some of the parties I ha¹ appointed to meet me not coming to their time. We however apprehended James May (one of the committee) and who acts as their clerk) upon the information of Thomas Bailey, who I either named or alluded to in my last letter as having been sworn in the committee by James May *to be true to every journeyman shearman, that they should not be hurted and not to divulge any secret.* May appears to have been a very considerable actor in forwarding the views of the Society. The printer who printed the Rules identifies May as the man who gave him the manuscript of the Rules to print them from ; he also, by order of May, got the Club tickets engraved, one of which as well as a copy of the Rules I understand have been forwarded to your Lordship. The printer says, the pattern ticket came from Yorkshire and had the word *Leeds* instead of *Trowbridge* at the bottom, which is the only difference between them. The printer has orders from a man (he pretends not to know) to get 400 tickets engraved, for Bradford. I have no doubt but May knows a great deal if he would communicate it. He said upon his examination that he worked for Mr. Waldon, who was a very honourable man, and if other clothiers had behaved as he had done the disturbances would *not* have happened. The Act of 37 George III, ch. 123, against administering unlawful oaths, I think applies to

May's case, and to all others of the committee who were present when the oath was administered, and I mean to-day or to-morrow when the meeting will be at Trowbridge, to identify and take up as many as I can. It will create a shock, and some of them thinking themselves in danger may probably come forward against the rest . . .[1]

These clubs are certainly not of many months' standing, and I think their government is at Leeds. A letter has been seen as coming from thence, directing the formation of clubs and committees of correspondence, and to write as sensible a letter as they could and direct it and any other letters to George Palmer, Duke Street, near St. Peter's Square, Leeds. The person who communicated this to me is a respectable clothier at Warminster, and as he did not come by his knowledge of the contents in an honourable manner, I at present can give your Lordship no further information about it, but I hope to do it at a future day . . . (H.O.42/66).

(56). *Earl Fitzwilliam to Lord Pelham*

Wentworth, 21 *August*, 1802.

I enclose for your Lordship's perusal two letters which I received yesterday : one, from Mr. Cookson, the Mayor of Leeds, the other from Colonel Dixon. Both these letters convey more distinct inform- ation on the subject of the management and organisation of the nocturnal meetings than had ever before reached me ; and likewise more direct evidence of one meeting having actually taken place. Mr. Cookson makes his report from the mouth of a person who was an eye-witness, at least as much so as he was permitted to be. Mr. Dixon has an account likewise of the same meeting : for though there may be found to be a difference of dates, that is, the one making it on Friday, which was the 13th, the other the 14th, this difference may be accounted for by the meeting having been held in the night between the 13th and the 14th, but I conceive both letters refer to the same meeting, as the situation, though described in different manners, is the same. Whether each of these gentlemen has his report from the same person, or not, is more than I can ascertain, but certainly Mr. Cookson's informer gives a very distinct account of the transaction, as far as he was permitted to see into it ;

---

[1] James May and four others charged with administering an unlawful oath were subsequently acquitted, ' owing to our witness (the accomplice) failing in his testimony. He had evidently been tampered with.' (H.O.42/70. J. Read to J. King, Tuesday afternoon [8 March, 1803].)

and Colonel Dixon's speaks positively of the fact. From the latter
likewise the names of some active parties have been disclosed. Upon
the whole, I hope some little progress is made towards the end we
all desire, and that these gentlemen by their vigilance and activity
will soon attain it completely . . .

According to Mr. King's request, I enclose Hirst's tickets. I enclose likewise a ticket your Lordship sent me, with some observations on it, in Mr. Cookson's handwriting . . .

[*Enclosures.*]

William Cookson to Earl Fitzwilliam

Leeds, 18 *August* 1802 (*Copy.*)
I have now to return the ticket and papers which your Lordship did
me the honour to transmit to me. The ticket was fabricated three
years ago at Leeds and bears the Borough arms, to which the device
of cross shears, such as the clothworkers use, forms a crest. The
whole system upon which the shearmen in the West act, was, I am
afraid, engendered here, being perfectly congenial to the threats and
tone of language they use on any occasion attracting their hostility.
From a perfect conviction that their threats would be carried into
execution here, if any merchant infringed the clothworkers' pre-
scriptions, I have, within these last nine months, by my own personal influence, privately prevailed upon one or two houses who
meditated the adding a gig mill or a shearing machine to their
works, to desist for the present, or I am firmly convinced we should
have had such horrid outrages to deplore here, as have been practised
in the West.

George Palmer is a shoemaker, through whose medium their correspondence with the West is carried on. Every class of workmen
make a common cause with that of the clothworkers, and every
turn-out for advance of wages is supported by general contribution
from almost every other class. From a respectable house near
Trowbridge I learn that a sum of money was received there last
week from Leeds, and this week (Monday evening) a letter
to Trowbridge, with a bill enclosed, was put into the office, which
there is reason to suspect was directed by Palmer. The letter to
acknowledge receipt may perhaps afford some opportunity of closer
observation.

With respect to the nocturnal meetings, they continue, though the place is never known to others till they take place. On Friday evening at or near midnight a meeting was held in a hollow way or narrow valley about six miles from Leeds and two from Birstall, at some distance from any public road. A man of perfect veracity assures me that he attempted to form one of the party, but found that scouts were stationed on all sides at some distance, the outermost of whom accosted him and aimed at drawing him off in a different direction. On his persevering he found another irregular and moving line of scouts, who asked his business, and upon his continuing to proceed towards the ' Black Lamp ' of men, a whistling was made, and he heard expressions and tones of voice that quite deterred him from his purpose. That some particular persons whom they called gentlemen were expected and were not then arrived, he could easily collect from what he overheard on the way, as he advanced and receded.

From another quarter on which I can depend, I learn that the committee forming the ' Black Lamp,' and which on Friday night might be composed of about 200 men, consists of those who have discoursed on the subject with nine others, and have sworn them in, each of which again, *ad infinitum*, becomes a Committee man on the same grounds. ' Abolition of all taxes, and the full enjoyment of their rights,' are the subjects on which the leaders hold forth, and the cement which holds them together. 'By Christmas they should be able to carry their points, and on one night the rise was to take place in every quarter.'

All is carried on by messengers verbally, and the business committees, consisting of a small number, meet in the larger towns.

I have a channel open, from whence I shall learn more, as occasion arises—but as every link of the working community are disposed to take part with those who profess to raise the price of labour and lower the price of provisions, the utmost secrecy is necessary, and were it suspected that anyone gives or receives information on the above matters, the source would soon be dried up.

Colonel Dixon to Earl Fitzwilliam

19 *August*, 1802. (*Copy and Extract*).
Mr. Scatchard sent the man he mentioned to us at York to Mr. Beckett[1] on Tuesday for his examination, the purport of which

---

[1] John Beckett, who became Under-Secretary of State for Home Affairs in 1806, and who succeeded his father as second Baronet in 1826, came from a well-known Leeds family, and had several brothers.

chiefly was 'that there were three houses at Leeds and three at Wakefield where the committees met—that one of them was expected to be searched some time since, and that their papers were hid under a trapdoor in the floor of the house and amongst the coals ; that each member paid 1d. per week to the fund ; that there were many committee men made, and that each committee man got ten more ; that they were then divided again into committee men, and each again got ten, and so on ; that Leeds was the head place ; that they came from his district, viz., Morley to Leeds every week to receive orders ; that there was a night meeting at Hawden Clough on the 14th inst.; that they carry their weekly pennies to Leeds ; that there would be a rising all over the country on the same night, and everything overturned the next morning.'

The above is the principal information he gave, except giving the names of two men who were the principal active men amongst them, and that £300 or £400 had already been expended out of the fund produced by the penny contributions. Mr. Beckett offered him a guinea for his trouble of coming over, but he refused taking anything. He promised to bring further intelligence soon. (H.O.42/66).

(57). *A. Graham to John King*

¾ *past* 8 *p.m.* [*Endorsed, 24 August,* 1802.][1]
I have the satisfaction to inform you that the shipwrights have acceded to the builders' terms and have promised to go quietly to their work to-morrow morning.

The caulkers still hold out, but they are not considered of sufficient consequence to occasion any uneasiness. (H.O.42/66).

(58). *Earl Fitzwilliam to Lord Pelham*

Wentworth, 30 *August*, 1802.
. . . The measure which the Mayor [of Leeds] has already taken, of sending information to Mr. Jones of Bath will probably be of great utility towards the end of breaking up the combination of cloth-workers, which is become very alarming in the West on account of the outrages used for its support. From this communication it appears, however, that the combination is merely for a partial purpose, according to the opinion of the Mayor of Leeds : from the enclosure,

---

[1] There is another endorsement : ' Copy sent to Sir E. Nepean, 24 August.' The note was therefore probably written on the 23rd.

no judgement can well be formed : it may be partial but it may be general. Having passed the last week at York Races, I took the opportunity of conversing with gentlemen on this subject. I cannot say that even from those to whom I had been referred, as having knowledge of these transactions, I collected any information that tended to corroborate the certainty of their existence : everything rested upon hearsay and from accounts given by persons who spoke from no direct knowledge. The accounts given in the Mayor of Leeds' letter of the 18th and in Colonel Dixon's of the 19th, which your Lordship has seen, are more specific than any other information I am able to get at : but yet the credit given by several very respectable persons, biasses my mind so that I know not how to withhold my own belief ; and I must believe that there are in existence Committees, having great general changes for objects, unless this combination of the clothworkers (about which there can be no doubt) has given ground for the reports of conspiracies for general change. Probably this will soon be cleared up . . . (H.O.42/66).

(59). *James Read to Lord Pelham*

Bradford, (Wilts.), 1 September, 1802.
. . . Six shearmen were sent to gaol last week under the Combination Act, four of them for offences, and the other two for refusing to give testimony, and we have had one pecuniary conviction for paying a shearman to keep him out of work. I am bringing forward as many cases as I can under the Combination Act, and by forcing some to give evidence against others, I hope to provoke some quarrels amongst them, and by that means to be able to bring some of their deeds to light . . . (H.O.42/66).

(60). *Lord Pelham to James Read*

Wimbledon, 2 September, 1802. Confidential. (Copy).
I have received this day a letter from Lord Fitzwilliam enclosing one from the Mayor of Leeds, in which he gives the same account of the utility of the machinery, and of the objections to it on the part of the shearmen, that I received from the two gentlemen who came to me from Wiltshire.

It appears to me from these accounts that the successful establishment of the machinery is a subject of great national importance inasmuch as the pre-eminence of our cloths in great measure depends upon it ; at the same time the immediate interest of the shearmen and others who may be deprived of their accustomed support and means of living is not to be disregarded, however irregular and dangerous their mode of maintaining their interest may have been. It has occurred to me that a meeting of some of the principal clothiers from Yorkshire and Wiltshire might be of use in devising means for satisfying those people who are likely to be affected by this machinery, in order that, when Government shall have convinced those who have attempted to redress themselves by acts of violence, that the laws cannot be transgressed with impunity, there is a disposition to attend to their reasonable complaints, and to prevent a recurrence of the same outrages.

I wish you would collect the sentiments of some of the principal clothiers upon this point, and I am sure that I need not suggest to you that in doing so, you should take care not to create any suspicion that Government is disposed to sacrifice their interest by any premature compromise until the existing spirit of insubordination is overcome. (H.O.42/66).

(61). *James Read to Lord Pelham*

Bradford (Wilts.), 5 September, 1802.
In answer to your Lordship's letter of the 2nd inst., I have the honour to inform your Lordship that the manufacturers of Wiltshire and Somersetshire at a meeting held in Bath nearly three weeks ago came to a resolution (which has been printed and circulated through the two Counties) to find employ for all persons who should be thrown out of their accustomed work by the introduction of machinery, in some other branches of the manufacture and at reasonable wages. It therefore appears to me that the manufacturers have already met the case which your Lordship's plan proposes to provide for, and in regard to the grievance alleged (viz., the introduction of gig mills) I think it is in a great measure imaginary both as to the introduction of gig mills as well as to the effect of them, because I find that from amongst the clothiers in this County not more than five or six have introduced them, and Mr. Jones is the only one in the neighbourhood of the two populous towns of Trowbridge and Bradford. In Trowbridge, where Mr. Naish resides (who has suffered so much injury) they have not been introduced. Mr. Jones, before his mill was completed, sent his cloths into Gloucestershire to be dressed, where gig mills have always been in

use. Therefore his present dressing by gig mills in this County may be said to be a new trade and cannot have had the operation of displacing any shearmen from their accustomed labour ; and Mr. Hill, another very considerable manufacturer near Malmesbury, who dresses his cloths by gig mills, was the first founder of a manufactory in that part of the County.

The generality of manufacturers who continue to dress by hand allow that cloths dressed by gig mills are better done and have the preference in the market. The effect upon the labour of shearmen is, that four men are required to dress a piece of cloth in the old way, and one man by attending the gig, does what is called the roughing part, but then I understand that as the gig works quicker there is more cutting after the gig, and the labour of shearmen is not very considerably reduced by it, but such is the prevailing prejudice that no shearman in Wiltshire will shear cloth that has been dressed by gig mills, and Mr. Jones at this time has not a single shearman at work for him. That part of their labour therefore he is obliged to supply by shearing frames set in motion by machinery where one person attends four pairs of shears and that person need not be a shearman. Although it appears that any shearman thrown out of employ by the use of the gig mill might be provided for in some other branch, yet I think if shearing frames could be brought into general use (which would require a great deal of time to accomplish) it might entirely cut off the artists in that branch of the trade. Mr. Jones has introduced them here (as I am informed) and the manufacturers at Warminster are doing the same to sustain their business because shearmen will not work for them, and your Lordship will recollect the case of the seven delegated shearmen who met Mr. Jones, that he promised never to use his shearing frames when he could get shearmen to do his work, and to employ every man in Bradford Parish out of work—stated by them to be about thirty. This promise with respect to Mr. Jones ought I think to have satisfied them, and the public engagement of the manufacturers by machinery to find employ for such as by their machines are deprived of labour, ought also to remove the general prejudice which I have shown your Lordship exists even in towns where neither the gig mills nor shearing frames have been introduced. The master shearmen who are a class of middlemen between clothiers (who do not dress and shear their own cloths) and the labouring shearmen, are, I believe, considerably instrumental in keeping up the prejudice behind the curtain, and I also believe that the smaller manufacturers are not dissatisfied with the opposition. . . The disbanding of the army and navy has occasioned an increase of workmen before the manufacturers were ready for them, which is, I believe, the present temporary grievance, although almost every labouring manufacturer, but particularly the shearmen, are impressed with an opinion that the use of machinery is the only cause of their being out of employ (H.O.42/66).

(62). *James Read to Lord Pelham*

Bradford (*Wilts.*), 6 *September*, 1802.

. . . About the 14th July last, upon a dispute between the clothiers of Trowbridge and their shearmen respecting their wages, the latter left work, and continued out of work until after the 22nd July. In the night between the 21st and 22nd July, Littleton Mill, the property of Mr. Naish, was burnt down.[1] On the following morning (the 22nd) the clothiers being alarmed, five of them met a like number of shearmen deputed by their body, when the clothiers acceded to the terms of the shearmen, and they went to work again. The shearmen afterwards printed and circulated papers of what had been agreed to . . .

On the 31st July, Howell (who appears to have been the spokesman of the five shearmen) went in company with another shearman named James Murray, to the Assizes at Salisbury, and presented a paper writing [*sic*] to the Grand Jury, which complained of the introduction of gig mills and shearing frames, and alleged that numbers of manufacturers were thrown out of employ from the use of them . . .

About 600 persons are thrown out of employ from the destruction of the two mills belonging to Mr. Naish.[2] (H.O.42/66).

[1] See *Annual Register*, 1802, Chronicle, p. 67, where he is described as Mr. Nash.

[2] Mr. Read enclosed a printed handbill, which stated that a meeting of the West of England woollen manufacturers was held at the White Hart Inn, Bath, on 16 August, John Jones in the chair. It cautioned all persons against illegal contributions, subscriptions and combinations. It resolved ' to defend the machinery already introduced, and any which, from its utility, may be judged advisable hereafter to introduce, into the woollen manufactures, against the attacks of any person or persons whomsoever ; the manufacturers engaging to find employ for all persons in their respective employment in some other branch of the manufacture, of which such person shall be capable,

[*Continued on p. 59*]

(63). *Earl Fitzwilliam to Lord Pelham*

Wentworth, 9 September, 1802.

I could not so well express your Lordship's wishes for a meeting in London of the merchants and manufacturers of Yorkshire with those of the West of England, nor so well convey your reasons for those wishes, as by transmitting to Mr. Cookson, the Mayor of Leeds, your letter to me on that subject. I have now the honour of transmitting his reply. I was confident there would be no backwardness on the part of Yorkshire to such a meeting, but the reasons which Mr. Cookson has stated to its being summoned in a manner that may not leave it liable to the construction of being originated by the merchants and manufacturers for the purpose of forming a combination among themselves, appear so forcible that I have little doubt of your Lordship's agreeing with him in sentiment, that to avoid that appearance, it had better be called by Government. Certainly there exist causes sufficient for such a summons on the part of Government. The disturbances, that it is notorious have happened in the West, and the suspicion of illegal meetings in Yorkshire, call for inquiry into their causes, and I should hope that, summoned by Government, the parties who attend will not suffer in property or in other concerns, from that sort of vengeance which they seem to dread, were they to appear themselves the authors of such a meeting. It is a subject of infinite moment and at the same time of the greatest delicacy.

[*Enclosure.*]

William Cookson to Earl Fitzwilliam

Leeds, 8 September, 1802.

. . . Perhaps it would be proper that all appearance of the measure originating with the clothiers and merchants should be avoided: an idea of combination on their part might present itself in the momentous shape which the spirit of combination amongst workmen of almost every class (but particularly amongst shearmen) has

[*Continued from p. 58*]

at ample and sufficient wages, in case by the introduction of machinery the services of any such persons shall be rendered unnecessary in the particular branch of the manufacture in which they are now or have lately been employed.'

now assumed—would not your Lordship advise that his Majesty's Ministers should take up the subject ? . . . Such are the powers and terrors exercised by the workmen here, that I am convinced few if any desirable parties would be found except it were to act under the immediate *direction* of his Majesty's Ministers.

During the last winter I had opportunities of observing the progress, and I may say maturing, of the combination system amongst workmen : such indeed as could only fall in the way of a magistrate acting in a highly populous jurisdiction. Seriously impressed with the conviction that evils of great magnitude would arise if the working people were allowed to feel and make known the extent of their power, I applied to the late Mr. Bayley, a highly revered magistrate in Lancashire, stating the difficulties and dangers that must ensue unless some effectual and timely remedy were not applied to repress if not extirpate the combination system. Mr. Bayley was of opinion that the laws in force were adequate. I suggested several important points, in which we found here that the laws were inefficient, and that, conscious of this, we were unwilling to urge any person to prosecute, where the proving the combination was doubtful, the punishment trivial compared with the extent of the offence, where it was remote in point of time, and where during the interval (if not much longer) the prosecutor would be obliged to suspend his business entirely, and be exposed to incalculable injuries. I had likewise some correspondence with our County members on the subject, who strenuously supported our representations, and had some discussions with the then Mr. Law[1] and his predecessor.[2] My friend Beckett saw every letter that passed, and wrote several himself to Mr. Lascelles,[3] corroborating my statement of grounds for apprehension. However we made no impression. I trust that under your Lordship's auspices we shall be more successful. Indeed the evils call aloud for a cure or would soon extend beyond computation. Perquisites, privileges, time, mode of labour, rate, who shall be employed, &c., &c.—all are now dependent upon the fiats of our workmen, beyond all appeal ; and all branches are struggling for their share of these new powers. It is now a confirmed thing that a

---

[1] Edward Law, first Baron Ellenborough (1750–1818). Attorney-General, 1801 ; Lord Chief Justice, 1802-18.

[2] Sir John Mitford, afterwards (1802) first Baron Redesdale (1748 – 1830.)

[3] A son of Edward Lascelles, Baron Harewood, who was made an Earl in 1812.

bricklayer, mason, carpenter, wheelwright, &c., shall have 3s. per week higher wages in Leeds or in Manchester than at Wakefield, York, Hull, Rochdale, or any adjacent towns. It is in orders too that bricklayers' and masons' labourers at Leeds shall have 2s. per week extra. No workman will or dare deviate from these terms, no matter from whence he comes, and there arrived here last week two delegates from Carlisle on their way to Manchester, summoned by the Lancashire cotton printers, to agree upon certain advances in their wages, who made no secret of their mission . . .

We are all desirous that the labouring poor should earn wages fully equal to the advance of provisions, but there is a rate of wages beyond which every noxious effect would ensue—dissipation, idleness and disorder generally prevail where the means and time are at their command. Extravagance, whilst work is abundant, renders them unwilling and unable in many cases to sustain scanty subsistence, and the poor rates in all places are high in the same ratio as wages—and unless some radical means can be devised to keep wages within proper limits, the poor rates will prove a canker to the property and morality of this country and will fatally prey upon its vitals . . . (H.O.42/66).

(64). *James Read to John King*

Bradford (Wilts.), 13 September, 1802.
. . . Two or more Justices meet daily at one or other of the manufacturing towns, and as the Combination Act affords a very convenient pretext for summoning and examining upon oath any suspected persons, I have continually some before them. It answers the double purpose of keeping the magistrates at their post and of alarming the disaffected. We have six in confinement for offences against the Act, and three for refusing to give testimony . . . (H.O.42/66).

(65). *Earl Fitzwilliam to Lord Pelham*

Wentworth, 27 September, 1802. (Copy).
. . . Whilst I was in conversation with Mr. Beckett and Mr. Markland the other day, at Leeds, Mr. Gott, a most extensive manufacturer and considerable merchant, came to us to communicate an occurrence that had taken place in his manufactory that very morning,

to him a very serious one. *All* his croppers[1] to a man, 80 in number, had given him notice that they would quit as soon as each had finished the job he had in hand. Henceforward not one of them would strike a stroke for Mr. Gott. The menace did not stop here. They gave him to understand their place should not be supplied by others, for that they would not permit others in their line of business to work for him, nor would they suffer him to evade the effects of their displeasure by getting his cloths finished at the workshop of another merchant, his friend. Any person presuming to do so would incur the same penalty : he likewise should be proscribed. Did this sudden denunciation of vengeance arise out of resentment for harsh treatment or any ill usage ? Was it meant to extort advance of wages ? For no such cases, but it took its rise and was the consequence of what one should have considered as a most innocent because a most legal, and indeed a daily practice : because Mr. Gott had ordered indentures to be prepared for binding two boys apprentices ; both of them were 14 years turned (though in fact neither of them were 15). For a breach of this regulation decreed by their pleasure, Mr. Gott is declared by the croppers under the ban of their empire.

The striking of workmen is certainly to be considered usually as a business of a private nature. The public has nothing to do in disputes between master and man, where breaches of contract, or some circumstance of that nature does not bring the case within the cognisance of magistrates. But on this occasion I must say it appears to me (as I hear it from the report of one of the parties) that the manner, the motives and the nature of the denunciation give it a very different character. It is for the infringement of a law made by parties incompetent to make any law ; a law (if I may so call it) subversive of the general rights of all his Majesty's subjects, and to be enforced by violence, not only against the party denounced, but against all other people. Single men will not dare to face the menace of so numerous and so powerful a band, without some good assurance of public protection. That this is the [case] is proved (according to the report of Mr. Gott) from the case of some few of the very [sic] eighty. Upon the occurrence happening, Mr. Gott took the measure of examining each of the parties by himself. Some few lamented this combination against him, but declared they did not dare to swerve from it. On this examination, which he took in the

---

[1] The Yorkshire name for shearmen. See No. 46. The disturbances in Yorkshire and Wiltshire were similar and connected.

presence of two creditable witnesses, the cause of the measure that the indenture was so generally avowed that about it there can be no doubt : and as for the denunciation, that was much more publicly declared, both as to extent and means, was by no means blinked [*sic*] ; it is supposed it is held out in terrorem.

To Mr. Gott this is a very serious concern : as the business done by the cropper is the finishing stroke of the manufacture, Mr. Gott is not only precluded from manufacturing in future, but there remains upon his hands all that has passed through the first stages of manufacture, without the possibility of its ever being rendered saleable. In Mr. Gott's case this is a great concern ; exclusive of croppers, he employs daily more than 1000 persons in his manufactory. Great as will be the injury to Mr. Gott, injury arising out of this act of the croppers is not confined to him alone—1,000 people are thrown out of employ to gratify the resentment or perhaps the policy of the croppers, they are doomed to starve. I say the policy, because the business of the croppers really continues to exist, but through the medium of terror, and I am sorry to say, this system of terror has answered to them in Yorkshire for a considerable time. Your Lordship has certainly heard that of late years it has been found that the business done by the croppers is *better* done, as well as cheaper by machinery than by hand. Several merchants of Leeds have had [it] in contemplation to erect machinery for this purpose— but the outcry of the croppers, and their menaces, have deterred them from putting their plan into execution. By terror, then, the croppers have already perpetuated an expedient mode of doing business. They are now going a step further, and by the same system of terror they mean to perpetuate in their present number the monopoly of that business.

Mr. Gott, with great magnanimity and laudable disinterestedness declared his readiness not to submit, but to resist the croppers on the occasion, if the other merchants would support him in it. It was a matter likely to be immediately taken into consideration, but I left Leeds too early to know the result. I confess I felt a strong inclination to have suggested the propriety of bringing the subject of machinery to the test, and to have made this the occasion of bringing it into use : but so great will be the risk attending the attempt, that it was a wish not to be broached by a person who could not be a party to the risk, still less by a person who has not the power of offering adequate means of protection. However, I have little expectation that any measure of vigour to that extent will be taken at Leeds just now : the intimidation is too strong. I know that it has been a measure among some of the magistrates to stop any merchant from erecting a shearing mill, for fear of the consequences. There must be some strong encouragement held out before any one will make the attempt. It is indeed unfortunate the masters have yielded so often, that they have lost all superiority. The journeymen are now masters. The masters feel the inconvenience and repine at it, but it appears to me that they have no thoughts of meeting the evil sternly, but are thinking of application to Parliament for further restrictions against the combination of journeymen. Laws to this effect have been amended, and amended over and over again, but still they remain inefficacious. So they will for ever. The system of restriction is vicious. Parliament always feels it so, and whenever it touches upon the subject, its better principles are always a check upon its worser propensities. But though masters cannot be vested with an unfitting authority over their servants, they may and ought to be protected in the full exercise of their own just rights against all violence and against the effects of terror. I cannot help feeling a strong opinion that all the meetings, and suspicion of meetings, take its rise in the combination of the very men I am now speaking about, the croppers. They are the tyrants of the country ; their power and influence has grown out of their high wages, which enable them to make deposits that puts them beyond all fear of inconvenience from misconduct. They are, however, an order of men not necessary to the manufacture, and if the merchants had firmness to do without them, their consequence would be lost, their banks would waste, their combinations would fall to the ground, and we should hear no more of meetings of any sort or description . . . (H.O.42/66).

(66). *James Read to John King*

3 *October*, 1802.

. . . I have seen Richards, the agent of Messrs. Wormald and Gott, and learn from him that their want of hands arises from the shearmen at Leeds refusing to work for those manufacturers who have taken apprentices after the age of 14, and for a shorter period than is directed by the Statute of Elizabeth,[1] unless such apprentices are discharged ; but he informed me that he did not expect to get many recruits.[2] (H.O.42/66).

[1] 5 Eliz., c. 4.
[2] [*See p. 65*]

(67). *James Read to John King*

Melksham, 4 October, 1802.

. . . Beaumont . . . is a Bradford man. He was one amongst others that left Mr. Jones's factory under a pretence that they had been threatened and forced to do it. I had Beaumont under examination about it but he would not fix upon anyone ; indeed he at first refused to give testimony and was committed, and after being in prison about three weeks he relented. Mr. Jones, after this, conceiving that apprehension for the security of his person was the only cause (as Beaumont alleged it to be) why he did [not] go to work again, offered to protect him within the walls of the factory, and to give him constant work and a guinea a week instead of 14s., his former wages. Beaumont agreed to accept the offer but never went to work. I mention this merely to show what strict discipline they carry on.

I shall endeavour to learn when Beaumont returns, and get hold of him if I can before he unloads himself. He has a wife close by Bradford. If she has any letters I think the Postmaster at Bradford should intercept them. (H.O.42/66).

(68). *John King to James Read*

Whitehall, 5 October 1802. (*Draft.*)

I gave the necessary orders yesterday for stopping the letters you suggested[1] at Trowbridge or Bradford. If Beaumont could be met with on *the road or immediately on his arrival* and thoroughly searched, it might prove of great service. (H.O.42/66).

[Footnote refers to p. 64]

[2] He enclosed the following printed handbill :

WANTED IMMEDIATELY at LEEDS in *Yorkshire.*

A NUMBER OF JOURNEYMEN SHEARMEN

sober, steady, good workmen, will meet with *constant employ and good wages,* by applying to Messrs. Wormald, Gott and Wormalds, at their manufactory NEAR LEEDS.

Further particulars may be known by applying to Jacob Richards, at the George Inn, Trowbridge, or to Mr. Henry Richards, near the Market Place, Frome . . .

28 September 1802.

[1] In an earlier letter.

G

(69) *Richard Carpenter Smith to Sir Richard Ford*

Union Hall, Southwark, 12 *October,* 1802.

. . . Two of the shipwrights were tried yesterday at the Quarter Session at Newington for an assault upon two men belonging to Messrs. Randall and Brent's yard on their return from work. The jury very reluctantly found them guilty and recommended them to mercy. The Court . . . ordered them to be fined 6s. 8d. each and to be imprisoned twelve calendar months in the House of Correction. Some of the jury, after the Court broke up, declared they would not have found the men guilty if they had thought so severe a punishment would have been inflicted. The Court was crowded with caulkers and shipwrights during the trial. (H.O.42/66).

(70). *James Read to John King*

Melksham, 18 *October,* 1802.

I understand that a deputation from the Bath meeting of manufacturers are about to set off to London for the purpose of submitting a case to the Secretary of the Treasury for the repeal of some Statutes which, as they imagine, cripple the present state of their trade, and I learn that their first visit is likely to be made either to you or Lord Pelham upon the subject . . .

The shearmen continue to have meetings, particularly at Trowbridge, but I do not find that there is at present any disposition to riot. In the town of Melksham, where the usual manner of working does not furnish sufficient employ, I expect to influence some shearmen to cut cloths after the gig mills, and the combination once broken, many others I dare say will follow.

The shearmen's wives begin to get impatient and complain that the clubs take away their husbands' earnings, and there appears a disposition in some of the Warminster shearmen to go to work again. It cannot therefore be too strongly impressed upon the minds of the deputies who may come to you to recommend to the body of manufacturers not to harbour any resentment against those who may be willing to return to their labour and to concert measures for their employment . . .[1] (H.O.42/66).

---

[1] Mr. Read explained the situation further in a letter to Lord Hawkesbury, dated 19 February, 1805 : '. . . The struggle between the shearmen and their employers (the manufacturers) began many years ago from a prejudice of the

[*Continued on p.* 67]

[*Continued from p. 66*]

former against the introduction of machinery which they pretended (as to the gig mill) was prohibited by Statute of 5 and 6 Edward VI, ch. 22. The discontents have been increasing ever since, and in the year 1802 broke out into acts of great violence against the property of several manufacturers in Wiltshire. Some of the ringleaders were taken and one of them was afterwards hanged. The principal manufacturers in Wiltshire and Somersetshire having formed a large fund to give rewards for apprehending and carrying on prosecutions against the rioters, and a very small part of it having been exhausted for those purposes, the committee for managing the fund (most of them manufacturers by machinery), thought it a favourable moment, and suggested an application to Parliament for a repeal of the Statutes alluded to in the enclosed letters (18 in number). Upon this scheme they were joined by the Gloucestershire manufacturers. About this time the weavers formed a subscription to prosecute those manufacturers who had offended the Statute of 2 and 3 of Philip and Mary by having more than the prescribed number of looms and by employing unapprenticed weavers, and several actions were brought against the Gloucestershire manufacturers, but only one action, I believe, came on to a trial. The shearmen of Wiltshire and Somersetshire also threatened actions against unapprenticed men, but none, I believe, were commenced. The shearmen and weavers petitioned separately against the repeal of the Statutes sought for by the manufacturers, and they were represented before the committee of the House of Commons by different Counsel. The opposition of the former was directed against the use of machinery and to prevent a repeal of the Statute of Elizabeth respecting apprentices, and the latter to prevent a repeal of the Statute of Elizabeth and also of the Statute of 2 and 3 Philip and Mary. The manufacturers attacked all the Statutes without proposing any others, and complained against any interruption to the progress of machinery, although in fact there was not any law against its use except the Statute of 5 and 6 of Edward VI, ch. 22, which only prohibits the use of gig mills for the perching and burling of cloth, whereas the gig mills now complained against, perform a different operation, namely, that of dressing cloth, which is part of the employ of shearmen when it is done by hand. About twelve years ago an action was commenced and carried on at the expense of the shearmen of Wiltshire against a manufacturer in that county to recover penalties alleged to have been incurred for using a gig mill contrary to the Statute of Edward VI. The action was brought to trial and became a subject of great notoriety, but the plaintiff, after going through his evidence, was non-suited, and as no other action has been brought since, it operates as a pretty strong circumstance to show that the gig mills of the present day are different from those the use of which are prohibited by the Statute of Edward VI   (H.O.43/83).

(71). *Earl Fitzwilliam to Lord Pelham*

Milton, 30 January, 1803.

. . I am sorry to say that the combination of the cloth croppers continues in full vigour, and produces the effect of complete submission on the part of the merchants. The latter might easily have prevailed had they had perseverance to stick out against the former : 1500 of these had once struck work, and were living upon the principal of their fund. The demand on it was so great that it would have been quickly exhausted ; when the merchants compromised the subject in contest between them, and have thus given time for rendering the croppers still more their masters by a renovated fund. By the reports I receive, it does not appear that the croppers commit any acts of violence, nor do I know upon what principle the measures they adopt, and which renders them so powerful, can be restricted or even reprobated. What is objectionable in bodies of men laying up in the days of prosperity against those of adversity ? Within these few years Parliament has sanctioned and encouraged the principle to the full extent of anything these people appear to do.[1] However, I fear it will be productive of serious evil hereafter. The advantage these people derive from their system of combination becomes an example to every other branch of trade and manufacture, and the pains they take to disseminate their system amongst other trades, gives just cause for apprehension that the trouble they take in this cause will not be without its consequences. Others will do as they have done. Wages will increase universally, and of consequence the prices of manufacture. The question that arises is, how far can the foreign market bear increase of price ? It is an alarming incitement to the industry of other nations. There is the evil—I see little else to be uneasy about. (H.O.42/70).

---

[1] The reference is to the Friendly Society Acts of 1793 and 1795 (33 George III, c. 54 ; 35 George III, c. 111.) George Rose's Act of 1793 recognised the existence of numerous Societies, gave them encouragement in various ways, and relief from taxation. The Preamble began : ' Whereas the protection and encouragement of Friendly Societies in this kingdom, for raising, by voluntary subscription of the members thereof, separate funds for the mutual relief and maintenance of the said members in sickness, old age, and infirmity, is likely to be attended with very beneficial effects, by promoting the happiness of individuals, and at the same time diminishing the public burdens . . .' The Act of 1795 was a short amending Act ' for more effectually carrying into execution' the previous Statute.

(72). *Charles Thomas to George Palmer*[1]

Bristol, 17 March 1803. (Copy[2]*)*

We received your kind letter the 5th instant, and am sorry to hear that you have so many enemies to contend with, as it must be very expensive to you when so many men is out of employ. Hope you have had liberal supplies from most towns in the kingdom ; if you should be in want we have no objection of making you a small remittance. Hope you will in a short time be able to give us an account of your having met with good success, and be able to let the merchants and manufacturers know they are in the wrong, and be ashamed of their nasty mean conduct. We shall always be happy to hear from our brethren the cloth dressers of Leeds, as they are a set of men which ought to be esteemed, and I hope is by all trades. Gentlemen, wishing you health and respect, I remain your most obedient, Charles Thomas, President. (H.O.42/70).

[1] Addressed to Duke Street, near St. Peter Square, Leeds, Yorkshire.
[2] The original letter, after being intercepted by the postal authorities, was sent on to its destination in order to prevent suspicion.

III. SHOE-MAKERS AND
LANCASHIRE COTTON WEAVERS, 1804-1808.

1804. The journeymen in the hemp and flax manufacture. The shoe-makers and boot closers.

1808. The Lancashire weavers' strike.

(73). *Joseph Moser*[1] *to John King*

Public Office, Worship Street, 28 February, 1804.

. . . Last Sunday, a Mr. Gamson, a very respectable sacking, &c. manufacturer in Kingsland Road, came to my house (Princes Street, Spitalfields) and after producing the letter (No. 1), a copy of which I enclose, stated to me that in consequence of his having intercepted it, and his former observations respecting his journeymen, of whom he employs a very great number, and among whom circumstances had arisen which had for some time indicated that they meant to strike for wages, he was apprehensive that they would assemble according to the intimation in the said letter, and combined with the numerous artisans in the hemp and flax branches of manufacture, proceed perhaps, in a manner more overt than they had hitherto attempted. I accordingly sent Armstrong and Vickery, two very intelligent officers, twice in the course of Sunday afternoon and evening to the White Bear public house behind Whitechapel Church. They reported to me that although many persons were there assembled at an improper hour (during divine service) there was no appearance of any proceedings hostile to the peace of the district.

Last night Mr. Gamson called again at my house and produced the letter (No. 2) which he had intercepted, a copy of which I also enclose. By this you will observe that there seems to be an organised, systematic combination among the journeymen in the hemp and flax manufactories, that they collect money, and as Mr. Gamson states to me, are resolved to set their employers at defiance, and

---

[1] The London magistrate who presided over the Worship Street police court.

that this idea had spread to all these manufactories in the kingdom, through the same medium, that they meant to apprise his journey-men of it.

Knowing, Sir, in the first instance, that a compliance with the unreasonable demands of these men would only operate as a temporary paliation and excite further demands, and in the second, that the maritime strength, the safety and the commercial riches of the nation would receive a material shock from the suspension of the labour of these men, and an irreparable injury if it was continued for any length of time, I have deemed it advisable to lay the case before you, that this evil, if you think it, may be stopped in the outset by his Majesty's Secretary of State directing the proper officers to proceed against them.[1] (H.O.42/78).

(74). *Thomas Hudson's Affidavit*

9 *August*, 1804.[2]

Thomas Hudson of Whitcomb Street in the Parish of St. Martin's in the Fields in the County of Middlesex, boot closer, on his examination saith that he has followed the said occupation for 28 years, and that for the last 18 years has worked for Mr. Rymer of Cockspur Street ; that in or about the year 1792 this informant was applied to to become one of the Society[3] whose Rules are hereunto annexed ; that after seeing the violence and injustice of such Society which induced a prosecution in 1799 when several were tried and found guilty, but the Court, on motion of Mr. Erskine,[4] permitted the defendants to be bound in their own recognisance to appear to receive the judgement of the said Court when called on, the cause of such mercy being extended was a promise that such combination should in future be done away, in consequence of which this informant did not attend any meeting for two years and upwards, but this informant is informed and believes that the same system of combination, so far from being abated by the mercy of the Court, did exist within a few months after, if not a few weeks ; but this informant was at length compelled to attend through threats which tended to deprive him of the means of getting a livelihood. But

---

[1] The enclosures are missing.

[2] This document is very badly written : hence the blunders.

[3] The Society of Journeymen Boot and Shoe Makers.

[4] Thomas Erskine, first Baron Erskine (1750-1823), the Whig lawyer. Lord Chancellor, 1806-7.

finding their principles so inimicable to the laws of his country and their combination carried to such an extent so as (in his opinion) to be dangerous to the State, he felt himself in duty bound as a faithful subject of his Majesty to withdraw himself from that Society, which he found from their principles and various demands made on him in consequence of their correspondence from different parts of the kingdom to be so formidable as to put all law at defiance. In their meetings, if any man dared to be bold enough to say or even give a loyal toast or sentiment, he immediately became a marked character. On the contrary, should anything be given tending to subvert the Constitution and to tend to an overthrow of all civil power, the same was received with enthusiasm . . . This informant further saith that he will, if duly authorised, undertake to produce evidence to facts far more extensive as to the power and extent of this combination, and its dangerous tendency on the community at large, by proving that the first masters in the said trade, after having endeavoured to resist, have joined such combination, and are now the supporters of those illegal meetings, one in particular, who, having indicted his men, now actually having the warrants in his possession to the number of 107, withholds the same for the avowed purpose of preventing justice taking place, and protects the same men who are at large and are now the defienced [? defiant] upholders of those illegal meetings.

This informant further saith that the system is conducted as follows. Every man working for those masters whose men join in this combination is obliged to meet once in 14 days under a fine for non-attendance. This fine is doubled every time until the fourth meeting, and if the person does not attend he is by this combination declared inimicable to them, and they depute two men to give information to the said master that such a man has not complied with the rules of the said men, and that if the said master does not immediately discharge the said man, they will no longer work for him. This has so frequently been the case, and if the said man shall quit his former employ and go to another, he must produce a certificate that he is regularly admitted a member of this combination, otherwise he will not be allowed to work at his trade ; and this informant further saith that this combination has extended to every principal town of Great Britain ; that there is a regular correspondence conducted by persons calling themselves delegates, who hold secret meetings, and those meetings are held with such secrecy that should anyone of the said delegates communicate the place of meeting to any other person not a delegate, he will be fined one guinea ... From every shop's meeting one person chosen as a delegate attends those secret meetings where all general questions are determined, and wherever assistance is necessary to carry on the said system of combination, by this means orders are sent to the shops' meetings, that such sum or sums of money are wanted in different parts of the kingdom, and that the sum fixed on is never less than £20 at any one remittance. Giles Jerman, of King Street, Golden Square, in the County of Middlesex . . . saith that at one of those shops' meetings held at the Carpenters' Arms, James Street, Manchester Square, it was proposed and agreed to to raise by subscription money to help those men who were found guilty with Colonel Despard,[1] and this informant having refused to subscribe, incurred their displeasure.

Witness, John Welch,   Thomas Hudson
    at Eton, Bucks., 9 August, 1804.   Giles Jerman[2]
                                                          (H.O.42/79).

(75). *Giles Jerman, Thomas Hudson and David Prentice to the Attorney-General (Spencer Perceval)*

London, 27 July, 1804.
[The Cordwainers' Combination][3] . . . Its various ramifications extend to all the principal towns in the kingdom, and on a strike they are supported at shops working for lower wages till the masters have submitted to their illegal exactions, which hitherto has always been the case ; and it is a fact no less extraordinary than true that a general meeting of the trade can be convened at any time to the amount of several thousands in less than two hours.

. . . We beg leave to call your attention to the tyranny they[4] are at present exercising towards the boot-closers, a set of men who now

---

[1] With six of his fellow-conspirators he was executed for high treason in February, 1803.

[2] The documents which follow were communicated to the Home Office with the above, but, to avoid confusion, they are numbered separately (Nos. 75-83). The Home Secretary sent them to the Law Officers of the Crown (See No. 84).

[3] The early part of the letter covers much the same ground as the previous affidavit.

[4] That is, the illegal meetings.

are endeavouring by every legal means to extricate themselves from the thraldom to which they have so long reluctantly been forced to submit. At most of the principal shops they have been off work for several weeks and are determined to fine every man five guineas whose habits of industry and inclination to support himself and family induce him to work for their maintenance and support rather than thus daringly outraging the laws of his country. It may probably be thought that the masters ought to prosecute on these occasions, but a recollection of what was the fate of Mr. Newcome, who, for undertaking to prosecute, was, being deserted by the masters, entirely drove out of the trade, as no man would afterwards work for him. The masters, therefore, fearful of similar treatment, submit to their exactions . . .

At the shops' meeting money was subscribed for the infamous purpose of supporting those men[1] who had basely aimed at the life of their Sovereign—and when the well-known inclination to republican principles which unfortunately prevails but too much among the journeymen shoe-makers is considered, it will afford a strong presumptive proof that many of them were well acquainted with the treason at that time hatching . . .

At the last Quarter Sessions held at Hick's Hall a great number of these men were indicted for a conspiracy and combination in preventing the closers from working and several of them have been apprehended. The indictment was laid under the Act of the present King's, commonly called the Treason and Sedition Act.[2] But such is their daring conduct that it is scarce safe for any man to work, and being supported by the contributions of the combinations in London as well as all parts of the trade in the country, they boast they can (as they have hitherto done) set at defiance every effort of the law, and the more particularly as deprived by their illegal conduct of the means of getting our bread, we feel ourselves in the cruel necessity of submitting and again joining a combination contrary to law and repugnant to our feelings, if you should not think we have made out a case sufficiently strong for the interference of Government.

---

[1] Colonel Despard and his fellow-conspirators.
[2] 39 George III, c. 79.

(76). *To the Secretary of the Shops' Meetings in London*

Bath, 29 November, 1803.

Sir—We are requested by the body of our Society at large to inform you that we have established shops' meetings in this city for the benefit of the trade in general. Be pleased to make it known to the body at large that we will expect every man coming here from town to bring his clearance[1] with him, and every man going to town from here to produce *his* clearance from here. Gentlemen, we hope we are going to do something for the good of the trade in general. Gentlemen, we sincerely hope and wish to keep a regular correspondence with you, and to be in unity with you, and hope that you will send us the best advice for the good of our cause. With the best wishes to you from our body, we remain, gentlemen, yours to command,

Thomas St. John,	Signed in behalf of this body by
No. 22, Corn Street.	Thomas St. John, Clerk.
	John Whittingham, President.
	Lewis Richards, Clerk to the Committee.

(77).

Loving shopmaites, Liverpool, 14 November 1803—I hope you will excuse our neglect in not wrighting before now to return you our gratefull thanks for your timley asistance in our last contest with our tyrant, hopeing you will retain the same regard wich you have shown in your last contribushion towards us at a time when we was so much nesseated at aney time should aneything of the kind happen to you, you lose no time to inform us of your sittuashion that we may shew ourselfs as much in your intrest and wellfaire as lyes in our power, and we still and allways shall think our[selves] indeted to you for the suploys we received from you without wich we must a suffered verray much as we did not receive the suploys from the other towns as we expected, but since we have got partley through our distresses, we hope you will not omitt wrighting to us as we shall be obliged to you for your asistance in all cases to conduct us as we are but indiffrientley situtated, for we have so maney disarters, the cause on a count of contribushions but this we dispise for if a

---

[1] Presumably, a written permission from the secretary or clerk of his branch of the Union to join another branch when changing his job.

man will not contribute to the suport of his fellow shopmaite he is better at a distance than preasant.

Amongst disarters Wm. Hall, our last preasident, has gone to phillipps purposley to instruct his aprentises on a count of wich he is going to ogment them to 30 he is hired for some time at so much pr week to instruct 2 boys at one time and John Welch and Thomas Richards and all the others has reduced thare wages 2 pence pr paire wich we [hope] you will make as publick through your meetings what villands we have had amongst us.

I supose you have heared of the death of Mr. Taylor our last clark wich has put us much about or we should a rote before.

P.S.—at the request of Mr. Richardson our seckeretarey I was to inform you of the conduct of Charls Duggeon wo with 2 others dubblin bootmen has gone to our tyrant phillipps a longue with the other scabbs.

So I conclude hopeing this will find you in good health.

I remain yours truley

Thos. Freasor   in defence of the traide
Clark.   F. Capper.

(78). [Printed handbill.]

18 June, 1804.

At a General Meeting of the Master Boot and Shoe makers of the cities of London and Westminster, held this day at the Crown-and-Anchor Tavern, Strand,

Mr. George Hoby, in the Chair ;

It was unanimously resolved,

That the present combination of the journeymen boot and shoe makers to prevent the masters from employing such boot closers whom they think proper, is unjust and oppressive, tending ultimately to destroy the free principles by which trade in general should be governed, and must therefore be resisted, by a most vigorous appeal to the laws now in force against such illegal conduct, in order to bring the offenders to that severe punishment they so justly deserve.

That lists of the public houses &c. where the General, Shop and other meetings of the journeymen are held, be immediately delivered to the magistrates, so that such meetings may be suppressed and prevented in future.

That prosecutions be immediately commenced in the Court of

King's Bench, Sessions of the Peace, and in such other way as shall appear advisable, against all journeymen and others, concerned in such illegal meetings and Societies, and particularly against such persons who act in the capacity of Chairman, President, Treasurer, Clerk or Delegate ; and that such prosecutions be brought under the Act of Parliament of the 39th George III, c. 79, s. 8, whereby all such persons who are in any manner concerned in, or privy to, such illegal meetings, or Societies, are subject to be transported for the term of seven years, or be imprisoned for two years.

That every encouragement and protection be granted to all such well-disposed journeymen as have already withdrawn, or who shall immediately withdraw themselves from such meetings and Societies, and return to their former employment.

That the master boot and shoe makers in the country, where such illegal meetings are held, be recommended to aid in the accomplishment of the above most just and necessary measures.

That another meeting of the trade be convened on Monday the 25th of June instant, at 6 o'clock in the evening, at the above place, at which all masters are earnestly requested to attend.

George Hoby, Chairman.

(79). *Thomas St. John (Clerk), C. Swiney (President) and L. Richards (Clerk) to Mr. Ried, of Blackmore's Head, Jermin Street.*

[*Bath, n.d.*]

Sir—I received your letter and made it known to the body at large, and they all return you thanks for your accepting them into your Society, and likewise for your generous offer to support them in case of necessity. Sir, I have to inform you that they are all determined to a man to redress the grievance they labour under from the present low state of wages, which I am ordered to lay before you. Messrs. Brownlow and Mr. Whitehead can inform your body of the work (I mean boots) that is done here for such low wages as making feet for 4s. 6d. and feet of Hessians 5s.—which, a good deal of this work if done in London, would draw your wages, closing equally so. Sir, the body has come to this resolution, to advance 6d. on feet and 6d. on closing per pair on boots and 6d. per pair on shoes, and fully determined (with your approbation) not to work for less, as soon as we receive your consent.

Sir, I have likewise to inform you that from the great number of our body we are obliged to have two houses, the women's men has [*sic*] taken a house for themselves, though we continue as one body to support each other in every lawful measure and all abide by the same rules, and we adhere strictly to them.

Sir, we have ordered 500 clearances to be printed which shall be strictly attended to. Your Rules shall be our laws and most strictly adhered to. Sir, we wait your answer to this, and that you will be pleased to lay this before your body as soon as possible, as we wait your consent to strike, Some of the masters here seems to intimate as much should the men strike they would give the wages [*sic.*]

Sir, I remain in behalf of the body, yrs. truly,[1]

For it, 40

Against, none.

(80).

Bath, 10 *February* 1804.

Sir—Your letter dated the 23 of January I received, and communicated it to the trade at large, and I am ordered to return you thanks for your generous encouragement. Sir, we have struck last Monday. Both men's men, and women's men determined to stand by each other to the last extremity. I am ordered to beg you would be so good as to send circular letters to every city and town that are in a correspondence with you, to inform them that we are out on the strike. Determined not to give it in to the last, the masters here at their meeting last night sent two of theirs for our statement, which was given to them, which was shamefully curtailed on both statements with such we never will comply [*sic*].

Sir, I am ordered to inform you that those men of both meetings who can leave town are preparing as fast as possible, and some are gone already. There is one thing that is a little against us, we having no fund prepared to give a little relief to those whose situations will not admit of their leaving town. Sir, we will act according to your advice in respect to avoid law suits or combinations. Sir, I hope your speedy answer will give spirit and animate all to stand nobly in defence of a good cause. We hope to bring two or three of the masters to compliance in a little time. I have thought it proper that this letter should be signed by a few members who are known to you at your meetings in town, that you may rely on the truth of this letter.

Sir, I am ordered to inform you that our meeting was very sorry to hear of the unjust accusation laid against them to you by the

---

[1] *Three* signatures follow.

trade of Bristol, as we did not deserve it, nor I believe not one of our meeting had any such idea. There is not one of our [members] gone there as yet, nor no man shall go there. I remain for our body at large, your obedient and humble servant to command.

Thomas St. John, Clerk.
Joseph Hussey, President.
John Weaver, C. Swiney, John Flannagan.

P.S. Sir—When this letter was dated, we had a report that some of the masters was agreeing to give the wages, consequently the letter was detained from going to post until we should know the result of their intentions, Mr. Moore, Bath Street, Mr. Love, Mr. Benton, Mr. Flook, Mr. Ralph has signed to our statement agreeing to give the wages, Mr. Sloper to women's men, and the above masters the rest seems determined to stand some time, but we hope they will soon come to . . . [sic].

Monday night, 13 *February*.

(81).

Portsmouth, 28 *October*, [1803]
Sir—We are desired to inform you for the information of the traide of a shops meeting being carried on here, and that it will be nessarey for tramps comming this road to bring their clearances with them. You will likewise demand clearances from aney that may com from here it is likewise the disire of this shops meeting to form an alliance with you the same as the diffrent towns in the north, and if at aney time you should want aney assistance for the procecushion of aney thing that may be for the generall good we will be verrey happey to subscribe *our mite*. We will take it as a favor if you will send us a few printed clearances to serve us for a little as we have got none of our own our meeting being in its infancey but wee meet with better sucksess than we at first expected if you can spaire us a few you will be so good as to deliver them to James Ashley as he is going to send down a parcel to one of our members it will save som expence you will be so good as to make this as publick through the trade as possible as sevrall has maid this excuse for not bringing thare clearances that did nont knowe there was a shops meeting here—if you think us deserveing of you correspondances you will be so good as to send us an answer soon as possable.

From yours
T. Weston, J. Laidley, Thos. Freasor, Clark.

[H.O.42/79.]

(82). *Rules of the Society of Journeymen Boot and Shoe Makers.(Copy)*

Rules and orders to be observed by the different shops meetings.

1. That we do agree to meet every second Monday night at 8 o'clock, the Clerk not attending by half-past eight or not send his book, to be fined 1s.; in not attending by 9 o'clock fine 2s. 6d. Members not attending the first night fine 2d., second night fine 6d., third night fine 1s.; then to be visited by the Clerk of the shops meeting, the visitor to be paid 2d. by the visited member. Roll to be called at 9 o'clock. Any member coming after, fine 2d. extra to his night's spending money.

2. A President to be taken by rotation, and hold his office for two nights, and take the chair by half-past eight, or fine 4d. The President or delegates not attending for the night, fine 2s. 6d. each. Business to commence immediately after the roll is called. Members not to leave the room till the business of the night is fairly discussed, or fine 1s.

3. All delegates to be elected and paid 1s. 6d. from their shops meetings, for their committee-meeting nights, and exempt paying at their shops meeting. Two delegates from each shops meeting to form the committee for two months. The first delegate out of office to propose another, and if approved of by his shops meeting to stand the office or fine 2s. 6d.

4. The Clerk of the committee to be ballotted, and to be paid 2d. from each shops meeting, every delegate-meeting night ; and hold his office six months, the Clerk of the different shops meeting to be elected, and to be paid 1s. every shops meeting night, and hold their office six months.

5. In all debates the speaker must stand up and address the President, keep strictly to the question, in default thereof, the President is authorised to call him to order. After being called to order three times he must sit down and fine 6d. And any member interrupting another while speaking to the question to be fined 2d. for each offence.

6. Any member using any abusive language to another during meeting hours, or advance any political sentence, swear or act in a riotous or indecorous manner shall be fined 6d.

7. The committee may propound anything they think proper, or order a general summons, provided always that 2/3rds. of the committee agree to the same ; and no general summons to take place without the authority of the s[ai]d committee ; and any member of

the committee making known to any person not belonging to the said committee the place appointed for their meeting, or communicate their proceedings before the next shops meeting shall be fined one guinea.

8. Any member making known the private concerns of his shops meeting to a person that is not a member of this body shall be fined not less than 5s. and not exceed one guinea, agreeable to the nature of the offence.

9. That every member shall give his place of abode to the Clerk of his shops meeting ; when changing his lodgings shall acquaint the Clerk the next shops meeting night, or fine 6d., and the Clerk screening a member shall fine 1s.

10. Any member being called on extra business shall be allowed 6s. per day, half-day 3s., for an evening 1s. 6d.

11. Any member being guilty of scandalising a brother member in public or private of a breach of any of our rules, and cannot prove the same, shall fine 5s. Any member causing another to be brought to trial, and can prove nothing against him or them, such person shall fine 5s., and the acquitted shall be paid for his loss of time, and should any witnesses be summoned to attend by 8 o'clock, they shall be allowed 1s. each, and if each party do not attend at the time and place appointed they shall fine 2s. 6d. each.

12. If any member of these shops meetings shall purloin or embezzle his master's stuff or shall leave his work unfinished that is paid for, shall not be allowed to meet as a member till he has reimbursed the same, or pay a fine of 10s. 6d. and clear the books.

13. That no closer instruct a maker while he professes closing, on any pretence whatsoever.

14. Any member leaving his shop and going on for another shall produce his clearance the next shops meeting night, or fine 1s. 6d., and not producing it the second night shall fine 2s. 6d., and any clerk giving false clearance shall fine 5s.

15. If any branch or body of men should withdraw themselves from the general body without the mutual consent of the same shall fine one guinea, each individual.

16. Any Clerk of a shops meeting neglecting taking the number of votes for or against any motion, shall fine 2s. 6d., or any Clerk or delegates leaving their office without delivering up their books shall fine 10s. 6d., and no member shall hold two offices at one time.

17. Any member being proved *a scabb* shall not pay a fine less than one guinea nor more than 5 guineas, and any member screening

H

a scabb, knowing him to be one shall fine one guinea, the shops meeting a scabb belongs to, shall have the power to enforce the fine, but scabb fines shall be sent for the use of the trade.

18. No shop or shops to strike for wages without the consent of the trade ; in acting otherwise they must stand on their own bottoms. Shops meetings may strike against scabbs without the consent of the trade.

19. Any expenses that may occur on general concerns in the trade, to be levied by the committee on the shops meeting, agreeable to their strength, any shop calling a meeting of their own must defray their own expenses. (H.O.42/79).

(83). *Articles of the Friendly and United Society of Cordwainers, in-stituted at Westminster on 4 June, 1792, and associated for the laudable purpose of serving the trade in general.*[1]

PREFACE

Though the following Articles evidently explain the end and design of this Society, it may not be improper to take a more enlarged view of the subject, in order that such as are disposed to become members may perceive at once the advantages that are likely to result from such an Institution. We are sorry that in doing justice to our design we are obliged to advert to the late disturbance in the trade. We disclaim all intention to revive animosity, but, in order to prevent the return of similar evils, we are determined, in the first place, to raise a FUND.

If the laws of this country were much more perfect than they really are, still we must *purchase* their protection ; and it is much to be lamented that the expenses of a law-suit far exceed any journey man tradesman's ability. Hence it often happens that power over-comes right, and innocence itself proves no real security from punishment. When therefore a fund is collected, the money becomes the joint property of every individual member of the Society, and will be employed (if occasion requires) to shield him from injustice and oppression.

This then is one great end answered ; the master will then be cau-tious of accusing the guiltless when he knows the accused has it in his power to do himself justice ; and we shall then be no longer shocked with the account of journeymen being sent to Newgate as associates for common felons.

[1] Printed in pamphlet form, 31 pp.

82

If we look at the conduct of other trades (such as hatters, curriers, &c. who have established a *fund* for the benefit of those of their own profession) we see that all *their* journeymen take a lively and active concern in everything that interests their trade ; and none of *their* members are suffered to wander like vagrants when out of employment, or stoop in case of sickness or accident to solicit uncertain charity. They likewise wisely foresaw that when time, and a rise in the price of provisions rendered an advance of wages absolutely necessary, it would be but a poor dependence to expect to support a public cause by the subscription of their own journeymen, who, when their assistance is most wanted, are themselves out of employment.

We have experienced those evils. We have felt their effects, and should an attempt be made to reduce our wages, it is but prudent to prepare for our own defence. Almost every other trade takes care to secure (to their own journeymen, who have served a legal apprenticeship) the exclusive privilege of following the profession, and all the advantages accruing from regular employment. But in our trade, the servant without a character or the soldier worn out in the service, who can command a guinea or two, will at any time be taught the business, and (to the great prejudice of legal men) be suffered to follow it without interruption.

This is an evil that has been long and justly complained of, and which past experience has convinced us, nothing but a public fund can ever enable us effectually to reform. This then is another object the Society has in view ; we are determined to raise the trade to a more respectable rank among mechanical professions, by excluding unqualified intruders, by procuring proper and legal journeymen for the masters, and more constant employment for the men who are entitled to it.

In this part of our scheme there is nothing novel, for in many trades (some of whom are nearly as numerous as our own) both the masters and journeymen have long agreed to and established the same Regulation, and it often happens, when a master in any of those trades, from motives of partiality, employs a man not legally qualified, the rest of the men will leave the shop until such a one is discharged. To make us equal to any trade, and to accomplish all the designs we have in view, it requires but unanimity and perseverance, and the members of this Society having already accumulated a sum sufficient to purchase a portion of stock, have given a strong and honourable proof of their ability for such an undertaking.

We are convinced that nothing short of a general Fund can lay the foundation of a lasting union among journeymen of any trade ; but when that is once effected, every man will feel an interest in being connected ; he will see that a master cannot then easily take advantage of him ; and should it be attempted, the Society will be able, in some shape, to do him justice which he could not do for himself. In short, such a Society holds out a community of interests where the members are encouraged to promote each other's welfare. The next object of this Society is to raise a distinct Fund by small and separate subscriptions for the benefit of any of its own members in distress, and as their place of abode must (by the Articles) be always known to the Society, they will receive relief, without the painful circumstances attending the practice of begging.

Should it now be asked, what security can we have for the proper application of the money, one answer is that we have taken care to make it every member's interest to be honest, and therefore none has any temptation to act otherwise : there ought to be as much integrity in a Society of Shoemakers as one composed of any other tradesmen. You have therefore the same security as in other Societies of a similar nature, and surely it is full time to show the world that we can look forward to benefits more lasting and advantageous than even the substantial enjoyment of a supper ; and we trust the time is now arrived when shoemakers can (as well as cabinet makers and others) assert their rights and regulate the concerns of their own trade.

Some of the Articles make mention of scabs. And what is a scab ? He is to his *trade* what a traitor is to his *country* ; though both may be useful to one party in troublesome times, when peace returns they are detested alike by all. When help is wanted, he is the last to contribute assistance, and the first to grasp a benefit he never laboured to procure. He cares but for himself, but he sees not beyond the extent of a day, and for a momentary and worthless approbation, would betray friends, family and country. In short, he is a traitor on a small scale. He first sells the journeymen, and is himself afterwards sold in his turn by the masters, till at last he is despised by both and deserted by all. He is an enemy to himself, to the present age and to posterity.

Of such characters this Society will not be composed, being determined to admit of those only, whom we have strong reason to believe are friends to the real interest of the trade in general.

Preface to the Second Edition. [1794].

Brothers and fellow-citizens,

I beg leave to congratulate you on the success with which your efforts and perseverance in our laudable cause, is at last crowned. The many bars that lay in our way rendered our undertaking at first rather doubtful, such as the many fruitless attempts that had been made at former periods. Our master's vigilance to suppress us, and lastly, so great a number of disaffected journeymen who, in place of joining us like men, sneered at the proposition, but these very persons are now glad to sue for admission. Our masters also view us with a more favourable eye, witness their lately agreeing to employ none but Society men ; they see and experience that our institution is calculated to promote their interest as well as our own.

Although it is our lot to earn our bread by the sweat of our brow, it must be allowed that Providence has endowed the lower class of mankind with the faculty of discerning between right and wrong, as well as those that move in a higher sphere. We view our master's interest congenial with our own, their success is our advantage, and if they suffer, we must in our turn suffer with them ; but there is still a few masters, although but a few, that think our proceedings hostile. These men being destitute of that benevolence and liberality that constitutes a good member of society (which is to be found in the breast of every honest man) such characters are apt to think that all men is possessed with the same wretched disposition as themselves, and in course can never entertain a favourable opinion of their fellow creature.

Many are the advantages and good effects of our Constitution, that barbarism, with which the trade has been but too justly branded for centuries past, is now totally dispelled. There is no more working on Sundays, nor sotting and swearing in public houses on Mondays like vagabonds as usual ; this attainment must give infinite pleasure to every sober thinking man. Our rules, if strictly adhered to, has a tendency to improve the morals and cultivate the manners, and we are happy to acknowledge the great change that is among the trade in general in both these points, since our associating together. Another advantage arising from our union is that both customer and master is better served, and it is hoped the masters will in return be more tender in trifling with the journeymen's time ; this is an old and heavy grievance, and stands much in need of being redressed.

What remains for us to do, but to persevere in the laudable plan. Let us beware of forward hot-headed men, whose arguments in general consists of mere sound and emptiness when strictly examined. Let us conduct ourselves in all matters of importance, with judgement, coolness and deliberation. Let everyone lay aside his own private interest, and study the good of the whole. And lastly, let us study friendship and unanimity with one another; this will cement our noble structure and render it permanent. Make us the joy of the present and the praise of ages to come.

J. Cowie, Secretary

RULES AND ORDERS

ARTICLE I.—That every person wishing to become a member of this Society must be introduced and recommended by a member, as a person every way proper for admission.

II. That every person intending to become a member of this Society shall pay at his admission 5s., which when paid, each person shall receive a ticket to show that he has been legally entered a member of this Society.

III. That if any person, who wishes to become a member cannot make it convenient to deposit the sum for his admission on the first night of his appearance in the Society, he shall be indulged till the next half-yearly night, and then, when the money is paid, such member shall receive his ticket.

IV. As we have thought it expedient to admit scabbs on paying a fine of 10s. 6d., being desirous to bury their former conduct in oblivion, it is enacted that any person reproaching them or any other member, in or out of the Society, by calling them scabbs, shall pay a fine of 2s. 6d.

V. Any member knowing another guilty of a breach of our Rules, and does not report the same next meeting-night, shall be fined 2s. 6d. or be excluded.

VI. That one Steward shall be chosen and appointed every quarterly night, by each division, to act as a committee in transacting the necessary business, and if such Steward shall neglect to attend at the stated time of meeting, they shall forfeit for every such offence 1s.

VII. That any Steward who shall come to their respective division disguised in liquor, shall be fined 2s. 6d., and for that night excluded the room; any other member guilty of the same shall be fined 6d. and leave the room.

VIII. That all monies paid in for the use of this Society shall be deposited in the hands of such persons as the majority of the Society shall think most proper for that purpose, till a sum sufficient is raised to be put out at interest.

IX. That the names of such persons as are entrusted with the money shall be communicated to the committee by the represent-atives of each Society, that it may be known when a sum sufficient to bear interest is collected, and that such money, when raised, shall be put out in any way most agreeable to a majority of the whole.

X. That no member of this Society shall take any person to in-struct, or cause any to be instructed in the knowledge of the trade, for the space of one year from the date thereof ; and if, at the ex-piration of one year, it should be thought necessary by the Society at large to admit of any scholars, no member shall then be allowed to take one, unless such intended scholar has himself been a member of this Society for three months. And any member acting contrary to any part of this Article shall pay one guinea and turn away such scholar, or be excluded.

XI. That if any master should attempt to oppress the journeymen by reducing the price of labour, such journeymen shall immediately give notice to their Stewards ; and the said Stewards are hereby required to call a committee without loss of time, which committee shall, on such an occasion, give every necessary support to the oppressed.

XII. That no member of this Society shall presume to help any person to a seat of work unless such person be a member of this Society ; and any member so offending shall forfeit, on conviction, the sum of 2s. 6d. for each offence.

XIII. That no member during Society hours shall throw any ill-natured reflection, or use any abusive language to a brother member, and should anyone continue to violate this Article, after being repeatedly called to order by the Stewards, such a member shall be fined 6d. for each offence.

XIV. That for the security of the committee it is unanimously resolved that no member of this Society shall mention the business of the committee but in the Club-room. That no member shall mention the name of the Clerk, or Stewards, or the place of meeting, to any person unconnected with this Society on forfeiture of 10s. 6d. for each offence.

XV. That the Society shall meet at 8 o'clock in the evening pre-cisely, and the book be opened immediately to receive subscriptions, and shall continue open for that purpose till 10 o'clock, at which time it shall be closed for the evening, and no money to be taken afterwards.

XVI. That no member during Society hours shall be guilty of cursing, swearing, obscene songs, toasts or sentiments, under the penalty of 2d. for each offence.

XVII. That the Clerk shall be paid 3d. from each member every half-year night, and if the Clerk does not attend each meeting-night at 8 o'clock, he shall be fined for every such offence 2s. 6d.

XVIII. That on the entry of each member he shall give in the place of his abode, and the Clerk shall register the same in the book ; and when any member shall change the place of his abode, he shall give notice to his Society of the said change in the next meeting-night, or be fined 6d. The Clerk screening any member shall pay 1s.

XIX. That if any member should go into the country and afterwards return to town, he shall give notice of his return to the Society the first meeting-night after his arrival, or forfeit 6d.

XX. That every member who is absent on the Society meeting-night, and sending his money by another, shall, exclusive of the Society's subscriptions, pay 2d. to be spent for the good of the house.

XXI. That our Societies may not be charged with overlooking the interest of the masters, but especially to show our own attachment to honest principles, it is unanimously resolved that if any member of this Society shall purloin or embezzle his master's stuff, he shall be deemed a vagabond, and expelled the Society. And we further promise and engage that if any member should suffer such a loss by any of our members, this Society will re-imburse him, provided he employs only such journeymen as are members of this institution.

XXII. That each member shall pay 6d. every half-yearly night, to go towards establishing a fund for the relief of members in distress.

XXIII. That when any member is in distress he is to represent his case to his own Society, and the Stewards of which, by describing his situation to the committee will obtain such relief for him as from the whole of the case may be judged necessary ; and any steward, or others making an improper application, knowing it to be so, shall return the money and pay 2s. 6d. fine.

XXIV. Any member that has been absent for six months shall pay a fine of 2s. 6d., besides clearing the books, and for twelve months, 5s., provided he resides in town.

XXV. When any Steward or Clerk are called upon any extra business [they] shall be allowed from the general fund 4s. per day for their trouble, for half a day 2s. 6d., an evening, 1s. 6d.

XXVI. That each division shall consist of 60 members, and as soon as there is an overplus sufficient to make a new division, the same shall be done by ballot or otherwise, and take a fresh letter.

XXVII. If any member shall impose on the Society by lending his card, such member shall be fined one guinea.

XXVIII. That no person or persons shall strike from any shop or shops for more wages or otherwise, without the advice of the Society taken in the following manner, a teller to be on each side the question, the numbers carried to the committee, and a majority always to be decisive ; and anyone violating this Article shall be fined one guinea.

XXIX. That if any grievance should occur between individuals or otherwise, the committee, then in existence, shall have full power to decide on such matters.

XXX. All members above the age of 55 shall be exempted from paying anything to the general fund.

XXXI. That every member shall pay up all deficiencies on the half-yearly night, or be fined 6d.

XXXII. That such members as do not pay up all their deficiencies on the half-yearly night shall pay the whole the next succeeding meeting-night, or be excluded. And that therefore the Clerk shall send such members, a written notice a full fortnight before the time, informing them of their situation, and desiring them to prepare for the payment of all arrears, or be fined 1s.

XXXIII. That the Societies shall meet every fourth Monday, reckoning from 22 October 1792, and every member pay 6d. each meeting-night, all fines to be paid first.

XXXIV. That all fines and forfeitures shall, without exception, go to the general stock committees excepted.

XXXV. That the Secretary be allowed two guineas per year out of the joint stock. He shall keep a clear and distinct account of all monies in the funds, general collections, disbursements, &c., &c.; that he may pay to the amount of 5s. between meeting-nights to any members in distress, on a proper application being made by a Steward.

XXXVI. That he write in each Steward's Memorandum book the sum collected, likewise the minutes of the night.

XXXVII. If at any time the committee or stockholders should be guilty of a breach of the Articles, the Secretary shall pay the same before the different divisions next meeting-night, under the penalty of 10s. 6d.

XXXVIII. That if any case should occur, not comprehended in any of these Articles, the majority of the Societies shall then determine for themselves what is most proper to be done ; and the said majority shall have the power of altering, enlarging or adding to these Articles, when such majority are fully convinced that the good of the whole Society requires such a power to be exercised. (H.O.42/79).

(84). *Spencer Perceval (Attorney-General) to Lord Hawkesbury*[1]

5 *October*, 1804.

I have had the honour of receiving your Lordship's letter of the 22nd ult., accompanied with several papers relative to the combination formed by the boot and shoe makers in the metropolis, which your Lordship thereby submitted to the consideration of the Solicitor-General and myself, who were requested to state our opinion as to the steps most proper to be taken thereon.

These papers contain a statement of a very extensive combination existing amongst the boot and shoe makers in the metropolis who are in correspondence by means of delegates, committees and otherwise with similar combinations, or rather branches of the same combination in different parts of the kingdom. The system seems to be established upon the plan acted upon by the Corresponding Society and other United Societies,[2] which have been formed to act with such mischievous concert in England, Scotland and Ireland, upon political points which were the objects of their union ; and there appears to be no doubt that the plan of the present combination is capable of being applied in support of any object to which they may be disposed to direct it. The present objects seem to be the increase of wages, some regulations with respect to the number of apprentices, and imposing an obligation upon the masters to employ no journeyman who, not being a member of the combination, or refusing to comply with its rules and submit to its authority, has made himself obnoxious to its members. This latter object, it is plain, is immediately directed to the establishment of the strength of the Society, by putting into their hands the means of compelling every journeyman in the trade and through the journeyman, every master in the trade, to submit to their terms, under peril of ruin, by loss of employment to the

[1] Home Secretary, 1804-6. Created Baron Hawkesbury, 1803 ; succeeded his father as 2nd Earl of Liverpool, 1808 ; Prime Minister, 1812-27.
[2] See No. 32n.

journeymen, and loss of workmen to the masters. The general evidence of the existence of such a system seems to be very strong and convincing, but is not given with that detail and particularly with regard to individuals, as to enable me to point out to your Lordship the persons (whom if it should be thought fit for Government to take it up as a subject on which they would direct a prosecution) it would be proper to select as objects of that prosecution. But the papers contain the offer of more information, and I think it may be reasonably concluded from what they contain, that sufficient particular information against individuals might be procured.

Upon the point of law I have no difficulty in stating to your Lordship that the combination is illegal, and that the parties, if particularised by such evidence as I above suppose to be within reach of being procured, are liable to be prosecuted for a misdemeanour.

With respect to the policy of Government's instituting such a prosecution, my mind is in too great a degree of doubt to permit me to state any opinion, or to do more than to submit it to your Lordship and his Majesty's Government to determine it, suggesting some of the considerations which create my doubts.

If the effect of prosecuting or not prosecuting by Government was to begin and end with this case alone, it might perhaps be immaterial who carried on the prosecution ; the source of evidence is open to Government and the public prosecution would probably be able to procure sufficient evidence to convict. But as it will be viewed as a precedent of what the masters in this trade and in others will expect Government to do in future, it seems to me to deserve very serious consideration—for it is not only to be collected from these papers, but it is otherwise too notorious that similar combinations exist in almost every trade in the kingdom. And if Government attends to this application on the part of the boot and shoe makers, similar applications must be expected from every other trade, and it will lead to an opinion that it is not the business of the masters of the trade who feel the injury to prosecute, but that it is the business of Government. And it seems to admit of no doubt but that either as it regards the authority and weight of the masters, or the facility of securing evidence to prosecute with effect, that such prosecutions had better be in the hands of the masters than of Government. It must be admitted indeed that the offence has grown to such a height and such an extent as to make it very discouraging for any individual to institute a prosecution—as the persons whom he would prosecute would be supported at their trial and during their imprisonment by the contributions of their confederates, and his own shop would probably be deserted by his workmen. But then it is clear that it is owing to the inertness and timidity of the masters that the conspiracy has reached this height, and it may well be feared that this inertness will be rather increased than diminished by the interference of Government. The same timidity which disposes each at present to wish to leave it to some other masters to prosecute, lest by prosecution they should lose their workmen, will dispose them to leave to others the equality [*sic*] if not more obnoxious duty of informing, and when they once think the punishment of such offences to be the business of Government, they will think it also the business of Government to procure the evidence, and not theirs to give it, so that the future detection and prosecution of such offences would probably be rendered more difficult. Besides in all these cases they [*sic*] are always, whether well founded or not, complaints on both sides, and the impartiality of Government would be awkwardly situated, if, after undertaking a prosecution at the instance of the masters against the conspiracy of the journeymen, they were to be applied to on the part of the journeymen to prosecute the same masters for a conspiracy against their men.

These are some of the considerations which lead me to doubt whether it would or would not be politic to institute a prosecution by the public in this case, and I take leave to submit them to your Lordship's better determination. Upon the illegality of the conspiracy I have had an opportunity of knowing that the Solicitor-General agrees with me, but not having been able to see him since I have read the papers myself, and being pressed by the persons who submitted these papers to your Lordship not to delay my opinion upon them, I have reported upon the whole of the case without waiting to confer with the Solicitor-General upon the expediency of the Government's engaging in the prosecution. (H.O.42/79).

(85). *William Dawson, J.P., to Lord Hawkesbury*

Wakefield, 15 *October*, 1804.

Having long had reason to suspect there was an illegal combination amongst the cordwainers in this town, I have taken some pains to ascertain the fact, and having obtained information where I might probably meet with the box and rules of the Society, by a search warrant I got possession of the articles and letters I have the honour to enclose together with two books, one, an account of disbursements, the other, merely the names of the members against each of which was a check showing who had paid their subscriptions and who were in arrear.[1] George Foster, who appears to have been Secretary to the Society, and one Stephenson, were, on the evidence against them, and their own confession, convicted before the Rev. Mr. Wood and myself, but in consequence of their great contrition, promising to do their utmost to break up the Club and never to attend it again themselves, as well as their general good conduct, we only committed them to the House of Correction for fourteen days to hard labour, but we thought it right to summon before us the President, Stewards and Committee, on the complaint and information of Joseph Parkinson. Copies of the information, summons and examinations of witnesses are also enclosed. The defendants were assisted by counsel, who, I understand, had a general retainer from the Club and advised them to make no defence before Mr. Wood and myself, but in case of conviction, to appeal to the next Session. We did convict, and sentenced them to three months' imprisonment in York Castle ; and they appeal. The informant as well as the rest of the witnesses are all in very low circumstances, complain of the loss they have already sustained from being called off from their business, and fearful of expense (though we have directed our clerk to take no fees) and now proceed with unwillingness, which makes us fear that unless they are supported, our convictions stand little chance of being confirmed, the consequences of which we beg leave to submit to your Lordship's consideration, as also the propriety of taking any notice of the contents of the enclosed letters as far as they relate to the Societies of London and York.

This Club was at first instituted merely for the purpose of assisting each other in sickness or when unavoidably out of work, but like most Societies whose views are extended to illegal purposes, has its verbal as well as written laws. So cautious are they now become, no general striking or communication with masters is necessary ; it is done in a way perfectly intelligible to the master, but so as impossible to be given in evidence to prove a combination. I am sorry to say there are similar combinations equally extensive in other trades even in this town. So dangerous have we looked upon them in their consequences, we are anxious to suppress them, and feel it our duty to make this communication to your Lordship from the poverty of the prosecutor in the present instance. (H.O.42/79).

---

[1] The enclosures are missing.

(86). *Spencer Perceval to Lord Hawkesbury*

20 *October*, 1804.

I have had the honour of receiving your Lordship's letter of the 17th instant referring me and the Solicitor-General to the reference made to us on 22nd ultimo, of the combinations of journeymen shoe makers and boot closers in the metropolis, and to our report thereon, and transmitting to us the copy of a letter[1] with its enclosures from Mr. Dawson, a magistrate of Wakefield, relative to a similar combination amongst the cordwainers in that place, which shews the extent to which these combinations are carried in different parts of the kingdom ; at the same time desiring our opinion how far these additional facts operate as to the mode of proceeding which it may be advisable to adopt to check this very serious and increasing evil, and more pressingly submitting for our immediate consideration and opinion whether it will be advisable under the present circumstances to order Mr. White under our directions to proceed with the prosecution and to support the convictions of the magistrates in this case which are represented as likely to fall to the ground from the poverty of the prosecutors and witnesses.

The pressing manner in which your Lordship requests our opinion upon the latter question induces me to return to your Lordship my report upon this reference, without waiting to communicate with Mr. Solicitor-General, who is at present at some distance from town.

Mr. Dawson's letter only impresses more strongly upon me the opinion expressed in the former report of the necessity of his Majesty's Government taking it into their serious consideration whether they will or will not direct prosecutions of this kind to be openly taken up by the Solicitor for the Treasury. On the one hand it shews that the extent to which the mischief has arisen may perhaps deter private prosecution, but on the other it shews to a certainty that there must be so many cases in which the same interference on the part of Government would be applied for, if consented to in this, as would be extremely inconvenient for the reasons suggested in the former report. With respect to these particular convictions, perhaps your Lordship might not think it inexpedient to take a middle course, and to write to Mr. Dawson, informing him that if the prosecutions in question are in the hands, or could be placed in the hands of a respectable solicitor, that that solicitor

[1] No. 85.

might correspond with Mr. White, the Solicitor of the Treasury, who should have directions to give him the necessary assistance, and also to discharge his bill. This, though not wholly free from all the inconveniences of a more avowed prosecution by the public, is from the circumstance of its not being attended with such notoriety, exposed to fewer of them and in a less degree.[1] (H.O.48/13).

(87). R. A. Farington, J.P., to Lord Hawkesbury

Manchester, 24 May, 1808. 6 p.m.
. . . The rejection of the Weavers' Bill[2] is the avowed cause of the disturbance, and an increase of wages in that branch of the manufactory is called for. They profess a determination not to work longer at the present prices, and endeavour to prevent the well disposed from continuing at their looms . . . (H.O.42/95).

---

[1] The following unsigned and undated note is in H.O.42/131 : ' The journeymen boot and shoe makers and boot closers have for a considerable time past, formed themselves into various illegal Societies (chiefly held at public houses) for the express purposes of raising their wages ; and have at each of the said Societies nominated and appointed a chairman or president with a deputy, and a treasurer or clerk to receive and account for monies paid in by subscription : and have likewise bound themselves to each other by various laws and regulations, and have affixed fines of money when any of their members have acted contrary to their said laws.

'They have in consequence of forming themselves into these aforesaid Societies adopted every means in their power (either by threats of personal violence or by persuasion) to prevent and hinder every industrious journeyman from obtaining work from any shop within the metropolis, unless he would consent to become a member and receive a ticket to signify his admission therein.'

[2] A Bill to guarantee a minimum wage. The wages of the handloom weavers had fallen from an average of 2/4½d. per day in June 1805, to 2/3d. in January, 1806, 1/7½d. in February 1807, and 10½d. in January 1808. (H.O.42/95. Col. Fletcher to Lord Hawkesbury, received 24 February, 1808). 'It is a very unfortunate circumstance,' wrote Mr. Farington on 26 May, 'that a very considerable rise has taken place very lately, in the price of flour and oatmeal.' (H.O.42/95). He reported on the 25th that there had been disturbances in Manchester, one man being killed who attacked a dragoon with brickbats, and another being severely wounded. 'They again (as yesterday) intimated their intention of meeting tomorrow. Parties of them went about early this morning, took away the shuttles and compelled many to leave their looms.' (*Ibid.*) Another correspondent, Ralph Wright, said that the trouble in Manchester was due to Irish weavers. 'It is reported that the weavers in the neighbouring towns are much unhinged.' (*Ibid.*, 25 May).

(88). *The Rev. Charles Prescot and John Philips to Lord Hawkesbury*

Stockport, 28 May, 1808.

As magistrates acting for this and the adjoining County of Lancaster, we think it a duty we owe to Government to acquaint your Lordship with the state of this town and neighbourhood, which, since the Bill, lately before the House of Commons for fixing the price of the labour of the cotton weavers, was thrown out, have been under continual alarm and terror, owing to great bodies of the weavers having assembled for the purpose of obliging the manufacturers to raise their wages, and in the meantime neither working themselves, nor suffering others to work, and of course their families starving . . . (H.O.42/95).

(89). *R. A. Farington to Lord Hawkesbury*

Manchester, 28 May, 1808. 6 *p.m.*

Yesterday and this day have passed without any materially riotous proceedings. No general assemblage of the weavers has taken place, but the whole of the town and neighbourhood, so far as the weaving branch is concerned, are in a state of confusion. No work is carried on, and the well-disposed families, who are inclined to pursue their labour, are prevented doing so by the threats and intimidation held out to them. It has become necessary in many instances to distribute immediate relief to families of the above description until order can be restored. The merchants and manufacturers have formed a committee with the view of assisting the civil power, and of devising some mode of meeting the claims of the weavers, but the accomplishment of this appears to have many difficulties . . . (H.O.42/95).

(90). *Henry Norris to Spencer Perceval*

Davy Hulme Hall, near Manchester, 30 *May,* 1808.

I am just now returned from a large assembly of the people near this house, collected with the avowed intention to prevent weaving being carried on. When I first got up to them some symptoms of resistance appeared, but upon a quiet representation of the impropriety of their conduct they attended to reason. In the course of conversation they agreed immediately to disperse upon condition that I would represent to Government the real state of the country. This I most readily agreed to.

It is certain that from the very low wages paid for weaving, the weavers are in the greatest distress, and quite unable in many cases to procure necessary food. The language they held forth to me was this—that for the last six months their distress had been well known, and no prospect of being relieved appeared, that, driven to the miserable situation in which they stood, it was indifferent to them which way they perished ; they acknowledged the law was against their present conduct, but extreme want was the cause . . . (H.O.42/95).

(91). *R. A. Farington, J.P., to Lord Hawkesbury*

Manchester, 31 May, 1808. 9 p.m.
My last letter would inform your Lordship that it was understood a meeting of certain individuals would take place on this day, to offer conciliatory measures to the weavers. It has taken place, and although I cannot at this late hour enter into the details, it appears to have stilled the disposition to riot for the present. An advance of wages in certain articles has been proposed, averaging about 20%. But as this will not bind the great body of manufacturers to give full employment, or indeed any, to the weavers, I am very apprehensive it may lead to future disturbances, and those at no great distance of time . . . (H.O.42/95).

(92). *R. A. Farington, J.P., to Lord Hawkesbury*

Manchester, 1 June, 1808.
. . . I remain of opinion that no great length of time will elapse before the magistrates are again called upon to use measures for preserving the peace of the country. The discontents, as I have before stated, extend to every part of the manufacturing districts in the County of Lancaster, and although a great proportion of the weavers may be satisfied with the prospects held out of an advance in the prices, many will be otherwise, and as it is impossible to bind the masters at large by the Resolutions and recommendations passed yesterday, or to fix with any precision, prices which must vary, not only from the quality of goods of the same species, but the demand for them in the market, I fear these ill-judging people, incited perhaps by some mischievous spirits, will again be troublesome . . .
We have reason to believe there is now a strong division among the leaders of the weavers, that is, between those satisfied with the

J

results of yesterday, and those who differ in opinion . . . Some intelligence has been conveyed to the magistrates, as if the dissatisfied part of the weavers, or perhaps their leaders, had an object in view beyond an advance in wages, something of a political nature. I am unwilling to think this can extend far, but we are taking pains to gain some more certain information . . . (H.O.42/95).

(93). *J. Silvester to Lord Hawkesbury*

Manchester, 2 June, 1808.

. . . I have great pleasure, in the absence of my brother magistrates, to state that peace seems in a great degree restored in this town, though few, if any, of the weavers, are yet permitted to return to their looms, by small menacing parties, mostly to the lowest description of Irishmen, who are so well organised as to be able to elude the vigilance of the Peace Officers. I should not, however, omit to state that of the description of persons desired to return to their work (perhaps 4/5ths of the whole or more) have been relieved by a very liberal distribution of money issued from the parish table.

Many acts of depredation and violence have been committed in the neighbouring towns, and the levies have been very heavy and frequent upon the troops at the barracks, who in every instance have happily succeeded in dispersing the rioters, who now seem composed of every description of woollen, cotton and other weavers and spinners, who become every day more extensive and formidable . . .[1] (H.O.42/95).

[1] The following printed handbill is enclosed in the above letter :
ROYTON.
At a meeting of the weavers and other inhabitants of the Township of Royton, it was agreed to submit the following statement of our sufferings, and the cause thereof, to our fellow-countrymen :

As we have been called upon to take part with you in your present proceedings, we, the said inhabitants, feel it our indispensable duty to address you at this important crisis, upon the subject of our mutual distress ; a subject that demands the most serious attention of every one of us, and upon which depends our happiness or misery. While we lament the general distress, we beg leave to suggest that it is our opinion your proceedings are not likely to obtain you relief ; for that distress can only be removed by removing the cause—which cause we have no hesitation in pronouncing is the WAR. To prove which, we need only refer to our dependence upon commerce, and how it is obstructed by the War ; and it is our humble opinion that it is impossible for either the Legislature or commercial characters to remedy the evil by any other means than that of the restoration of peace.

[*Continued on p. 99*]

(94). *R. A. Farington to Lord Hawkesbury*

Manchester, 4 June, 1808.

[The Weavers] . . . Some have returned to their looms satisfied with the arrangements both in the town and country ; others are still idle, and endeavour by various means to prevent and intimidate the well disposed from working. But with all the endeavours we have used to obtain information so as to identify the persons, hitherto we have been unsuccessful. A committee sit who direct operations, as we believe, but no discovery has been made so as to enable us to seize them. They are in an equally disturbed state in all the villages round Manchester, [as] well as Bury, Ashton-under-Lyne, Rochdale, &c., &c. But as the dissensions among the weavers and their committees are considerable, I hope and trust these will lead in some part to the restoring order and industry ere long.

We have a great number of Irish weavers, who are the foremost and most turbulent in all the proceedings. A considerable fund has been, as I hear, for some time collecting, and is now distributing, but in the whole of their proceedings, there is such secrecy and arrangement, that we find the utmost difficulty in detecting or gaining any information to found proceedings upon . . . (H.O.42/95).

(95). *Thomas Drake, D.D., and J. Entwistle[2] to Lord Hawkesbury*

Rochdale, 4 June, 1808.

We beg leave to lay before your Lordship the late alarming situation of this populous town and neighbourhood, occasioned by the recent

[Continued from p. 98]

Fellow countrymen—We have been misrepresented and treated as enemies to our King and country, but we can safely say that our only wish has invariably been a termination of the contest in which we are unfortunately engaged ; and are now convinced that it is an object equally the wish of the major part of the country ; and which we believe has been withheld from us by those whose counsels have too long prevailed in this country. Yet notwithstanding, we are ready at all times to forward, in any constitutional manner, that which is likely to be productive of the good we all aim at. But [we] will never lend our aid to any illegal measure ; therefore, by your permission, we will advise you to desist from your present proceedings—return to your families and respective employments, as the neglect so to do will, we fear, only tend to your misfortune and distress.   30 May, 1808.

[2] Magistrates for the County of Lancaster.

riots and disturbance here. On Monday an outrageous mob of several thousands broke open the private houses of weavers, carried off their shuttles and other implements of weaving. The civil power made every attempt to quell it but in vain. In the evening of that day the Police Office was attacked, the windows demolished by large stones thrown at the magistrates sitting there, who narrowly escaped at the hazard of their lives ; soon afterwards the prison was broke open[1] and entirely burnt down. During the night money was extorted by a furious mob, menacing to burn the gentlemen's houses, factories, mills, &c., and the lives of individuals were not only threatened, but in most imminent danger.

These illegal proceedings continued until last Wednesday morning when half a troop of cavalry arrived from Manchester, and also the Halifax volunteers . . . These illegal and alarming proceedings took place in consequence of the cotton and woollen manufacturers requiring an advance of wages from the merchants who employed them . . . (H.O.42/95).

(96). *Henry Fielden to Lord Hawkesbury*

Blackburn, 6 *June*, 1808.
I think it necessary to enclose for your perusal a letter,[2] copies of which have been very generally distributed in this neighbourhood. In this, the motives are plainly avowed and the meetings appear to be [no] longer for the purpose of getting an advance in the wages of the weavers but to excite and spread revolutionary principles. Considerable excesses have been committed here, and it will require an immediate and strong military force to prevent a recurrence. (H.O.42/95).

---

[1] To release a number of riotous weavers who had been committed.

[2] '*Bolton*, 4 *June*, 1808 : Oppressed brethren—We, the inhabitants of Bolton and its vicinity, do intend to meet upon Charters Moss, near this town, every Sunday morning for the space of two months, and hope that our brethren (the poor and oppressed weavers of Blackburn and its neighbourhood) will join them ; at which meetings they intend to discuss the following questions, viz.

1. What is the cause of our present disastrous, unhappy, miserable condition ? Is it not the protracted War, the most unsuccessful and ruinous that has spread devastation over Europe, and rendered our once flourishing country a scene of misery ?

2. What will be the best mode of redress, as the calamities of the people call aloud for reformation ?

[*Continued on p. 101*]

(97). *R. A. Farington to Lord Hawkesbury*

Manchester, 9 June, 1808.

Nothing of a tumultuous nature has taken place in this district since I last had the honour of addressing your Lordship. Some weavers are discontented and have not returned to their looms, and are still clamorous for prices of their own fixing, viz. 6s. 8d. in the pound at least, more than the current prices previous to the disturbance. But I have great satisfaction in stating to your Lordship my opinion that all serious apprehensions have subsided. We have reason to believe that the numbers inclined to work are daily increasing. The appearance of a strong military force has contributed most materially in producing this effect amongst some, and an advance in the wages having taken place is a cause for content with others . . . The avenues to Manchester are patrolled by dragoons and special constables to protect people bringing in and taking out their work ; and every measure we can think of is adopted to give the well disposed confidence and security. These have become necessary as many instances occurred of work being taken, and destroyed or damaged by utter strangers to the parties.

Many people, some of them ringleaders, have been taken into custody, and are admitted to bail, or committed for trial according to the nature of the offence. We understand that money for subsistence becoming a scarcity among the weavers, applications are making for assistance from the funds of the Friendly Societies, but these, I think, must prove as fruitless as illegal, for there are few if any consisting wholly of weavers . . . (H.O.42/95).

[Continued from p. 100]

3. Is not the British Cabinet the cause of this War ? Did it not spring from that originally, and is it not the inflexibility of that nest of adders, that cripples our trade and commerce, and shuts the foreign markets against our manufactures ?

4. Do not our merchants and manufacturers deserve to lose their property for their parasitical nonsense presented to his Majesty and the Parliament, in which they propose to support the War with their lives and fortunes ?

5. Is it not time to drag the British Constitution from its lurking hole, and to expose it in its original and naked purity, to show to each individual *the laws of his forefathers* ?

These, and several other questions of the like nature, will be the business of those meetings . . .'

(98). *R. A. Farington to Lord Hawkesbury*

Manchester, 10 *June*, 1808.

. . . The weavers continue quiet, greater numbers have returned to their looms, and the advance in wages becoming general will, I trust, keep them so. Yet there are still many who are restless and dissatisfied, and over whose conduct it is necessary to keep a watchful eye. We have not ascertained that anything of a disloyal or seditious nature has mixed itself in the present disturbance . . . (H.O.42/95).

(99). *Lord Ribblesdale to Lord Hawkesbury*

Manchester, 10 *June* [1808].

. . . In this town and in its vicinity the greatest part of the populace have quietly returned to their respective employments. Nor is it in the least probable they should again attempt to disturb the tranquillity of this town or its neighbourhood. At Bolton, however, considerable discontent still prevails . . . The price of grain is much reduced, and the wages of the manufacturers have been increased which collectively have had the happiest effect in restoring tranquillity . . . (H.O.42/95).

(100). *R. A. Farington to Lord Hawkesbury*

Manchester, 14 *June*, 1808.

. . . A very considerable number of weavers assembled yesterday in the neighbourhood of Stockport, but dispersed without committing any outrages.

The weavers in many parts are yet discontented. They require the whole of the manufacturers to sign an engagement for prices, of the weavers' fixing, appear determined not to work until this is entered into, and labour to create fear and uneasiness amongst those who are disposed to be content. In other parts the weavers are generally at work, but this depends a good deal upon the nature of the goods they are weaving . . . In some instances I learn the weavers have drawn money from their Friendly Societies' funds . . . (H.O.42/95).

(101). *The Mayor of Wigan to Lord Hawkesbury.*

Wigan, 15 *June*, 1808.

. . . In this borough and the neighbourhood the principal employment of the people is in the cotton manufactures, and we have within the borough 3,000 weavers. The rejection of the Bill introduced into

Parliament to fix a minimum of the wages to be paid to weavers in those manufactures immediately created universal discontent amongst them. And on Monday, 30 May, many of them from the adjacent villages entered the town in different parties and expeditiously collected as many shuttles from the weavers residing here as they could obtain, which they marked with the owners' names and locked up near the places from whence they were taken. Most of the owners of the shuttles were as ready to deliver them as the collectors were to receive them, but in some few cases the owners were intimidated to part with their shuttles by the number of the collectors and the general voice of the people that all shuttles should be taken, and there are few instances where any resistance was made by any of the owners. On the next day many weavers of this town began to collect shuttles at the extremities of the town in a similar manner, and I appointed and swore about 200 special constables and called out the volunteers, and we traversed the town and pursued the weavers, to have apprehended them, but they fled.

We however discovered the places where many of the shuttles had been left, and we seized and afterwards restored them to the owners. We endeavoured to identify the persons who had taken the shuttles, but all the owners (except one) pretended that they did not know any of the offenders. I have committed one of the shuttle takers to Lancaster Castle for felony in taking two shuttles.

. . . In travelling the streets with the military and constables I was sorry to see so great and general a ferment amongst the lower order of the inhabitants. Their common cry was, 'Give us bread, we are starving !' And though the streets were afterwards quiet, yet the people appeared to be full of rancour and insubordination, and they manifested a disposition to commit acts of violence if they had not been restrained by the apprehensions of exemplary punishment. It must be admitted that the earnings of an industrious weaver are but small, and that provisions are high, and that such a man with a wife and two children can scarcely provide bread for himself and family, and that the present distresses of the weavers and their families are such as were never before experienced, but the trade of this country is now so depressed and confined that the manufacturers must either pile up their goods in their warehouses, which will require an extraordinary capital and can only be adopted by a few individuals, or vend their goods for the reduced price that can be obtained, and under such circumstances the manufacturers are paying as great wages as their trade will bear . . . (H.O.42/95).

IV. LANCASHIRE & SCOTTISH WEAVERS, AND THE FRAMEWORK-KNITTERS

1809. The journeymen hat manufacturers of Stockport. The Tyne-side keelmen (lightermen).
1810. The Sheffield cutlers. The Lancashire weavers.
1811. The beginnings of Luddism.
1812. The frame-work knitters. The Lancashire weavers. The journeymen hatters of Manchester. The miners in the Forest of Dean. The Scottish weavers. The West Riding wool-combers.

(102) *Daniel Cooper's Memorial to the Earl of Liverpool*[1]

Stockport, 31 *January*, 1809.

The humble Memorial of Daniel Cooper, of Stockport in the County of Chester, hat manufacturer, one of the sect of people called Quakers, sheweth

That your memorialist carries on the trade of hat-making in the town of Stockport, and has employed divers journeymen and work-men in such manufacture.

That a considerable manufacture of hats is carried on in the town and neighbourhood of Stockport and several thousand hands are employed therein.

That a great number of the journeymen hatters and others have entered into an unlawful combination and conspiracy against their masters, and have refused to work and have been out of employ for three months last past [*sic*] and continue out, and are supported by contributions and subscriptions from those who are suffered to re-main employed.

---

[1] Enclosed, together with the following printed document, in J. Lloyd's letter to Lord Liverpool, dated Stockport, 5 February, 1809, and transmitted through his agent, Mr. Wilson, of 16 Greville Street, Hatton Garden. The letter is endorsed, 'Refer to the cases wherein a pardon has been offered to an accomplice—for sending threatening letters.'

That no legal steps whatever have at present been taken against any of the offenders as your memorialist knows of.

That your memorialist has not done any act calculated to offend, provoke or irritate any of them. Yet on the 7th day of January instant there was found by a person (not a Quaker, and consequently capable of giving his testimony in a criminal prosecution) thrust under the door of his house, a written paper in the words and letters following :—

'Danel Coper if you do not turn of your nob sticks we have agreed to burn your hous and warehouse and if you do not turn them of the matter is to late we will do for you and your son to the first opportunity we will dammed if we do not the first time we can see you peg drunc then goes Danel to the pot think what our families have suffer we shall nor forget you nor the other masters nether we put one in the cannell remember some you will next we have done for John[n] and we will do for Fleter.'

Directed on back, 'Danel Cooper.'

That the expression 'We put one in the cannell' is supposed by your memorialist to allude to one William Williamson, a master hatter, who was found in the canal near Stockport in the month of June, 1807, supposed to be drowned accidentally till certain facts transpired that led to the suspicion of its being wilfully done by some journeymen hatters or workmen of that trade in consequence of evidence he was about to give that would implicate some of them in crimes.

That your memorialist is under fear of bodily hurt or harm by reason of the letter so addressed to him . . . (H.O.42/99).

(103). *At a General Congress of the Journeymen Hat-makers and Finishers, of Stockport, and its vicinity, held the 19th of September, 1808, at the Royal Oak, in the Hillgate, the following Rules and Regulations were agreed to.*

PREAMBLE — Whereas the very being, end and existence of every Society consists in a steady, strict and uniform compliance with such Rules, Orders and Regulations as such Society shall, upon the most mature consideration, think necessary to adopt, for the better carrying the design of their Institution into execution : the following Rules, Orders and Regulations are therefore hereby agreed to be most impartially and punctually observed, by every member of the Friendly Associated felt-makers of Stockport and its vicinity.

RULES AND ORDERS

ARTICLE FIRST — It is agreed that we shall altogether treat to one book, and that we shall take turn as it shall come in order.[1]

2. And we agree that one plate shall be deposited in one box, and the other be destroyed ; and we have unanimously agreed that the finisher's plate and tickets be kept for the use of the trade.

3. That each party shall settle their own business except when it shall concern prices, apprentices, subscriptions, men that have not served their legal time, or any general turn-out ; and that each man shall subscribe to the support of all turn-outs, in any case that shall be agreed to at any general meeting.

4. And in any case that concerns a maker or finisher, they shall call seven shops of their own (that is, on any trifling matter) such as calling a man a rogue, creep[2] or thief, or any such like petty offence ; and should the fine be under one guinea the said seven shops to drink it ; but if the fine be one guinea or above, the whole trade to drink of the same ; but if any dispute arises betwixt a maker and a finisher, the person that dozens[3] to call four of his own branch, and three of the other, that is, if a maker dozens to call four makers and three finishers, and if a finisher dozens, the same to be observed on his part.

5. And it is further agreed, that if either maker or finisher accuses any man of his time,[4] and cannot make his accusation good, to be under a fine of one guinea.

6. And any person accused must take his dozening shilling[5] before he goes to his work after such accusation has taken place, to the next fair shop, on or before 4 o'clock on that day ; when that shop shall warn the next fair shop, and so on till seven shops are got together : but if it should so happen that the person is not accused in time for his dozening shilling to be taken by 4 o'clock he is to take his dozening shilling at the time he is accused, and it must rest there till 4 o'clock on the day following, when such seven shops must be

---

[1] They agreed, that is, to book all work in one book and pool the wages, all receiving equal.

[2] A creeping fellow, a sneak.

[3] Dozening means arbitrating. The dozen consisted of representatives of the shop, and the person claiming the dozen (or jury) had the right to nominate a proportion of it.

[4] Accuses him, that is, of taking work out of his turn. It was, and is, a custom in the trade to share the work equally.

[5] Both the accused and the accuser were to deposit a shilling when a dozen was called.

called together, but if any person is accused of his time, he may take his shilling to the next shop, and have the shops called together immediately. It is to be observed that the seven shops must be called together by 7 o'clock in the evening, and any person that dozens let the person he dozens know, and each party to bring their witnesses by 7 o'clock.

7. And it is further agreed that any person dozening another, the person brought down shall pay the fine that the seven shops lay him under before he proceeds any further, but if he thinks himself injured he may dozen again at 14 or 21 shops, and the person that cast to be at all the expense that may have been incurred, and neither of the 7 or 14 shops to be laid under any fine, and this decision to be final.

8. And it is agreed that when any congress is called, no man shall be at liberty to leave the turn house[1] before 11 o'clock that evening, except business is settled before that time : nor no man to be compelled to stop longer than that hour, whether business is settled or not. Any man leaving before the above-mentioned time, except business is settled, will be under a fine of 2s. 6d.; and for the future all congresses to be called at 6 o'clock in the evening, and an hour allowed as usual for the men to come together. All notes to be issued out from the turn house by 12 o'clock at noon, in order that there may be a proper time for them to go round the trade in, and no fine to be drank before 7 o'clock in the evening, and notes to go round the trade in the same time, and in the same manner as for a congress, and any man or men stopping any such notes in any shop above five minutes, to be under a fine of 2s. 6d. Any man or men larking in the congress room, to be under a fine of 2s. 6d., and any man or men fighting in the said room, to be under a fine of 5s. It is to be understood that no fine of any description is to be drank before 7 o'clock in the evening, even from seven shops.

9. And it is unanimously agreed that all women are to be knocked off against,[2] to knock one woman off at one shop at a time, till it is gone round the trade, and so on till they are all done away with. Any person neglecting to be conformable to this, will be deemed under a fine of 5 guineas, and no woman shall be allowed to pad[3] from either town or country.

[1] The meeting place of the Union. This term is still used.
[2] If women were brought in to do work usually done by journeymen, there would be a 'knock-off,' or strike.
[3] 'To pad' was the term used by a workman when he took back to his employer work he had done at home.

10. And any man knowing of a foul[1] shop of any description within this district, is to make it known to the men of the shop where he works, that in case they should come to be asked for, they may be knocked off against. Any man so neglecting to make such case known will be deemed under a fine of 10s. 6d.

11. And whereas it has at many different times occurred, that some out-door men hearing of a master that has plenty of work to deliver out, they will go and get work out from such master, and perhaps the said work is in haste to go off again ; these men neglecting to take in their work at the time ordered by such a master, prevents the order from going off, to the great detriment of both master and man, as it prevents others from coming down, which would have come in case such an order had been completed at the time appointed, and therefore causes many a man to wait ; therefore it is ordered that any man taking out work from any master and neglects taking in the said work again within eight days after such master has ordered him (the master allowing him sufficient time to do it in) such man in default thereof shall be under a fine of 10s. 6d.

12. And it is agreed that when any piece-master takes an apprentice, the said apprentice shall be bound to serve his whole time, or seven years, with the said master unto whom he is first bound, unless the said master shall happen to die before the said apprentice shall have duly served his time, or that the said apprentice is unjustly used by his said master ; in either of which cases, then it shall or may be lawful that the said apprentice be assigned over to another master, his indenture being made exactly the same as his former indenture, according to the contracts therein mentioned, and to no other purpose whatever. And whereas it has been the practice of some corrupt apprentices to damage their masters' work, in order to incite their masters to assign them to other masters, merely to procure to themselves extraordinary wages, it shall not for the future be lawful for any apprentice to be assigned to another master, without his other master die, or that the said apprentice can give sufficient proof of some ill usage uncommon (as before specified). And whereas several masters have made a practice of assigning over their apprentices to other masters purely for gain, which practice doth prevent men who have served lawful apprenticeships from being employed, to no small detriment of them and their families ; therefore, any master or masters guilty of the said offence, or for every

---

[1] A foul shop was presumably one where the rules were abused.

offence contrary to the above articles, shall be under a fine of 5 guineas, and no person who acts otherwise, shall be stood by in the trade till such fine is duly paid ; and any master striving to persuade a lad away from his present master, on any pretence whatever, shall be deemed under the said fine. That there shall be no more journeymen apprentices at all, and those already bound shall be conformable, or their time will be deemed illegal. And in case an apprentice should enlist for a soldier, or go to sea, and will not stop to serve his time, his bonds to be cancelled by a magistrate or the trade, the master allowed to take another apprentice, and a memorandum made on the indenture, specifying the day of the month and the year of our Lord when such apprentice left his said master, and the indenture to be lodged in the box belonging to the trade. And in case such apprentice shall return, and come to his business again, his indenture to take date from the time he left his former master, to the full end and term of seven years, and be bound exactly as by his former indenture and if in case any master and apprentice shall at any time agree between themselves to cancel such indenture, without consulting the trade, or a magistrate, such master shall not be allowed to take another apprentice till the time of the one he has discharged be expired. It is deemed requisite that every piece-master should have a copy of the above Articles, and that he place them in some eligible part of his house or shop, in order that an apprentice by perusing the same, may have a better knowledge of his duty to his said master ; and every master who shall reckon with the apprentice, or allow the apprentice to reckon for work, shall be under a fine of 5 guineas.

13. Any person shall be allowed to take his own son to the trade, at any time he may think he is useful to him, but he shall not be at the trade any longer before he is under bond indenture than the age of 13 years, or within one month after that time at farthest ; but no person shall be allowed to have a foreigner above one month before he is put under bond indenture. The master neglecting to comply with the above, to be knocked off work and under a fine of 5s. 3d.

14. And it is unanimously agreed that any lad being bound apprentice to any master who has served a legal seven years, and that it appears that such lad was bound in every respect fair, such lad's time shall be deemed fair, though it should happen after that lad was bound that the said person should take above the legal number of apprentices : but no other apprentice's time to be allowed fair save the first apprentice, and in case such first apprentice should stop in

opposition to the trade, and teach other illegal apprentices, or men who have not served a legal time, then his time will be deemed foul also.

15. Any person or persons going into any shop and teaching a number of illegal apprentices or men of any description that have not served their time, they shall not be stood by on any account whatever ; or any man or men standing by any such person or persons, to be under a fine of 5 guineas.

16. And for the future, a list of all the shops to be inserted on a paper, purposely for the use of the trade to call the shops over by at a general congress ; and any person neglecting to attend such general congress and answer to his name the second time of calling over, to be under a fine of 2s. 6d.; and the names to be called over by a chairman chose by the trade : and the chairman that sits to-night to have it in his power to choose a chairman for the night following, by the consent of the trade, and no dozenings to be allowed to be brought on the committee at a congress : and any person neglecting to keep good order when called upon by the chairman, to be under a fine of 2s. 6d., and all the shops to be called over after business is settled, and any person neglecting to be there to answer for his shop, will be under a fine of 2s. 6d.

17. And when any person comes wishing to be asked for, the person that goes and asks for him, to take his ticket, and in case that man is shopped,[1] he must leave his ticket at the place he is shopped at, and some of his shopmates must come and inform the turn-house when such man is shopped, that they may know when to call upon him for his eight-day turn, and any man neglecting to give such information to the turn-house, to be under a fine of 2s. 6d., and in case such man stops at such shop above eight days, his shopmates shall see that his ticket is destroyed, or they will be under a fine of 2s. 6d.

18. Any person quitting a shop and leaving his work to get up, the master is at liberty to go and knock such man off when he sees proper, and the man that is knocked off to be obliged to go the day after such master has knocked him off, or in default thereof he will be under a fine of 10s. 6d.; and any man standing by such man after he is knocked off, to be under a fine of 5s. 3d.; and any man leaving any walking to pay, or any other shop dues, to be knocked off in the same manner.

[1] *i.e.* employed.

19. That for the future, if piece-masters, journeymen felt-makers, hatter or hatters whatsoever, shall be found guilty of purloining, wasting, destroying or embezzling any stuff of any kind whatsoever committed to his or their care to work for hire, or selling the same, either wrought or unwrought, such persons found guilty of so doing shall from that time be under a fine of 5 guineas, and make good the stuff he has had made away ; and if any journeymen of the said trade shall hereafter be known to connive, wink at, or be privy to any waste as aforesaid, and doth not make due and immediate discovery thereof to the owner or proprietor thereof, or to the piece-master, or to whom such stuff was delivered out, such journeyman guilty of the same concealment, shall be deemed under a fine of 5 guineas, and any man standing by such a man, and knowing of it, to be under a fine of £2 12s. 6d.

20. Any man coming with another man for a ticket, when that man is not in every respect entitled to one, such man shall be under a fine of 10s. 6d.; and the person declining his office as steward must give an exact account to the stewards next ensuing, of all letter sheets and tickets that remain in hand. And be it observed, that when any stewards are counting their tickets or letter-papers, no person to be allowed to come near them, nor to handle such tickets or letters ; and any steward or stewards neglecting to give a proper account to the succeeding stewards, of the tickets and letter-papers left in hand, to be under a fine of 10s. 6d., and an entry made in a book provided for that purpose of all tickets and blank papers going out, and which are remaining in hand. And if in case any letters, papers or tickets may be missing, and such stewards cannot give a satisfactory account of them, such stewards to be under a fine of 10s. 6d. (H.O.42/99).

(104). *Isaac Cookson, junr., Mayor of Newcastle-on-Tyne, to Richard Ryder*[1]

Newcastle-on-Tyne, 11 *November*, 1809.
I am honoured with a letter from Mr. Beckett[2] communicating your wish that I should lose no time in reporting to you the particulars of the disturbance amongst the lightermen (or keelmen as they are here called) employed on this river, and whether tranquillity has been restored.

---

[1] Home Secretary, 1809-12.
[2] [Permanent] Under-Secretary of State for Home Affairs, 1806-17.

For three weeks that class of men have combined with a view to obtain an advance of wages ; and in furtherance of their object have absented themselves from their services, and in one or two cases they have proceeded to acts of violence in preventing the well-disposed from returning to their work, and in rescuing persons apprehended under warrants issued by the magistrates. Several of the offenders have been committed to the House of Correction, and I would persuade myself that the bulk of them are about to return to order and their duty.

The magistrates of this town and the two adjoining counties met a deputation of the keelmen to-day, and the conference seems to have produced a determination on the latter to return peaceably to their employment, which I have much reason to think will take place on Monday . . . (H.O.42/99).

(105). *Thomas Sutton to the Rev. Stuart Corbett, J.P.*

[*Sheffield, April,* 1810.][1]

. . . The manufacturers in this place are in a sad situation. The men are all associating together for an increase of wage, and the masters to resist them. They are now completely at issue. How the contest will terminate I think it would be difficult to say. In a riot most probably. They are writing upon the walls, 'Cutlers stand true.' Their plans are, I understand, very well organised. Amongst the grinders, Mr. Brownell informs me, there is a regular Committee appointed to examine the work; and if it is sufficiently well done, as they suppose, for the price given, they send a note to the master signifying their approval of it. Mr. Rhodes, the late master cutler, has one of these notes, commencing with, 'We the Committee,' but bearing no signatures. The master manufacturers have entered into some spirited Resolutions which are given in to-day's paper, and have entered into a subscription (amounting already, I understand, to £3,000) to resist, as they say, 'the exorbitant demands of the workmen' . . . (H.O.42/106).

---

[1] The address and date have been torn off. The letter is enclosed in the Earl of Effingham's letter to John Beckett, 14 April, 1810, and is endorsed, ' Disposition to combination amongst the workmen at Sheffield.'

(106). *Daniel Williams to John Beckett*

Police Office, Whitechapel, 6 July, 1810. 9-30 *p.m.*
. . . The labourers in the docks have certainly struck, demanding an increase of wages, but you may rely upon every exertion being paid to the preservation of the public peace.[1] (H.O.42/108).

(107). *W. Kinnaird and J. Longley to John Beckett*

Thames Police Office, 7 July, 1810. 1-45 *p.m.*
. . . Yesterday evening four persons were apprehended and held to bail for riotous behaviour, upon which the multitude dispersed and peace was restored.

To-day everything hitherto has been orderly and quiet. It is however apprehended that about 4 o'clock some further attempts may be made by those who have struck work to intimidate those who do not join in their combination ; but from the arrangements we have formed, we trust we shall be able to prevent any serious mischief. (H.O.42/108).

(108). *John Harriott, W. Kinnaird and J. Longley to John Beckett*

Thames Police Office, 9 July, 1810.
. . . In regard to the labourers at the London Docks we find that a considerable number of them still refuse to go to work, but we are disposed to think that from the wholesome interference of this Office they are deterred from entering upon any mischievous projects . . . (H.O.42/108).

(109). *John Harriott and W. Kinnaird to John Beckett*

Thames Police Office, 10 July, 1810.
. . . Everything in this district is quiet, though a number of the London Dock labourers assemble round the docks but do not appear disposed to riot.

[1] *The Times,* 7 July, had the following paragraph : ' Yesterday the workmen employed at the London Docks struck for an increase of wages. They demanded an advance of from 18s. to a guinea per week. The number employed amounts to about 1,000, and such as were backward in approving the conduct adopted by the ringleaders were roughly treated. Constables were called in, and we are happy to say the malcontents did not betray any spirit of outrage other than that of persisting in the demand for an increase of wages.'

113

The Directors of the London Dock Company have come to a resolution not to advance their wages and have given notice to the purpose, and that those men who are disposed to work in the docks will be protected.

Ibid. to Ibid., 12 July, 1810 : . . . Very considerable numbers of the labourers have returned to their work without any previous stipulation or condition, and without any hindrance or molestation . . . (H.O.42/108).

(110). *Henry Feilden [sic] and John Fowden Hindle to John Beckett*

Blackburn, 23 August, 1810.

[Respecting the circulation of handbills in Blackburn and other manufacturing towns] . . . These prove a degree of system and combination which in our opinion ought immediately to be checked, and we feel it our duty to submit them to the judgement of his Majesty's Ministers. (H.O.42/108).

[The following handbill was enclosed in the above letter :—]

Blackburn, 16 August, 1810.
To the Manufacturers of Blackburn.

Gentlemen—We, the undersigned, being the committee of weavers, of Blackburn, on behalf of our fellow-workmen engaged in the cotton weaving, beg leave to state,

That from proper information received, they have reason to apprehend a reduction of their wages (small it is, God knows) will shortly be attempted by a few of those who have ever acted as if their sole wish was to destroy commerce, ruin the fair trader, and bring both themselves and the community at large into a vortex of destruction.

Gentlemen, the committee have always considered the true interest of the master and workman as one, therefore when the workmen are poor and wretched (as has been the case with weavers for a long time) the masters' property inevitably suffers. To make this clearly understood, suppose a manufacturer employs 200 weavers on 60 reeds, at 24s. per cut, and sells the same at about 50s. per piece, we may reasonably suppose such a master turns over £250 weekly ; then admit he abates his workmen to 16s. per cut, he will at least lessen his returns £40 per week, or near £2,000 in one year ; now let it be granted that money in commerce is worth 10%, and he sustains an absolute loss of £200 a year, by the unjust system of reducing his wages on every little slackness in the market.

To this loss might also be added the increased number of paupers and consequent rise of poor rates, &c., &c.

Having proved thus much, we have only to add that by an Association of the manufacture[r]s of Lancashire and cordial co-operation of the workmen, such dreadful evils might at any time be prevented ; accordingly we submit the following plan to your serious consideration. It is simply this : reduce the quantity of goods when the market is overstocked, and their value will undoubtedly increase with the scarcity.

Gentlemen, the whole body of weavers in this town have come to a determination not to submit to a reduction of prices, but will rather be limited in the quantity of their work, and will, in conjunction with their masters, bear every privation for a few weeks or months, until a change takes place in the markets.

They are willing immediately to enter into subscriptions for the relief of small families, who might in the first instance be hurt by the measure, and also to send proper persons and documents to all the towns in connection with *Blackburn*, so that the whole body may act as one in a cause so interesting.

The remainder, Gentlemen, rests with you. The moment is urgent : unite, therefore, instantly, and by your laudable endeavours preserve the trade from impending ruin, and secure yourselves the good wishes of 400,000 fellow-creatures.[1] (H.O.42/108).

[1] Twenty-three signatures follow. The worst fears of the weavers were justified. In 1811 about 8,000 Stockport weavers petitioned the Government about their distressed situation. For a considerable time, they said, they had laboured under the most severe privations and had suffered hardships unequalled in the history of commerce. Their wages had been progressively reduced, whilst house rent, taxes, poor rates and the necessaries of life had regularly increased. The constant succession of bankruptcies had resulted in an extraordinary increase in the number of applications for parochial assistance. Great numbers were out of work ; the wages paid to those still employed, had in six months been reduced by half. The petitioners were unable to procure enough food for themselves and families, and they were contracting debts which they would never be able to repay. Thomas Bentley signed the petition on their behalf ; it was transmitted to the Government in April, and Mr. Beckett forwarded it to the Board of Trade on 2 May. Three weeks later the Board replied that it was unaware of any measures that could be taken to relieve the weavers beyond those which Parliament had recently adopted—an advance of Exchequer Bills to enable manufacturers to keep their workmen employed. (H.O.42/115).

(111). *The Duke of Newcastle to Richard Ryder*

Clumber, 9 December, 1811.

. . . The grand difficulty is the almost impossibility of obtaining information respecting the movements and intentions of the rioters, everything is so well organised amongst them, and their measures are conducted with so much secrecy, added to which, that no one dares to impeach for fear of his life, that it is scarcely possible to detect them.

A sort of negotiation is now carrying on between committees formed of delegates from the discontented framework-knitters (as they are called) and the hosiers and masters. This may lead to something, and as this business cannot be terminated without some sort of agreement between the parties, it is much to be hoped than an understanding may be established between them, if it can be done without an appearance of conceding anything to them in consequence of intimidation . . . (H.O.42/118).

(112). *Henry Sedley to Spencer Perceval[1]*

Nuttall Temple, 16 December, 1811. (Copy).

. . . It is the general opinion of the magistrates that if any check could be given to the committee meetings, whence measures against the public peace originated and are organised, it would contribute most materially to suppress the disturbances.

Some of the magistrates request to be informed whether the 39th of the King, chapter 79, applies, in any degree, to such committees as have been formed on the present occasion.

Of combinations and committees answering the words of the Act, we have sufficient evidence, but we doubt of the application of the Act, though a just alarm has extended to a great part of the counties of Nottingham, Leicester and Derby. (H.O.42/118).

(113). *The Rev. R. Hardy, J.P., to Richard Ryder*

Loughborough, 19 December, 1811.

. . . We have been several days employed in examining two persons apprehending upon charges of collecting money by threats for the support of the rioters, but we find the class of men to whom we are obliged to look for information, in general very unwilling to give it.

[1] Prime Minister, 1809-12.

The loss of their time, and the dread they have of the vengeance of the ill-disposed among their own class, operate together against their speaking the truth, and it is not without summonses and great pressing from the magistrates, that any truth can be extracted.

We have however this day committed the two men for *a felony*, in extorting small sums from brother stockingers *by threats* . . .

A spirit of combination to dictate to their employers and to raise the price of their wages, has within these few days shown itself among the *women*, who are employed in what we call *running lace*. Meetings have been called and emissaries sent into all the neighbouring towns and villages to unite and collect money for their purpose. I have thought proper to issue a handbill to warn persons against such illegal meetings. . . The numbers employed in this branch of manufacture may amount to several thousands in this county. (H.O.42/118).

(114). *H. C. Litchfield*[1] *to John Beckett*

Lincoln's Inn, 20 December, 1811.

In obedience to Mr. Secretary Ryder's directions, signified by your letter of the 19th inst., I immediately laid Mr. Sedley's letter therewith transmitted before the Attorney and Solicitor-General, and beg leave to acquaint you that they are of opinion that the meetings alluded to in Mr. Sedley's letter of the 16th inst. are not within the purview of the Act 39 George III, c. 79, although they are not prepared to say that they may not be brought within the words of it. They think the attention of the magistrates should be called to the 39 George III, c. 81, expressly made for the suppression of combinations of workmen, by which a summary jurisdiction is given to the magistrates, or the parties may be proceeded against by indictment. (H.O.42/118).

(115). *The Duke of Newcastle to Richard Ryder*

Clumber, 21 December, 1811.

. . . The hosiers are coming into the terms required by the workmen, and it is very probable that this may be the cause of concluding the business. Added to this, the rioters certainly begin to be very much alarmed, and what is very desirable, their fear arises from distrust. (H.O.42/118).

---

[1] The Treasury Solicitor. He retired towards the end of 1817.

(116). *William Milnes to Sir Joseph Banks*[1]

Ashover, 22 December, 1811.

I am extremely sorry to inform you that the stocking frame-breaking system which has caused so much alarm and disturbance in the neighbourhood of Nottingham has extended its baneful effects into this neighbourhood. At Pentridge, about six miles from hence, a person of the name of Topham has had frames destroyed to the amount of £500 . . . Two men came to this place who called themselves inspectors from the committee; they went to every stockinger's house and discharged them from working under such prices as they gave them a list of, and said they should come again in a few days, and in case any of them were found working without having a ticket from their master saying that he was willing to give the prices stated in their list, they should break their frames. They summoned all the stockingers, about 12 or 14 in number of master men to a public house with as much consequence as if they had had a mandate from the P~ince Regent. When they got them hither, all I can learn at present, was for the purpose of collecting money from them for the support of those families who were deprived of getting their bread by having their frames broken. Where they found a frame worked by a person who had not served a regular apprenticeship, or by a woman, they discharged them from working, and if they promised to do so, they stuck a paper upon the frame with these words written upon it—'Let this frame stand, the colts removed'— colt is the name given to all those who have not served a regular apprenticeship . . . (H.O.42/118).

(117). *Viscount Bulkeley to Richard Ryder*

Stockport, Thursday, 26 *December,* 1811. *Private.*

Two delegates from Nottingham have certainly been here and held a meeting with some delegates of the weavers of this town in Union Street last Saturday, and returned before any information had come to the ears of the magistrates that they had been here . . (H.O.42/118).

---

[1] President of the Royal Society, 1778-1820 (1743-1820).

(118). *G. Coldham (Town Clerk) to Richard Ryder*

Nottingham, 14 January, 1812.

... The framework-knitters appear to be as much dissatisfied as ever. Such of them as are out of employment are many in number and are disposed to inflame the discontent of those who [are] in work in order to exist upon their contributions in support of the system carrying on ... They have lately exercised great judgement and discretion in the selection of their victims in the town, by fixing upon the property of individuals on some account obnoxious to popular resentment. The last frames destroyed in the town belong to persons who have been in the habit of paying the workman in part or in whole in goods generally inadequate in value to the price of his labour. The general system adopted for coercing the hosiers is so closely embraced by the great mass of the mechanics that these feel a confidence which is hardly ever abused in each other, and refuse to trust any person not concerned in the trade . . .[1] (H.O.42/119).

[1] The Rev. J. T. Becher, Vicar of Rumpton and of Midsomer Norton, explained in a letter of 11 February 1812, that the Luddite disturbances in Nottinghamshire were due to over-production. The workers had been prosperous before the War, when the demand for hose exceeded output. The restriction of the Continental market hurried on the crisis, which had become inevitable in any case. Warehouses became glutted with unsaleable goods. The masters had begun to reduce wages in 1805, and although the workers offered as an alternative an increased rent for their frames, this solution failed to take into account the excessive productive capacity of the industry. Wages were reduced in 1810 and many workmen lost their employment. (H.O.42/120).

Moreover, a new kind of frame had been introduced, which required less manual labour, and women were employed instead of men, at a reduced rate of wages. The hosiers thrown out of work, or those who refused to work at the new rates of pay, started the frame-breaking. These disorders spread into Lancashire, Cheshire and the West Riding, and machinery worth more than £100,000 was destroyed. But Luddism was more than a violent protest against the introduction of labour-saving machinery. In Nottinghamshire and Leicestershire machinery was broken as a means of coercing employers into granting higher wages. Unemployment, distress and low wages were the chief causes of the disturbances that marked the last years of the Napoleonic Wars and the first years of peace.

On 21 February 1812, Donald Cook wrote to the Home Secretary, asking that the Bill to make frame-breaking a capital felony should be extended to Scotland for the protection of the Glasgow stocking manufacturers. ' This we are induced to solicit your attention to, as an indication at different times of the same spirit of combination has shown itself amongst our operatives, which has been so hurtful to the manufacturers in Nottingham.' (H.O.102/22).

(119). *J. Mayer to Unknown Correspondent*

Manchester, 11 *February*, 1812. (*Copy*).[1]

. . . Wages must be raised or we shall have a general *turn-out of the weavers*. Already we have plenty of Nottingham, Carlisle and Glasgow delegates, who are holding private meetings *every night* and instigating ours to riot and confusion . . . For our part we are not at all personally afraid, for we believe the weavers have no antipathy to us. But this we know, that an *honest, industrious fellow* by *hard labour* cannot get *bread* much less *clothes* for himself and children, and there is a point beyond which human nature cannot bear. Nothing but an advance will do, and this can only be accomplished by your helping the *poor manufacturers* to get a little additional advance upon every succeeding sale till goods are come up to a reasonable price. Nobody will be hurt by it except the *Jews* and the poor slaves of this country will be made comfortable and kept *good subjects* . . .[2] (H.O.42/120).

(120). *J. Lloyd[3] to Richard Ryder*

Stockport, 26 *February*, 1812.

. . . The weavers have latterly evinced a very restless and refractory spirit—have met in small bodies to deliberate on their grievances, and, on Monday afternoon, there was a general meeting in an open piece of ground near the town . . . Threatening letters continue to be sent to particular individuals, but, at present, it has been deemed unnecessary to notice them specifically . . .

---

[1] Forwarded by Spencer Perceval, the Prime Minister to Ryder, the Home Secretary, on the 13th. It had been sent to him by a commercial house in the City.

[2] Colonel Fletcher, the magistrate and Colonel in the Bolton Militia, wrote to Mr. Beckett from Bolton on 21 January : '. . . The example of Nottingham is certainly dangerous and would have been still more so to such a manufacturing neighbourhood as this, had not the demand for cotton goods a little increased, the consequence of which has been a decrease in the number of those unemployed, and a small increase of the wages. These circumstances, added to the stoppage of distillation from grain which tends so effectually to prevent any very material advance in the price of all the necessaries of life, will, I trust, prevent any risings of the disaffected and preserve the public peace . . .' (H.O.42/119).

[3] Clerk to the Rev. Charles Prescott, the Stockport magistrate.

I fear the bad spirit is kept up by some few desperate characters from Ireland that have got among the weavers here.[1] They certainly do meditate the destruction of the looms worked by steam and employed in factories[2] . . . (H.O.42/120).

(121). *Francis Ronaldson, Surveyor, to Francis Freeling*[3]

Post Office, Glasgow, 1 *June*, 1812.
Private and Confidential.
I beg to send you the enclosed copy, with the only observation I can make, of its being connected with another of the same description from Stockport formerly transmitted, and although it is evident that such a correspondence implies a combination for the particular purposes mentioned, yet [it] does not reach the length of any general purpose of insurrection, nor can I by any means discover that such dangerous mischief is really in agitation here . . .

[Enclosure.]
Secret and Confidential copy.
A blue ground plate on the top with figures of a traveller and a man sitting before a table in the act of making entries into a book—motto—'We assist each other in time of need.' Underneath the plate, 'United Feltmakers of Manchester, No. ——.' 'Gentlemen—From daily experience of the various impositions practised upon the

---

[1] Mr. Farington had written to the Home Secretary from Manchester on 27 June, 1808 : ' In the early part of last week some few refractory weavers, principally Irish, molested the people then at their looms, and gave hindrance in one of the districts of the town to several weavers bringing in and returning with work.' (H.O.42/45).

[2] The weavers complained that the introduction of steam-driven machinery was creating unemployment. The magistrates ordered them to appoint two persons to call on Mr. Ryder, the Home Secretary. They did so, but they received no satisfactory answer : he thought that the new machinery was of great service to the State. A Bolton weaver, Robert Waddington, said on 7 October that at a meeting on 2 March of from 25 to 30 persons, mostly unknown to him, it had been agreed to meet every evening 'after they had done their work by daylight and before they lighted up candles, and by that means they thought they could frighten their masters to give them more wages.' (Enclosure in Sir Richard Clayton's letter of 18 October 1812 to Lord Sidmouth, from Adlington, near Wigan.) Samuel Kay, of Bolton, also reported in October that there had been meetings of weavers ' who intended to shout to frighten their masters and make them raise their wages.' (H.O.42/128).

[3] Secretary to the General Post Office.

trade by means of so many blanks[1] and turnhouses being kept in country places about this town where there are such quantities of foul men who in slack time obtain blanks and travel the country to the great injury of the trade, we have determined as far as lays in our power to put a stop to them and compel the men to join the turnbooks of either this town, Rochdale, or Stockport, and by that means prevent these frauds—therefore we request you not to treat any blanks from the under-mentioned places dated after the 1st of June, 1812, they being under twelve miles from Manchester, nor clear any man who shall come from any of the places mentioned until you have first wrote to one of the three places above-mentioned, enquiring whether they have served their time and treated to any of the three books. Names of places to be treated—Gorton, Geecross, Denton, Drylsden, Hoolyhill, Marple, Ashton, Bury, Oldham, Chedleham, Romily, Barton, Newton Moor. In doing your utmost endeavours to detect these imposters you will much oblige yours,

The journeymen hatters of Manchester.'[2]

(122). *Edward Protheroe[3] to John Beckett*

Conduit Street, 29 June, 1812.
. . . The colliers in the Forest of Dean are returned to their work without rendering it necessary to call for assistance from the military . . . (H.O.42/124).

(123). *A. Colquhoun[4] to Viscount Sidmouth[5]*

Edinburgh, 4 *July,* 1812. (*Private*).
. . . There exist in Scotland associations of operative weavers, who, as far as I have been informed, take no unlawful oaths, neither do they elect their office bearers in a secret manner, nor conceal their proceedings from the members of the Society at large, nor do they form different divisions or branches of what may strictly be called

---

[1] Certificates of good character from the Union, which unemployed men took with them when seeking work.

[2] Addressed, ' Journeymen hatters of Glasgow with speed,' and stamped Manchester, 28 May 1812.

[3] M.P. for Bristol in the 1812-18 Parliament.

[4] Lord Advocate of Scotland until June 1816, when he was appointed Lord Clerk Register in Scotland, and was succeeded by Alexander Machonochie.

[5] Home Secretary, 1812-22.

the same Society. They do not therefore fall under the Statute,[1] but they form a numerous Society in one place, and that Society corresponds with other Societies in other places. Delegates are sent by the one to the other, or delegates from different Societies meet together but so as not to bring themselves under the words of the Statute ; although the system is as dangerous in its nature as any of those associations which exist and are struck at by the Act in the year 1799, and may be easily made instrumental for accomplishing seditious or treasonable designs.

The avowed object to which such Associations at present direct their immediate attention, is an increase or rise of wages. In the month of February last in Glasgow, public notice was given of an intention to assemble an immense body of operative weavers to parade through the streets of the town of Glasgow, in order that they might present a petition or make an application to the magistrates of that city, with a reference to an increase of wages. The magistrates on the other hand very properly gave public notice of their intention to prevent such parade from taking place, and as a precautionary measure made application to Lord Cathcart, the Commander of the Forces in Scotland, for additional troops to be sent to Glasgow and its vicinity. The consequence of the measures adopted by the magistrates was that no parade or assemblage took place, and there was no riot or tumult. Since that time an application has been made to the Justices of the Peace in that district by the operative weavers for fixing a rate of wages, and the point has lately been under the consideration of the Court of Session.

The same spirit which was manifested in Glasgow in February, having also then displayed itself in Paisley and Ayrshire, similar applications were made to the Commander of the Forces by the Sheriff of Renfrewshire and by the Lord Lieutenant of Ayrshire, and troops having been sent, no acts of violence were committed, nor has there been any riot or tumult in any part of Scotland.

Such Societies or Associations still exist, and have, I believe, a regular communication with Associations in England, the intercourse being carried on in an organised and expeditious manner. In a large town they can in a very short time give notice to all the members of a numerous Society of resolutions or intentions which may have been formed ; and accordingly in the town of Paisley, which is a large populous manufacturing town, when it was intended

[1] 39 George III, c. 79. 'An act for the more effectual suppression of Societies established for seditious and treasonable purposes.'

last winter to collect a large meeting, a printed notice was rapidly circulated, by each person receiving it being desired by the printed notice to pass it to his next neighbour, and menaced with punishment if he failed to do so.

It appears that one of the objects which they endeavour to accomplish is to raise funds which may be at the command of such Associations. I enclose copies of some papers obtained possession of by the Sheriff of Selkirkshire, in the course of a precognition taken by him. Besides these papers, there was recovered on that occasion a printed paper from Nottingham dated 13 April, 1812 ; and a person of the name of William Kind, who had been a weaver for two years in Selkirkshire and who was a native of Nottinghamshire, had, it appeared, from the precognition alongst with others, been endeavouring by menaces to deter stocking weavers in Selkirk from working at lower wages than those fixed upon by the operatives in general.

The operatives in Scotland consist of natives and of a numerous body of Irishmen. The last, although they shewed some disposition to riot and tumult, have been kept quiet and peaceable by the former, and at present I am disposed to hope from the information I have received from different quarters, that no acts of violence are to be apprehended . . .

[Enclosures.]

Copies of Papers obtained possession of by the Sheriff of Selkirkshire in the course of a precognition.

Glasgow, 9 March, 1812.

Sir—I am ordered to transmit to you an extract of a letter received from Nottingham :—

Nottingham, 19 February, 1812.

Sir—I am directed by the committee of framework knitters to inform you that on Monday 17th instant there was a meeting of the trade of the Counties of Nottingham and Derby to take into consideration the propriety of petitioning Parliament for a redress of grievances ; it was carried that application should be made to Parliament for a Bill for the better regulation of the trade—that a subscription should be entered into to defray the expense, and information and aid should be solicited from the most distant places, and that the whole should be solicited to make it a common cause, &c., &c. Signed, G. Henton.

It would also appear that they labour under great difficulties by being paid their wages with goods, and by introducing fine cotton much beyond the size, adds considerably to their distress. A general meeting was held here on the 2nd instant. It was resolved to collect 2s. 6d. each for their interest to be raised in three months. We hope that on receiving this letter that you will call a meeting of your brethren within your bounds, and have the goodness to give us an account of your proceedings. Mr. John Aitken, stocking maker, Kent Street, Gallowgate, is appointed collector. You will please address your letters to him.

I am, Sir, for the Committee,

Your obedient servant,

James Richardson.

(This letter is addressed : 'Mr. James Kennedy, Stocking Maker, Selkirk.')

Selkirk, 12 *March,* 1812.

The committee appointed by the stocking makers of Selkirk having met, they unanimously adopted the following Resolutions :

1st. That although the evils arising from the general stagnation of the trade of the country has as yet been but little felt by us, yet that we deeply feel for the distress of the great majority of our brethren who have been involved in these calamities, and that we will cordially join in co-operation with the great body of the trade in any measures which they may deem proper to pursue for attempting to remedy the evils under which they labour.

2nd. That for this purpose we agree to enter into a subscription of 2s. 6d. each besides expenses, to [be] raised in three months, which money is to be placed in the hands of a general collector, and to be at the disposal of a general meeting of the subscribers.

3rd. That we earnestly request the whole of the journeymen in Selkirk and Galashiels to subscribe the above Resolutions and to concur in any other measures which may ultimately be deemed necessary for furthering the common cause.

(This paper is signed by 43 persons).   (H.O.102/22).

(124). *Kirkman Finlay*[1] *to A. Colquhoun*

[*c. October,* 1812.] (*Copy*).

I think it my duty to apprise your Lordship that a decision has lately been given by the Justices of the Peace here in a cause brought by the operative weavers against their employers, by which a certain rate of wages is found to be moderate and reasonable, and ought to be paid where no express agreement has been made.

[1] Lord Provost of Glasgow.

I understand from some of the manufacturers that these prices are in very many instances considerably above those which the present state of demand can authorise them to pay, and that although they would not, for their own sakes, venture to offer less, that they must for the present decline giving out work. The weavers are, on the other hand, determined to accept only of this regulated price, and in several instances they have prevented the beaming of webs (an operation preparatory to the weaving) which had been agreed to be wove at a price under the rate fixed by the Justices.

With this evidence of a disposition on the part of both parties which would in a very short time lead to the putting a great body of people out of employment, the magistrates here have felt a very strong apprehension lest the public peace might be destroyed, and however confidently I rely on the endeavours of all classes of well-disposed persons here, I have thought it right that the military force should be such as to enable us instantly to suppress any disposition to riot or illegal proceedings on their first appearance. (H.O.102/22).

(125). *A. Colquhoun to Viscount Sidmouth*

Edinburgh, 9 *November*, 1812. (*Private*).
The Sheriffs of Lanarkshire and Renfrewshire have set out this morning for their Counties, the conduct of the operative weavers having rendered it necessary that an investigation should be made with a view to a criminal prosecution. By the letters I had yesterday, the weavers were coming into Glasgow, to the number of 20 in a body, carrying with them webs which they had cut out of the loom, and none of the manufacturers had then ventured to complain of such outrages, which evidently proceed from an illegal combination to raise the rates of wages. The Sheriffs are immediately to seize such papers as may afford evidence against the delegates and leading members of the Association, and they will of course apprehend some of them for examination and imprisonment until they find bail, as the crime is a bailable offence.

I shall inform your Lordship afterwards of what passes, but in the meantime it may be proper to have a power to open letters at the Post Offices of Glasgow and Paisley, as they correspond with one another from a distance. This is a delicate power both to be granted and used with discretion, and can only be given by the Secretary of State. (H.O.102/22).

(126). *A true copy of the articles to be observed by the Woolcombers in Great Britain, as appointed by the Congress, which was composed of Delegates from several different Societies, in various parts of the Kingdom ; held at the City of Coventry, on the tenth and eleventh of August, in the year of our Lord 1812, and fifty-second year of the reign of our Sovereign George the Third : published by order of a meeting of the Worsted Manufacturers, held at the Devonshire Arms Inn, in Kighley, on Wednesday the 11th of November, 1812.*

READ, AND THEN JUDGE!!

GENTLEMEN,

The Congress, deeply impressed with a sense of the importance and necessity of an union upon a firm and liberal basis, between all the woolcombers in Great Britain, are desirous that the same may be communicated to every individual woolcomber, who is now in society, or whom societies may think proper to receive, consistent to the following articles.—Considering that union in itself is so essential, not only to the peace, but also to the prosperity of any community, society, or firm. The principle of union has the sanction also of divine authority, being inculcated in the sacred pages of holy writ ; it is there said, "can two walk together except they be agreed," and as by walking together, we must understand, all the transactions and connections of men, (both civil and religious) in their social intercourse one with another ; and, if unity is so essential to the peace and good understanding of two only, how much more so to ten, twenty, a society, community, or nation ! !

Brethren, while the principal inhabitants and trades of the nation are uniting and exerting all their power and influence in the establishment of various institutions, for the avowed purpose of promoting the peace, prosperity, and happiness of the people ; shall we as a body, still be divided ; shall we still continue to tear and devour one another, by working against each other to the injury of the whole ; shall we still continue to be wanderers in the land, as sheep having no shepherd, no control, no head, nothing to which we can refer, no place to which we can fly for shelter or security in time of peril or disaster ; but still continue to expose ourselves to be torn, devoured, annihilated by the wild ungovernable passions of pride, malice, tyranny, and oppression ? "Tell it not in Gath, publish it not in the streets of Askelon," suffer it not to be said in the nation, that at a time like the present, when all that can be lawfully obtained, is necessary, the woolcombers refuse to be united.—But brethren, we are persuaded better things of you, although we thus speak, things which accompany unity, peace, and concord.

There never was to our knowledge, any well-regulated articles, which took into their cognizance so many particulars, and on such an extended and liberal plan, as these now presented for your candid consideration, in which, we have endeavoured to consider every general circumstance, and particular usage in the trade, and adopt such measures as appeared to us, best calculated to promote a good understanding, and prevent infringements.—If any of the following articles in their execution, should fail, every society is humbly invited to point out such failures, and propose any amendments.—If we have exceeded our limits, we hope every society or individual will attribute it to our zeal for the public good.

Signed in behalf of the congress,

Daniel Lord.
Samuel Perry.
John Hewes.

ARTICLE I.

The eldest son of any woolcomber, who is received by the trade as a fair man, shall be received by the trade as fair, provided he commences working at woolcombing trade, at not exceeding fifteen years of age, and continues till he is twenty-one, under the tuition of his father, or any other person properly appointed.

2. Second sons of woolcombers apprenticed to their father, are not to be received, except their father employs them upon wool that is his own property.

3. That no other person shall be received into the United Societies of Woolcombers, or permitted to work at the trade, or receive any benefit therefrom, but such as have served a lawful apprenticeship of seven years, to a master or mistress, who, during their apprenticeship, employ them upon wool that is their own property, except those who are brought up under the first article.

4. If a youth learns the business under either of the preceding articles, and does not continue his full time in it, but engages in his Majesty's service, and continues therein, till the term of his apprenticeship is expired, he shall be received by the trade as a fair man.

5. No master or mistress to be permitted to have more than two apprentices at any time, who may board them either in or out of their own house, as may best suit their convenience.

6. Every woolcomber who is a member of any society in Great Britain, at the date of these articles, shall be received by the United Societies as a fair man ; and every man who has a right to the trade, who does not belong to any society, shall be permitted and invited to join the nearest society to him, without any extent of limits, and free of any expence, provided he join within three months from the date of these articles.

7. In order thoroughly to unite the trade, and maintain its privileges, there shall be one general acting society ; and the congress has appointed W A R W I C K to be the general acting society.

8. Every society in union, shall make a return annually to the acting society, of all their member's names, (both christian and surname, and what county they come from), alphabetically arranged together, with what club benefit they allow, on or before the 14th day of November next, and every succeeding year, on or before the 10th day of August, which annual list shall be printed, and every society in union, shall have a copy, so that every society may know what benefit is allowed by any single society, or by the whole of them.

9. To prevent imposition, by false blanks, there shall be provided a good copper-plate, on which shall be suitable emblems of the woolcombing trade, which shall be kept by the acting society, and every society in union shall be supplied with blanks from the acting society, and the society who issues them to fill them up as usual.

10. No man that is not enrolled, and in the printed list, shall be entitled to the benefit of any of the United Societies, when on the walk for labour, except he has a certificate with his blank, shewing that he has been regularly entered, and for such certificate, a copper-plate shall be provided by the acting society.

11. Every apprentice, and father's eldest son, when in the last year of their time, shall have their names enrolled with the words apprentice, or eldest son, subjoined, in order, that if they travel before the ensuing enrolments are printed, they may do it with safety, without a certificate, as every society will know where to refer to for their names.

12. Every man in our United Societies shall allow, when in work, one halfpenny to every stranger that crosses him with an union blank, over and above the regular club benefit.

13. The eldest sons of woolcombers who are brought up to the business under their father, or any other person properly appointed, shall allow one halfpenny to every stranger, from the time of his

first commencement at the business, till he is twenty-one, and if the father is obliged to travel, the son shall be entitled to the same relief of one halfpenny from every man, and nothing more.

14. That no society shall be allowed to give less than six-pence as a club benefit, to every stranger that crosses them with an union blank. If any society be not large enough to allow six-pence, they shall join the nearest society to them.

15. No man shall be permitted to cross for labour, or to receive a benefit, oftener than once in thirteen weeks.

16. If any man who is enrolled, shall ask for work within the limits of any of our United Societies without his blank from the last Society whereunto he belonged, he shall forfeit and pay the sum of one pound, forthwith to be sent to the acting society for general expences.

17. If any man who is not enrolled, makes application to any of our United Societies for a blank, and the society he applies to, approve of his right, they shall be at full liberty to give him one, on condition that he pays the sum of one pound, to be forthwith sent to the acting society for general expences, and the expence of sending to and from the acting society, for the certificate of his enrolment.

18. If any man offer himself to become a member of any of our United Societies, after three months from the date of these articles, and the society to whom he offers himself approve of his right, they shall be at full liberty to take him in ; and if he draws his blank before he has paid three succeeding months deficiencies, he shall pay the sum of one pound, to be forthwith forwarded to the acting society, for general expences, and the expence of sending to and from the acting society, for the certificate of his enrolment.

19. To render the woolcombing business more respectable, and prevent as much as possible the disgrace of cutting. If any man who is enrolled, gets work within the limits of any United Society, without a blank, the society in whose limits he is, shall ask him where he was enrolled, and what society he belonged to last, and the society where he then is, shall be bound to send immediately to the society he came from, informing them that they have such a member, and who came without a blank, and whether the man was muffled at a disadvantage or cut ; the society he came from shall send an account of all just debts due to master, society, shopmates, or lodgings, and the society where he is then a member, shall remit the whole of the debt, within one month from the receipt of the account, in order that the debts may stand against the man in that society where he

is then a member. Although a strict compliance with this article will necessarily require some sacrifices to be made by the societies where it may occur ; yet we are persuaded, if strictly adhered to, it will effectually remove the necessity of it ; for men who are disposed to cut, will know the difficulty they have to get work, because every society will be reluctant to receive a man without a blank, and that they will not thereby get rid of their debts.

20. If any man presumes to send to a person for a dozen of wool, or any man obtains a dozen of wool in any way that is not according to the general rules of the woolcombing trade, he shall not be permitted to enjoy it ; but if the society within whose limits he obtains the dozen of wool, shall after investigation, permit him to continue in it, he shall forfeit and pay the sum of one pound, to be forthwith sent to the acting society for general expences.

21. If any society in Great-Britain, shall think proper to become one of the United Societies after the fourteenth day of November next, when the articles and enrolments will be printed, they shall send a list of all their member's names, (both christian and sur-name and from what county they come) alphabetically arranged, and also what club benefit they allow to the acting society, and the acting society shall return them certificates to be given out with each of their blanks.

22. If any society, or shop, labour under burdens of any kind, from which they cannot extricate themselves by petition, or remonstrance, and they think proper to leave their employ, as the only effectual means of removing them, they shall give a fair and full statement of all their grievances to three of the nearest societies to them, and the societies to whom they write shall consider their case as soon as possible, and return them an answer whether they think they had better continue in their employ or not ; and if the majority of the societies to whom they write, are of an opinion that they had better leave, they shall immediately send all the answers received from the societies consulted on the business to the acting society, together with a clear and full statement of the number of wives and children who are dependent on their father's for support, and the acting society shall immediately send to every district society, and from thence to every society in union, on their behalf, and every society shall send their contributions to the district society, and from thence to the acting Society.

23. The relief to wives and children belonging to men who may leave their employ agreeable to the twenty-second article, and who

are dependent on their father's for support, shall be two shillings and sixpence each per week as long as the necessity of the case may require.

24. If any society in union, acts derogatory to these articles and regulations, or neglects to comply with them in a regular manner, the said society may be reported by an individual, or more, or by any adjoining society, to the acting society, who shall be bound to give the case a clear, full, and impartial investigation, and if the society who is indicted should be convicted, the acting society shall be empowered to levy a fine on them, of not less than one, or more than five pounds, which sum shall be sent within one month to the acting society, towards general expences, and if the fine is not paid, their blanks shall not be suffered to pass, and the acting society shall inform every society in union of the circumstance.

25. When the acting society are in possession of all the societies who join in union, they will immediately divide the societies into districts, in order to facilitate communication, and one society in each district to be denominated the district society, and all general communications to be sent to the district society, and from thence to every society within its district, and all contributions for general expences, and for the relief of societies in union, when in distress, to be sent to the district society, and from thence to the acting society, and all annual enrolments to be sent to the district society in like manner, and from thence to the acting society.

26. The acting society shall provide proper books to keep a regular and just account of all receipts and disbursements on public accounts, and of all enrolments and certificates granted, of which several particulars after being audited by proper persons, there shall be a faithful report given annually with the enrolments, &c.

27. As a check against the acting society, every district society when appointed, shall provide proper books, in which to keep a regular and just account of all monies received from every society within their district, for general use, and of all remittances to the acting society.

28. If a district society is accused of irregularities or neglect of compliance, or breach of trust, by any society, or by the acting society, there shall be a clear, full, and impartial investigation of all the charges alledged against them, by three of the nearest societies in the district, or by delegates from them, and if found guilty, a fine shall be levied on them, of not less than two, or mor than five pounds, to be forthwith forwarded to the acting society for general

expences and public uses, or their blanks shall not be suffered to pass.

29. If the general acting society is judged to be partial, irregular, or unfaithful in the discharge of the various important public concerns confided to its trust, they shall be subject to investigation, by delegates from five of the largest societies in union, and if proved to be guilty of any breach of public trust, shall be fined a sum not less than five, or more than ten pounds, which sum shall be paid before any of their blanks shall be suffered to pass, and the reasonable expences of investigation to be paid out of the fine, and overplus to go for general expences and public uses.

30. If any man who is enrolled, learns, or attempts to learn any man, woman or boy, so as thereby to bring them to the trade in an illegal manner, shall have his, or their names sent to the acting society, and from thence to every society in union, and if he should be found with an union blank, at any time after such public notice, any society will be justified in breaking it, and shall give information thereof to the general acting society, what society the blank was issued from, and the society that issued the blank shall be subject to a fine, levied on them by the acting society, of not less than one, or more than five pounds, to be forthwith remitted to the acting society for general expences and public uses, before any of their blanks shall be suffered to pass again.

31. If any man, or shop of men, suffer any man or men who are not enrolled or regularly entered, to turn in upon, and work with them, without the knowledge and consent of the society whereunto they belong, such man, or men, so offending, by passive submission, to such a breach, shall be subject to a fine levied on them, by the majority of the members of the Society within whose limits it may occur, if only one man, not less than one, and if a shop of men, not more than five pounds, to go to the acting society for general expences and public uses.

32. All the expences of printing blanks, certificates, general articles, annual enrolments, forms of petition for contributions and reports of public proceedings, together with postage of letters to the acting society, on public accounts, shall be paid by the societies in union, and all offences and forfeitures for public expence to go towards it.

33. As every society is liable to be called upon to meet on public accounts, or to consider disputes with, or concerning any other society or societies, every society shall pay the expence of their own meeting, and not charge any other society or societies with the expence of them, by way of fine or any other pretext whatever.

34. In order to strengthen the union between the members of society, let no young men, or any member who does not already belong to another sick society, be permitted to join any, but such as are purely amongst their own business. That is, let there be provision made for sickness in every United Society, and all the members who do not actually belong to a sick society already, whose articles forbid them to join in it.

35. If any dispute should arise, between any two or more of our United Societies, and the dispute be of such a nature as not to come within the cognizance of any of these articles, and they cannot settle it between themselves, each society shall give a clear and full statement of the causes of difference, or points in dispute, to one, two, or three of the nearest societies to them, and the society or societies which may be consulted on the business, shall be by the joint consent of the contending parties, or, one by each, and a third by both, and the decision of the societies consulted on the business shall be final; and if any society refuses to submit to such decision, because it is against them, their blanks shall not pass.

36. Every several United Society shall be at full liberty to appoint their own monthly, or other meetings, and payments and forfeits for non-attendance at meetings, or neglect of payments shall belong to the society where they are forfeited to be disposed of as the society may think proper.

37. If any man upbraid his shopmate, or any member of society, or stranger, of his country or anything relating thereto, or use any other abusive language, so as thereby to cause disgust, the same shall be reported to the first committee or body meeting, or on the regular meeting night, when an impartial investigation of the charges shall take place, and if the accused is found guilty, he or they shall be fined according to the enormity of the offence, and such fine to go towards the deficiencies of the society.

38. If any man is disposed to leave his employ, and finishes up his work, and pays all just debts to master and shopmate, so as to leave them in every respect in an honourable way, he shall not be under any necessity of explaining his reasons.

39. If any member of our United Societies, should at any time be guilty of any criminal misdemeanour against the laws of the land, it is hereby enjoined upon every member of society, to aid and assist the civil powers, in endeavouring to bring such offenders to public justice.

40. If any master who is situated at a remote distance from those

districts where woolcombers are more numerous, and employs men who are enrolled, and in union, should at any time be in want of men and cannot procure them, the men who may work for such a master, shall immediately communicate the same to the acting society, who shall make the same known to those districts where men are more numerous, and endeavour to obtain a regular supply of good workmen.

This Article is intended to stand as a check against, and to remove the cause of any Master introducing non-associates, or unfair Men.

41. Every society shall be answerable to their club-house to the amount of five shillings, that is, we will not suffer such a law as clearing the club-house with one shilling, but every club-house shall be indemnified by the society to the amount of five shillings.

42, If any shop or society, obtain the consent of the majority of the societies consulted on the subject of leaving to redress any grievances, the same being made plain and clear to the acting society, and registered in the public books, shall be considered sufficient, and the circular letter, petitioning for relief, will be all the evidence required by societies of the fact, until the yearly report is made.

43. If any society who receives a man who is enrolled, without his blank, and neglects to enquire into the cause, and to send to the society where he last came from, they shall be subject to investigation, and if proved guilty of neglect of compliance, shall be subject to a fine equal to all the debts that may come against the man.

44. If any stranger crosses any shop or society, and refuses to take a dozen of wool when there is one for him, the stranger so refusing shall not be entitled to the benefit of either shop or club, but if any shop or society make a pretext of there being work, because they will not give the benefit when there actually is none, they shall be subject to a fine, upon full proof, of not less then one, or more than two pounds, to be levied on them by the acting society, and the fine to be forthwith sent to the acting society for general expences and public uses.

N.B. No Irishmen to be admitted to society, after the date of these Articles.

FORM OF AN ADDRESS,

To any master, or firm, who has employed men who have been divided.

Sir, or Gentlemen,

We humbly hope you will have the goodness, in your clemency, to pardon us, in thus presuming to address you, nor attribute it to any undue respect to either your person or property, but for the avowed purpose of informing you, that there has taken place a general union amongst woolcombers throughout Great Britain, and that any master who employs such men, and such only, as are regularly enrolled and in union, agreeable to, both the wholesome laws of the land, and the woolcombing trade, may be ensured of having a regular supply of men who are capable of working well at the business, and their property indemnified.

We are, sir, your obedient and humble servants, The WOOLCOMBERS.

FORM OF A PETITION,
To obtain redress of any grievances, &c.

Sir, or Gentlemen,

Your humble petitioners, confiding in your clemency, hope you will take into your most serious consideration (here state the grievances) which by experience has been found to be so very injurious, (here state the particular bearings they have upon you, and the embarrasments you labour under through them, and endeavour to point out what you conceive would be a remedy) which your humble petitioners having confidence in your wisdom and goodness, hope you will endeavour speedily to adopt (or comply to, as the case may be).

(Here sign all your names, or some in behalf of the whole).

FORM OF THE CIRCULAR LETTER,
To petition contribution towards relieving any society, or societies, when in distress through leaving, or other causes.

Gentlemen,

The society of   within the district of   is in great need of your assistance, the cause is legal having had the approbation of those societies consulted on the business, we therefore hope you will have the goodness to contribute according to your ability, without delay, and remit the same to the acting society.

And you will greatly oblige, gentlemen, your's most respectfully,

Done per order,   D. L. Clerk.

WARWICK,   181

FORM OF GENERAL BLANK,
After the emblems, number, &c.
WARWICK, (or where issued from)
This is to certify that the bearer hereof A. B. W—kshire man,
was enrolled at C—y, and that he has a right to the woolcombing
trade, and has contributed to our charity stock.

Witness our hands this   day of   181

D. L. } Clerk.   A. B. }
                                                      T. G. } Stewards

FORM OF CERTIFICATE.
This is to certify that the bearer hereof A. B.   W—kshire
man has been regularly entered at C—y, and enrolled by the acting
society,

Witness our hands this   day of   181

D. L. } Clerk.   A.B. }
                                                      T. G. } Stewards

The acting society wishes every society who joins in the union to
state, when they send their enrolments, whether in their opinion, it
would be legal and advantageous, to have a general charity stock,
to be kept by the acting society, who should be accountable to the
trade for the whole stock. from which stock every society in distress
through leaving or any other cause should have their regular relief,
and all public expences paid, and whether you would be willing for
every member to contribute one penny per month ; it would certainly save a great deal of trouble and expence to the trade.

(127). *W. Kerr to Francis Freeling*

General Post Office, Edinburgh, 13 *November,* 1812.
I have this day a letter from Glasgow stating that the weavers are
in a ferment there, and will allow no one to work under a certain
rate. How it will terminate no one can say, but I trust without any
material disturbance. (H.O.102/22).

(128). *The Town Clerk of Glasgow to A. Colquhoun*

16 *November* [1812].
To-day the leading operative weavers continue to make the late
judgment of the Justices fixing rates, under the authority of the
Court of Session, a pretext not only for giving up work themselves,

but also for compelling other operatives to desist from working, and to return the materials they had received, and they have also attempted by intimidation to prevent different public carriers from conveying materials for weaving at a distance. There is likewise great reason to apprehend that in the course of the week, perhaps Wednesday or Thursday, the operatives will *in general* strike work. And their doctrine is that they are not bound, to take work at any lower rates than those fixed by the Justices, and that, if the master manufacturers do not choose to give these rates, they are entitled to come upon the parish for support.

To-day the Provost called another meeting of magistrates, Sheriff Substitute and Justices of the Peace, and it was resolved to issue another Proclamation to-morrow morning, pointing out the illegality of such proceedings, intimating that instructions had been given for the apprehension and prosecution of offenders, and on the other hand holding out protection to the industrious who are disposed to continue in the peaceable exercise of their trade . . . (H.O.102/22).

(129). *The Marquess of Douglas and Clydesdale*[1] *to Viscount Sidmouth*

Hamilton Palace, 22 November, 1812.
. . . In consequence of a decision of the Justices of the Peace fixing a minimum for the wages of the weavers, they have one and all insisted upon being paid in conformity to that decision. The manufacturers, on their part, not conceiving the present state of their trade sufficiently brilliant to enable them so to remunerate their operative weavers, have resolved not to acquiesce. The consequence is, the weavers have struck work, not only over all Lanarkshire, but over all that very extensive district of country that is employed by the Glasgow and Paisley manufacturer. I am sorry to say this whole population is now wandering about quite idle, refusing work at a lower rate than the minimum unfortunately fixed by the Justices, and will not return to their business without that price of wages that their employers do not feel disposed or do not choose to give. The magistrates of Glasgow have procured military force . . . (H.O.102/22).

[1] He succeeded his father as 10th Duke of Hamilton in 1819 (1767-1852).

(130). *A. Colquhoun to Viscount Sidmouth*

Edinburgh, 1 *December*, 1812. (*Private*).

By letters I have received from Glasgow dated the 28th and 30th of November it appears that on the 27th of that month the Justices of Peace pronounced a sentence finding that the operative weavers who had received out work prior to the 10th of November at prices agreed upon by the parties, were bound to execute their contract and were liable in penalties for refusing to complete their work.

On the other hand the delegates of the operative weavers have circulated a printed paper declaring that that sentence ought not to be regarded, as it had been pronounced without the operative weavers being heard.

The letters from Glasgow further state that several webs have been destroyed by sharp instruments introduced at the end of sticks, by vitriol and other means, but in so secret a manner as to prevent the possibility of obtaining proof against any individual . . . (H.O.102/22)

(131). *A. Colquhoun to Viscount Sidmouth*

Edinburgh, 12 *December*, 1812. (*Private*).

I enclose your Lordship copies of two letters from me to the Provost of Glasgow, which will explain how matters stand in that quarter. The Provost writes me to-day that he and other well-informed individuals are of opinion that the operative weavers will either soon return to their work or will commit such acts as will place their delegates in a situation of increased guilt and danger.

[*Enclosures.*]
A. Colquhoun to Kirkman Finlay.

Edinburgh, 11 *December*, 1812. (*Copy*).

. . . In your letter of the 10th you state that the information which you had given to me by a letter of the 7th, which I received before the Sheriffs left Edinburgh, has turned out on further investigation to be unfounded. The statement in your letter of the 7th was that the operative weavers had on that day come into Glasgow in bodies to the number of 20 at a time carrying webs which had been cut out of looms. Such a state of matters certainly led me to be of opinion that it was necessary that measures should be adopted without delay for checking such open outrages and such daring insult to the law of the country, that a precognition should therefore be taken without loss of time, a seizure of papers made, and the delegates apprehended for examination and committed to prison if that should appear to be proper, till liberated in due course of law, by their finding bail if their offence was a bailable crime. But after the statement made in your Lordship's letter of the 10th which I have this day received, and the desire there expressed, I shall only say that I have complete confidence that the magistrates of Glasgow and the Sheriffs of Lanarkshire and Renfrewshire will do their duty, and that they, being on the spot, must of course be the best judges both of the measures which should be adopted, and of the proper time for carrying into execution such measures as they shall deem to be expedient . . .

Though it may suit the views of the delegates to have extra-judicial and irregular communication with the magistrates or Sheriffs, it is necessary to observe great caution in that respect, and the less of such communication that takes place, the better.

Ibid. to Ibid., Edinburgh, 12 December, 1812. (Copy) : . . . I approve of no steps being taken respecting a precognition unless acts of illegal violence shall be committed, or other circumstances shall exist which, in the opinion of the magistrates of Glasgow and Sheriffs of Lanarkshire and Renfrewshire, shall render it expedient to have recourse to that measure . . . (H.O.102/22).

(132). *A. Colquhoun to Viscount Sidmouth*

Edinburgh, 17 December, 1812. (Private).
. . . I transmit a Proclamation which was issued soon after the Sheriffs of Lanarkshire and Renfrewshire had made the seizure of papers, and had apprehended some of the delegates or leading members of the Association.

By a letter I have from the Provost of Glasgow this day, it appears that the Sheriff of Lanarkshire is still occupied in taking a pre-cognition, and that a meeting of operative delegates having been held on the 16th, the Sheriff went and ordered them to disperse as having been convened for an illegal purpose, with which requisition they complied.

The Provost adds that there were many people on the streets of Glasgow, but no riot, and that there was some disposition evinced on the part of the weavers to begin work. The Sheriff of Renfrew-shire also writes that at Paisley the weavers had begun to work.

It appears that the members of the Associations in Scotland correspond with others in England and in Ireland, and a letter was observed at the Post Office in Glasgow from Newry to one of the delegates in Glasgow.

[*Enclosure.*]
PROCLAMATION.

By the Sheriff of the County of Lanarkshire, the magistrates of Glasgow and the Justices of the Peace for the lower Ward of Lanarkshire.

WHEREAS certain information has been received that, notwithstanding the Proclamation of the 16th November last, great numbers of OPERATIVE COTTON WEAVERS, pretending to have instructions and powers from other operative weavers in the city of Glasgow and suburbs, and in other towns and villages in the County of Lanark, have held VARIOUS MEETINGS, for the purpose of exciting and maintaining a GENERAL COMBINATION AMONG THE OPERATIVE COTTON WEAVERS IN SCOTLAND, to enforce an advance of the rates or prices of weaving by illegal means ; and WHEREAS, certain information has also been received, that numerous bodies, or bands, of people, have, for the said illegal purpose, and in prosecution of the plans adopted at the said meetings, gone about intimidating by threats of violence, great numbers of peaceable and well-disposed persons engaged in the cotton manufacture, and have thereby succeeded in preventing the said persons from exercising their lawful trade, and reduced them to a state of poverty and distress : and WHEREAS, information has likewise been received, that the said bodies or bands of people have, for the accomplishment of their unwarrantable objects, proceeded even to acts of personal injury, destruction of property, and open outrage, in manifest breach of the public peace, the SHERIFF OF LANARKSHIRE, the MAGISTRATES of GLASGOW, and the JUSTICES of the PEACE for the LOWER WARD of LANARKSHIRE, HEREBY INTIMATE that they can no longer refrain from exercising the powers with which they are by law invested, for the protection of his Majesty's peaceable and well-disposed subjects, and have determined, by the most vigorous and effectual measures, to suppress all such illegal meetings, plans of combination, and violent and outrageous proceedings, and to bring to immediate trial and condign punishment all such violators of the laws of their country ; and they hereby offer a

REWARD OF TWENTY POUNDS STERLING

to any person or persons, other than the parties concerned, who shall, within 14 days from this date, give such information as may lead to the apprehension and conviction of such heinous offenders : FAR-THER, the Sheriff, magistrates and Justices deem it their duty thus publicly to put the well-disposed operative weavers on their guard against frequenting such illegal assemblies in future, and hereby intimate to them that if, after this notice, they shall be found attending any such meetings, they will expose themselves to criminal prosecution, and will have themselves to blame for the consequences.

And WHEREAS it is notorious that numbers of OPERATIVE WEAVERS have for some time past been in the practice of calling at the houses of the inhabitants of this city and suburbs, and of other parts of the County, and of attempting by solicitation to obtain sums of money for the purpose of supporting themselves and their brethren in wilful idleness, and of promoting the objects of their illegal combination, the SHERIFF, MAGISTRATES and JUSTICES feel themselves called upon, in the discharge of their public duty, to declare, that men who, although in health and able to procure work, thus obstinately persist in idleness, and degrade themselves to the rank of public beggars, have no claim whatever to the maintenance provided by law for the industrious poor, who are by age or disease disabled from working ; and instead of being objects of compassion and charity, are guilty of an illegal act ; and the SHERIFF, MAGISTRATES and JUSTICES therefore hereby admonish the inhabitants, in general, that those persons who comply with the unreasonable demands of such mendicants, instead of fulfilling a duty, contribute to the support of the idle and disorderly, encourage proceedings illegal in themselves, and highly prejudicial to the welfare of the country, and assist in enabling a few designing men, still farther to mislead their deluded brethren.

COURT-HALL, GLASGOW, 14th December, 1812.

Printed in the *Courier* Office

(133). *John Joseph Dillon to Viscount Sidmouth*

Glasgow, 18 *December,* 1812, *(Confidential).*

Having witnessed, whilst lately on a visit to the Marquess of Douglas, the *alarming* state into which so large a portion of this country is plunged by the disputes subsisting between the manufacturers of Glasgow and the operative weavers in this city and its populous environs, I was induced from curiosity to inform myself *thoroughly* upon the nature of the existing differences among these people.

Having taken some *pains* to investigate the matter, I have not hesitated in troubling your Lordship with a letter, conceiving that it might be satisfactory to receive a communication from an Englishman, a barrister, a person altogether *impartial* and *disinterested*, known also personally to your Lordship, upon the introduction of his Royal Highness the Duke of Sussex.[1]

It must of course be *officially* within the knowledge of your Lordship that 40,000 persons have struck their work, determined to submit to *every privation* rather than yield to their employers—that the manufacturers, at least most of them, are equally determined *not* to concede, and that an army of 6 or 8,000 men are quartered within this city, marched from all parts of Scotland to support order.

Conceiving, however, from the spirit which prevails on this subject, that *accurate*, or at least full reports, may not have been transmitted to your Lordship's Department, I shall endeavour briefly to state occurrences, as far as they have come to my knowledge.

I therefore shall begin by observing that disputes having long subsisted respecting the price of work between the manufacturers and the operatives (as the weavers are here called), the latter, at the commencement of the year presented a petition to the Provost and magistrates of Glasgow, praying them under certain powers of a judicial nature vested in them by the law of Scotland, 'to fix by their official authority reasonable prices for weaving the different fabrics of cotton cloth agreeably to the spirit and letter of the Acts of Parliament stated in their petition.'

The Provost and magistrates by a letter dated the 20 January, 1812, dissuaded the weavers from presenting their petition in an aggregate meeting, but recommended them to *appoint a committee* to confer with a committee of manufacturers.

This recommendation was adopted, and a memorial being presented to the Provost and magistrates, an intimation was made by the latter 'that in a matter of such consequence as that referred

---

[1] The sixth son of George III (1773-1843).

to their consideration in the memorial of the operatives, they thought it right to consult *three of the most eminent counsel*, who had all given their unanimous opinion that the magistrates had no legal power to regulate the rates of wages, as requested by the operative weavers.'

This opinion is supposed to be that of the Lord Advocate, the Dean of Faculty and Mr. J. Clerk,[1] late Solicitor General, AN OPINION PRONOUNCED ERRONEOUS BY THE COURT OF SESSION, as will presently appear.

Not satisfied with this, the committee of the weavers took the opinion of other Counsel, and in consequence commenced a regular judicial proceeding before the Justices of the Peace for the County, to which a considerable number of manufacturers were made parties . . .

On the 12 May 1812 the Court, having heard Counsel on both sides, pronounced the following interlocutor, or decree :

' In the action, &c. the Justices having considered, &c. REPEL the objections to the competency and relevancy, and before further procedure on the merits, APPOINT the defenders to state specially in a minute their objections to the printed table or statement of prices given in and founded on by the pursuers, and A L L O W the pursuers to see and answer such minute.'

From this interlocutor the manufacturers appealed by bill of advocation to the Court of Session, who, after most solemn consideration DISMISSED THE APPEAL AND CONFIRMED THE ORDERS made by the Justices in the Court of Quarter Sessions, *confirming* the opinions entertained by the Counsel of the weavers, and *deciding contrary* to that supposed to be given by the *Lord Advocate* and others.

The cause being therefore remitted by the Court of Session, a considerable body of evidence was produced by the weavers, after perusing which, and hearing Counsel, the Court on the 10th November 1812 pronounced the following interlocutor :

'Having resumed the consideration of the petition, remit of the Court of Session . . . we . . . find that the rates of wages and prices specified in the printed table referred to in the petition, as modified and restricted in said minute are MODERATE and REASONABLE . . .

Such is the history of the late judicial proceeding between the weavers and the manufacturers. The infatuation under which the

---

[1] John Clerk, Lord Eldin (1757-1832). Solicitor-General for Scotland, 1806-7 ; a Lord of Session, 1823-28.

latter have proceeded, has been such that whilst they repudiated all offers of amicable arrangement, previously to its commencement, and having had the weakness to dispute a point so clear as to the competency of the Court of Quarter Sessions to interfere, even AFTER its competency had been solemnly decided by the Supreme Court of Scottish Judicature, they were so badly advised as not to meet the case made by the weavers. They took no steps before the Court to meet any discussion upon the *merits* of the case. They entered upon no proof—they made no representations—they did not deny that the prices demanded were fair, nor did they attempt to shew any inability, to afford what was demanded, and they did not attend by their Counsel, even the hearing of the cause.

Every *judicial* mind must consider that in consequence of this omission, the manufacturers are concluded both in *law and reason* by this decision, and that they cannot *now* aver that they ought not to be called upon to pay those prices. Every *loyal* mind must hold that a Court of COMPETENT JURISDICTION having decided what was fair and reasonable, it was incumbent on the manufacturers to *respect* the decision of such a tribunal. Every *prudent* person must condemn a conduct which, while it tends so obviously to a breach of the peace, must diminish the respect of the lower classes towards established laws, and drive them into acts of violence.

Upon the publication however of this interlocutor the manufacturers resolved *not* to pay the prices awarded by the Justices.

The weavers on their side held a meeting and determined, as they have done, to *strike their work* unless the manufacturer consented to *pay the prices fixed by the Justices* ...

I conceive it to be a *principle clearly established* that it is lawful for weavers, or any class of persons, to *associate and combine* for the purpose of *resorting to those remedies* which the law and Constitution have established for regulating the price of labour. In this case the Court of Session has *recognised* the lawfulness of such an association. I conceive it to be equally lawful to *continue* such an association for the purpose of obtaining the benefit of a decision in their favour, and until the *end* of the association be accomplished.

On the other hand it is, I conceive, equally clear that a combination of masters to reduce the price of labour, or to defraud the workmen of the fruits of their decree, is a crime punishable by indictment, and requiring on the part of Government the most severe animadversion.

145

M

The law declares that although it cannot compel *individual service*, it can punish an *agreement* between two persons not to serve unless upon an advance of wages. The same law applies to *employment*. An agreement between two or more manufacturers not to employ weavers but *under* the rate fixed by the Justices is certainly an *unlawful* combination.

Such a combination however has actually been formed in this city on the part of some of the manufacturers. Some indeed have yielded, and others from the beginning complied with their demands, but the majority hold out, and I cannot sufficiently describe the imprudence of their partisans, who talk of *starving* the people into an abandonment of their claims, although sanctioned as they are by the sentence of the law. It chills one's blood to hear the language prevalent upon this subject, and to behold in the streets the poverty, distress and yet patience with which one is surrounded.

I can attribute the obstinacy of the manufacturers principally to the *facility* with which, upon their unfounded representations of riots and disturbance as likely to occur (and which would be the effect of their own imprudence) they have obtained the presence almost of an army. They seem anxious for an appeal not to justice but to A R M S, and the selfishness of many would have been highly gratified, had any breach of the peace been committed, and the weavers crushed by an overwhelming force.

The people however have been too wary, and although out of employ, never was this place in such a state of profound tranquillity. I was prone at first to conceive that these weavers might be under a pernicious influence, impelled by crafty persons with mischievous designs. This, I am now persuaded, is *not* the case. The people of Scotland are superior to the English in reflection and discernment. They have the superior advantages of education, and the leading men of their body are persons of wonderful coolness and ability. They pride themselves on patient endurance, and upon the contrast which their conduct has afforded with that of their southern neighbours. They manage their own concerns, and have retained advocates of superior talents in the Court of Session, men of great eloquence in the forum but of great *prudence* in the closet, with whom they have advised upon all points necessary for the regulation of their conduct in any event. The battle which they seem inclined to wage is one of *law*.

The commonalty of Glasgow support the weavers by credit and by subscription. There has not yet appeared the slightest indication of tumult or open violence. If any acts of intimidation have been used against individuals disposed to work at the rates proposed by the manufacturers, they are disavowed by the committee, and though generally alleged by their adversaries to have been practised, I believe no case has yet been made out by evidence.

The organisation of the weavers is very peculiar. They act in concert with wonderful unanimity, and they seem to have established an interior system of police in order to prevent disturbance or breach of the public peace by individuals ; they consider themselves *legally justified* in their proceedings, and seem particularly cautious to avoid *Luddism*. They *correspond* with England and Ireland, but seem to *act* upon *distinct* grounds. They profess to act openly and to have no secrets.

The landed interest rather take their part, and have given them employment in agriculture, to which they resort with pleasure and activity.

They seem determined to undergo the last privation rather than work under the prices fixed by the Court of Quarter Sessions, and the *obstinacy* of the Scottish character is beyond expression.

The manufacturers on the other hand seem divided among themselves. Some from the beginning have acquiesced in the demand of the weavers, and others are yielding. Those however who persist in standing out, evince in all their proceedings the same infatuation which governed them at the commencement of the process. They have wished to raise alarms of plots and conspiracies of which as yet no evidence has been procured, and which no sensible person believes, and, as always happens when parties proceed upon a *wrong principle*, every step taken increases instead of suppressing the mischief. Proclamation has followed Proclamation without effect ; delegates have been apprehended and discharged, orderly and peaceable meetings have been dispersed, and none, I understand, are to be allowed. The committee originally formed at the *suggestion* of the magistrates, recognised by them, treated with by them, is suddenly pronounced unlawful, and the members seized, with papers which amount to nothing. The Crown lawyers, the magistrates have been already, the Government itself even will be *committed* most seriously, unless your Lordship shall send down without delay a person in your confidence to examine matters upon the spot. Such a step I conceive to be of the *most urgent necessity* . . .

Pending the process before the Justices, certain work was given out to be manufactured, with the price as usual, under the Act of

1803 mentioned in the ticket. The weavers at first thought the order of the Justices extended to this work. The Justices published an explanation purporting that it did not. In this the weavers appear to acquiesce, taking however a distinction as to work *finished* at the time of the decree.

The plan of *starving* the weavers into the *necessity* of working at less wages than *the law has pronounced reasonable*, can never meet the support of Government.

On the other hand, the situation of the manufacturers in consequence of the American War is such that many of them, who have adventured without capital, *cannot afford* to give the prices fixed by the Justices. The general state of the trade is *worse* than is generally supposed, and this, many persons who have engaged *beyond their means*, are disposed to confess. It is upon this consideration alone I can account for the conduct of the manufacturers before the Justices, but I think it will occur to your Lordship that if *such be the case*, the evil must be increased by this sort of *double dealing* with the workmen, who say that they ought not to contribute to the *losses* of the manufacturer whilst they are not admitted to a participation of the *profits* . . . In society it is common to hear that the MANUFACTURERS ARE GLAD THE PEOPLE HAVE STRUCK, AND THAT THEY DO NOT wish them to return to their work as THEY CANNOT DISPOSE OF THEIR STOCK.' This may be a reason for employing fewer workmen, but is none for not paying to those whom they employ, the *full price* awarded by the law . . .

Something must be done, or in a few days the clamour for peace will be so loud as to be irresistible, and greatly embarrass the Foreign Department at this critical conjuncture of affairs upon the Continent.

. . . There is a disposition on the part of many to make *the law* and *the power of Government* the instrument of oppression, and of a mean, selfish narrow-minded mercantile cupidity . . . (H.O.102/22).

(134). *John Joseph Dillon to Viscount Sidmouth*

Star Inn, Glasgow, 20 *December*, 1812.
. . . I have the honour of transmitting to your Lordship the Proclamation to which I alluded in my former letter, and on which I shall take the liberty of making a few observations.

To me the first Article appears peculiarly objectionable. The means declared *illegal*, are not specified, nor does it appear to what the expression alludes. If to the proceedings within the courts, it is manifest that the Proclamation proceeds upon an *erroneous conception of the law*.

No lawyer can doubt that a combination of workmen to institute legal proceedings in order to establish through a competent jurisdiction the rate of wages, is a proceeding perfectly justifiable.

It is also clear that a determination on the part of a body of workmen not to work under the rate of wages fixed by a court of competent jurisdiction, is also legal and justifiable, certainly not exposing those by whom it is formed to the accusation contained in the latter part of the Proclamation of raising 'unreasonable demands' and of '*obstinately* persisting in *wilful* idleness.'

I have the less difficulty in laying down these positions, having bestowed during the last two years considerable attention on the law of Scotland and being confirmed by the following passage, in the judgement of the Lord Justice Clerk in 1803, in the case of the paper makers. His Lordship expresses himself as follows :

'It is admitted on all hands that an individual workman may refuse serving a master, if the wages offered to him are not agreeable to him. *I see nothing criminal or blameable* if he makes known his opinion to his fellow servants, and if *they*, concurring in the same opinion *combine*, that is, take *joint* measures to obtain redress of this evil, which affects *them all in common*.

'Now what are the measures to which a combination of workmen may *lawfully resort* ? They are equally obvious and *efficacious*. They are *pointed out* by the law and *Constitution* of this country, and ensure *complete redress* to the workman if the evil really exists without injustice to the master, or detriment or hazard to the public. Workmen legally and honestly combined in this manner will naturally, in the first place, go to their master and state their reasons for requiring an augmentation of their wages. If they do not agree with the master, they may then, very *lawfully* and *properly* make an application to the *Justices of the Peace*, or *Judges Ordinary*, the JURISDICTION in which the LAW and CONSTITUTION of the country place the POWER OF REGULATING WAGES, and which they *never* exercise but on *due enquiry* and *proof as to the fact*. If the Justices are of opinion that the wages are too low, THEY WILL RAISE THEM, and the MASTERS OF COURSE MUST PAY THEIR WORKMEN according to a HIGHER RATE.'

What can be a more clear justification of the conduct adopted, ostensibly at least, by the weavers, than the above judgement of the Justice Clerk, and at the same time a more severe critique upon this Proclamation ?

I have really thought it incumbent on me as an *impartial* spectator of these proceedings to lay the case *accurately* before your Lordship, that you may be enabled to *stop* the mischief, which these and other measures are calculated to produce. The Proclamation thus worded is the last proof of the *spirit of Party* and *prepossession* which appears to prevail in this city.

The acts of violence stated, are not established, as far as I have been able to discover, by *any evidence*. They are *assumed*, and I have found that it is the practice of many weavers, those the *most obstinate* or *standing out*, to excuse themselves with their masters, whom they wish not to offend, by *pretending* that they are *afraid* to work at less than the price established by the Court of Session.

The manufacturers have been incessant in their assertions to make out a case of violence, and the Proclamation offering *rewards* is the best proof that evidence of such violence cannot be obtained. The dwellings of the committee are entered without *legal* warrant ; their papers are *seized and detained* contrary to law. Their persons are apprehended, and they cheerfully submit, and even voluntarily, to every inquiry, concealing nothiug, and even offering the search of their habitations.

I have not yet traced anything *political* in the object of their association, but it *may become so*, and this is with me a principal source of apprehension. Should the association adopt any *political* and *ulterior* views, it will be one much more *serious* and *even tremendous* than anything we have ever witnessed in England. I have endeavoured to study the national character, and I believe I know it well.

It may be proper to inform your Lordship that *representation*, *delegation* and *correspondence* are usual and *congenial* to the institutions and practice of Scotland. The Counties are in the habit of *corresponding* with each other through an officer next in rank and consideration to the member for each County, called the 'CONVENER.' The members for Burghs are elected through the intervention of *primary assemblies*, who appoint *delegates* to choose their representative in Parliament. The weavers of Glasgow have held an organisation and have been in the habit of acting by representation and delegation *during the last ten years*, and the Act of 1803 was obtained *by themselves*. They have during ten years been anxious to obtain an Act of Parliament fixing a *minimum* of labour. These points are *material* to be borne in mind, as they tend to prevent misconception in an English mind, and they explain the nature of the present conflict . . .'[1] (H.O.102/22).

(135). *Sir Thomas Plumer (the Attorney-General) to John Beckett*

Lincoln's Inn, 21 December, 1812.

I send enclosed for the information of Lord Sidmouth the communications received from the Rev. Dr. Collins, a magistrate in Yorkshire.

These combinations are mischievous and dangerous, but it is very difficult to know how to deal with them.

[*Enclosure.*]
Dr. Collins, D.D., to the Attorney-General

Gisburne, Yorkshire. 12 *December,* 1812.

Having the honour of acting as a magistrate for the County of Lancaster as well as for this West Riding of Yorkshire, I think it my duty to transmit you a document put into my hands by some most respectable woollen manufacturers at Burnley [No. 126].

Whether the names of the chief framers of this dangerous and desperate conspiracy be fictitious or not, the gentlemen who have solicited my attention to it are not informed—but they express to me the most serious apprehension as to its effect upon the conduct of their workmen, who are extremely numerous in their neighbourhood and the adjacent districts on the borders of Yorkshire.[2]

---

[1] Sidmouth replied, on the 28th : ' I think myself particularly obliged to you for your letters of the 18th and 20th instant, containing information and suggestions deserving of very serious consideration. To the principle of fixing a minimum for the price of labour, I confess myself to be strongly adverse ; and the law under which this authority has been exercised appears to me to have had a considerable share in occasioning the irritation and distress which I am concerned to find still exist amongst the operative weavers in Scotland.' (*Ibid.* [Copy.])

[2] Writing to the Under-Secretary of State from Gisburne on 27 June, 1808, he had said : ' You, Sir, I believe, may know that this part of the Riding where I partly reside is chiefly in pasturage and but very thinly inhabited. The lower orders of society have more reliance on their superiors, and in fact at the present moment have less occasion to complain of wants either of provisions or work—but within a few miles—the instant we get near the borders of the manufacturing parts of Lancashire we meet a fresh race of beings, both in point of manners, employments and subordination . . .' (H.O.42/95).

You, Sir, will best judge as to the offence of forming such a systematic Congress or acting as delegates at it—as well as of framing, or procuring signatures to such extraordinary articles. I therefore have the honour of most respectfully requesting the favour of your directions on any points you may think necessary or requisite on this subject—but especially what process you would wish a magistrate to pursue in case either of proof being ascertained of subscriptions being either asked or put to such a paper, or of offenders acting upon the rules therein contained.[1] (H.O.42/130).

---

[1] Lieutenant-General Maitland, who commanded the troops in the north of England, wrote from Wakefield on 21 December : ' What will give us more aid than anything is the very great change that has already taken place in consequence of the Russian news. [Napoleon's retreat from Moscow.] Everything is up, and I understand that in some of the cotton parts of the country they are even working long days. Here, the people, from having nothing to do, are full of business. If this continues, all will go well, notwithstanding the high price of provisions.' (H.O.42/130). But Mr. Coldham could report no improvement in the hosiery trade : he wrote from Nottingham on 29 December : 'The trade of this town is in the most lamentable state, and the distresses of the poor and working classes severe beyond the power of description.' (*Ibid.*)

V. THE LAST YEARS OF THE NAPOLEONIC WAR

1813. The Scottish weavers. The Friendly Societies finance turn-outs in Lancashire.

1814. Strikes in Sheffield. The journeymen calico printers. The framework-knitters. The Nottinghamshire bricklayers.

(136). *A. Colquhoun to Viscount Sidmouth*

Edinburgh, 2 January, 1813. (Private).

... Of all these occurrences I was ignorant till after they had taken place, and I certainly would have objected to their taking place had I known of the measures proposed to be adopted. For though Mr. Thomson was only sent to prison for a short time till examined after the seizure of some papers, yet I do not think he ought to have been so sent at all, nor should this investigation, into which the Sheriffs were incidentally led when searching out for evidence of an illegal combination on the part of the operative weavers, have been prosecuted. There is no help for it now that it has been done, and as the Sheriffs were acting with a view to check dangerous practices, as much support must now be given to them as the circumstances of the case will admit of ...

Ibid. to Ibid.:—Edinburgh, 2 January, 1813. (Private):—The Provost of Glasgow,[1] who is member for that District of Burghs, goes to London, and will probably wait on your Lordship before the middle of this month.

He will bring under your Lordship's view what he stated to me at length yesterday, that it would be expedient to prevent the interference of Justices of Peace in regulating wages and to prevent meetings of delegates of a numerous body of the lower class such as the operative weavers. I informed him that should his Majesty's Ministers deem it proper to adopt any legislative measures on those subjects, such measures could not be confined to Scotland, but

---

[1] Kirkman Finlay, M.P. (1773-1842).

behoved to extend to England also, and to be general measures affecting Great Britain ; that they would require deliberate consideration, and that the actual state of the law in England relative to the existing powers of Justices of Peace in such matters ought to be ascertained by a reference to the Crown Council there before any steps were taken.

Certainly it would be most desirable that all such meetings of delegates should be prevented, as they must produce the most dangerous consequences to the public peace and to the Constitution and government of the country—but it will be very difficult to draw a line in such matters.

The interference of Justices of Peace except in fixing a maximum in branches of trade connected with the necessaries of life so as the public may not suffer by improper combination, is also to be deprecated. On the present occasion much evil has resulted, and I fear will continue to result from the late injudicious interference of the Justices of Peace of Lanarkshire, and which I learn has been followed by an injudicious interference of a different nature in some respects in Stirlingshire.

Your Lordship will find Mr. Finlay an intelligent, sensible man. He carries on trade to a very great extent, and has hitherto almost always got access with his commodities into the Continent. (H.O.102/23).

(137). *A. Colquhoun to Viscount Sidmouth*

Edinburgh, 17 *January,* 1813.

The precognitions relating to the operative weavers in Lanarkshire and Renfrewshire have been under the consideration of the Crown Council, and as soon as circumstances will allow, criminal trials of some of the ringleaders will take place for an illegal combination to raise wages, followed by acts of violence towards those who did not enter into that combination but who continued to work as weavers.

I am sorry to learn that although the operative weavers are now finishing more webs they had contracted for before the Justices gave a sentence declaring certain wages reasonable, that it is the determination of the Association not to work after those webs are finished, at lower prices than those declared to be reasonable by the sentence of the Justices of Lanarkshire pronounced last November, nor to allow any weavers to work at lower prices . . .

A similar attempt to that made in Lanarkshire has lately been made before the Justices of Peace in Perthshire, but they have acted more wisely by finding it was inexpedient to attempt to regulate the rates of wages, after fully considering the pleadings of both parties. Mr. Jeffrey, the editor of the *Edinburgh Review*, who was Counsel for the operative weavers at Glasgow, went as Counsel for the operative weavers to Perth, and pleaded their cause before the Justices of Peace there, but without success. He is to be their Counsel when tried in the Court of Justiciary here for illegal combination . . .

[Enclosure.]
An unknown correspondent to the Lord Advocate of Scotland

Glasgow, n.d. (Copy.)

Since writing you I have had communications with different people here, and I find the combination amongst the weavers [in Glasgow] is stronger than ever. Your Lordship may be apt to suppose that because no outrage has taken place, matters are gradually coming round, which is by no means the case. They have indeed agreed to work out the webs in the loom, but not a man can work at a new web but at the full price, as they call it, and not even at this, unless he signs a bond for money borrowed to subsist those who will not work, and joins the Association. They manage the business thus. The committee, who consist of five persons, who direct the whole, have divided out the country into districts, in which they appoint one or more beamers in each. The beamers are those who put the webs upon the beam and prepare it for working, and the necessary utensils for which, belong to the Association, and no person dare offer to beam a web, but those appointed by the committee. When a person therefore gets out a web from the manufacturers, he must satisfy the beamer and others appointed with him, that he has become a member of the Association, and produce the ticket to show that it is to be worked at the high price, otherwise he cannot get it beamed. Vast numbers of the most industrious have not only for six weeks been prevented from working the webs they had in the loom until now, that the committee permitted them, but they cannot get working the new webs offered them, now the old is done. These utensils for beaming being private property of the Association in the district, we do not think the beamer can be forced to beam any person's web that offers, and if they were willing they dare not do it. (H.O.102/23).

(138). *The Procurator Fiscal to the Sheriff of Lanarkshire*

18 *January*, 1813.[1] (*Copy*).

. . Nightly instances occur of windows being broken and webs destroyed, but I have hitherto been unable to trace any of these to any individual.

In Govan, Anderston, &c., the village drummers have been ordered by the managers of the weavers to alter their hours of beating their drums, &c. They did this at 8 o'clock, and it was candidly avowed that any person continuing to work after that hour ran a great risk of getting his windows destroyed. (H.O.102/23).

(139). *Viscount Sidmouth to A. Colquhoun*

Whitehall, 20 *January*, 1813. *Private.* (*Copy*).

. . . It cannot be reasonably expected that the operative weavers will return steadily to their work till the trials for illegal combinations are over. The magistrates of the County of Perth have acted most judiciously, and I trust that the discretion supposed to be vested in Justices of the Peace in Scotland to fix the rate of wages, will not be exercised in any other quarter, as it has unfortunately been in the County of Lanark . . . (H.O.102/23).

(140). *The Rev. W. R. Hay, J.P., to Viscount Sidmouth*

New Bailey Court House, Manchester, 4 *February*, 1813.

In obedience to the directions of the magistrates at the last Manchester Sessions, I have the honour to address this letter to your Lordship, and to enclose the heads of a Bill which we hope will be soon presented to the House of Commons, and for the success of which we are peculiarly anxious . . .

The Bill has for its object to prevent the Friendly Societies from being perverted to purposes of public mischief. The attention of the magistrates here has for some years past been drawn to this subject under various pressing applications. In the years 1810 and 1811, combinations among the journeymen in almost every branch of trade were peculiarly alarming, and there was strong reason to suspect that these persons held their meetings under the rules allowed to them in pursuance of the Friendly Society Acts. In the course of

---

[1] In the Lord Advocate's letter to Sidmouth, 21 January, 1813.

inquiry, we had opportunity to see the printed rules of several of these Clubs which had for some years back been allowed at the Quarter Sessions ; and it was found that through want of sufficient attention in those who were more especially relied on to peruse the articles before they were admitted, they in many instances contained clauses directly binding the members to combinations in respect of trade. On this, the Acts were looked into, and advice taken ; and it appeared that the Quarter Sessions had no power of calling in or revising the rules they had so imprudently allowed, and that, although the original rules allowed had been unexceptionable, it was in the power of the Societies at any time to add or substitute others ; while it depended on the Societies themselves whether or no they would submit the new rules to the Sessions for approval. In consequence of this, and of a great variety of pressing representations, I was directed to apply to Mr. Perceval on the subject, which I did personally in July 1810, after Parliament broke up. I had further communication with him by letter towards the close of the year, and after learning his sentiments on the subject, which were laid before the magistrates in January 1811, the draft of a Bill was ordered to be prepared. An unexpected delay took place in preparing this, and it was late in May before I could present it to Mr. Perceval for his perusal. It was his opinion that before the Bill was offered, it should undergo considerable alteration. The Session of Parliament was far advanced. These, in addition to other considerations which at that time presented themselves, made it advisable not then to press the subject further.

After that time, from the depressed state of trade, these combinations were for the most part, if not entirely, discontinued ; and the subject, though repeatedly and strongly mentioned to us, was not pressed upon us till about the month of May last, when the committee which regularly sat at the Police Office here to assist the magistrates during the disturbances, feeling that the abuse of these Societies might have contributed materially to the furtherance of the mischief then experienced, strongly called the attention of the magistrates to the subject. This happened about the time of Mr. Perceval's assassination.[1] Mr. Bootle,[2] and I believe some other member of the House of Commons, was communicated with, and it

[1] Perceval, the Prime Minister, was assassinated on 11 May, 1812.

[2] Edward Wilbraham Bootle, of Lathom House, Ormskirk, Lancashire; M.P. for Clitheroe in the 1812-18 Parliament ; created Baron Skelmersdale. 1828 (1771-1853).

was considered that such was the state in which the public business then was, that it would be best to defer the measure for the present. On the 8th of June the committee, pressed as strongly by resolutions to promote the measure, and feeling that there was no likelihood of getting a Bill passed that Session, recommended that we should learn the sentiments of magistrates in other populous districts. This we did by applying to those at Sheffield, Huddersfield, Bolton, Macclesfield and Stockport, and met with their full concurrence in the expediency of applying to Parliament. The suggestions offered by different parties were laid before the Counsel who has revised his original Bill. He has materially altered it, and the rough draft, since corrected, was that which was approved at the Sessions. In the instructions given for preparing the draft, it was particularly desired that no clause should be introduced which could in any way affect the genuine objects of the Friendly Society Acts . . .[1] (H.O.42/132).

---

[1] The proposed Bill provided for the compulsory registration of all Friendly Societies and for the submission of their Rules to the Quarter Sessions. Unregistered Societies would be deemed unlawful assemblies. The Preamble of the proposed Bill said that ' whereas it appears that the funds of many of the said [Friendly] Societies have been dissipated in improvident adventures in trade, with intent to reduce the price of provisions and in the support of unlawful combinations of workmen with intent to enhance the wages of manual labour—and whereas it also appears that many of the said Societies being respectively composed of persons employed in one and the same trade and business under colour and pretence of associating for the charitable purposes aforesaid, have entered into Rules for controlling workmen and others in the lawful exercise of their respective trades and occupations, and have assembled together for the purpose of carrying on such illegal combinations as aforesaid and have also elected delegates or deputies to be convened with others deputed in like manner by other like Societies far and near, in a general convention or assembly in order to confederate numbers of the said Societies together in more numerous and extensive combinations and conspiracies whereby the beneficial purposes of the said Act are likely to be frustrated and the means of effecting the same perverted from the maintenance of the industrious poor in age, sickness and infirmity to the support of idle and improvident workmen who refuse employment for the purpose of extorting exorbitant wages from their employers, and the peace and good order of the realm has been of late greatly disturbed and may hereafter be again endangered by such confederated Societies unless the timely aid and authority of Parliament be applied for remedy thereof. Be it therefore enacted . . .'

(141). *Kirkman Finlay to Viscount Sidmouth*

30, St. Albans Street, 5 February, 1813.

The accounts I yesterday received from Glasgow represent the operative weavers in that city and neighbourhood in a similar situation to that which lately excited so much apprehension.

This alteration in their conduct is principally produced by an opinion generally, but I hope erroneously entertained, that the Lord Advocate does not mean to proceed against certain delegates and others lately apprehended, and will probably subside when that error shall be corrected.

But we all feel persuaded that the short and effectual measures to compose the present unhappy differences are the two measures which I had the honour to submit to your Lordship, namely,

1. To declare that by law in Scotland Justices of the Peace have not the power or authority to regulate the rate or prices of weaving in the cotton manufacture.

2. To extend to Scotland the provisions of the Act of the 43 of the King, chapter 86, relating to combinations in Ireland.[1]

The first measure, to which I trust there does not exist any objection, would go a great way to allay that ferment in the minds of those persons which the second would, I am persuaded, completely remove, and I trust to your Lordship's indulgence when I add that its early introduction into Parliament will be a most acceptable measure in the west of Scotland. (H.O.102/23).

(142). *A. Colquhoun to Viscount Sidmouth*

Edinburgh, 13 March, 1813. (Private).

Yesterday the trial of five of the operative weaver delegates came on here in the Court of Justiciary. We met at 9 yesterday morning and got out of Court this morning at 7 o'clock. The most guilty of the five had fled and was accordingly fugitated (outlawed) . . .

---

[1] The Preamble began : ' Whereas the laws now in force in Ireland against unlawful combinations, by and amongst artificers, workmen, journeymen and labourers, have been found to be inadequate to the suppression thereof ; whereby it is become necessary that more effectual provision should be made against such unlawful combinations in Ireland, and for preventing such unlawful practices in future, and for bringing such offenders to more speedy and exemplary punishment . . .' Offenders were to be committed to the common gaol for a period not exceeding six calendar months, or to be committed to a House of Correction and be kept to hard labour for a term not exceeding three calendar months.

Ibid. to Ibid., Edinburgh, 14 *March* 1813 : . . . The jury yesterday returned a verdict finding the operative weavers guilty, and the Court are to pronounce sentence to-morrow.

Ibid. to Ibid., Edinburgh. 16 *March* 1813 :—Yesterday the Court of Justiciary sentenced Johnston, the Treasurer of the Association, to 18 months' imprisonment, and the other three pannels,[1] one to 9 months' imprisonment, and two to 4 months' imprisonment each, and all of them, on the expiry of their imprisonment, to find security to keep the peace for three years . . .

This day the trial of four more of the operative weavers came on. Three of them having fled, were fugitated, and their bail bonds forfeited. The fourth, and least guilty, pleaded guilty to part of the charges in the indictment, and he was sentenced to two months' imprisonment . . . (H.O.102/23).

(143). *Viscount Sidmouth to A. Colquhoun*

Whitehall, 17 *March,* 1813. *(Copy).*
. . . The conviction of the delegates of the operative weavers at Edinburgh will, I trust, have the effect of at least checking that disposition to, and system of combination so prevalent in most of the manufacturing parts of the kingdom, and this effect is likely to be aided by the Bill now before the House of Commons for repealing the Acts authorising magistrates to fix the wages of labour . . .[2] (H.O.102/23).

(144). *A. Colquhoun to Viscount Sidmouth*

Edinburgh, 20 *March,* 1813.
On Thursday last the third trial of the operative weavers came on, when the two persons indicted, who had been members of the Select Committee, pleaded guilty, and the jury, having of course found them guilty, they were sentenced to five months' imprisonment.

After the trial was over I stated that I did not mean to proceed

---

[1] The accused.
[2] 53 George III, c. 40. Sidmouth said that the existence of these Acts had, until lately, been unknown, particularly that of 1563, which had fallen into desuetude, 'and the existence of which was unknown to the magistrates and even to high authorities in the law, as well as to the Committee of the House of Commons which had the subject of wages under their consideration last Session.' (*Parl. Deb.* XXV. 594 [6 April 1813].)

to the trial of any more of those who had been implicated in such illegal conduct, but would suspend any further criminal proceedings, trusting that no such crimes would in future be committed, but that if there should be a repetition of such offences, the persons guilty of them would be liable to be brought to trial both for the offences which had been now committed, and for any crime of a similar description, in which event, as the Court had declared, there would be inflicted a severer punishment, but that I trusted such combinations would be completely abandoned and never formed again . . . (H.O.102/23).

(145). *Memorial respecting Combinations and Benefit Societies*

Museum Tavern, 27 May, 1813.

We, the undersigned, being a committee of the trade of mechanists and engineers resident in London and its immediate vicinity, beg on behalf of ourselves and the said trade to submit the following Memorial to your consideration, and to request your assistance to give efficacy to its several objects. Your memorialists have long deplored the combinations that have been systematically organised and carried on for several years among the major part of the journeymen not only in your memorialists' trade but in most of the manufacturing employments pursued in the metropolitan part of the empire ; combinations which have engendered not only insubordination but created a refractory and oppressive spirit in the conduct of journeymen, and which have operated in a way equally injurious to them and their employers. Your memorialists were anxious to believe that the existing laws of the realm would have been adequate to repress these evils, but they are sorry to declare after long and painful experience that these laws are artfully and efficaciously evaded and defeated by and under the mask of Benefit Societies, institutions which have created, cherished and given effect to the most dangerous combinations among the several journeymen of our district, to the great injury and annoyance of ourselves and the generality of manufacturers, and by which the welfare and tranquillity of the country are materially endangered. Immense numbers of journeymen embodied under the legal protection of Benefit Societies congregate together under the specious pretexts of discussing and forming plans and regulations for governing these Societies, and which give to them on all occasions the advantage of conferring and forming any resolution on any point either connected

N

with their particular or general employments. Meetings for promoting these combinations are called with facility, and under the existing laws they are held with perfect safety to those who attend them. They are conducted with a secrecy and a dexterity that place the master manufacturers at defiance, and your memorialists have long found it a matter of the greatest difficulty to conduct their respective journeymen by those wholesome regulations and ancient wages that heretofore constituted the line of duty between master and man. Your memorialists respectfully but earnestly assure you, Sir, both for themselves and others, that they have in their individual characters been of late years accustomed to see with sincere regret and profound astonishment continued exactions and demands made by journeymen upon their masters, which have been invariably followed by the masters being compelled to yield to these demands. Concession has been followed by concession till the journeymen have attained nearly the power to demand with one hand and to enforce with the other. This state of things cannot long exist, and if there is not shortly some legislative regulations adopted, your memorialists are deeply impressed with the most serious apprehensions that absolute ruin will overtake the master manufacturers of the empire, and the journeymen will assume an overbearing, oppressive and mischievous character that will be alike dangerous to the prosperity and tranquillity of the country. Your memorialists are fully persuaded that the recent mischievous associations, disgraceful riots and ruinous burnings in the neighbourhoods of Nottingham and Manchester have had much of their origin in compacts of this nature, and as long as bodies of journeymen are allowed to constitute themselves into Societies under any denomination of Benefit while the present laws for the management of such Societies exist, your memorialists have no hope of having the evils redressed which they have lamentably experienced. Your memorialists respectfully suggest that if some law was formed which should enjoin that all monies paid and subscribed on account of any Benefit Society should be funded as soon as it might amount to £40, and that the persons in trust for the time being of such Benefit Society should be compelled to state on oath the precise purpose for which such money was collected, and that no such money should be disposed of but for the purpose for which it was collected. [sic.] Your memorialists are fully persuaded that the present laws for registering the objects, rules and regulations of Benefit Societies are greatly defective . . .

Your memorialists are fearful that much mischief has resulted from permitting any Benefit Society to be composed altogether of persons of one line of business to the exclusion of all other persons. It is by such exclusions that such Societies are enabled to promote illegal and dangerous measures with a safety and a secrecy that would never be attempted nor attained by mixed bodies. It will be obvious to you, Sir, that journeymen so embodied, with considerable funds at their command, are sufficiently powerful not only to control their particular masters but the whole body of masters are more or less at their mercy. Their mischievous influence and overwhelming power is greatly augmented by a system of delegation. A convention of delegates has been sitting in the heart of the metropolis for some months composed of two persons from every trade and profession carried on in the metropolis and its neighbourhood. That convention was called together solely to consider of the best means of applying to the legislator [sic] to enlarge the powers and to extend the operation of the Statute of the 5th of Elizabeth, yet your memorialists have well-grounded reasons for believing that various other objects have come under the consideration of this convention. Its meetings have been protracted, and discussions have been instituted, and have given to the journeymen of this metropolis the means of identifying their several interests, ascertaining their strength and consolidating their power, and by which the masters of any particular trade will now have not only to combat with the power and property of their own class of journeymen but with the whole journeymen of the metropolis, who will form an irresistible phalanx, and greatly superior to the united energies of the masters, if such an Union was either attainable or legal [sic]. Your memorialists are apprehensive that this system of powerful and dexterous association is rapidly diffusing its spirit and extending its power through the whole country. Benefit Societies have been made a successful weapon, and the Statute of the 5th of Elizabeth a constant and prosperous rallying point to further the measures of the journeymen against their employers . . .[1] (H.O.42/133).

---

[1] The Memorial is signed by five engineers : Henry Maudslay, Alexander Galloway, J. Collinge, Bryan Donkin and Timothy Bramah. It is docketed : 'This appears to me to be worth supporting. The policy of requiring apprenticeships in these days is most questionable in any trade. And Benefit Societies (unless better regulated) will be the ruin of the country.'

(146). *Colonel Fletcher, J.P., to John Beckett*

Bolton, 16 December 1813.

. . . The Jacobin leaders during the prosperous state of affairs with which it hath pleased the Almighty to bless this country, cannot find many followers, nor dare now (as, during Bonaparte's career of conquest, they used to do) openly express their malevolent sentiments against their country and its Government for fear of that immediate chastisement which would be likely to follow from the hands of that order of men (the lowest) which in some instances they had before too successfully cajoled.

In conversation with the persons employed, they confess that the prosperous state of the trade, enabling men with common industry to earn a comfortable subsistence for themselves and their families, has considerably diminished their hopes of revolution, which yet, however, they affect to think will ultimately be accomplished by the catholics of Ireland. Indeed, whilst Bonaparte shall remain in power, so long there will be danger from his machinations, and particularly in that quarter of the United Kingdom.

In this manufacturing part of Lancashire there is reason to apprehend that the mischievous activity of the seditious will be principally exerted in promoting *turn-outs* (what in town you call *strikings*) for a further advance of wages, in different branches of the manufactures. In matters of this sort, men of this description generally take the lead, thereby keeping up some consequence with the working manufacturers, who are but too prone to regard those persons as benefactors, who even pretend to procure for them more wages for their labour. (H.O.42/136).

(147). *John Beckett to the Rev. W. R. Hay*

Whitehall, 14 March, 1814.

Lord Sidmouth having directed a reference to be made to the Attorney and Solicitor-General on the subject of the 'Rules for the conducting of the Union Society of Printers, Cutters and Drawers in Lancashire, Cheshire, Derbyshire, &c.' which you transmitted to his Lordship in your letter of the 20th of last month, I have received his Lordship's directions to acquaint you that the Law Officers have received his Lordship's directions to acquaint you that the Law Officers have reported that the Articles entered into are illegal by the Statute of 39 and 40 George III, ch. 106.

The object of these Articles is to prevent the masters from using machinery by agreement of the workmen who are parties to the Articles not to work for such masters, and so to prevent the workmen from working in certain sorts of work described in some of the different clauses of the Articles. This combination for controlling and affecting persons who carry on the trade or business, &c. as such is illegal, and any of the persons who can be proved to be members of the Society or to have subscribed their money for the purposes of the combination are guilty of an offence for which they may be convicted . . . It would be very desirable that the magistrates should take measures for ascertaining who are the individuals composing the Society in question, and that sufficient evidence should be procured so as to bring the fact home to one or more of the parties of their being members of the said Society or of their having subscribed money for the purposes set forth in the Rules, in order that a case may be made out for immediate prosecution, and as soon as the magistrates have collected any information on which they conceive a prosecution may be instituted, Lord Sidmouth requests that it may be transmitted for his information with as little delay as possible. (H.O.43/22/449-51).

(148). *John Spencer to Viscount Sidmouth*

Makeney, near Derby, 14 *March*, 1814.
From the increased demand for the labour of our mechanics of late, it is to be expected that some inconveniences, if not tumult, will occur, but I presume to call the attention of your Lordship to a subject which, if not timely checked, will at a future period render all your efforts to do so fruitless, and will eventually destroy our superiority over other countries in manufacture. What I allude to is the combination of workmen to demand an increased price for labour, or what the manufacturers term 'striking.' This is now taking place to a considerable extent in our principal towns, and will spread to all, if not prevented ; and certainly nothing will be more fatal to the real interests of our country than this misfortune . . .

In Sheffield, where I was the 8th inst., I find that three bodies of workmen had struck, and their employers have complied with the terms they demanded ; another body called the file makers have demanded an increase of wages, to take place 2nd May next ; and they have sent out to the masters the terms they will work for in future after that period ; a printed paper of which I beg to enclose, and which these workmen have sent out to their employers. These file makers get at present in six short days 25s. to 35s. per week ; the enclosed paper is 15% above that price. Other workmen in Sheffield are preparing to follow this example ; they are also doing the same at Nottingham.

The Act of Parliament to prevent unlawful combinations of 22 George II[1] and others, are not of sufficient strength to meet this evil, and besides there are several reasons why masters of manufactories will not prosecute, particularly since the late treatment in Yorkshire[2] and Mr. Trentham being shot at Nottingham . . . (H.O.42/138).

(149). [*Printed handbill*]
Manchester, 22 March, 1814.

At an adjourned meeting of the Master Calico Printers, for the consideration of the recently increased and highly injurious restrictions imposed upon the trade by the combined body of journeymen, and stated in their late printed regulations.

It was unanimously resolved as follows,

1. That the ill-advised and unwarrantable proceedings of the journeymen printers, cutters and drawers, are now carried to an extent so alarming as to render it impossible on our part to submit to them without being justly involved in the charge of contributing to the destruction of the block printing branch of the trade.

2. That, after the most mature deliberation, aided by the best legal advice, we are fully convinced the duty we owe to ourselves, and to

---

[1] The Act 22 George II, c. 27 was an Act 'for the more effectual preventing of frauds and abuses committed by persons in the manufacture of hats, and in the woollen, linen, fustian, cotton, iron, leather, fur, hemp, flax, mohair, and silk manufactures ; and for preventing unlawful combinations of journeymen dyers and journeymen hot pressers, and of all persons employed in the said several manufactures . . .' The Act extended the provisions of the Statute 12 George I, c. 34 (' to prevent unlawful combinations of workmen employed in the woollen manufactures . . .') to journeymen dyers, journeymen hot pressers, and all other persons employed in the woollen industry, in the making of felts or hats, in the manufactures of silk, mohair, fur, hemp, flax, linen, cotton, fustian, iron and leather. Persons guilty of unlawful combination were, by the provisions of both Statutes, to be kept to hard labour in a House of Correction, or to be committed to gaol for a period not exceeding three months.

[2] On 28 April, 1812, William Horsfall, a mill-owner at Marsden, was shot at, and died on the 30th. An attempt to murder William Cartwright, another Yorkshire mill-owner, was made ten days earlier ; during this month, too, William Trentham, the hosier, was murderously attacked.

the various working classes who are so materially interested, imperiously calls upon us to exert our united endeavours for the preservation of the print trade.

3. That the necessity of such a union is, at this moment, still more obvious, from the prevailing efforts of rivalship in other countries, where the price of labour is so comparatively low, and where the means of producing work by block and machine printing combined, are unrestricted, and the right of employing any number or description of hands is perfectly unlimited.

4. That it is utterly impracticable to preserve the block-printing trade from ruin, unless those who are concerned are left at full liberty to exercise their own discretion and ingenuity, by which the superiority which this country has established, may be maintained.

5. That the arbitrary restrictions now imposed by the journeymen as to the number of our apprentices, the employment of our machinery, the abatements for spoiled work, and in other material instances, are wholly incompatible with the welfare of the trade at large, and must be absolutely abandoned.

6. That we are not actuated by vindictive motives, in reference to what is past, but are compelled by the pressure of the occasion to avert, if possible, the dangers which threaten the continuance of the block printing business.

7. That the journeymen, by immediately desisting from their inconsiderate and unnatural efforts to deprive their employers of their own discretion in the management of their several concerns, will prevent the institution of measures called for by the illegality of their proceedings ; but if, after the sentiments of these Resolutions are made known to the journeymen, they may nevertheless think fit to persevere, we shall feel obliged to adopt such steps as are calculated most effectually to remove the grievances complained of, and, by so doing, to save the country the incalculable injury of ultimately banishing the cotton trade.

8. That these Resolutions, after they are signed by the master-printers generally, be printed, and copies sent to each establishment, that they be delivered by the masters, or managers, to their journeymen, and the committee are especially authorised to attend to the result.[1] (H.O.42/138).

[1] Thirty-seven signatures follow.

(150). *The Rev. W. R. Hay to John Beckett*

Ackworth, 28 *March,* 1814. (*Private*).
... In another instance, a roller for the purpose of printing was in use at some very extensive works. The men insisted that, inasmuch as that roller was not made by such persons, and under circumstances as they approved, it should not be used. The master remonstrated, and with apparent firmness ; but at length he judged it prudent to give up the roller. The men, not satisfied with this, would not continue to work for him (or, probably, as the term is, would have declared him in a state. of blockade) unless he paid the expenses of their combination, £1 16s. od. This he did, and I have since been informed that some other demand for expenses was insisted upon and paid ... When the masters, with the law in their hands, dare not put it into force, the case is very serious. The evil complained of is vital : it will run through every branch of trade ... (H.O.42/138).

(151). *C. Swainson and Co. to Viscount Sidmouth*

Bannister Hall, near Preston, Lancashire, 31 *March,* 1814.
... A demand having been made by the journeymen calico printers for five guineas being paid to them for each apprentice when taken into our service, not being the son of a printer (one guinea only being demanded if the apprentice be a printer's son) we have refused to comply with so unjust a demand.

Delegates were immediately sent by the journeymen, to take '*the sense of the trade*' as to whether they should turn out in a body and refuse working for us or not. Thinking that this mode of proceeding might not injure us so much as some other plan in consequence of many of our journeymen having been employed by us for a very considerable number of years, it was supposed they might by some offers from their employers be induced to desert the combination, it was agreed that from time to time our journeymen should be withdrawn from us and no other printer be allowed to be taken in their stead, until in a few weeks the works should be entirely deserted. The whole of our apprentices are to be carried off, and we believe Ireland is fixed upon for the purpose of preventing if possible our discovering them. We are in hourly expectation of these plans being put in practice—for already some few of the men have left the works . . .[1] (H.O.42/138).

(152). *George Coldham (Town Clerk) to John Beckett*

Nottingham, 7 April, 1814.[2]

. . . It is simply an attempt on the part of the men to induce their masters to raise their wages, to accomplish which they have had recourse to entreaties and means to intimidate. Messrs. Needham and Nixon are amongst the most respectable hosiers in the trade, but they have been one of the leading houses in refusing to advance 2d. a pair to a certain description of the workmen who have requested and demanded it of their masters. Their frames have been broken to intimidate them into a compliance with this demand. From a considerable intimacy with Mr. Needham I know that this line of conduct would not have had its desired effect upon them, but the trade have pretty unanimously determined to agree to the advance, and in consequence they have reluctantly and against their judgement been compelled to submit with the rest.

I have reason to think that this submission, which I lament as a most ungenerous mode of procedure towards Messrs. Needham and Nixon's on the part of the general body of hosiers, and a most impolitic act on the part of themselves, will however for the present, produce a total cessation of all hostile movement on the part of the framework-knitters, and I have reason to know that the hosiers entertain the same opinion on the subject . . . (H.O.42/138).

(153). *Lewis Allsopp, J.P., to John Beckett*

Nottingham, Friday evening, 22 April 1814.
. . . There is a regular communication with these people of Sheffield, where the workmen have struck, and it would be desirable to obtain information therefrom. Lord Sidmouth's attention should be directed to this, and to the propriety of examining at the post offices here and at the different places where committees of this Society are

---

[1] A combination to prevent a master from employing apprentices except on certain conditions, might be prosecuted before the magistrates by the Act 39 and 40 George III, c. 106.

[2] Three days earlier he had reported to Beckett that ' the organised system of combination amongst the framework-knitters has begun to act in the former mode of breaking frames.' (H.O.42/138).

established, the letters, as some may by chance be sent in that way, though they are doubtless communicated by the coaches and by private hands. A great difficulty is, what afterwards can be done. Lord Sidmouth must consider whether the magistrates have sufficient power to seize these people and their papers ; if not, such power ought to be given by Parliament, as well as the punishment made greater than the law seems now to inflict upon persons guilty of unlawful combinations . . . (H.O.42/138).

(154). *George Coldham to John Beckett*

Nottingham, 28 April, 1814.
. . . It is a most difficult matter to find a framework-knitter upon whom we can rely to obtain and give us information. Every constable as such is known, and is more or less an object of suspicion. It is astonishing how clearly we can perceive that some of the leading characters, as we believe, of these formidable Societies are engaged almost continually in watching the movements of all persons evidently acting in opposition to them. I have little doubt that the late breaking of frames were directed by the executive committee of the Union . . .[1] (H.O.42/138).

(155). *George Coldham to Viscount Sidmouth*

Nottingham, 10 *May,* 1814.
. . . Through a secret and confidential channel Alderman Ashwell has learnt and desires me to communicate the same to your Lordship, that the sums collected the week before last by the Union Society in Nottingham alone amounted to £115. It appears that when any men turn out, as it is called, against their masters, that the Club furnish them with subsistence . . . (H.O.42/138).

---

[1] The Union was a federation of societies of framework-knitters, founded in 1813.

On the 27th, William Walker, Mayor of Leicester, reported that James Rawson, jun., a hosier in the town, had received a threatening letter, and said that this ' spirit of mischief ' must be crushed in the bud. ' This is the first manifestation of it in this town, but I am sorry to add that some serious disturbances have taken place at Hinckley upon the same subject, and I understand that the hosiers there have in consequence yielded to some of the men's demands.' (H.O.42/138).

(156). *John Beckett to George Coldham*

Whitehall, 17 May, 1814.

I am directed by Lord Sidmouth to acknowledge the receipt of your letter of the 11th inst., submitting for his Lordship's consideration the suggestion of the Mayor and Aldermen of Nottingham, that the publicans of Nottingham should be required on applying for a renewal of their licences, to give in an account of every Club or Association meeting at their respective houses, and of the nature and design of such Clubs, with other particulars respecting them.

Lord Sidmouth having given the fullest consideration to this suggestion, I have received his directions to acquaint you that in his opinion it would be by no means advisable to adopt it. It appears to his Lordship that in all probability no account of the Associations in question would be rendered by the publicans sufficiently accurate or satisfactory to enable the magistrates to put them down, or to punish the members of them for acts already done ; and that the enquiry so made of the publicans would in all likelihood have the immediate effect of driving the Clubs which have hitherto assembled at public houses, to meet in future at private ones, where it will be much more difficult if not impossible to get at them or to procure information respecting their proceedings. His Lordship thinks that too much caution cannot be used in the mode of procuring information respecting these Associations, and that without such caution every source of information will be of necessity dried up. His Lordship hopes however that no pains will be spared to collect evidence of their associating, though the difficulty of doing so may be great—relying as he does with much confidence on the vigilance of the magistracy of the town of Nottingham. (H.O.43/23/9-11).

(157). *George Coldham to John Beckett*

Nottingham, 22 May, 1814.
Private and confidential.

I write to inform you that on Wednesday last a very numerous meeting of the hosiers was held at the Police Office Tavern at which a very liberal subscription was set on foot to counteract the formidable combination in force and activity amongst the frameworkknitters. At this meeting a Secret Committee was appointed upon the plan which was last year adopted by the Corporation, by a very small number of the original meeting selected by the Chairman without the knowledge of the body forming the meeting ; and this select number nominated the Committee, which consists of a still smaller and in fact a very inconsiderable number . . . Its plan is to obtain information and to act upon it by calling upon the executive power to appeal to the Legislature for such an amendment of the law as they may deem adequate to remedy the evil . . . (H.O.42/139).

(158). *George Coldham to Viscount Sidmouth*

Nottingham, 23 May, 1814.

As Secretary of a committee lately appointed by the hosiers of Nottingham in consequence [of] a public meeting in London of gentlemen connected with this manufactory, in order to oppose the present alarming and dangerous combination amongst the framework-knitters, I am directed with the utmost deference and respect to suggest to your Lordship's consideration that it has occurred to the committee that the immediate disbanding (if it could be accomplished without any material inconvenience to his Majesty's service) of the Leicester and Nottingham and Derbyshire Regiments of Militia, but particularly the Nottingham Regiment, would very much tend to frustrate the system upon which the Nottingham Union Society is at present acting. They have lately compelled large masses of the framework-knitters working for different houses to strike and give over working for them. Already the hands of Messrs. J. and G. Ray and Co. have struck at their suggestion or commands. It is rumoured that they are about to force the hands of another house, Messrs. Beardmore and Co., to come to a similar determination. Under these circumstances the more framework-knitters were at home in a situation to receive work, the more equal would the hosiers be to meet the efforts of this formidable combination, and the more likely would they be to find persons ready to supply the places of those whom these committees may be enabled to persuade to act upon their system. Every accession of numbers of persons wanting employment, which can be sent home and placed in such a situation as to be enabled to supply the deficiency in the regular workmen withdrawn from their masters by the combination, must, in the judgement of the committee, be a powerful occasion of embarrassment to the system that the framework-knitters are pursuing . . .[1] (H.O.42/139).

[1] Coldham communicated to the Home Office the names of the secret committee, on 7 June : Thomas Carpenter Smith and Joseph Churchill, of Nottingham, and Matthew Needham, of Lenton ; these three co-opted John Parker, jun., and James Hooley (H.O.42/139).

(159). *The Rev. John T. Becher to John Beckett*

Southwell, 24 May, 1814.

. . . The Union Society, as it is styled, does not conceal its existence . . . The principal leader is stated to be Grosvenor[1] Henson . . . Henson does not now work at his trade, but is maintained by the Association at a weekly allowance of about three guineas. In connection with him are many desperate characters, who are strongly suspected of being the frame-breakers and the instruments of popular vengeance upon all who, in the language of the Society, are 'denounced' . . . It is not imagined that this Nottingham gang has ever been broken up by the prosecutions formerly instituted, and the terror impressed upon the minds of the manufacturers by the existence of such a daring conspiracy has placed the masters in a state of almost unqualified submission to the demands of the workmen, who dictate their own terms. Every branch of the lace and hosiery trades is represented by a set of delegates, and these sub-committees hold a regular communication with the grand executive committee . . .

Mr. Nixon ascribes the demolition of his frames to the modification of the Frame-Breaking Bill by substituting transportation for life instead of capital punishment at the renewal of the Act . . . He feels convinced that the order for demolishing his frames was issued by Henson, and that the evidence which he gave against the Bill for regulating the framework-knitting trade, and his non-compliance with the exorbitant demands of the workmen are the sources of provocation. He has now been compelled to advance the prices of labour in defence of his property, though the Nottingham hosiers are manufacturing at from 10 to 20% above those at Tewkesbury, and the rate of workmanship is such as to preclude the prospect of a successful competition with the foreign markets.

In the silk-stocking trade, all the workmen of Mr. Ray have struck because he rejected their application for an increase of wages.

The framesmiths have discontinued their employment for similar reasons, and are collecting money to sustain themselves.

The bricklayers, encouraged by the success of the journeymen in the hosiery trade, are endeavouring to effect their purpose by a conspiracy of the same description. I enclose one of the handbills which they are now diligently circulating . . .

Such an extensive system of insubordination and terror will, I

---

[1] Generally spelt Gravener.

conceive, be deemed incompatible with the existence of our manufactures ; and apprised as we are of the industry and success with
which these principles are disseminated throughout the empire, the
expediency of some remedy will unquestionably be acknowledged.

To devise the means of prevention constitutes the difficulty.
Specific regulations between the masters and the workmen appear
to be utterly impracticable. Labour must find its own value in the
market, but the standard ought to be established by free competition, unrestricted by combination on either side. With this view I
have strenuously urged some of the manufacturers to prefer an
application to Parliament . . . To render the Bill palatable, the
masters as well as the men should be prohibited from combinations,
and to secure efficiency, the existing punishments should be considerably augmented.

For my own part I attribute the late as well as the present outrages to those Jacobinical principles with which the inferior orders
have been sedulously inoculated by our Nottingham Reformers, who
have, in many instances, become the objects of that secret organisation and malevolent confederacy which they fostered by their
pernicious examples, their licentious harangues, and their seditious
Press for the attainment of their factious projects. Thus have the
evils, of which I complain, been introduced and cherished until they
have become intimately incorporated with the state of society in
this and other manufacturing districts. I do not apprehend that the
result will produce any general tumult, but I foresee that the
ferment will not subside without it be coerced by the interposition
of the Legislature.[1] (H.O.42/139).

---

[1] The following printed handbill, enclosed in the above letter, was circulated
at Southwell on 22 May, 1814, by an emissary from the Society at Nottingham.
There is a printer's error in the date :

To the Journeymen Bricklayers of the Town and County of Nottingham, the
Town and County of Leicester, the Town and County of Derby, the City and
County of Lincoln, or elsewhere.

Gentlemen—Your brother journeymen of the same branch in Nottingham,
having experienced a very severe winter, and the price of provisions being so
high, we have solicited our masters to advance our wages to 4s. per day. We
therefore hope you as brothers in the same trade, that none of you will come
from any County at a lower price, whilst we are striving for the good of the
trade.

We are, Gentlemen, your most obedient humble servants,

The Bricklayers of Nottingham.

10 April, 1813.

(160). *George Coldham to John Beckett*

Nottingham, 21 June, 1814. Private and confidential.
Ever since about the 26th of April the efforts of the combination
here have been directed against the house of J. and George Ray of
this place, who are manufacturers of plain silk goods to a very great
extent, but manufacturers whom the combination have thought
most particularly assailable by them because they are not, correspondent [*sic*] to the extent of their business, proprietors of frames,
but manufacture their goods from what are here called independent
frames. Such persons are therefore at all times more dependent than
the owners of frames, upon the master and journeymen frameworkers.
The blow which has been struck by the combination upon this house
is a very heavy one, for it has reached to deprive them of the work
of between 200 and 300 hands. Messrs. Ray were fully aware of the
nature of their situation, and Mr. John Ray, the partner here to
whom the management of the business of the manufactory is almost
exclusively confided, was very much disposed to give the advanced
price demanded by the combination, with a view to prevent the
temporary derangement of their business. It was however very important to the Secret Committee and the great body of the trade
not only ultimately to frustrate the plans of the combination, but to
prevent if possible their succeeding in them as connected with the
house of Messrs. Ray. With this view I have been in constant communication and treaty with Mr. John Ray from the 24th of May to
the present moment. There was considerable difficulties in the way
of this arrangement. The bulk of the houses possess very considerable property in frames, and through them contrive to acquire the
entire control over their workmen. Perhaps the most effectual manner in which the combination could coerce them was their former
manner of carrying on war by destroying their frames. Mr. Ray
however was not accessible to this mode of attack, but then he was
still more accessible by the system upon which they acted against
him. They applied to the workmen employed by him, and they
engaged these to leave off working to him unless he should advance
their wages, and to induce them to do this they undertook to pay
their weekly wages for being idle, or to employ them in performing
the business of the combination. Messrs. Ray were not at all in-
sensible to the extent of the value of their opposition to the demands
of the workmen, to the rest of the trade, and indeed it is but justice
to them to admit that the consciousness of their peculiar situation

with their workmen had placed them in a very unpleasant predicament in this respect, for Messrs. Ray had proposed in consequence of an engagement, as I believe, with their workmen to do so, the very advance which the combination demanded, and which the great body of the trade had refused to grant to the framework-knitters. Mr. John Ray therefore required of the Secret Committee and the rest of the trade that they should state those facts to the public in the manner most calculated to vindicate Messrs. Ray, and show the peculiar ingratitude of the attack of the combination as directed against those who had been the best friends of the workmen. This, however, the secret committee positively refused doing, because they felt that it [would] endanger the transferring the whole odium of the refusal from Messrs. Ray upon the rest of the trade, because it seemed in some degree to countenance the propriety of the advance demanded, and because they were of opinion that there were other parts of the conduct of Messrs. Ray's conduct to their workmen [sic] which would admit of the trade identifying themselves with the defence of their general conduct to their workmen. In the difficulty which these clashing opinions produced, the secret committee appealed to a still larger body of the trade than themselves, and communicated from them to him a full and complete vindication of the conduct which the secret committee proposed to adopt. I had given up the whole arrangement for lost when on the 10th of June I was fortunate enough, with the concurrence of the secret committee, to come to an entire understanding with Mr. John Ray, effected, I have little doubt, in consequence of the sincere and zealous co operation we received from the committee in London. This agreement produced the printed address from the secret committee which I enclose, and it has also produced an order from Mr. Ray to his warehouseman to give evidence against some of the leading master framework-knitters with a view to the reaching through them some of the most reprehensible of the workmen engaged in this conspiracy, not without hopes through them of reaching some of the principal actors in the combination. This has only been done yesterday, but I shall proceed without loss of time to try our legal strength upon the evidence by an appeal to the magistrates. In the meantime the support of the combination by the great body of the framework-knitters seems evidently upon the decay, for this week they have been forced by their necessities to make their collections in the town and country by eight or ten of the hands who have used threats to induce the framework-knitters to keep up their usual contributions. We had prepared a handbill to set this matter at rest, but upon a perfect knowledge of the manner in which the pulse of the people beats, the secret committee have adjourned the commencement of their attack upon this part of the system of the confederacy until Friday next, when I hope to obtain the co-operation of the magistrates to the same point, and it will appear at the very same time when the combination will also be attacked through the medium of the conviction of some of their abettors, either for neglecting their work or for being otherwise engaged in the combination. In the meantime the secret committee are extremely impatient that they have learnt no tidings of a communication made by them very early indeed after their appointment, to the committee in London, with a view to its being transmitted to Lord Sidmouth, which communication contained some hints of what they were of opinion would be the best means of giving general legislative relief from the dreadful effects of such extensive combinations as the present . . . (H.O.42/139).

[The following printed handbill was enclosed in the above letter.]

Nottingham, 16 June, 1814.

It having been unanimously determined at a large and respectable meeting of hosiers, held in London on the 21st day of April last, convened to take into consideration the propriety of a proposal then made for advancing the price of manufacturing plain silk hose, that such advance should be resisted by the trade at large ; and that in consequence of the recent renewal of the practice of breaking frames, a Society should be formed for the purpose of prosecuting framebreakers and other purposes connected therewith, and such deteration having been sanctioned by the approbation of a subsequent very numerous and highly respectable meeting of the hosiers and lace manufacturers resident in this town, held at Nottingham on the 18th day of May last for the same purposes, at which last meeting a committee, secretary and solicitor were appointed for the conduct and management of the general business of the Society then instituted. And it appearing to that committee, that in consequence of the adherence of the house of G. and J. Ray to the general determination of the trade not to give the advanced price, that the plain-silk workmen of that house since the 26th day of April last—and that subsequently part of the plain-silk hands of Beardmores and Parker, have combined together and ceased to work, with a view to compel those houses to give the advance. The committee appointed by the

O

meeting held in Nottingham on the 18th day of May last, being fully aware that the houses of Messrs. G. and J. Ray, and Beardmores and Parker, have suffered inconvenience—been rendered unpopular and harassed by the combination, in consequence of their acting in conformity with the unanimous opinion of the meetings of the persons engaged in the manufactory; have felt it their duty to declare that it is still the full purpose and resolution of the trade in general, in conjunction with the aforesaid houses, to resist the advance of price—to decline every appearance of a compromise or settlement thereof—and to pursue all legal means to break up a combination so fatal to the true interests of hosiers and framework-knitters.

The committee for themselves and the great body of the plain-silk hose manufacturers feel bound to refuse employment to any work-man who shall appear to have struck for an advance of wages, or who are otherwise engaged in this illegal combination; and to give every assistance and support to the houses of G. and J. Ray and Beardmores and Parker, by every accommodation in their power with respect to the conduct of their trade, so long as they shall be the object of attack by the present combination.

By Order of the Committee,

George Coldham, Secretary.

(161). *George Coldham (Town Clerk) to John Beckett*

Nottingham, 2 July, 1814.

On Friday sennight last we summoned before the magistrates in the name of Messrs. Ray's, but in reality under the direction of the secret committee, a great number of Mr. Ray's master hands, under a charge made against them by the managing warehouseman of Messrs. Ray's, of having neglected their work in the hope that these men could have been induced as one man to step forward and put an end to this nefarious combination. At first we seemed likely to be successful. One of the master hands came forward and told us the plain truth. He acknowledged that he believed that they could if they chose put a stop to these proceedings by forcing the men to work and preventing the contributions to the combination, but he called upon us to obtain for him a fair and reasonable pro-portion of the other master hands to act with him. He expected their co-operation, but he was mistaken: there was only one other heartily disposed to act a similar part, the rest appeared devoted to the combination and had committed themselves beyond the power of retracting. There was some satisfaction in coming at the truth, although it boded us much more trouble than we at first anticipated. But we had taken up some also of Mr. Ray's journeymen in consequence of being possessed of some private information respecting them . . . By the mouth of one of these I obtained information which implicated three of the leading members of the committee, three of the leading managers and directors . . . of the whole Society.

The state of the trade is putting them down and I hope they can't stand long, but we must not, I am well aware, slacken our vigilance on account of any appearances of stillness.

Ibid. to Ibid., Nottingham, 5 *July*, 1814 :—. . . The magistrates . . . apprehended two of the committee[1] in their general weekly night of assembling, and brought away all their books and papers, which, from the hasty looking at them we have yet been enabled to give, contain the accounts from 1812 [of] the origin of the Union Society to the present moment.

Ibid. to Ibid., Nottingham, 7 *July*, 1814 :—. . . On Tuesday evening late the magistrates heard their cases, the third person implicated in these charges, Samuel Simpson, not having been apprehended, and they convicted them both upon the evidence of William Robinson, the warehouseman of Messrs. Ray, and Joseph Brookhouse, a framework-knitter working to Mr. Ray, who had been employed by the committee in collecting for [*sic*] receiving money of the said Joseph Brookhouse for these illegal purposes. As this was the first prosecution under the Combination Act, it was not thought politic to push the conviction up to the full extent the law would have warranted, either on the part of the prosecution or the magistrates, and they were accordingly sentenced to one month's imprisonment to hard labour in the House of Correction . . . I hope a great deal of good has been done, although the combination does not yet seem prepared to dissolve itself.

Ibid. to Ibid., Nottingham, 11 *July*, 1814. I herewith send you for Lord Sidmouth's information a short memorandum or note[2] of the contents of such of the papers as have appeared upon our inspection of them most material in developing the nature and extent of the

---

[1] George Gibson and Thomas Judd.
[2] This is not reproduced as it is not particularly illuminating.

late operations of the combination as applied to the turning out and supporting the hands of Messrs. George and John Ray in striking upon a demand for an advance of price which the members of the combination now admit in all its bearings to have been exorbitant. I also send for Lord Sidmouth's inspection an account of the funds of the Society extracted from their books during the existence of the application of their means to the purpose above stated. The main prop of the Exchequer has been borrowing money for the purpose of being applied to manufacturing, and by this means they have produced a great many silk hose which are now sent to London to be sold . . . [1](H.O.42/140).

(162). *L. Allsopp to John Beckett*

Nottingham, 31 *July*, 1814.

I have taken the opportunity of having some conversation with Mr. Coldham on the subject of the degree of punishment inflicted by the magistrates on the two men convicted of the unlawful combination. He informs me that he appeared before the magistrates in the situation of prosecutor as secretary to the Association of the hosiers, that upon this subject he had no communication with the magistrates, and that he was much disappointed at the punishment. As far as I could make out there was some communication between the magistrates and the parties implicated, and the former proceeded upon a mistaken hope that lenity might be productive of good. The

---

[1] The copy of the accounts starts on 25 April, 1814. It shows that money was collected practically daily to assist the strikers, the largest amount collected in one day being £53 4s. 5d. on 2 May. Subscriptions to the Society, together with collections, amounted to the substantial sum of £1,302 10s. 7½d. between 25 April and 4 July.

Those who collected money were paid for the work. The total amount paid out between 25 April and 4 July was £903 12s. 2d. Early items in the account on the expenditure side were as follows :

			£	s.	d.
April	25	Bellman		5	3
		Paid collectors	1	4	6
	29	Paid for collecting		14	9
		Paid cash drawn of Rollett	60	1	0
		—————————————— for Rayner	1	5	0
		——————————————————	15	15	8
May	4	Drawn of Rollett for Mansfield	10	10	0
	5	—————————————— Derby	20	0	0

proceedings of last Tuesday night . . . must have satisfied these gentlemen of their error. Coldham says the committee affects to be broken up. The conduct of these deluded men on Tuesday night was most daring and atrocious[1] (H.O.42/140).

(163). *H. Enfield (Deputy Town Clerk)*[2] *to Viscount Sidmouth*

Nottingham, 11 August, 1814.

The Mayor having received an important communication from Mr. Thomas Fraser, the Procurator Fiscal of Dumfries, relative to the alarming combination at present existing amongst the workmen in the hosiery manufactory, has directed me to transmit to your Lordship a copy thereof for the information of Government . . . (H.O.42/140).

[*Enclosures.*]
S. Simpson to Unknown Correspondent

Nottingham, 16 *June*, 1814. (*Copy*).

Sir—Having seen a letter you have sent to your brother Timothy expressing the disposition of the trade of Dumfries to join their friends in England in uniting themselves under the Union, I feel it my duty to give you every information on the subject. You will see

---

[1] Two days later the Town Clerk of Nottingham reported that frame-breaking had started again. He added, ' I have reason to believe that the combination are about to abandon their attempts to regulate the prices of wages by turning out the workmen, and I am apprehensive that more frames will be broken. I regard, however, their change of plan as indicative of their weakness.' These combinations were not broken up, as Major-General Sir Henry Fane's letter to Lord Sidmouth, dated Nottingham, 24 October, 1816, shows : . . . 'In respect to Nottingham and its vicinity, I have made all the enquiry I can, and especially relative to the recent outrages committed upon the frames of manufacturers. It appears that certain combinations exist, professing to have the object of regulating trade, and the dealings between the master manufacturers and the workmen ; that the persons so combining have agreed upon a *minimum* of wages to be paid for certain descriptions of work ; and that when a master manufacturer employs workmen at a less rate than this fixed minimum, his frames immediately become in danger from the machinations of the aforesaid combinations. It is not a war against any particular description of loom but against all looms let for work below certain fixed rates of wages. Therefore it is to *the power of dictation in respect to wages* to which these outrages are directed, and they are upon the same principle as those which have recently been detected in the hat trade'. (H.O.42/154).

[2] He became Town Clerk in 1815, following the death of Mr. Coldham.

by the Articles that the intent of the Institution is to unite every branch for the support of each other in times of distress. The Institution has been found to be very beneficial to every branch, as we have all received a small advance on our work except the plain silk hands, which we are now contending for. We have had 300 hands out of employ for more than six weeks because the hosiers have not the honour[1] to give a reasonable advance. The hosiers have formed a powerful combination against us, but this we have not cared for, we have persevered, and resolved to persevere until we accomplish the object in view which we hope is not far distant.

The Union is well established in Nottingham, Derby and their Counties, and is making very rapid progress throughout Leicestershire, London, Godalming, Tewkesbury and Northamptonshire have all formed themselves, and we have long wished to form an interest in North Britain in order that the principle may be diffused throughout the north ; and we are happy to find that Dumfries is anxious to set the example, and hope when you have formed yourselves, you will disseminate the principle through all Scotland ; for depend upon it, if the trade are united and true to their own interest, we shall be able to make our trade as respectable as any other in the kingdom, and no longer be designated by the application of 'stracking stockingers.' According to request I have sent four Articles and 60 Diplomas,[2] that you may form yourselves as soon as possible . . . I hope you will excuse us not writing sooner, as we are now so throng, we have scarcely time to attend to anything but the turn-out.

N.B.—Direct for me, Newton's Head, Glasshouse Lane, Nottingham.

Thomas Fraser to the Mayor of Nottingham

Dumfries, 6 August, 1814. (*Copy*).

A correspondence having lately been discovered to have commenced here betwixt the journeymen stocking makers and their brethren in Nottingham, for the purpose of forming an Association of the trade to be connected with and dependent upon the General Society of Nottingham, the master of the trade became alarmed, and made application to the magistrates of this town, who, upon a complaint from me as Procurator Fiscal of the Burgh, granted a

---

[1] Probably ' humour ' in the original.
[2] Trade Union membership cards.

warrant for apprehending and bringing before them the persons complained upon for examination. There were accordingly five journeymen brought forward, who stated that although they had had some correspondence with the Nottingham journeymen, they had entered into no resolutions in consequence thereof, nor formed themselves into any Society. They at the same time produced a letter from an S. Simpson, a Secretary of one of the committees in Nottingham, strongly urging them immediately to form themselves into an Association connected with the principal Society there ; they also produced some printed Regulations and 60 what Simpson in his letter calls Diplomas.

The magistrates as well as the masters here, who are anxious to prevent as much as lies in their power the diffusion of principles so injurious to the trade and so subversive of the peace of the country, have desired me to hand you a copy of Simpson's letter which is prefixed. I enclose at the same time one of the Diplomas for your information.

(164). *Viscount Sidmouth to Kirkman Finlay*

8 October, 1814. (*Copy*).

I thank you for your letter of the 4th instant, which I received by the post of yesterday, which also brought me letters from the Lord Advocate and Mr. Connell,[1] all relating to the discovery, recently made, of a system of combination amongst the calico printers in England, Scotland and Ireland to raise their wages. The vigilance and promptitude of Mr. Connell upon this occasion have been highly meritorious ; and I trust that the information already obtained, will furnish a clue to further discoveries. I shall avail myself of it for this purpose without delay.

What is already known will be extremely useful when the subject of combination is brought, as in my opinion it must be, under the consideration of Parliament.[2] (H.O.42/140).

---

[1] Sheriff Depute of the County of Renfrew.

[2] Sidmouth wrote that day to the Lord Advocate of Scotland, saying that the Postmaster at Glasgow would be directed to stop all letters addressed to Alexander McGregor at Anderston ; to Kitchen, of Penny Street, Blackburn, Lancs.; and to a calico printer named Downs, of Dublin. Such letters would be transmitted to the Lord Advocate, who would be asked to send copies to the Home Office.

(165). *Viscount Sidmouth to the Earl of Lonsdale*

Richmond Park, 27 October, 1814. *Confidential.* (*Copy*).
. . . Of the combination you mention[1] I have long been apprised.
Three active members of it were apprehended at Glasgow about a
month ago, through the vigilance and activity of the Sheriff of
Renfrew, and no doubt is entertained of their being convicted. Copies
of the papers found upon them were sent to me, and by means of the
information thus afforded, very important information has been
obtained.

The immediate object of the combination is to dictate the rate of
wages ; and it comprehends the calico printers and weavers of
Glasgow, Manchester, Blackburn, &c., and of Dublin. Persons of that
description at Carlisle are deeply engaged in it ; and it is material
that great caution should be observed in seeking for information
there, as the excitement of alarm would destroy the means which
we now possess of obtaining intelligence from that quarter . . .

The Attorney-General is out of town, but the Solicitor-General
is to be at the Home Office to-morrow, as I wish to consult him as
to the course to be pursued. I incline to think that more *rope* must
be given, but I am satisfied that, in the ensuing Session, the interference of Parliament will be indispensably necessary. (H.O.42/140).

(166). *A. Colquhoun to Viscount Sidmouth*

Edinburgh, 26 December, 1814.
I transmitted to your Lordship some weeks ago the indictment
against five of the combined calico printers whose trial stood for
this day. They were in Edinburgh yesterday, but, dreading the issue,
did not appear this morning and were fugitated or outlawed, and
their bail bonds forfeited. (H.O.102/24).

(167). *Viscount Sidmouth to A. Colquhoun*

Richmond Park, 1 *January,* 1814 [1815].
It gave me great pleasure to learn that the five calico printers whose
trials stood for Monday last, have, by their non-appearance, put
their guilt, and the means of proving it, out of the question. It would,
however, have afforded me still greater to have heard that they had
all been convicted and punished.

---

[1] In Lord Lonsdale's letter of the 25th.

The combination, in which I have no doubt these persons were engaged, unquestionably extends to England and Ireland, from various parts of which information has been received, which I have laid before the Attorney and Solicitor-General, together with sundry suggestions for alterations of the existing laws with reference to this evil. I shall be thankful for any information, observations or suggestions, with which your Lordship may favour me on this subject. The report of the Law Officers will be probably made towards the end of this month. (H.O.102/25).

(168). *Charles Swainson to Viscount Sidmouth*

Walton, near Preston, 31 *January,* 1815.
I think it requisite to inform you that as my partner Mr. Baxendale was getting upon the mail coach last night a gun or pistol was fired at him, too evidently, I fear, with the disposition to kill or wound him. I cannot entertain a doubt but the attempt was made by someone connected with the combination of the journeymen calico printers, and I much fear that unless strong means are used to put a stop to such lawless proceedings, we may shortly expect a similar disturbance to what occurred in this County a few years ago. There is, I am happy to say, a most promising disposition on the part of the masters to suppress the combination, and I doubt not they will succeed, but a recurrence of it must shortly be expected unless the masters are supported by strong legislative measures, and the earlier these measures are adopted, the sooner may we expect that the men will return to their employment.

In addition to this unpleasant attempt on the life of Mr. Baxendale, our concern has had to regret an assault made upon some of the workpeople we now employ[1] . . . (H.O.42/142).

---

[1] A reward of 200 guineas was offered to anyone giving information leading to the conviction of the offender, and the master calico printers soon combined to offer an additional reward of 500 guineas. But on 4 February Mr. Swainson wrote again to the Home Office, saying that the supposed attempt on the life of Mr. Baxendale had been satisfactorily explained. The gamekeeper of a neighbouring gentleman had discharged his gun near the mail coach.
The following printed handbill was enclosed :
To the Various Bodies of Mechanics.
Gentlemen—It is generally known that we, the journeymen calico printers as a body of workmen, have had frequent occasion to oppose those proceedings
[*Continued on p. 186*]

[*Continued from p. 185*]

of our employers, which to us have appeared of an arbitrary nature ; and so far we have been successful. But our masters of late have united to overwhelm us, and are now endeavouring to put their oppressive plans into practice. Their grand scheme is to have us all out of work at once, so that we shall not be able to render any assistance one to another.

We are about 1,800 journeymen, and out of these there are about 1,600 men already discharged, besides apprentices. Now you will see that it is impossible for the few that are in work to give any adequate support to the rest that are out.

Our employers have taken the advantage of the depth of winter, because they know we can get no other employ. The state of our finances must be well known to them, as we have had of late a deal of domestic broils to contend with, and our brethren in the sister kingdom, as well as Scotland, to assist and support for a long time back ; so that we deem it expedient to appeal to all the friends of liberty and freedom in whatever way you may be disposed to lend us the right hand of fellowship, either in way of *loan* or *gift*, and it shall not be forgotten. If a *loan*, there shall be an exact account kept and faithfully discharged. If a *gift*, our hand shall always be ready to assist in return, whenever you see it necessary to call upon us, and by so assisting each other in the time of need, we trust we shall yet be like a three-fold cord that cannot be broken. All our men are cool and firm, and in good spirits.

We submit these few general remarks to your candid consideration, and trust that the result will be favourable towards us, assuring you that your assistance will be thankfully received and remembered.

From yours with the greatest respect,

The Journeymen Calico Printers.

VI. THE FIRST YEARS OF PEACE (1815-1817).

The following is a copy of a printed handbill, issued by the Thames Police
Office on 3 August, 1815 :—]
(169).

CAUTION.

The magistrates, being informed that a considerable number of
seamen have for some days past assembled themselves together for
the purpose of obliging the shipowners to dismiss foreign seamen
from the merchant service, and to raise the price of wages, think it
necessary to caution them against persisting in their unlawful
attempts . . . Those who choose to enter into the merchant service
may do so, upon such terms as may be agreed upon between the
shipowners and themselves. On the return of peace the number of
foreign seamen allowed by law to be employed in the merchant
service, must not exceed one fourth of the crew.

Any attempt to compel the dismissal of foreign seamen, by force,
is illegal.

The magistrates are determined, under the authority of Government, to resort to the most effectual means for preventing such
practices in future, and for bringing those concerned in them to
condign punishment. (H.O.42/145).

(170). *Benjamin Sorsbie* (Mayor of Newcastle) *to Major-Gen. Riall*[1]

Newcastle-upon-Tyne, 11 *September*, 1815. (*Copy*).
I beg leave to inform you that the seamen at this port are at present

[1] Enclosed in the Major-General's letter to Sidmouth, York, 13 September,
1815.

in a very alarming state of riot, in consequence of disputes respecting wages between them and the shipowners. The latter have represented to me that the seamen collect together at Shields, to the number of several thousands, and prevent by force any ships going to sea, besides maltreating all well disposed seamen and committing other acts of violence.

The shipowners urgently request the interference of the civil power, and the magistrates at this town are very desirous of doing their duty, but being almost entirely unsupported by military force, I have to request the favour of you to send such troops under your command, as can be spared, without delay. Cavalry is always found particularly serviceable, but it may also become necessary to man the batteries at Shields very effectually, as the seamen threaten to take possession of them in the event of a frigate being sent by the Admiralty, as is expected.

(170a). *Benjamin Sorsbie to Viscount Sidmouth*

Newcastle-upon-Tyne, 15 *September*, 1815.
. . . Matters have remained in nearly the same state, but it is evident that the seamen mean to prevent the ships going to sea, until the issue of their petition to the Lords of the Admiralty is known. (H.D.42/146).

[*Three Enclosures*].
Benjamin Sorsbie to J. W. Croker, Secretary of the Admiralty

Newcastle-upon-Tyne, 14 *August* [*sic*], 1815. (*Copy*).
I beg leave to state to you for the information of the Lords of the Admiralty, that a deputation from the British seamen at this port have waited upon me with a Memorial in which they state that 'from the number of foreign seamen employed in the ships of this port, the memorialists cannot find employment, but are reduced to great distress, and trust that it is in your power to direct the owners and masters of the ships to discharge the foreign seamen so employed.'

To this I have of course replied that I do not possess any such power, but that if, upon enquiry, their case should appear to merit attention, I would make an application in their behalf to his Majesty's Government.

As I find upon enquiry that there really is a want of employment for the full number of British seamen at this port, I trust that such measures as may be deemed expedient will be adopted by their Lordships with as little delay as possible, since very serious consequences may arise if the unemployed seamen should be driven to extremities.

They have already proceeded in some instances to discharge the foreign seamen by force from several ships, and even in cases which bear particularly hard upon the owners, as a certain proportion of foreign seamen is required by law in foreign-built ships navigated under British licenses . . .

R. B. Roxby[1] to Benjamin Sorsbie.

Northumberland Arms, North Shields, 8 September, 1815. (Copy). A meeting of the General Committee of the shipping interest of this port has been held this day in consequence of the very alarming and riotous behaviour of the seamen. The Committee have directed me to communicate to you that the ships have for several days been stopped, and their crews forcibly taken out, and not any seamen are permitted by the rioters to assist even in the common harbour duty of the vessels.

Propositions have been made by the seamen to the shipowners, most of which are utterly inadmissible, but from the great numbers which are assembled and which are daily increasing, it appears absolutely necessary to call for the active co-operation of the civil power having jurisdiction on the river . . .

Jonathan Cockerill to Benjamin Sorsbie

North Shields, 12 September, 1815. (Copy). . . . Not any ships coal laden have yet been permitted to sail except one or two chartered for the Baltic, which by leave from the delegates of the seamen have been allowed to depart. The small Scotch sloops and some coasting ships have also gone. The mates have all been taken out of the vessels by the rioters, and the General Committee have recommended the owners not to load any coals until peace is restored . . .[2]

---

[1] Chairman of the Shipowners' Committee.

[2] The Mayor of Newcastle-on-Tyne informed the Home Secretary on the 22nd that the number of seamen on strike was 'considerably increased in consequence of the arrival of many ships at the port. All seamen are immediately

[*Continued on p. 190*]

(171). *Jos[ep]h Raworth to Earl Bathurst*[3]

Sheffield, 18 *Septemver*, 1815

I hope you will excuse the liberty I have taken in wrighting you, but as a loyal subject I think it my duty to inform you as one of his Majesty's Government the stat of combination in Sheff[iel]d. About 6 week ago my brother and myself thought it prudent to discharge one of our men for combining with the rest to compel us to give a price that they think wright, it not being in their statement* as he had one month's notice to provid for himself according to the custom of this town, but whent, it was only two weeks gon he was orderd by the committee of their combination to strike is work on the Monday. This we did not know untill the Wednesday night, but on the Tuesday we sent him a note saying if he did not com to his work we should put another man in his place. he being the borer of scissor, in which line of business we succeeded Mr. John Humfry about 18 month ago, and one borer is sufficient for an extensive manufactory, in consequence of which we began to be at a stand on the Wednesday. We got a man to take his place, he being ignorant of an order of the Committee order [*sic*] that we should have him or now [*sic*] so he being informed by the men he immediately informed us that he dare not continue any longer as the other had struck work by order of the committee, this being the first information we got of it, and at the same time informed us that there was going to be a meeting of the whole of the workmen in the trade that night at the Rose and Crown Inn . . .

You will naturally say we should appeal to the law, but the law is inefectual, for the utmost punishment is three months imprisonment, and they would send them in chaise and four there and the same back again and support there familys and would fulley stop you from ever making anything more, so if we was to do that it would be the loss of our establishment, which which [*sic*] having so recently bought would be our ruin . . . (H.O.42/146).

[*Continued from p. 189*]
after their so arriving, induced or compelled to join the discontented body, and no ship is permitted to proceed to sea if bound for London or other ports in the south of England.' (H.O.42/146).

[3] Secretary of State for War and the Colonies.

* 'Statements are printed lists which the men have got printed and compell us at their pleasu[re] to pay . . .'

(172). *John Connell[1] to Kirkman Finlay[2]*

Garscube, 2 October, 1815.

You will probably recollect the combinations which took place last year among the calico printers, and with respect to which you had some correspondence with Lord Sidmouth. These combinations were of an extensive and dangerous nature, pervading the greater part of the three kingdoms, but were fortunately put down in Scotland by the measures which were then and afterwards taken.

The system was so well organised in Scotland that although they had reduced their masters almost to a state of dependence upon them, the masters were wholly unacquainted with the detail of their measures, or with the persons most active in the combination ; and for the discovery which then took place, and the beneficial consequences which followed, we were entirely indebted to one of the operatives who communicated the information at first partially by anonymous letters, and afterwards in a more detailed form in the course of several interviews with myself. In consequence McGregor was apprehended, and all the books and papers of the Association were seized.

I was satisfied that the discovery made by this man proceeded from a conviction of the evil consequences which might follow from such a combination, or, to use his own words, might tend 'to shake the State,' but the part which he acted was attended with considerable personal hazard, as from the violence of the people concerned there was reason to believe his life would have been in danger had his good offices been made known.

. . . If it be thought right to reward this man, I can point out a particular fund from which this may be done. A few years ago there were similar combinations among the operative weavers in Scotland. Some of the offenders in Renfrewshire who had been put under bail, did not stand trial, were in consequence fugitated, and their bail bonds forfeited ; and I have now in my possession £100 sterling of bail bond money which I lately received . . .

There was another of the operatives who communicated to me a great deal of useful information both as to what passed here and in England ; and a small part of this sum might perhaps be given to him.[3] (H.O.102/25).

[1] Sheriff Depute of Renfrewshire.

[2] In Finlay's letter to Sidmouth, 12 October, 1815.

[3] Sidmouth wrote to Finlay on the 17th, saying that the sum of £100 should be placed at Mr. Connell's disposal, to be divided between the two informers in such proportions as he should judge proper. (H.O.102/25).

(173). *The Mayor of Yarmouth to Viscount Sidmouth*

Yarmouth, 5 October, 1815.

In consequence of an information on oath this day given before me that a seaman had been taken out of a ship at this port by a large assemblage of mariners to the amount of between 300 and 400, whose object is declared to be an advance of wages and to compel each ship to carry a larger number of hands than usual, I have entered into an examination of the matter, and find that what is passing originates from an example set in the port of Shields . . .

A vessel belonging to this port, and bound here from Shields, was prevented [from] coming to sea from thence, till the master had made an affidavit of his destination and received the inclosed Certificate from a committee consisting of seamen ; and another vessel, also belonging to this port, is now detained there, the crew having refused severally to pay 10s. out of their wages, which was demanded by the committee as a fund for the sailors now standing out for the above purposes at Shields. If this is permitted to continue, similar conduct may ensue, as well at this port as at all other ports on the coast . . . (H.O.42/146).

(174). *H. Cramlington (Mayor of Newcastle) to Viscount Sidmouth*

Newcastle-upon-Tyne, 7 October, 1815.

Since the communications which my predecessor in office, Mr. Sorsbie, had the honour to make to your Lordship of the disturbed state of the seamen of this port, the magistrates of this town and those of the adjoining counties of Northumberland and Durham, have, (influenced by their desire to avoid the necessity of measures of coercion) acted as mediators between the seamen and their employers. Some approach towards a conciliation had been made, but the shipowners of the port having this day at a very numerous meeting come to a general resolution that the demands of the seamen cannot be complied with, and having called for the protection of the magistrates, it seems now to be their duty to seek for such a naval and military force as will enable them to act with effect . . .

The present state of this part of the country is already sufficiently alarming, and each coming day adds to the number of the tumultuous. But, my Lord, the mischief must spread—the great bodies of keelmen or lightermen, of pitmen and of waggon men, whose bread depends on the coal trade (now entirely stopped) must in a very few days be without employment, and it is greatly to be feared that their strength will be added to that of the seamen . . . (H.O.42/146).

(175). *Dr. Robert Gray*[1] *to Viscount Sidmouth*

Rectory, Bishop Wearmouth, 11 *Ocober,* 1815.
. . . I feel it incumbent on me to state to your Lordship that as the conciliatory measures now in contemplation here at Shields at length embrace a sufficient pledge to the sailors that a competent number of men will be employed aboard the ships, and that the surplus number will be provided for, but little hope of an amicable adjustment will remain, unless it should be deemed expedient by his Majesty's Ministers to sanction under the peculiar difficulties of the case, the intervention of some persons of higher rank in the naval and commercial departments, and who, under the expectation which prevails that the affair must come before Parliament, might settle a temporary arrangement.

The combination is the more formidable as the men have had just grounds of complaint and suspicion, and the shipowners have slowly and reluctantly consented to measures which were judged necessary by all impartial persons. In consequence of these circumstances the prevailing sentiment is in favour of the sailors, and your Lordship will perceive that there may be reason to apprehend that the influence of that sentiment may spread where it would be most serious . . .

Ibid to Ibid., Bishop Wearmouth, 14 *October,* 1815 :— . . . My wish as I believe that of all the magistrates, has been that the shipowners should give some pledge of the sincerity of their intentions to man the ships in future sufficiently for security ; and by some explicit assurance, or publication of their plan, do away the complaints and suspicions which unhappily had arisen. It was evident that such measures were necessary to deprive the sailors of the only reasonable ground on which they stood, and thereby dissolve the strongest bond which unites them together.

A scale has at length been agreed upon by the shipowners here and offered to the sailors, and it has been rejected by them as too low, with a declaration that they will not accede to any terms but those which they themselves have proposed, and in conjunction only with the seamen of Shields.

[1] Rector of Bishop Wearmouth and Prebendary of Durham.

P

From the information which I have received I do not despair of an adjustment at Shields, where the head committee of the sailors sits and where warrants are issued to be executed, if conciliatory measures should fail; but some of the shipowners here propose to bring forward informations upon which the magistrates must act immediately. Every measure, however, will be tried which may prevent a contest of which the effects would be most serious and permanent, and to detach if possible the well disposed from those mischievous men who control them. As the subject for regulating the number of men to be employed aboard the ships with some reference to the keelage or tonnage will probably come under the consideration of Parliament, it may possibly be of some use that your Lordship should know that the principle was approved, and the scale adopted at the public meeting of the shipowners by a majority of 38.

I take the liberty of sending the two extreme scales,[1] that of the shipowners and that of the sailors, and a third recommended by an experienced man.[2] (H.O.42/146).

1

Keels	Shipowners' Scale		Sailors' Scale		Mr. Moore's Scale	
	Men	Boys	Men	Boys	Men	Boys
6	4	2	5	1	5	1
7	5	2	5	2	5	2
8	5	2	6	2	6	2
9	6	2	6	3	6	2
10	6	3	7	3	7	2
11	7	2	7	3	7	2
12	7	3	8	3	8	2
13	7	4	9	4	9	3
14	8	3	9	4	9	3
15	8	3	11	4	10	3
16					10	3
17 & 18					11	3
19 & 20					12	3

Wages 4 guineas per voyage. Proposed at a meeting of the committee of shipowners on the 11th, and adopted by them on the 13th. (H.O.42/146).

[2] In another document the seamen stipulated that boys above the age of 17 or 18 should be reckoned as men, provided that they had been two years and upwards at sea; and two boys under the age of 17 should be reckoned as one man.

(176). *H. Cramlington to Viscount Sidmouth*

Newcastle-on-Tyne, 14 October, 1815.

. . . The proposed arrangement between the seamen of this port and their employers continues to hold out to us the gratifying prospect of terminating the unhappy differences between them, and of restoring order to the port. The shipowners have taken the necessary preliminary measures to carry their regulation into effect, and it is hoped that by Monday next the ships will have received on board their increased complement of men, and that they will soon after be got to sea . . .

5 *o'clock p.m.* P.S. I am this moment informed that some of the seamen have to-day shown a strong disposition to be dissatisfied with the arrangement. (H.O.42/146).

(177). *John Cartwright to Viscount Sidmouth*

North Shields, Saturday night, 14 October, 1815.

. . . During the war the masters of colliers have been accustomed to make their voyages with very few hands, giving those few good wages, viz., from £7 to £9 for the voyage ; and the number of hands has commonly averaged in the ratio of about 3 men and a boy for 100 tons.

The first question in the negotiation was the wages, which they succeeded in settling at £5 per voyage. The next, the number of hands. The shipowners promised their vessels should be *sufficiently manned,* and always *liable to the judgment of the harbour master* in this point—but the men peremptorily say it shall be fixed at 6 *men and a boy* for the hundred tons (the transport service, I am told, requires 5 men and a boy). Report says the owners have this afternoon, as an ultimatum, offered to fix it at 5 and a boy. In the meantime, my Lord, these men meet regularly every morning, when the names are called over. They have appointed a committee which, after the meeting, adjourns to a public house, and remains all the day, ready to grant passports in certain cases to ships which are allowed to go to sea after paying 10s. for each of the crew. All absentees from the morning meeting are sought up and brought before this tribunal, and summarily punished for that or any other offence. Many have been tarred and feathered, and last week 3 men were exposed for some hours in a hastily constructed pillory in Sunderland, of which no notice has been taken. A vessel was sent out to sea a few days ago, that they might bring her forcibly back and that the offenders might be punished. They did so and the matter was dropped. They (the seamen) keep up constant guard boats and patrols, and certainly under the circumstances maintain admirable order. They have quietly and civilly collected a good deal of money among all classes.

Yesterday two circumstances occurred, very likely to throw a brand of discord among them, and a moment of disunion, if judiciously seized by an active, spirited magistrate, would unravel all this confusion. A very large party desire to go to sea on the terms proffered them, and at yesterday's morning meeting, the managing committee consented that they might do so if they would constitute them a permanent committee to watch over their interests and allow them a certain portion of their wages, which was indignantly rejected. It was then proposed and resolved to appropriate to their present use the funds of their Benefit Societies. The different associations met last night but found they could not effect this, and did not separate without a good deal of quarrelling.

From what I have heard, my Lord, I cannot help thinking that the morning meetings and roll callings at present are the *bond* of union—and that these, dispersed daily as illegal, would enable the best disposed to repair to their ships and go to sea. But now, as soon as a ship arrives, her men are taken away, their names added to the list, and they are obliged to answer to the call the next morning. It is true these are a body of men formidable from their courage and natural hardihood—but I am convinced that the best disposed might be detached from it by reason, and the civil power backed by a sufficient military force ready to support it would at once (directed by a man of energy) disperse the rest. But, my Lord, the civil power has slept so long, it is unnoticed and despised . . .

The Shields refractory seamen, when they attended the general meeting last week at Sunderland, were counted one by one as they passed the wicket at the bridge. Their number is 3,900. It appears by calculation that the ships now ready for sea would require this number within about 200, manned as the *owners* propose. And it is ascertained that the ships now in the *Wear*, manned as the *seamen propose*, would require more by 1,800 hands than there really are . . .

Ibid. to Ibid., Norton, near Stockton, 17 October, 1815 :— . . . I had misconceived the fact of the wages being *now* proposed to be reduced. They *were* £8 and £9 per voyage in January and February last, had been reduced very low before the commencement of the dispute, and the proposition at present is to raise them at Shields to £6 for the winter voyages and £5 for the summer ; at Sunderland to £4 and £5. I understand the wages at the latter place have always been about £1 below the other, and this circumstance accounts for the number of seamen at the former place being more numerous in proportion to the shipping. It appears to be the general opinion that there are few, if any, surplus hands at Sunderland, even if the ships go to sea with only their accustomed number of men.

I am of opinion there cannot be more than $\left.{}^{3,500}_{2,500}\right\}$6,000 men at both ports. I said to your Lordship that 3,900 men from Shields had passed the wicket of Sunderland Bridge to attend the general meeting, but I have since learnt that in this number many men from Monk Wearmouth, which is on the Shields side of the river, mixed with them as they arrived, and went over the bridge with them.

As a disinterested stranger, I have been in crowds of seamen, heard their complaints, views and intentions, and witnessed their proceedings, and setting aside the absolutely intolerable violence and illegality of the power they have assumed to restrain the trade and business of the ports, I feel myself compelled to bear my testimony to your Lordship, in favour of their principles, and in other respects good conduct, as well as the solidity of their grounds of complaint . . .

Ships from these ports have gone to sea shamefully deficient in strength to navigate them, and, should ever this subject excite the attention of the Legislature, hundreds of cases may be produced in which avarice has risked at sea a helpless insufficient crew, in a crazy but *highly-insured* ship . . .

I must observe, however, to your Lordship that the system, even with its abuses, has greatly encouraged the increase of the numbers of seamen by the advantages derived from navigating the ships by so large a proportion of apprentices . . .

Your Lordship has too much humanity to fix an eye exclusively on the crime these poor men are committing in search of redress, without giving some consideration to the circumstances out of which that crime has arisen . . . I deeply lament that they have made such advances in error (stimulated by unprincipled advisers, and, let me add, the shameful supineness of the magistracy, which they have construed into a tacit approbation of their conduct) that the most violent measures of coercion will be resorted to. There is confessedly a *large proportion* of the men would rejoice to be permitted to join their ships, and accept for the sake of their starving families (your Lordship will know the private misery which six weeks suspension of labour will produce) any terms they could obtain, and I am further convinced that the *honest real seamen* are merely passive. There are numbers of idle, dissolute fellows whom few will employ, good for nothing at sea, and who, conscious that whilst there is so great a number of prime seamen, they must be out of employ, feel an interest in keeping up this mischievous proceeding. There are besides great numbers of *tradesmen in sailors dress* even more active than the rest . . .

I found my way yesterday to a public table at Sunderland, where except myself all were shipowners, and heard a full discussion of the subject. They openly, to my deep disgust, avowed the base dissimulation with which they are acting, and that they intend to observe any terms they may *agree to* only till the present compact association and consequent danger are dispersed. The unprincipled avarice and want of integrity in this class of men, as a body, appears to be one reason of the bias observable in favour of the seamen, perhaps too of the *negligence of the magistrates* till it became questionable whether the means they were in possession of, could avail as a remedy for the evil . . .

The reports of remittances of money and advice transmitted from London, are so very current in all the disturbed places, that I may be permitted to suggest to your Lordship whether this matter could not be investigated at the Post Office. I have always been strongly impressed with the idea that there is somewhere a party so entirely abandoned to faction, and desirous of overturning the existing order of things, as secretly to stimulate all the popular discontents we have lately seen in the country.

It is not quite irrelevant to the subject to call your Lordship's attention to the adroitness with which the lower order of people accomplish the organisation and manage the machinery necessary to give effect to combinations. So accurate is the *surveillance* by which each man is in this case controlled, that *I saw* a sailor travelling by the mail ten miles south of Sunderland, obliged to produce his ticket of leave of absence to a party of three, who seemed in their turn to think it necessary to account for themselves and produce their vouchers. Your Lordship will have before learnt that when mechanics have struck for wages or the redress of real or fancied grievances, they seem at once to have arranged every grade of authority necessary to enable them to act with unity.

I have alluded to this subject because it has appeared to me capable of becoming dangerous to the State, and to be in fact only a modification of democratic and republican associations, whose objects, though now of a private nature, by a very easy transition may become political.[1] (H.O.42/146).

(178). *Memorial (to Lord Sidmouth) of the General Committee of the Shipping Interest of the Port of Newcastle-upon-Tyne*

North Shields, 17 October, 1815.

... On the 4th September last a body of seamen consisting of about 50 men collected at the mouth of this harbour and forcibly prevented ships laden with coals for the London market from sailing, unless the owners would comply with certain demands made by the seamen both as to the quantum of wages and the number of seamen to be employed on board each ship.

On the 7th September a petition purporting to come from the seamen of South Shields and its vicinity was presented to your memorialists, praying 'That the ships should carry five men and one boy for every 100 tons ; that no foreigner be employed in this trade unless he produces documents of his servitude ; that no person be employed as a waterman on this river, without producing an indenture, and that no pilots be permitted to act as foymen or temporary assistants to ships coming in or going out of harbour except in cases of necessity.

This petition was taken into consideration by your memorialists on the 8th September, when they entered into the Resolutions annexed, and numbered with the figure 1.

... The seamen's wages in this port have for many years past been at least 20% higher than those in any other port in Great Britain,

---

[1] In a printed Address the seamen of Sunderland said that they desired only £4 per voyage during the summer, and £5 during the winter ; and that ships should be adequately manned. ' Innumerable instances have occurred where the vessel, by not being "sufficiently manned" has not been able to outride the storm, the men on board, being benumbed with cold, fatigue and the hardship of their duty, have not been able to steer or navigate the vessel.' (Enclosed in the above letter).

Lord Sidmouth replied to Cartwright on 20 October : '. . . The authority of the laws, to which the seamen at Shields and Sunderland are in a state of open disobedience, must be re-established before their complaints can receive the attention to which they might otherwise be entitled, but, when their conduct in this respect is changed, they will, I trust, experience the liberal consideration which is due to men who have a claim upon the gratitude of their country . . .' [H.O.42/146. (copy.)]

and this has always created an influx of seamen, and which is now beyond what the trade can employ.

. . . Your memorialists beg leave here to observe to your Lordship that the shipowners conceive if they were to allow the seamen to have a controlling power over their property, which they evidently aim at, by pressing the adoption of a scale and by the mode in which they wished the magistrates to regulate that scale, as the mediator between the parties, it would be admitting a principle calculated to deprive the shipowner of exercising his own judgment in the mode of employing his own property, a principle subversive of the general law of property, and which if admitted, the shipowners conceive would extend itself to every branch of trade, and be ruinous to the whole commercial interests of the kingdom.

Should the mode of manning the vessels be entrusted to the opinion of the magistrates, who from their situation in life are necessarily incompetent to judge upon nautical affairs, and more particularly upon such parts as are *practical*, your memorialists are of opinion that the jurisdiction would not be competent to judge the question, and if even the magistrates were capable, the mode proposed could not from the nature of the trade be carried into effect.

Your memorialists beg leave to lay before your Lordship, as far as the same has come to their knowledge, the system which the seamen have hitherto pursued, and now continue in impeding the navigation of the river, and disturbing the public peace. When the wind is favourable, and opportunities present themselves of getting ships to sea, numerous bodies of the seamen are collected on each side of the river, in the narrowest part, while others are employed in boats upon the water ; as ships come down under sail they are hailed, and if found not to have obtained previous permission from the committee of seamen to proceed to sea, are immediately boarded by large parties and forcibly brought to anchor and the crew threatened with punishment and forcibly taken out. At other times the seamen assemble to the amount of some thousands and parade the streets of Newcastle and South Shields with flags and music, and should any of their own body not attend their muster or act contrary to the regulations adopted among themselves, his face is blacked, his jacket turned, and thus paraded through the streets as a marked object of their displeasure. On the 16th instant they assembled, as they have before done, on the river in upwards of 100 boats, containing from seven to ten men each, with which they

formed a line within a short distance of his Majesty's ships, manoev-
ring upon a boat carrying a Union Jack.

Your memorialists further shew that a Committee of the seamen
meet at certain houses in North and South Shields, and should the
master of any vessel bound coastwise wish to depart he can only
do so (except through the protection of the civil power) by making
an affidavit that he is not bound to London, with his cargo, and by
depositing with the Committee a certain portion of the wages of his
crew, the number of which is regulated by the Committee, and upon
so doing he receives a ticket or passport partly printed, and partly
written, to the following effect—'Permit the Ship —— of ——
whereof —— is Master bound for the Port of —— to sail. By Order
of the Committee of Seamen of North and South Shields.' It is true
that the act of applying to this Committee is a voluntary proceeding
on the part of the shipmasters, but still it is illustrative of the
seamen's system.

Thus is the control of this most important harbour in the hands of
a lawless and misguided set of men, and there is at this moment
about 90,000 tons of shipping thus detained, seven-eighths of which
are moored near the towns of North and South Shields, which are at
least eight miles from Newcastle, the residence, as has been before
stated, of the only magistrates who are authorised to act upon the
river . . .

Your memorialists have felt it their duty on behalf of the shipowners to enter thus into a detail upon the present important crisis,
for a system exists calculated to excite the most serious alarm in
the minds of every friend to good order and society. A property of
great value and importance to the country at large is threatened
with destruction, and it is seriously to be apprehended that if the
riotous spirit now existing is not speedily subdued, it will extend its
baneful effects among the keelmen, pitmen, caster of coals and
ballast, and to every ramification of the important trade of this
very populous district, thereby increasing the seamen's strength to
an incalculable extent. R. B. Roxby, Chairman. (H.O.42/146).

[*Four Enclosures.*]
[No. 1].
Northumberland Arms, 8 *September*, 1815.
At a meeting of the General Committee held this day, Mr. R. B.
Roxby in the chair, a petition from the seamen of South Shields and
its vicinity delivered to Mr. Roxby by Mr. Francis Robinson, of

South Shields, praying that the ships do carry five men and one boy to every 100 tons—that no foreigner be employed in this trade unless he produces a document of his servitude—that no person shall be employed as a waterman on this river without producing an indenture, and that no pilots be permitted to act as foymen except in case of necessity, having been read and fully considered—

Resolved—That this meeting is of opinion that as the above petition purports to be from the seamen of South Shields and its vicinity only, no answer can be given to the above petition until it be clearly shewn that the resolutions entered into by the shipowners of North and South Shields at a meeting held on the 7th September have been finally rejected by the seamen both of North and South Shields . . .

[The following is a copy of a printed handbill :]

Northumberland Arms, North Shields, 9 September, 1815.
The General Committee of the Shipping Interest of the Port of Tyne have taken into consideration the petition of the sailors of South Shields and its vicinity, respecting their claim for wages and other matters, and, after mature deliberation, they are of opinion that the shipowners of the port will have no objection to pay the seamen £5 per voyage, and if the sailors are satisfied with this, the Committee will call a general meeting of the shipowners (if necessary) and recommend them to pay £5 per voyage.

With respect to manning the ships as transports, say, five men and a boy for every 100 tons, it is a request that can never be complied with, and the Committee are of opinion that instead of affording the sailors relief, it would have a contrary effect, inasmuch as it would compel the shipowners to lay their ships by, at least three months in the year, and would also compel them always to load best coals, by which means the ships would only make five or six voyages at most, instead of eight or nine voyages in the year ; the sailors must therefore perceive that instead of an advantage, it must be a great disadvantage to themselves. However, to afford the sailors as much relief as possible, the General Committee will recommend to all the Insurance Clubs upon the river that their Committees shall go on board all their ships, and order, and also see, that the ships are well manned.

With respect to the pilots acting as foy-men, the Committee can only say that they will recommend to the shipowners to employ the common foy-boats when they are to be got, and only to employ the pilots as foy-men when there is a necessity for doing so ; but the sailors must be aware that there can be no compulsion in this, as all his Majesty's liege subjects have a right to employ themselves upon the river Tyne in any way they think proper, provided they conduct themselves with propriety, and in a lawful manner.

With respect to the scullermen,[1] the General Committee cannot interfere, as such interference would be contrary to law, and consequently of non-effect.

The General Committee will strongly recommend (and have no doubt but it will be carried into effect) that no foreigner shall be employed on board of any ship belonging [to] this port ; they will also strongly recommend that the seamen belonging to the towns of North and South Shields, and the Port of Tyne, shall be employed in preference to any strangers.

The General Committee do assure the sailors that they feel great regret that so many seamen at this time should be out of employment, and that they will, with much pleasure, at any time, endeavour to give them all the assistance in their power—and hope the time is not far distant when there will be a more extensive trade for British shipping, and consequently better employment for British seamen.

[A printed handbill.]
Northumberland Arms, North Shields, 19 *September,* 1815.
Seamen's Wages, &c.

It having been represented to the General Committee of the Shipping Interest of the Port of Tyne that many reports are spread abroad which tend to prevent the seamen of this port coming to a good understanding with the shipowners, the Committee think it their duty to declare their sentiments publicly, with a view to conciliate the sailors and give them immediate employment, provided they will accede to what the Committee will recommend to the shipowners.

The Committee will recommend the shipowners to pay the seamen £5 per voyage, and they have no doubt but the shipowners will accede to their recommendation.

The General Committee do assure the seamen that no foreign sailor will be employed by the shipowners of this port, and they will

---

[1] Men who plied sculling-boats for hire.

recommend the Insurance Clubs on this river to direct the Committee to go on board all their ships and order them to be well manned, by which means a large additional number of seamen will be employed. The General Committee are of opinion that by manning the ships in this manner, it will not only employ all the seamen who are residents in the Port of Tyne, but also a great number of strangers, the Committee being desirous to afford employment to as many seamen as the trade can possibly allow ; but the sailors must be aware, and their own good sense must point out to them that it is impossible for the shipowners of the Port of Tyne to give employment to all the strangers that may resort here in times like the present ; and it certainly is extremely hard that the seamen belonging to the Port who are generally employed in the coal trade, and the other working men upon the river should be deprived of employment, and their families put to many inconveniences merely for the sake of a few strangers.

It is reported that the seamen, having failed in their application to the Admiralty, mean to lay their grievances before Parliament, but they ought to consider that in all probability it will be next January before Parliament will meet for business, and even then the sailors may be assured their request will not be complied with, that is, with respect to manning the ships with six hands for every hundred tons registered measurement, as such a proceeding would enable foreigners to navigate their ships upon better terms than the British shipowners ; and consequently the greatest part of the trade of Europe would fall into the hands of foreigners, and nearly one-half of the British shipping would be compelled to lay by the walls for want of employment, which would not only be extremely detrimental to British seamen but to the whole trade of the Kingdom . . .

Mrs. Carr's, North Shields, 13 *October*, 1815. (*Copy*). At a meeting of the Committees of the different Insurances held this day in pursuance of a circular letter sent by the Secretaries to the General Committee to these Committees to take into consideration the proper means of manning the vessels agreeable to the proposals of the shipowners, in consequence of Captain Caulfeild having communicated that the seamen of this town had abandoned their scale and that they were willing to accept the shipowners' terms provided they had an earnest that the shipowners would carry their plan into effect, Mr. Donkin communicated to this meeting what had passed between him and Captain Caulfeild yesterday, and stated that he was requested to see Captain Caulfeild again this day and to show him what the shipowners meant to pursue in carrying their proposal into effect.

Resolved, that the following communications be made to Captain Caulfeild through Mr. Donkin : 'Mrs. Carr's, 13 October 1815. The Committees of the various Insurances have met this day to adopt measures for carrying into effect the printed proposal of the shipowners, and have agreed to appoint Committees of Inspection to proceed immediately on board the different ships and to leave a printed or written order on board of each ship directing the complement which must be taken. The Committee will request Mr. Ostle to go on board the ships immediately after the Committees have performed their duty as agreed to before the magistrates on the 4th instant, and make his report to the seamen if requested as to the state in which he finds the ships.'

Mr. Donkin having returned this day from Captain Caulfeild with a communication from him that he had seen a deputation again from the seamen this day expressing a desire to return to their duty on the shipowners shewing a determination to put their proposal into execution.

Resolved, that a select party of the Committee meet tomorrow at Mrs. Carr's to arrange the plans, &c. for going on board the ships on Monday next.

R. B. Roxby, Chairman.

(179). *The Rev. R. Gray to Viscount Sidmouth*

Bishop Wearmouth, 21 *October,* 1815 :—As I have good reason to hope from the train in which affairs were put yesterday at Newcastle that intelligence will be sent to your Lordship by this day's post of a dissolution of the combination at Shields, it may be of some use that your Lordship should at the same time be informed that the shipowners at Sunderland, by consenting last night after many refusals, to print the scale which they proposed on Friday to the seamen, have afforded them that pledge which it was their chief object to obtain, and to which I have no hesitation in saying that after what has occurred they had a reasonable claim, had they presented it by legal means. Some discussions remain, but I have little doubt that the competition which will immediately take place between the

Port and Shields will expedite the termination of the dispute, and that some vessels will sail this day.

Your Lordship will, I trust, allow me to assure you that the authority of the magistrates has not been committed, since we have had no informations upon which we could act. It would have been useless to attempt to force the Port unless sailors could have been procured to man the vessels, and hitherto we have not had the power or the prospect of success as to other measures of a decisive character . . .

Ibib. to Ibid., 23 *October,* 1815 :—I have the satisfaction to assure your Lordship that about 100 vessels sailed from the port of Sunderland by the evening tide of yesterday without the least obstruction from the seamen, and that there can be no doubt that as many as are ready will proceed to sea this day . . .

Allow me to express the hope that your Lordship will see in this amicable adjustment under the existing circumstances, much that is to be approved, and that in the consideration of the conduct of these misguided men, your Lordship will admit some excuse, though their measures have been utterly reprehensible and insulting to the authorities of the country, since the chief object of the main body of them has been to procure the establishment of some pledge for a future attention to the preservation of their lives, and that in looking to a plain and simple principle, they have obtained the admission of a scale which, if it be fully confirmed and acted upon by their employers, will effectually contribute to the tranquillity of the port and promote the advantage of his Majesty's navy. The shipowners contend for the principle themselves in the Transport Service . . .[1]

Ibid. to Ibid., 23 *October,* 1815 :—. . . Notwithstanding the adjustment of differences between the shipowners and seamen, the magistrates have considered it to be their duty to proceed against the principal offenders against whom informations might be obtained. I therefore with another magistrate issued warrants last night against eight of the Committee. Two of them have been apprehended and will be examined this morning. (H.O.42/146).

[1] *[See p. 207]*

(180). *The Duke of Northumberland to Viscount Sidmouth*

Syon, 24 October, 1815. (*Private*).

. . . I dare say your Lordship is thoroughly acquainted with the origin of the business, which is really a private dispute between the shipowners and the seamen, which regularly happens at the commencement of every peace. The ships belonging to Shields and Sunderland, being of a large size and great capacity, and manned likewise by excellent seamen, are particularly adapted to the transport service. Great numbers of them (particularly from the former port) are taken up by the Transport Office during a war ; which, being paid off upon the signature of a treaty of peace causes such an influx of seamen at those ports, that it is impossible for the owners of ships to find employment for them. Besides, having been long used to the superior advantages derived from the Transport Service, they are always very troublesome in endeavouring to establish the same regulations with respect to pay and the ratio of seamen per ton, which they have been used to in that service. Formerly, this kind of disturbance was easily quieted in a very short time by arbitration, and I am convinced this might as easily have been done

---

[1] On the 21st the seamen accepted the terms offered by the shipowners the previous day :

Ships of 6 keels	4 men and 2 boys	
7 to 8—	5	2
9	6	2
10	6	3
11	7	2
12	8	2
13	8	3
14	9	2
15	9	3

Apprentices of 20 years of age having been one year at sea, and those of 17 having been two years at sea, were to be considered as men. As for apprentices under 17 who had been three years at sea, two of them were to be reckoned as one man. The owners offered wages of £4 10s. 0d. per voyage, until 25 March, 1816.

Major-General Riall, in a letter to Lieut.-Gen. Wynyard, dated 23 October, said that the conduct of the seamen ' has been peaceable to an extraordinary degree. Some have been apprehended by the civil power for tearing down notices issued by the magistrates and for some other breaches of the peace, but nothing at all serious.' Wynyard wrote to Sidmouth from York on the 23rd, 'The conduct of the shipowners in shifting this distressing business from their own, to the shoulders of the Government, appears to me as disgraceful as it is cowardly.' (H.O.42/146).

upon the present occasion, from the private information I have received. Unfortunately, a different mode has been adopted. From the length of the war, and the large employment of transports, the body of seamen now paid off is more numerous than usual, and the shipowners have taken fright, and have applied to the force of power instead of the voice of persuasion. The Mayor of Newcastle was applied to, from the mistaken notion that the whole of the river Tyne made a part of the town and county of the town of Newcastle [*sic*], and that the Mayor has the sole jurisdiction upon that river, whereas I have in my Evidence Room here the decision taken in the reign of Henry I 'that the northern half of the river, with its shore, belongs to the County of Northumberland, and the southern half to the Bishopric of Durham, but that one-third of each half, next the centre, shall be free for ships and boats to pass along.' The Admiralty likewise claim the jurisdiction on the river Tyne, and empower their Vice-Admiral to hold Admiralty Courts for the trial of offences committed on that river. The Mayor, I am afraid, my Lord, was unfortunately persuaded to step beyond his legal power, and having gone down in state to both North and South Shields, found he had no jurisdiction, especially on shore in the counties of Northumberland and Durham, and returned again without issuing a warrant, or venturing to act against the seamen. This, my private information mentions, both enraged and encouraged the sailors, and they assumed a more regular and threatening aspect. Ships and troops were applied for, and thus, what was really in the origin a private dispute between the shipowners and the seamen, has become through mismanagement a serious riot, which may possibly be attended with very disagreeable consequences. Your Lordship may rest assured that unless great care is taken to prevent it, the final issue of this business will be the departure of a large body of most excellent seamen from this county to the United States of America. I understand this idea is already talked of amongst them . . . (H.O.42/146).

(181). *Viscount Sidmouth to the Duke of Northumberland*

White Lodge, Richmond Park, 25 October, 1815. ½ *p.* 11 *p.m.*
Private. (*Copy*).

. . . Allow me to assure your Grace that I am extremely thankful for the valuable information which you have had the goodness to afford me, especially with respect to the jurisdiction of the harbour of Shields, which I had before supposed to belong exclusively to the Mayor and Corporation of Newcastle.

Of the origin of the recent disturbances I was not unapprised. Upon the commencement of the differences which took place, as usual, upon the paying off the Fleet, there was no disposition to an accommodation, manifested by the shipowners, nor to mediation on the part of the magistrates. The former saw, without regret, the blockade of the harbour, the effect of which would be to raise the price of coals in the metropolis, as of the augmented price they would have the benefit [*sic*] ; and the latter did not choose to interfere. In the meantime the sailors increased in number and audacity. A Committee was formed ; a regular system of embargo was established. Watch and guards were mounted and relieved ; unlawful oaths were administered ; permits granted to ships to sail upon certain conditions, which they imposed ; and for these permits contributions were exacted ; delegates were appointed to discuss the terms of an arrangement with the shipowners, who at length became alarmed at the effects of their own inertness. Terms were agreed to and then renounced, till at last the magistrates, who appear to me to have been strangely supine, were insulted ; the King's naval officers and the British flag treated with contempt and defiance, and the indispensable necessity created of such measures as might have been prevented by timely mediation or timely vigour.

The combination is, I trust, at last dissolved, and it is now my earnest wish that no prosecutions may be instituted except against the most prominent offenders, and that, as the law is no longer violated, that consideration and liberality may be manifested by the shipowners which is due to British seamen . . . (H.O.42/146).

(182). *Viscount Sidmouth to the Rev. R. Gray*

Whitehall, 25 October, 1815. (Copy).
. . . It is now my earnest wish that no prosecution may be instituted except against prominent and flagrant offenders, and that the seamen who have been engaged in the late unhappy disturbances, having experienced the power of the laws which they had violated, may find that all resentment has ceased with their misconduct, and that they have not permanently forfeited the confidence and goodwill of their former employers. (H.O.42/146).

Q

(183). *The Rev. R. Gray to Viscount Sidmouth*

Bishop Wearmouth, 26 October, 1815.

. . . By the mismanagement or neglect of the constables (who are ill-regulated and ill-paid here) only three persons were apprehended on Tuesday evening. The examination yesterday produced, I am sorry to say, a most alarming disturbance, in which it was necessary to call out the military to protect the person of the informer. The tumult however subsided with his departure without any mischief, and the seamen are perfectly quiet and I hope well disposed.

I am persuaded that your Lordship will concur with me in opinion that the authority of the magistrates was not to be compromised to extend impunity to the chief offenders, and that it is desirable to ascertain if possible by what secret views and agents the men have been directed. The papers are I fear destroyed. No evidence has yet been brought forward, but the oath of the informer, proving that two of the men apprehended were members of the Committee, and that one of them ordered punishment to be inflicted on the informer. . . . The men apprehended are not of the worst description.[1] (H.O.42/146).

Ibid. to Ibid., Bishop Wearmouth, 3 November, 1815. Being sensible that your Lordship has been exposed to much trouble by a polite attention to individuals, I feel great hesitation in indulging a wish to state some further circumstances which may enable your Lordship to judge fully of the line of conduct towards the seamen, which has been adopted here.

Your Lordship is apprised that the men, after some appearance of combination in September, returned to their employment, and assembled again, as they alleged, because the promises made to them were not observed. After illegal measures were again resorted to, so far back as the 6th of October, a gentleman of this neighbourhood, who has much influence with the sailors, informed a committee of the shipowners, which had been appointed at a public meeting at my request to act for the whole body, that the men would return to their ships if from 50 to 100 gentlemen would pledge themselves by their signatures that the ships should be sufficiently manned, allowing £4 10s. per voyage, which was not then deemed an unreasonable sum, but no attention was paid to this communication.

---

[1] The seamen arrested at North Shields were either bailed or discharged. Five were charged with misdemeanours under the Act 33 George III, c. 67.

When proposals were at length imparted to the men, they would soon have been acceded to by the well-disposed, at least, if the shipowners would have consented to do away the distrust which existed, by printing them. On the 18th the seamen sent up two of their men to the Rectory to request that I would undertake as a mediator to obtain this security. This I was then endeavouring to effect, but after admitting the men, with some difficulty, I informed them that I could not undertake any direct *office* in their favour while they persisted in their illegal conduct, that I expected to be called upon to act against them as a magistrate, but that perhaps there might yet be time, if they made a respectful application to the shipowners by the interference of some other gentleman. They then addressed themselves to Mr. Nesfield, who, though a magistrate, does not act in this district, and a meeting being called, it was at length agreed to print the terms offered, and the men professed themselves satisfied. It is to be regretted only, that no signatures but that of the chairman were affixed to the agreement, and complaints still continue that it is not generally and faithfully observed, and we are still embarrassed by near 300[1] men without employment,

---

[1] In a subsequent letter (9 November), after further inquiry, he corrected this figure to 126 (belonging to the Port of Sunderland). He added that the Commissioners of the Wear had decided, on the 7th, to engage 100 of these men to remove ballast and cleanse the course of the river. ' There are besides, many strangers who, it is hoped, will soon disperse.'

It was because of the great distress of some of the strikers that some smaller vessels belonging to Scotland and ports to the south of Sunderland were allowed to go to sea, on payment of 10s. for each man on board, to support the seamen ashore. Vessels going to foreign ports also paid their quota. Ships laden with Government cargo, bound for London, and Newcastle traders, were allowed to sail on payment of 20s. for each man aboard. The following Articles were made at the beginning of the strike :

1. 'Finding so many seamen out of employment and in great distress, we have altogether agreed not to go on board any ship or vessel until every man can be provided for ; to certify which, we individually sign our names to the annexed list, paying 1d. as an acknowledgment to the same.

2. It is expected, every man will meet at any time and place the majority of seamen shall think fit to appoint.

3. Every man missing his muster shall pay 6d. the first time ; 1s. the second, and the third time he shall be tarred and feathered.

4. If any man shall be found on board of ship after he has been taken out or has been joined to this body, he shall have his jacket turned, his face blacked, and marched through the town ; if found again on board he shall be tarred and feathered.

[*Continued on p. 212*]

and who, I fear, could not now be induced to enter the navy unless it could [be] for a limited time.

I have stated these circumstances in order to shew to your Lordship that if legislative regulations (either with respect to the number of men to be employed, or the mode of ensuring by companies) should be deemed expedient, they will not be superfluous. Whatever difficulties there may be in parliamentary interference with a body of men so jealous and susceptible as that of the shipping interest, it may be remarked, if your Lordship will excuse my presumption, that in the coal trade, no competition with foreign Powers, with a view to freightage, is concerned, and that while it is well able and ought to bear the expense of sufficient complements of men for security, it will, by being considered so to do, only become a better nursery for the navy. The propriety of the principle has at length been admitted here, and if it be not acted upon, disturbances will be renewed.

When the ships return, other offenders might perhaps be apprehended if deemed necessary, and I fear that if any enquiry take place, it will be found that some of the owners of the ships, who would not apply to the magistrates for a general redress, obtained licenses from the self-constituted committee of the seamen. If any oaths were imposed they were forced, I believe, upon the captains who sailed, enjoining them not to proceed to London. (H.O.42/147).

[Continued from p. 211]

5. If any man shall tell the names of any of the men appointed to transact business, he shall suffer such punishment as the seamen at large shall think fit.

6. If any man shall be known to divulge the proceedings of this body he shall be tarred and feathered.

7. As it is most likely the owners will find out some of the men during the business, and afterwards will not employ them, it is expected every man will contribute to their support after this business is settled, by paying the sum of 2s. each per voyage until they get employment.

8. Should any man be taken and confined during the business he is to be supported by the majority during his confinement, and his family (if any) to be taken care of.

9. No sort of gaming or *sky-larking* to be allowed during our meetings under penalty of 6d. for every offence.

10. Every man is to behave himself with the strictest attention, and walk peaceably in the streets and other places, after muster, under the penalty of suffering such punishment as the majority shall think fit ; as anything done amiss will get the whole body a bad name.'

(From a printed pamphlet, ' An Impartial Account of the late proceedings of the Seamen of the Port of Tyne. By a Tar.' Newcastle, 1815. 12 pp.)

(184). *John Beckett to Sir John Wrottesley*

Whitehall, 26 February, 1816.

I am directed by Lord Sidmouth to acknowledge the receipt of your letter of the 22nd instant, acquainting his Lordship in reference to the riotous proceedings which a short time since took place among the collieries, that some of the persons concerned in those trans-actions assembled in a tumultuous manner on the 21st instant, and attacked and ill treated those men who were engaged at work at the reduced prices ; and suggesting the propriety of introducing a Bill into Parliament for inflicting a heavier punishment upon offences of this nature. In reply, his Lordship directs me to acquaint you that as a subject with that you mention [*sic*] is now under the con-sideration of his Majesty's Attorney and Solicitor-General, Lord Sid-mouth has thought it advisable to lay before them your suggestions. (H.O.43/24/345-46).

Ibid. to Ibid., 12 *March,* 1816 :—. . . His Majesty's Law Officers have reported that they do not think it likely that the Legislature would be inclined to increase the punishment inflicted by the 39th and 40th George III, cap. 106, Section 3 (of three months' imprison-ment, or two months' hard labour) on persons who by intimidation prevent workmen from pursuing their employment. With respect to persons assembling to the number of ten to destroy any engines, if the assembly be riotous, it would be a serious offence, and subject the parties to punishment of imprisonment at common law, at the discretion of the Court before whom it was tried.

As to the fact of demolishing engines, it appears that the law at present in force would make such an act felony, for by the 9th George III, cap. 29, if any person or persons shall wilfully or malic-iously destroy or damage any fire engine or *other engine* for draining water from any colliery or coal mine (*or for drawing coals out of the same*) he shall be guilty of felony and be liable to be transported . . . (H.O.43/24/360-62).

(185). *Colonel Fletcher to John Beckett*

Bolton-le-Moor, 5 *March*, 1816.

In consequence of your query respecting Benefit Societies, I have procured from Adjutant Warr[1] the enclosed report relating to the application of the funds of such Societies in this immediate neighbourhood.

The members composing the Societies of which he speaks, are principally cotton weavers who, forming by much the largest class of persons in this manufacturing part of the county of Lancaster, have never been able for any considerable length of time and in any considerable numbers to *turn out* (or strike) from their employ, so as materially thereby to affect the interest of their masters. That period, alluded to by Mr. Warr (1808) was their greatest effort, when a Colonel Hanson, late of Manchester, deluded many of them into a tumultuous assembly—for which offence he was indicted and sentenced by the Court of King's Bench (I think) to six months' imprisonment.[2]

The classes of persons in the manufactures of this county that have been most formidable to their employers, by their combinations, are the calico printers and cotton spinners who, labouring in large numbers together in print works or cotton factories under the same masters respectively, have for many years past been almost every year in some place or other in a state of combination against their respective employers, as, in regard to the calico printers, will appear from the perusal of the correspondence seized lately in this town, and which I doubt not you will have perused. How far Benefit Societies (I mean such as are sanctioned by the Act of the 34th of His Majesty) have increased the facilities of forming such combinations, I am not fully informed so as to give a decided opinion, but although I have frequently heard of combinations amongst the calico printers before the enactment of the said Statute, yet as Sick Clubs or Friendly Societies prevailed in many parts of the country before any law gave them a sanction, so it is probable that such Societies, before the said Law, might have been the germ from which sprang originally such illicit associations . . .

---

[1] James Warr, of the Bolton Local Militia. For his expenditure of secret service money in 1812, see the account sent to the Home Office by Colonel Fletcher, in F. O. Darvall's *Popular Disturbances and Public Order in Regency England*, pp. 299-301.

[2] See Prentice, *Historical Sketches of Manchester*, pp. 31-3.

[Enclosure].

James Warr to Colonel Fletcher. Bolton, 1 March, 1816 :—Agreeable to your request I have made the enquiries contained in your note respecting Friendly Societies. I find at the time that delégates were sent to London with a petition from the weavers to get a fixed minimum of wages according to sorts and qualities of cloth worked. An application was made to them through the committee at Bolton to the different Friendly Societies for a sum of money to be advanced to them out of their respective funds. In consequence of which there was general meetings called of a number of the Societies for that purpose, and several Clubs agreed to lend them money on print notes [*sic*] being given for the same, by such of the members as would come forward and who were thought to be eligible, to which several of the members agreed to on condition they might be allowed to solicit subscriptions from the members the ensuing quarter day for the repayment of the same, but the delegates not succeeding in this application to Parliament—when they began to make their collections from the members. It came far short of their expectations and they had to make [good] the deficiency out of their own pockets. There were other Societies that advanced £5 each out of their respective funds, without any notes being required. But it has been a bone of contention ever since with those that were opposed to it, who declare there shall never any more money to go out again but for the purposes it was put in for, viz., to relieve the sick and bury the dead.

In the year 1808, at the general turn-out of the weavers, a number of families were brought into distress by having their shuttles, &c. took from them. There was general meetings of several Societies again called to consider of the propriety of assisting such of their members who were so distressed—when it was agreed to allow out of their respective funds 10s. to such member that would apply for the same, they repaying it back in six or twelve months with interest. The principal part of such money so advanced has been paid back, and when such members hath not repaid the same, it is deducted from their burial money. I cannot learn of any Society failing to relieve their sick or becoming bankrupt in consequence of any sums advanced to the weavers' delegates—as the largest sum advanced by any Society was £10. I learn there has been two or three Sick Clubs broke up—but it was owing to not having a sufficient number of young members joining their Societies, and being principally composed of old persons, their funds got reduced so low that they agreed to divide what little money they had left.

I believe the money raised in Friendly Societies in Bolton has been invariably applied to the paying of their sick and burying their dead, except in the before-mentioned cases—and I understand that those who were advocates for the advance of such money is convinced of the impropriety of letting any money go out of their funds for any purpose whatever but for what it was subscribed for. (H.O.42/149).

(186). *Opinion of the Law Officers of the Crown on a Memorial presented by the Merchants, Manufacturers and Inhabitants of the towns and neighbourhood of Manchester and Salford respecting unlawful combinations of workmen.*

2, Lincoln's Inn, 26 March, 1816.

We have considered this case with all the attention which its importance demanded. The subject is not new, but has frequently been brought under our consideration by his Majesty's Government, and particularly by the Secretary of State for the Home Department. We have very recently had a long and anxious consultation by his Lordship's express desire with a committee of gentlemen much interested in the subject, and maturely deliberated upon and discussed with them every project or suggestion communicated by them for remedying the evil.

No person can be more deeply impressed than we are with the great importance of the subject, or more sensible of the alarming extent to which the combinations of workmen in different branches of trade and manufactures have been carried, or the dangerous consequences which they threaten to the manufactures, the public interest, and to the deluded individuals themselves who are engaged in them ; but we have not been able to bring ourselves to recommend the adoption of any of the measures that have been proposed, or to think ourselves warranted in expressing an opinion in favour of any new powers for *suppression* of the evil.

The great danger and mischief arise from the combination of numbers to effect an illegal purpose. Now whenever this case exists and is capable of being satisfactorily proved, it amounts by the law as it now stands, to a criminal misdemeanour of great enormity, and would not fail to be visited, on a satisfactory conviction, by punishment of considerable severity. We do not think that it is necessary to increase the degree of such severity by any new law, nor do we believe that any proposition for such law would be favourably received by the Legislature. But it has appeared to some that the power to punish individuals convicted of offences against the Combination Act, is not sufficient, and that benefit might be derived from extending the punishment. We cannot recommend a proposal to give larger powers to single magistrates acting in a summary way without a jury, nor do we think a proposal to that effect would succeed. The great practical inconvenience which is felt arises from the difficulty of proving the necessary facts to convict offenders ; we dare not recommend a rule of evidence different in this case from any other ; or venture to suggest that less should be required than would be thought necessary to warrant a conviction for any other species of misdemeanour ; indeed it is obvious that the more heinous the offence, in that exact proportion the evidence should be satisfactory ; still less could we permit ourselves to suggest a departure from the usual course and nature of proof in a case of summary proceeding by a magistrate. We are of opinion that the law, as it stands at present, would be found sufficient, if duly enforced ; and we do not see any remedy for this most enormous evil but that which we are confidently persuaded would arise from an active, vigilant and well-regulated system, adopted and constantly acted upon by the masters in their various branches of trade and manufactures, to detect conspiracies and to prosecute by indictment such as could be affected by competent testimony ; we are persuaded that much might be done by encouraging persons who might be worthy of trust to collect, and from time to time to communicate in the most confidential manner the objects and meetings and correspondence of the conspirators, which would afford an opportunity of making examples in certain proper cases to be carefully selected, and which, in process of time might be expected to produce the most beneficial consequences by dissolving the combinations, by infusing into the minds of its members a great degree of jealousy and distrust of each other, and which would break up that confidence in their fidelity which at present binds them together. We cannot, from what we have heard and seen, venture to flatter ourselves that our sentiments on this important subject will convince, or be satisfactory to the very respectable gentlemen most interested in it ; we may have taken an imperfect or mistaken view of it, and shall be open to conviction, but these are our very deliberate opinions upon consideration. (H.O.48/17).

(187). *Viscount Sidmouth to William Johnson Edenson*[1]

Whitehall, 28 March, 1816.

I have the honour to acknowledge the receipt of the Memorial addressed to me by the merchants, manufacturers and inhabitants of the towns and neighbourhood of Manchester and Salford, upon the subject of the unlawful combinations at present existing amongst the working classes generally throughout the kingdom ; and I beg to acquaint you that after having bestowed upon it the fullest consideration, I judged it advisable to consult with his Majesty's Attorney and Solicitor-General with the view of being assisted with their advice and opinion upon the prayer of the petitioners, 'that his Majesty's Government will introduce and promote such amendments of the present laws as are best calculated to remedy the evils complained of.' This subject had previously been brought under the consideration of his Majesty's Law Officers, and they have recently had a consultation by my express desire with a committee of gentlemen much interested, and maturely deliberated upon and discussed every project or suggestion communicated by them for providing the remedy sought for. They have stated to me that they are deeply impressed with the great importance of the subject, and fully sensible of the alarming extent to which the combinations of workmen in different branches of trade and manufactures have been carried, and of the dangerous consequences which they threaten to the manufactures, the public interest, and the deluded individuals themselves who are engaged in them ; but they report at the same time that they cannot recommend the adoption of any of the measures that have been proposed, or think themselves warranted in expressing an opinion in favour of any new powers for suppression of the evil. Great danger and mischief arise from the combination of numbers to effect an illegal purpose, but, whenever this case exists and is capable of being satisfactory proved, it amounts, by the law as it now stands, to a criminal misdemeanour of great enormity, and would not fail to be visited on a satisfactory conviction by punishment of considerable severity.

[1] Borough-reeve of Manchester.

The Attorney and Solicitor-General further state that they do not
think that it is necessary to increase the degree of such severity by
any new law, nor do they believe that any proposition for such law
would be favourably received by the Legislature ; and although it
has appeared to some that the power to punish individuals convicted
of offences against the Combination Act, is not sufficient, and that
benefit might be derived from extending the punishment, yet they
cannot recommend a proposal to give larger powers to single magistrates acting in a summary way without a jury, nor do they think
a proposal to that effect would succeed.

The great practical inconvenience which is felt, arises from the
difficulty of proving the necessary facts to convict offenders ; but a
rule of evidence different in this case from any other, cannot be
recommended, nor would it be proper to suggest that less should be
required than would be thought necessary to warrant a conviction
for any other species of misdemeanour. Indeed it is obvious that the
more heinous the offence, in that exact proportion the evidence
should be satisfactory ; and still less would it be proper to suggest
a departure from the usual course and nature of proof, in a case of
summary proceeding by a magistrate.

The law as it stands at present, would, they are of opinion, be
found sufficient, if duly enforced, and they do not see any remedy
for this most enormous evil but that which would doubtless arise
from an active, vigilant and well-regulated system, adopted and
constantly acted upon by the masters, in their various branches of
trade and manufactures, to detect conspiracies and to prosecute by
indictment such as could be affected by competent testimony ; and
much might be done by encouraging persons worthy of trust to
collect, and from time to time to communicate in the most confidential manner the objects and meetings and correspondence of
the conspirators, which would afford an opportunity of making
examples in certain proper cases, to be carefully selected, and which
in process of time might be expected to produce the most beneficial
consequences, by dissolving the combinations, by infusing into the
minds of its members a great degree of jealousy and distrust of each
other, and which would break up that confidence in their fidelity
which at present binds them together.

I beg to assure you that I fully concur in the sentiments of his
Majesty's Law Officers, and I confidently trust they will prove satisfactory to all the gentlemen who have signed the Memorial before-
mentioned. (H.O.43/24/377-81).

(188). *J. Lloyd to John Beckett*

Stockport, 26 May, 1816.

Rumours are kept afloat of unlawful combinations and intended meetings of the dissatisfied workpeople. The weavers have petitioned the Parliament and their delegates have just received letters from the members, who give them no hopes of relief from that quarter, nor could it reasonably be expected . . .[1] (H.O.42/150).

(189). *Benjamin Hall to Viscount Sidmouth*

Upper Brook Street [*London*], 2 *July,* 1816.

I have an express from Merthyr that the puddlers of our Cyfarthfa works have struck, demanding an advance of wages. This is the same body of men thàt began the disturbances before, though not at that work . . . I have not yet heard of the stopping of any other Work, but there is no doubt a general understanding, and large bodies of men without wages will not long remain quiet. The magistrates there are active and intelligent, and will do their duty.[2] (H.O.42/152).

---

[1] Colonel Fletcher and James Watkins, two Lancashire magistrates, informed the Home Secretary on the 29th that 'in consequence of *failures* which have taken place within a week or two past, notices have been given to upwards of a thousand weavers that no more materials will be delivered out to them after those in the loom shall have been wrought, and also that like notices have been given by *solvent* manufacturers to upwards of two thousand weavers that they too, must not expect any more materials for weaving to be delivered out to them . . . From these circumstances *their* opinion is that before the end of three weeks one-half of the weavers of this town and neighbourhood (the whole estimated at 20,500) will be out of employment. They further state that the earnings of the weavers now in employ do not exceed upon average five shillings per week.' (*Ibid.*)

[2] Edward Kendall, High Sheriff for the County of Brecon, wrote to the Home Secretary from Abergavenny on 26 October, 1816 : '. . . I have communicated with some of the gentlemen concerned in managing the ironworks in this county and have received the following account : That the men have gone to work again partially, but not on the reduced wages (for they stopped on receiving notice that the reduction *would take place* in about a month hence, the usual way of such notices being communicated) because they conclude that when the time of reduction actually arrives, that more disturbances may take place. The men have got an erroneous idea into their heads, which I perceive has crept into the daily papers, that their wages are to be reduced to one shilling per day. Such is far from being the case, for I learn from one of the gentlemen managing a Work in my neighbourhood, to quote his own

[*Continued on p. 221*]

(190). *The Rev. William Powell to Viscount Sidmouth*

n.d. [? *Early July*, 1816].

. . . From Nantyglo I learn that the colliers met to the number of between 300 and 400 on an adjoining hill on Saturday, and continued a long time in deliberation, but committed no act of violence. On Monday morning they refused to work at the reduced prices, but being ordered by Mr. Bailey, junior, to deliver in their tools, they all, after a hesitation of a few hours, returned to the levels, but still declared that their future conduct should depend upon the result of the settlement of affairs at Merthyr . . . If the Merthyr men will work at the reduced wages, I think we may depend upon their example being followed at every other Work . . . (H.O.42/152).

(191). *J. C. Curwen, M.P., to Viscount Sidmouth*

Workington Hall, 11 *August*, 1816.

. . . There was a meeting of the sailors yesterday called by themselves, which I attended with the hopes of convincing them of the great impropriety of their conduct. I found them resolutely bent on resistance as long as their own means would enable them, 'and after that they would help themselves if the parish would not support them.' I have strongly recommended to the gentlemen to come forward and be sworn in as special constables . . . (H.O.42/152).

[*Enclosure.*]
The Workington Shipowners to J. C. Curwen

Workington, 10 *August*, 1816.

We, the undersigned, being principal shipowners of this port, beg leave to represent to you that, owing to the depressed state of the coal trade, we convened a meeting of owners and masters of vessels at the harbour house.

Amongst the regulations proposed to enable us to carry on the trade, it was thought right to reduce the sailors' wages from $4\frac{1}{2}$ to $3\frac{1}{2}$ guineas per man for the voyage to Dublin, and from $5\frac{1}{2}$ to $4\frac{1}{2}$ guineas to Cork, being a reduction of one guinea only on the voyage.

[*Continued from p. 220*]
words, ' that the wages are in fact from 2s. 6d. to 4s. per day and provisions not materially higher than in the adjacent counties,' but then that is what is the case *at this moment*—it is not *what may be* when the reduction takes place . . .' (H.O.42/154).

This was thought a liberal offer considering the present state of the trade. To our great surprise the sailors have refused to accept of those terms, in consequence of which the trade is at a stand. They have not only done so, but at a meeting amongst themselves have, as we understand, expressed their sentiments in a manner that calls forth every precaution and vigilance on the part of the peaceable and well-disposed inhabitants of the town . . .[1]

(192). *E. R. Travers (Mayor) to Viscount Sidmouth*

Preston, 13 August, 1816.

. . . In consequence of a reduction in wages of the persons employed in the manufacturing business, a great number of them have withdrawn from their employment, and have this morning been parading the streets, and assembling in groups and using the most threatening language . . . (H.O.42/152).

(193). *James Steel, J.P., to the Earl of Lonsdale*

Whitehaven, 13 August, 1816.

. . The shoemakers and several other tradespeople have struck their work, but there is no appearance whatever of disorder or intoxication . . .[2] (H.O.42/152).

(194). *John Beckett to E. R. Travers (Mayor of Preston)*

Whitehall, 16 August, 1816.

I am directed by Lord Sidmouth to acknowledge the receipt of your letter of the 13th inst., stating that a great number of persons who have withdrawn from their employment in consequence of a reduction of wages, have been parading the streets of Preston and assembling in groups, using the most threatening language, and you request that a troop of horse may be immediately ordered to Preston for its protection.

In reply, I am to acquaint you that Sir John Byng, who happens to be in London, wrote by last night's post to order some troops to move from Manchester to Preston. (H.O.41/1/263).

---

[1] Seven signatures follow.
[2] Enclosed in Lord Lonsdale's letter to John Beckett, 28 August, 1816.

(195). *E. R. Travers (Mayor) to Viscount Sidmouth*

Preston, 19 August, 1816.

. . . I have great pleasure in informing your Lordship that the discontented workmen have returned to their employments, and that every symptom of riot has disappeared, and we do not expect any further interruption to the tranquillity of the town.[1] The mob did not appear to be an organised one, and I have not been able to discover any symptom of *Luddism* in their proceedings. It seems to me that the disturbance arose entirely on account of a reduction of wages in one branch of manufacture. The wages are indeed very low, but few if any persons are out of work . . . (H.O.42/152).

(196). *The Earl of Lonsdale to John Beckett*

28 August, 1816.

The low price of coals in Dublin, and the exchange being so very much against that country,[2] the shipowners at Whitehaven, through the medium of a Committee formed for the better regulation of the trade, submitted to me the necessity, as it appeared to them, of lowering the price of coals. Although I thought it was incumbent on them to show in the first instance that every means in their power had been tried to render the trade productive, by making these deductions from their ordinary expenses which the circumstances of the times authorised, yet I was desirous of setting the example, and did actually make such abatement as gave them the fullest satisfaction. It was after this matter was arranged that they began to diminish the wages of the sailors. During a part of the war, when men were most wanted, the allowance was five guineas a voyage to Dublin, which on an average does not exceed three weeks, and they are fed on board and maintained at the expense of their employer. It was afterwards reduced to $4\frac{1}{2}$ guineas, at which it has remained up to this time, and the proposal is to take of[f] one guinea, which appears to me perfectly reasonable. Nothing in the character of riot has appeared at Whitehaven . . . (H.O.42/152).

---

[1] The house, though not the factories, of Mr. Horrocks, the cotton spinner, had been attacked by the mob, and about thirty squares of glass had been broken.

[2] The Irish pound was worth about 18s. 6d. in England.

(197). *R. Barker (Clerk to the Magistrates) to Viscount Sidmouth*

North Shields, 12 September, 1816 :—. . . A handbill[1] calling an un-lawful meeting of the seamen (a copy of which is herewith enclosed) has been written and posted up against the walls in North Shields ; in consequence thereof the magistrates have deemed it prudent to request Colonel Ramsey to inform the Officer commanding in this District to have such a force ready at the call of the magistrates as may be requisite to assist them in keeping the peace. And the magistrates have also, with the concurrence of a magistrate for the town of Newcastle-upon-Tyne, sent to the Commanders of two of his Majesty's ships of war now off Tynemouth Bar, to request that the ships may be immediately brought into the harbour.

P.S. The magistrates request me to intimate to your Lordship whether the assistance of an officer from Bow Street might not have a good effect in tracing out the ringleaders, as the constables acting for their districts have not the ideas requisite for such purposes.[2] (H.O.42/153).

(198). *H. Cramlington to Viscount Sidmouth*

Newcastle-on-Tyne, 14 September, 1816.
. . . An attempt has been lately made to excite new disturbances amongst the seamen at North Shields. It seems that their numbers have been increased by the discharge of the sailors employed in the

---

[1] 'It is requested by the majority of seamen that a meeting be held on the New Quay on Tuesday morning at ten o'clock to take into consideration for an advance of wages to £5 as the provisions is at such a rate it is impossible for to keep our families from starvation at this momentous crisis, and no credit to be obtained from any of the tradesmen. The seamen of South Shields meet this morning at ten o'clock, when it is requested every one will attend to this business that is concerned.

[2] The following is a printed handbill, enclosed in Francis Freeling's letter to Mr. Beckett, 11 September, 1816 :

TWENTY GUINEAS REWARD.

Whereas certain hand bills have been written and posted up against the walls in North Shields, calling a meeting of the seamen to consider of advancing the sailors' wages, NOTICE IS HEREBY GIVEN that a reward of TWENTY GUINEAS will be paid by the churchwardens and overseers of the parish of Tynemouth to any person or persons who will give such information to the magistrates as may lead to the conviction of the offender or offenders.

North Shields, 12 September, 1816.

Greenland ships lately returned from their voyages, and that these sailors are the persons who wish to create dissatisfaction amongst those who have employment in the coal trade, on the subject of wages . . . (H.O.42/153).

(199). *The Duke of Beaufort to Viscount Sidmouth*

Newport, Monmouthshire, 22 October, 1816. (At night).

. . . The only fear the gentlemen in this town appear to have of any additional riots is from the colliers in this neighbourhood, who are very numerous, and who struck work yesterday. They do not appear to have the least cause of complaint, as they have ample pay and constant work, but many of the workmen at the iron works have certainly had their pay much reduced, though perhaps they have been paid as high as their masters can afford to pay them at the present price the iron brings them in the market. The owners of the coalworks together with some magistrates have been endeavouring to-day to get the colliers to work again, but I have not heard with what success . . . (H.O.42/154).

(200). *Major-General Sir John Byng to the Under-Secretary of State for the Home Department*

Head-quarters, Pontefract, 4 December, 1816.

. . . Your correspondent[1] from Oldham has wrote to me, as doubtless he has to you, that the weavers of two or three townships have struck work on the 2nd inst. Denton, near Ashton, and Newton in the parish of Manchester are two of them. It has excited a strong sensation throughout the district of which Manchester is the centre, and it is feared the example will rapidly spread. . .

Connecting these reports with what occurred in London on the 2nd inst.,[2] I am led to believe that there has been some endeavour to excite a general rising on that day, which from some cause has failed. (H.O.42/156).

[1] William Chippindale. (This was his own spelling, though his name is generally given as Chippendale). He was a Captain in the Militia at Oldham.

[2] The Spa Fields riot. Arthur Thistlewood and the two Watsons planned an insurrection under cover of an agitation for parliamentary reform ; the mob was early put to flight.

R

(201). *Colonel Fletcher to John Hiley Addington*[1]

Bolton-le-Moors, 7 December, 1816.

. . . The striking of the weavers did not take place, at least not in any considerable extent of country. Neither do I think it practicable throughout the whole population employed in the cotton trade. Should such a suspension of work, even to the extent of *one half* ever take place (which may God avert) the consequences must be terrible in the extreme, but I think the agitators of mischief scarcely feel themselves ready for such an attempt. They say that the efforts of the people must be reserved for the *great day*, and had the insurgents succeeded in London, *that great day* would then have arrived, when a general movement would have been probably attempted . . .[2] (H.O.42/156).

(202). *J. J. Wilkinson to Viscount Sidmouth*

1, *Pump Court, Temple,* 12 December, 1816.

I beg to call your Lordship's attention to some attempts to raise the price of bread in the metropolis.

A letter (to all appearance a circular) was delivered some time ago by mistake to a person I know (who does not wish his name to be mentioned). On opening it, the contents were as follows—'Bread will rise on —— to —d.' The letter was for a baker in the parish of Chelsea.

Another letter has been subsequently opened. It was a printed circular, and to the best of my recollection stated that a baker at Ham near Richmond had been fined for selling bread of light weight, and requested the attendance of the bakers to a meeting of the United Bakers Association, a company in Red Lion Square, to

---

[1] Lord Sidmouth's younger brother, and Under-Secretary of State for Home Affairs, 1812-18 (d. 1818):

[2] See No. 200 and note. Ralph Wright reported to Lord Sidmouth on 11 January that the cotton industry in Manchester was reviving. 'The manufacturers tell me that a considerable demand for goods has arrived from Spain and Portugal for the supply of their colonies. and that the corn trade has brought already many orders for cotton goods. There is abundant evidence that things are mending. The little tradesmen all around me are taking on fresh hands to weave, some of them 100 and some 200 additional men, and although wages are not increased, yet the prospect of better times puts poor people into higher spirits.' He was writing from Flixton, near Manchester. (H.O.42/158).

consider the propriety of bringing actions against the persons who fined him (not upon the merits, my Lord) but for a supposed want of jurisdiction.

I have no doubt much public good would ensue if your Lordship would direct proper enquiries to be made, and if the parties were indicted for a conspiracy, I think bread would be lowered throughout the metropolis. (H.O.42/156).

(203). *William Todd (Postmaster at Sheffield) to Francis Freeling*

Sheffield, 4 January, 1817.

. . . For a long time, to the serious inconvenience of the trade and prosperity of this town, a combination has existed among the workmen belonging to various branches. The fact of this combination has been brought home to some of the parties, and the magistrates have condemned them to three months' imprisonment, against which they have appealed to the Quarter Sessions. I was present at the examinations held on this business, and have published some account of them in the *Sheffield Mercury* of the 14th and 21st December last, and January 4, 1817.

It is a complete system of Luddism, and an opportunity is now offered to check its progress in this town, and at the same time, to deter offenders in other places.

The magistrates, on passing sentence, recommended that the master manufacturers should prosecute all the persons, INDIVIDUALLY, for a CONSPIRACY, in addition to the combination. Now, the masters are afraid to do this, for fear that they may incur the displeasure of the workmen and be injured in their persons or property.

Should not the Attorney-General be ordered by Government to prosecute these men for the conspiracy ? . . .[1] (H.O.42/158).

[1] *Wheeler's Manchester Chronicle,* 18 January, 1817, had the following paragraph :

ILLEGAL COMBINATION.

At the Town Hall, Sheffield, on the 31st day of December, 1816, J. Barnsley and W. Pryor, journeymen scissors-grinders, were convicted before J. A. Stuart Wortley and H. Parker, Esqs., two of H.M.'s Justices of the Peace, of an illegal combination in controlling and affecting Messrs. Rhodes, Champion and Son, in their trade ; and also of attending an illegal meeting at the house of Joseph Holland.

Mr. Rhodes proved that the defendants, some time ago, both wholly refused

[Continued on p. 228]

(204). *Captain W. M. Henderson to the Under-Secretary of State*

Chester, 8 January, 1817.
. . . There is some discontent among the journeymen, as at this moment the masters in some trades are lowering their wages. There are partial combinations among them in consequence, but their meetings are neither secret nor is anything political mixed with it. To relieve those discharged from work by the declension of business we have a subscription, and we find employment in the Committee for all who have applied. The number is 420 . . . (H.O.42/158).

(205). *Sir Robert Baker[2] to John Beckett*

Public Office, Marlborough Street, 29 January, 1817.
A considerable number of journeymen carpenters, who meet periodically at the Argyll Arms in Argyll Street to regulate the concerns of their trade, met there yesterday evening for the express purpose of considering the propriety of joining in the measures for procuring a Reform, and in the course of the evening Mr. Hunt[3] paid them a visit. Their conduct, however, was peaceable and orderly, and they separated at an early hour, but as none were permitted to be present but members of their own fraternity, I have not yet been able to learn the result of their deliberations. (H.O.42/158).

[Continued from p. 227]
to work for him, and that the last time he offered work to Barnsley, the latter said that he could not take it out till the above witness has settled with Pryor. Witness said ; ' Then, I suppose, you are shelving us ?' Barnsley replied, ' I reckon so,' or in words to that effect. That Fisher took out work about four weeks ago, but returned it unfinished, saying, the grinders would not let him work, and that his tools had been damaged. Matthew Fisher proved the existence of the meeting at Holland's, and stated the object of the Society to be the upholding of the trade by punishing such masters as will not give the Society's prices, by *shelving them*, and to punish the men who disobeyed the Society's rules by *rattening them*—that is, breaking their tools. The Society is supported by weekly subscriptions of sixpence from each member, and has a President and Committee. Witness lately took out work for Mr. Rhodes, but had not been able to finish it, as he has been rattened.

[2] The Marlborough Street police magistrate. He soon became Chief Magistrate at Bow Street, but he was dismissed in 1821 for failure to display sufficient firmness and resolution in dealing with the mob on the occasion of Queen Caroline's funeral procession through London.

[3] Henry Hunt, the Radical agitator.

(206). *Thomas Powell, J.P., to John Hiley Addington*

Cantreff, 8 *February*, 1817.

Just as I left Brecon to-day I was informed by an inhabitant near Merthyr that he should not be surprised if there should be some disturbances next week or the week after. in consequence of the ironmasters proposing to lower the wages. You will excuse me, but I strongly suspect you above are grossly ignorant of the state of this part of the country. I do assure you my opinion is that the late disturbances originated with those persons who acted as magistrates, most of whom were ironmasters. And had not the military acted with more discretion than Mr. Hall and his brother magistrates, this country would have been in a state of confusion. As I am in the habit of acting more particularly for the Hundred which abutts on the town of Merthyr, and being a magistrate of the County of Glamorgan likewise, I will most assuredly go over should any disturbances happen. Nothing could be more untrue than the letter in the *Courier* signed Wm. Meyrick, with respect to wages per week, as the mode is to pay them by weight or measure, and that only monthly, which gives the ironmasters an opportunity of imposing on the people by obliging them to go to their shops. If the ironmasters mean by lowering their wages to force the people to apply to their parishes for assistance, the whole country will be in confusion . . . (H.O.42/159).

(207). *Sir James Lyon[1] to Viscount Sidmouth*

Lichfield, 17 *February*, 1817.

. . The County of Stafford is represented to me as generally well affected to his Majesty's Government. The disturbances which have taken place have been confined to the western part of the County, and are stated to me solely to have arisen from the high price of provisions or disputes of the workmen with their employers on the reduction of wages. This part has been much relieved by the County subscription, and its resources will not be exhausted before the middle of the month of April. Hopes are entertained, and it is very much to be wished, that before the expiration of this period trade will revive, for in a part of the district alluded to—Bilston, two miles from Wolverhampton, a numerous population—little gratitude has been evinced for the relief given, and it is feared that itinerant

---

[1] He commanded the troops in the Midlands.

demagogues may easily excite these people to tumult. The temper and disposition of the lower classes near Dudley and Wolverhampton is represented as bad, but it is not in any degree ascribed to anything of a political nature. There are as yet no political Clubs, neither have pamphlets or seditious publications been circulated . . . (H.O.42/160).

(208). *William Jackson*[1] *to Viscount Sidmouth*

Leicester, 20 *February*, 1817.

We have inclosed for the serious consideration of your Lordship and the Cabinet Ministers, No. 1, a copy of the Resolutions of the framework-knitters passed at their late meeting, and No. 2, the subsequent resolutions of the hosiers.[2] You will find in them a statement of matters of fact, and things as they really are in this town and neighbourhood. The framework-knitters in consequence of the reduction of their wages are reduced to the lowest state of misery and wretchedness, and if the present system of giving low wages is persisted in, the whole of the common people must soon become paupers. One cause of this state of things is the Combination Act, which is unjust in its principles, and impolitic in its application. If this Act had never been enforced, mechanics would in a great measure [have] been enabled to resist their employers in reducing their wages, and consequently the country would have been in comparatively flourishing circumstances. All ranks of people in this town see and feel the evil of the present system of giving low wages, and we can assure your Lordship from a personal interview we have had with the Mayor, that he and the other magistrates of this town are anxious that our wages should be advanced. The present system will eat up the vitals of the country, and your Lordship will find that a nation of paupers will ultimately produce an empty Exchequer and a national bankruptcy. It is not the want of employment of which we complain, but the lowness of our wages, the hands out of work being comparatively few. You have legislated to keep up the price of corn, and it is but just you should legislate to keep up the price of labour, and your Lordship will ever find in time of peace that the price of one is dependent on the price of the other . . . (H.O.42/160).

---

[1] A framework-knitter.

[2] The above-mentioned Resolutions are too lengthy for quotation. The Combination Laws are not mentioned. The arguments in the covering letter are otherwise elaborated.

(209). *Major-General James Willoughby Gordon to Viscount Sidmouth*

(Confidential) Merthyr Tydvil, 14 March, 1817.
. . . Hill, the late Sheriff, told me that all *his* men had struck work because he would not raise their wages, but that he could employ the lowest labourer at 12s. a week, and some as high as 25s., but this it seems will not do. Mr. Bruce told me, in Mr. Hill's presence, that two of his (Mr. Hill's) men out of employ had called upon him that very day with their families for parish relief, which he refused, having heard from Mr. Hill that he had offered employment to these very men at 25s. a week !

I hear that the *Calvinistic* Methodists have great influence amongst these men, and that their doctrines are dangerous, while in other parts of this Principality, and particularly amongst the peasantry, the Wesleyan Methodists inculcate patience, resignation, and strict obedience to the laws.

This place certainly gives the tone to the whole *iron country,* and I am fully convinced that your Lordship cannot keep too vigilant an eye upon it. Their numbers are formidable, and they have no other principle of action than what proceeds from their wants. In a moment of distress, therefore, they may be impelled to mischief, without combination or forethought, and they have the power (unless curbed by the presence of some force and by the apprehension of more) of doing the most extensive mischief, both private and national, in a very short time . . . (H.O.42/161).

(210). *W. Lloyd Caldecot's Statement.*

Princes Street, Hanover Square, 17 *March,* 1817.
Are there not meetings held at different houses, under *pretence* of their being Clubs or Societies, denominated *Provident* Institutions ?

Yes.—Numbers of journeymen tailors, indeed *all* journeymen tailors meet at Benefit Clubs in and round London every *Tuesday* night—at which meeting *each* Club elects its Deputy for that meeting—which Deputy goes to a house (named) on the following *Thursday* night, where all the Deputies first assemble, and then, receiving a *watchword* from a person there, they proceed to *another house,* where, with CLOSED DOORS they proceed to business, a sentinel being placed at the door, a *slate* being the only thing upon which they mark their proceedings. These general meetings of Delegates then form *select* or secret Committees of five or seven. Any Resolution settled by this Select Committee is then sent to the different Clubs on the following *Tuesday* to be acted upon. The Resolution of this Select Committee is committed in a short hand (of their *own* understanding) on the *slate*, until it is seen by the *Delegate* of *each Club*, who reports it to the Club, as the *law*. Shoemakers and other mechanics adopt similar plans to form *Unions*, but I am given to understand their method is not so well arranged as the Tailors' Societies. Upon any extraordinary occasion each union of trade [*sic*] elect *confidential delegates* to meet and form a *Grand Union of all the Clubs* of journeymen, of different trades, who then select of their number, *one confidential* as representative of their trade, *which trade* may have 80 Clubs. These Delegates or *representatives* of each trade then communicate their Resolutions to their constituents.

Did not the late attack on the Prince Regent[1] emanate from *these Societies*, and was it not *previously discussed* at a meeting of one of these Select Committees ?

Yes.—A detailed account of which I addressed to the Right Hon. H. Addington for the information of his Majesty's Government, but I was not at that time *acquainted* with the *extraordinary* mode of conducting their *secret meetings*, and their *power* of getting so many men to one particular spot, at *so short a notice as I now know they are enabled to do.*

Who were the Delegates sent from the Bath Union Club at that time ? Mr. Hunt and Mr. Allan.

Does not Mr. Allan of Bath supply Mr. Hunt with the *watchword* and other information ?

With *information he certainly does*, and I have every reason to believe he does with the checque (as they call it) to some things, but he will not *trust him* with *all* the secret.

Do you think Allan of Bath one of the *leading men* in regulating these Societies ?—Mr. Allan not belonging *immediately* to *any one of* these Clubs, cannot be said to regulate them, but he knows the *whole* of their *secrets*, and was *introduced* by Captain Wilson (as he is called) to some Societies, where there were a great many *sailors* present, a few days before the meeting of Parliament . . .

Did you not see a letter from Hunt, expressing *fears* that the *Benefit Clubs* would be done away with ?—Yes.

. . . If the *Benefit Societies* of shoemakers and tailors are not

---

[1] On his way back to Carlton House on 28 January, 1817, after opening the Parliamentary Session, a missile was thrown at his carriage.

altered, I know that the country will be always harassed, *as it now is.* They have a secret oath, which contains nine Articles.[1] (H.O.42/161).

(211). *Viscount Sidmouth to Joseph Marryat, M.P.*[2]

Lloyd's, Whitehall, 3 *May,* 1817.

I have to acknowledge the receipt of your letter of the 16th of April relative to a combination amongst the boatmen at Deal, and to acquaint you for the information of the Committee at Lloyd's that having had a conference with the Earl of Liverpool upon the subject, it has been thought advisable to refer the case for the consideration of the Board of Trade. The papers relative to it have accordingly been transmitted to that Department. (H.O.43/26/134).

(212). *Joseph Willday to Viscount Sidmouth*

Atherstone, 31 *May,* 1817.

I take the liberty of writing [to] you to request the favour of your interference respecting a public house in this place where the journeymen hatters meet for to combine together respecting the trade. The publican allows them to have *secret committees held at his house, and so secretly are they conducted that it is difficult to find them out.* My wish is that the license belonging to the house should be taken away. I am quite aware that these kind of meetings are the foundation of the disturbances at Manchester and other places, and I have now to suggest to your Lordship a way by which you may at once destroy the baneful effects of public houses. It is by not allowing any publican to draw any ale for any person in his house after six o'clock in the evening. . .[3] (H.O.42/165).

---

[1] ' I will have no hesitation in swearing to the foregoing, but for certain reasons respecting Mr. Allan, I would rather not do so, but as far as regards all the others I am willing to do so if the public safety requires it . . .' His address was Halton Lodge, Lincs.

In a letter from Ramsgate, 4 April, he told Sidmouth, ' The plans and *combinations* of these men are organised with so much *secrecy*, they also possess so much *cunning* and sagacity, and their fidelity " to the cause" is so great, I really do think it will be almost *impossible* to *enact* laws that will *reach* them . . . I am not quite certain, but I think Mr. Allan told me that it was these men who in the first instance furnished the Luddites with private signals, &c. . . .' (H.O.42/163).

[2] Chairman of Lloyd's, and the leading representative of the shipping interest in the House of Commons. Captain Marryat, the novelist, was his son.

[3] This town of 2,900 inhabitants then had 37 public houses.

(213). *Colonel Fletcher to J. Hiley Addington.*

Saddleworth, Yorkshire, 31 May, 1817.

'. . . The weavers in several parts to the eastward of Manchester have meditated a *turn-out* or *striking*, and have broken up some Friendly Societies, applying the money to their maintenance during their absence from work. Whether the scheme is connected with what is stated by the Nottingham magistrates (of which I suppose you have been acquainted) is not yet certain, but it seems to me probable, although the great bulk of the weavers may know little or nothing of the origin of the plan.' (H.O.42/165).

(214). *J. Johnston to the Under-Secretary of State*

Hoop Tavern, Park Street, Grosvenor Square, 9 June, 1817.

. . . A framework-knitter (called a stockinger) can earn at the present time from 7s. to 10s. and not more per week (if he is a fair workman) and to enable him to support himself and his family he is assisted out of the poor rates. It has been ascertained, however, beyond possibility of doubt, that at the present market prices of hosiery, the hosiers can well afford to pay the framework knitters such a price as will enable them to earn at least from 22s. to 25s. per week, and that the hosiers have long been taking a most unwarrantable advantage of the times in paying their workmen a much lower rate of wages than the market price of hosiery warrant ; and they are thereby enabled to undersell the fair trader, and whose goods have not been recently manufactured and under similar circumstances. In consequence of these and other circumstances which I am well acquainted with, the Overseers of the Poor of Leicester have come to the determination not to allow any assistance to persons who work at what they call under-price, and claim assistance from their parish. The overseers have therefore at a public meeting, set a sort of rate of wages for the different kind[s] of work, and it is to be observed that the statement of the prices they have fixed, are not speculative, but on the contrary are moderate and perfectly justified *by the present market prices of hosiery*, and the difference between the prices which are paid *at present*, and the prices *fixed* by *advertisement* is, that at the *present* prices, a framework knitter can earn no more than about *7s. a week*, and at the prices *now fixed* the same person will be enabled to earn in the same time about 25s.

The *Statesman* and other newspapers describe the hosiery manufactories to be in a decayed and deplorable state. This is a most infamous falsehood. I do assure you on my own knowledge that there has seldom, at any period for the last five years, been more orders for hosiery than at this moment, in so much that several advertisements and handbills have lately appeared inviting persons to take in their goods for sale, and which immediately meet such a market as fully to justify the proposed advance in the framework-knitters' prices . . . (H.O.42/166).

Enclosures

[Advertisements published in the *Leicester Journal and Midland Counties General Advertiser*]

Leicester, 3 June, 1817.

It having been represented to us by the HOSIERS and FRAME-WORK-KNITTERS that much of the EVIL COMPLAINED OF from LOW WAGES is, in consequence of Parishes sending men to get work at REDUCED PRICES, and as it is in contemplation to ADVANCE THE STOCKING MAKER'S WAGES (*a statement of prices having been drawn up, and printed for that purpose*), we, the undersigned OVERSEERS of the subjoined Parishes HAVE RE-SOLVED that we will not, after the first Monday in July next, employ our poor in the *manufacture of hosiery* (except those we are compelled to lodge and board in the House) and we pledge ourselves such goods shall be disposed of to the trade *only*. Neither will we give any relief to persons travelling as agents for the disposal of hose, but are resolved to render every assistance in our power to those who are thrown out of employment.

[17 signatures follow.]

STATEMENT OF PRICES

We, the undersigned, present the following corrected STATEMENT. OF PRICES which has been adopted by the FRAMEWORK-KNIT-TERS AND MET THE APPROBATION OF THE HOSIERS, *and is considered as a guarantee to the employer and employed for the better regulation of the trade.* The INCREASED PRICES *are expected to* TAKE PLACE ON MONDAY THE 7th OF JULY.

Signed on behalf of the framework-knitters,

William Jackson, James Snow, John Thorpe.

STATEMENT OF PRICES

PLAIN HOSE

Women's worsted dumps.

Gage	Width		Price	
18	68 to	70 leads	4d. per pair	
20	79	83	5d.	
22	92	96	6d.	unwelted
24	100	104	8d.	welted
26	110	114	9½d.	
28	116	120	10½d.	
30	122	126	12d.	
32	128	134	14d.	
34	136	142	17d.	
36	144	150	20d.	
38	152	156	23d.	

Ribbed worsted hose

18	54 to	56 ribs	7d. per pair
	60		8d.
20	64	66	9d.
20	68	70	10d.
22	77	79	12d.
24	83	85	14d.

Broad ribbed hose		*Narrow clocks*	
20	12d. per pair	From 18 to 30 gages	2s. per doz. extra
24	15d.	30 38	3s.

Men's Plain hose

From 18 to 22 gages, 1s. per dozen more than women's.

24 and upwards 2s.

Sized hose

6d. per size less than women's.

Men's and women's lamb's wool hose

1s. per dozen more than men's and women's worsted.

No straight-down ribbed hose under 6d. per pair.

Leicester, 4 June, 1817.

TO THE FRAMEWORK-KNITTERS OF LEICESTERSHIRE

Fellow Workmen,

In compliance with your wishes, we have made use of all the means in our power to BETTER YOUR CONDITIONS, and to prevent you and ourselves from *being burthensome to the Parishes*. We are happy to inform you that our mode of procedure has now met the approbation of most of our employers, as well as received the sanction of a generous public ; and that our exertions bid fair to be ultimately crowned with success. The great obstacle complained of by the hosiers, viz., *that of parishes giving premiums, and manufacturing hosiery*, BEING LIKELY TO BE DONE AWAY, as will appear by the *Resolutions of the Overseers of Leicester* ; and which laudable Resolutions, we trust, will be followed by the other Overseers throughout the County.

If any of you should be thrown out of employment, you have the satisfaction of knowing that you will be assisted in your difficulties by a generous public ; we trust, therefore, you will still continue that peaceable conduct which has gained you such high estimation, and that you will endeavour to secure the kindness which is manifested towards you.

> William Jackson, James Snow, John Thorpe,
> Framework-knitters.

Leicester, 3 June, 1817.

(215). *C. G. Mundy, J.P., to Viscount Sidmouth*

> *Burton, nr. Loughborough, 22 July*, 1817.

. . . I am sorry to say the dispute now existing in this County (Leicester) between the hosiers and framework-knitters takes rather a serious turn. The shop of a framework-knitter at Wimeswold, a village about three miles from Loughborough, who is working at the low prices, was last night broken open and the *jack wires* drawn out of his frames, whereby they are completely disabled . . . The dispute is a very unpleasant one. The workmen are supported by the parish officers who are of opinion (and I fear with some truth) that there exists a combination among the hosiers to keep down the prices of the workmen so low that the parishes are obliged to make up the earnings of the workmen so as to enable them to support their families, and thus carry on their trade in some measure out of the poor rates. Thus far is certain, that the hosiers have agreed that a yard of work shall consist of two-and-forty inches instead of six-and-thirty. In consequence, most of the parishes in this County, and I believe all those in the town of Leicester, have agreed to support the workmen who give up their frames in consequence of the low prices. Many of the hosiers have agreed with the parish officers to give an advanced price, but others still holding out, I fear unpleasant consequences may ensue. The demand for articles of hosiery is certainly greatly increased. A large quantity of goods have lately been sent out from Leicester, and I have confident hopes that the trade is decidedly advancing . . . (H.O.42/168).

Ibid. to Ibid., Burton, nr. Loughborough, 13 August, 1817. . . . I am sorry to say things are not on a good footing between the workmen and the hosiers. There is plenty of work but the prices in general given are so low that no workman can maintain a family. This has given rise to a sort of warfare between the parish officers and the hosiers, the former having proclaimed their intention of supporting the men without work whose masters will not give an advanced price. Some of the hosiers have adopted the advanced price, and I am assured by several very respectable hosiers that it is no more than the trade can well afford to give, but many of the hosiers, and those the most opulent and of the most extensive business, still give the low price. They have also enlarged the size of the pieces, making a yard of *work* to consist of 42 inches instead of 36—but when the piece is sold to the shopkeeper the yard is only 36 inches. I fear these disputes may without close watching lead to dangerous combinations again on the part of the workmen who at present are very quiet. (H.O.42/169).

(216). *C. G. Mundy to Henry Hobhouse.*[1]

Bowbridge, nr. Derby, 23 August, 1817.
. . . I hope the differences between the stocking knitters and the hosiers and the parish officers will subside. I am aware it is quite impossible anything can be done by the interference of authority, and was greatly surprised to learn at Nottingham yesterday that my name has been made use of by all the three parties to serve their own purposes. It is needless for me to say I have carefully avoided any interference with any of them, though a day seldom passes without my being applied to by some persons connected with one or other of them . . . (H.O.42/169).

---

[1] [Permanent] Under-Secretary of State for Home Affairs, 1817-27. (1776-1854).

(217). H. Enfield (Town Clerk of Nottingham) to Viscount Sidmouth

Nottingham, 10 September, 1817.

The magistrates wish me to make a communication to your Lordship of the present state of this town and its neighbourhood.

During the last three days there has been a general strike, or turn-out, of the framework-knitters for an advance of wages, and vast numbers of them have come into Nottingham from the adjacent villages and townships. It is reported that they have in some instances in the County used violence, and in very many instances threats, to bring out those framework-knitters who were reluctant to join them, and that there are Committees sitting in Nottingham who are the directors of the present measures, and supply the men with money for their immediate support. At present no violence or actual breach of the public peace has been committed. The men walk about in considerable numbers, and make their frequent applications to the hosiers—but the magistrates cannot expect this tranquil demeanour to be of long duration if the object in view shall continue ungained, and they have therefore taken, and will be constantly prepared with, means to the utmost of their power for putting down any commotion.

With respect to the question between the framework-knitters and their masters, the magistrates have not any *power* to interpose—and as individuals they do not conceive that they have any *right* to become parties. Their duty is, as they conceive, to watch the public peace and to preserve it—being ready, nevertheless, at all times to receive complaints, and to enforce the laws relating to combinations, &c. It may happen that each succeeding day will make the men more and more discontented, and the Committees more personal and threatening. This may become so overt as to *call* for the interference of the magistracy *without* a complaint—but should this not occur, the magistrates are of opinion that they should not officially take any active step. They will be happy to receive your Lordship's sentiments upon this subject . . .

P.S., 11 September.—I beg to enclose your Lordship a handbill. This handbill was carried about by the collectors of subscriptions to the framework-knitters' cause, and a copy left with the subscriber. Their collections were (and I believe *are*) by house-row. (H.O.42/170).

[*Enclosure.*]

John Parker to Alderman C. L. Morley, Nottingham, 8 September, 1817 . . . The magistrate, I am well aware, is entitled to answer me that his concern is only with acts which constitute a breach of the peace . . . My information is that the application of the workmen for an advance was suggested to them—nay even urged upon them by the conduct of the overseers of the Parish or Parishes of Leicester, and the framework knitters undertook by their Committees (which it was hoped had become dormant at least, if not extinct) that prices should have a correspondent [sic] rise in Nottingham and throughout the County—a point in which upon their failing, the Leicester and Hinckley houses, finding themselves imposed upon, recalled their advance . . .[1]

(218). *H. Enfield (Town Clerk of Nottingham) to Henry Hobhouse*

Nottingham, 14 *September*, 1817

. . . The military force here consists of the 95th and only one troop of cavalry (the 15th). The Yeomanry Corps, from the horses being out at grass, and from the busy state of the harvest, would not easily or speedily be assembled. If the present contest break out into violence, the points of attack may be dispersed—and if so—the presence of cavalry can alone be effective . . . The persons turned out may, in this *neighbourhood*, be from 8 to 9,000. (H.O.42/170).

---

[1] The following resolutions, amongst others, were adopted at a meeting of the framework-knitters held at the Bell Inn, Long Row, Nottingham, on 21 July, William Rayworth presiding :

' That it is with pleasure this meeting are informed by the deputation appointed to wait on the hosiers that most of them see the necessity of an advancement and regulation of the workmen's wages, and express a wish that it may be generally adopted.

' It is the opinion of this meeting that the present reduction of wages has not arisen from any desire on the part of the hosiers to injure their workmen, but rather from an eagerness to under-sell each other in the market . . .

' That it appears absolutely necessary, in consequence of what has taken place, that committees should be formed in each district for the purpose of maintaining such an advance of wages as the trade will admit of . . .'

On 21 August the committee informed their fellow workers that some employers had agreed to a regulation and advance of prices, provided that the others would fall into line. The committee, on 2 September, published a handbill 'To the philanthropic and feeling public of Nottingham and its vicinity,' appealing for aid, ' without which we cannot be extricated from our forlorn and distressed situation. Most of the manufacturers are giving the prices which we now crave FROM OUR OWN EMPLOYERS. The price we now ask is what we received in the year 1815 ; and in the year 1811 we received four shillings in the pound more than what we are now soliciting.' (H.O.42/170).

(219). *James Rawson to Viscount Sidmouth*

Leicester, 18 *September*, 1817.

... About two months ago there was an attempt made here to raise the price of labour, and meetings were called for the promotion of that object, and it was finally determined to raise the price of making stockings very considerably, in some instances 50%. In addition to this there was a rule prescribed by which every article was to be regulated, and no workman was to make any goods but what was specified in this statement. Of course several of the principal houses objected to this regulation, having to make goods for every climate in the known world, they were obliged to change and alter their goods according to the customs and wants of the markets they were intended for. This raised a violent opposition, and our warehouses were beset with stocking makers for two or three weeks. At length the magistrates issued a handbill which had the effect of bringing the men a little to their senses, but meetings of Committees were held weekly for the purpose of enforcing the original object. A Central Committee was found and district Committees in every street of the town, which communicated with the Central Committee. A regular register was obtained of every stocking frame, and who employed it ; and if any kind of work was attempted to be made which the stocking makers thought improper, a meeting was instantly called and handbills circulated to prevent such work being made. In this stage of the business we thought it right again to request the interference of the magistrates, and we caused the Chairman and good part of the Central Committee to be brought before them, when they were told their conduct was illegal and must be discontinued. They are now pursuing their object in a different way, and are extending all over the country. A man of the name of Snow has been sent to Nottingham to promote the same object, and after a great deal of discussion between the masters and men, they have this week *struck*. The same man has been to Belper, Derby, Sheepshead, Hathern, Loughborough, Shelton and Hinckley for the same purpose, and even as far as Tewkesbury in Gloucestershire. Your Lordship will naturally enquire how the men are maintained without work. There is a subscription amongst the hands *in work*, and the men unemployed are allowed a certain sum weekly provided they will not work[1] [?] agreeable to the prescribed rule.

[1] The MS. is torn here.

S

Your Lordship will immediately see the effect of these proceedings. It will of necessity be the means of very much cramping the trade and allowing no scope for genius, for if no goods are to be made but by a given rule, if those goods suit a warm climate they must necessarily be very improper for a cold one, it is making the hands completely masters of their employers, and if any regulation is attempted to be made, they do not approve, by means of this system, that person's hands are all stopped. I would be sorry to bring any charge against our magistracy for having fostered and encouraged this kind of conduct, but really such is their predilection for the stockingers (and the men are all aware of this) that it is next to impossible to maintain any kind of subordination. I hope the late terrible examples has [sic] had the effect of subduing the spirit of Luddism, but indeed, my Lord, we shall have something full as bad if this organised system is not effectually stopped . . .[1] (H.O.42/170).

(220). *E. Frere to the Duke of Beaufort.*[2]

Clydach Iron Works, 21 *October*, 1817.
. . . Our workmen in the iron works and mines are all at work, and, generally speaking, contented and grateful for having been enabled to weather the late terrible times—but the recently increased activity and profitable state of the trade has raised up expectations beyond what can be realised, and some strange propositions have of late been canvassed amongst the class of workmen (*puddlers*) with whom the former disturbances began, as proper to be submitted to their masters *by the whole of them.*

These circumstances, though far short of what would justify any appearance of distrust or wish to bring military into the neighbourhood, make me very glad to think they are already and as it were naturally at hand, and if any troops are to remain anywhere in the district of the ironworks, it does seem to me (though against the opinion of some of my brother magistrates for the County of Monmouth who, I fear, look to the popularity to be acquired by removing the burden of the military, which they much overrate, rather

---

[1] Mr. Enfield informed the Home Secretary on the 25th: '. . . The framework-knitters are said to be *dropping* in again to work. This is the case, I believe, with some—but the bulk still remain out. However, there is no violence.' (H.O.42/170).

[2] Enclosed in the Duke of Beaufort's letter to Lord Sidmouth, dated Badminton, 26 October, 1817.

than to the security of the country) that Abergavenny, situated
within eight miles of one-half the iron works, and within 20 miles
of the most distant, is a better situation than either Brecon, Swansea,
Cardiff or Newport, all of which are near twenty miles from any
of the works—for a permanent station . . . (H.O.42/170).

(221). *J. H. Spencer to Viscount Sidmouth*

61, *Piccadilly, Manchester, 23 October,* 1817.
I have occasionally written your Lordship letters for these two
years back and have frequently had interviews with your late
worthy secretary, Mr. Beckett,[1] upon a subject which I deem of
most serious importance to the country, viz., relative to the different
bodies of manufacturing men leaving their employ, or, as they
term it, striking for an advance of wages. Looking at this subject
in all its various bearings (supposing that no check is applied) the
manufacture of the country in the end must be ruined. Mr. Beckett
showed me the opinions of the Solicitor and Attorney-General, who
state that no remedy could be applied. I differ very much from such
opinion and think the remedy easy. There is nothing to dread seriously from tumult amongst the manufactories when the business is
bad or when the stomach is empty ; rioting amongst them always
takes place when their bellies are full. I look forward to very serious
disturbances when the business of the country is revived. There are
already more than 20 trades or manufactories that have formerly
struck and are regularly associated, demanding their own prices
from the master under whom they labour, and they have secretaries
who regularly correspond with Societies all over the country.

Handbills of the copy enclosed, are just stuck up all over this
town, and crowds are constantly standing before them . . .
(H.O.42/170).

[*Enclosure.*]
*The following Communication, so interesting to the labouring classes
of every description, is copied from The Globe, a London paper of
Friday, October 10th,* 1817 :—
'We have learnt that the revival of Trade and Manufactures has
not, in every instance, contributed much to increase the comforts
and profits of the Artisans, for the Master Manufacturers have, in

---

[1] He was appointed Judge Advocate General in 1817.

general, abstained from raising the wages of their workmen, beyond the miserable pittance for which they had laboured during the pressure of the late scarcity. This has caused the Labourers in some of the northern districts to refuse the work, and their resolution not to accept it under fair proportionate wages has been regarded by some persons as mere obstinacy, and the result of a disloyal and bad spirit.

'We have often thought that our laws against the workmen in favour of their Employers savoured too much of an aristocratic and oppressive character ; for in the nature of things, the numerous Workmen must be ever more in the power of the few Employers than the Employers in that of their Workmen. Labour is a marketable commodity, the only one which the poor man has to offer, and must, like all other articles, find its own level. Nothing, in our opinion, can be more severe than for a wealthy Manufacturer to extort from his poor Labourer all the industry and strength he possesses, and yet keep him on wages scarce sufficient to support nature. The labourer is undoubtedly entitled to a fair and proportionate share of the profits of the work ; nor should the laws countenance the combination of a few individuals to compel him to exhaust his strength for an inadequate compensation.

'During the stagnation of trade, the Labourers were contented with wages so low that they, in many instances, offered to *underwork even the machinery*. They are not generally inconsiderate, and they were aware that the Masters, having trifling profits, could not afford the usual wages ; but now they perceive a manifest alteration in the state of affairs, and they insist, and justly too, on a proper remuneration for their labour.'

Printed by William Cowdroy, Gazette-Office, 261, Deansgate

(222). *G. H. Allen (Town Clerk of Kidderminster) to Viscount Sidmouth*

Kidderminster, 2 December, 1817.
. . . The weavers are returning to their work. Informations have been given against some, and the magistrates are proceeding in the inquiries against them, and I hope in the course of a few days to inform your Lordship that there will not be any further occasion for the soldiers . . .

There are many Sick Clubs in this town, and nearly the whole of the men are members of them, and the funds are placed in the hands of the manufacturers and others at interest. As soon as the men struck, most of this money was called in for the purpose of maintaining the weavers out of employ, and it is feared a deal of it is spent. I am fearful, as they have found such funds useful to them, they may materially increase them and use them at some future combination. I submit it to your Lordship's consideration whether the Legislature would think it proper in order to protect the funds of such Societies and prevent them being used for such bad purposes to pass a law to inflict punishment upon Treasurer, Steward, &c. of any such Club paying any part of such funds to support persons then in combination or for any other purpose than what is provided for under the Articles. As the law stands now, these Clubs, otherwise of great use, may become injurious. (H.O.42/172).

(223). *The Rev. Charles Prescot, Thomas William Tatton and Robert Harrison, to Viscount Sidmouth*

Stockport, 16 July, 1818, 9 p.m.

We, the undersigned magistrates for the County of Chester acting for the Stockport Division, take the liberty of communicating to your Lordship . . . the following particulars relative to a riot and disturbance which happened here yesterday amongst the work-people chiefly employed at what are called power looms, and which from all appearances is likely to be repeated.

The cause of this tumult is attributed to a general turn-out for more wages;[1] but the vengeance of the workpeople has at present been confined to the factory of Mr. Thomas Garside only. His weavers in concert, as is supposed, with the rest in the town and neighbour-hood, a week or two ago gave him the usual notice of their intention to quit his service if their wages were not increased to a price equal to an advance of 50%, which he refused to accede to, in consequence of which they left his employ according to their notices, and he advertised for weavers, and procured eight from Burton-on-Trent by sending over for them. This measure so irritated his late workpeople that they, together with some thousands of others assembled opposite the factory, on Tuesday evening last, threatening violence to the new hands when they returned to their lodgings. They, how-ever, dispersed at a late hour without committing any violence. Yesterday evening about 8 o'clock they again assembled in greater quantities and repeated their threats in more violent language, as well against the new hands as against Mr. Garside.

The appearance of the people assembled being very riotous, and they having begun to assault Mr. Garside, the constables, special constables, and as many of the Stockport cavalry as could be col-lected, repaired to the place about 10 o'clock along with Mr. Harri-son, the magistrate, who, seeing their numbers and disposition, immediately began to read the Proclamation to disperse, in doing

---

[1] This was the first strike organised by power-loom weavers.

which he was assailed with, stones brickbats, &c., and he and many of the constables and cavalry were severely wounded by them. The mob, however, having been admonished by Mr. Harrison, dispersed about 12 o'clock without doing more damage than breaking the windows of the house where the new hands from Burton lodged, threatening, however, to pull down the factory and murder Mr. Garside to-night, in consequence of which, the magistrates have thought fit to send over to Manchester (seven miles from hence) for a detachment of cavalry which was promptly sent here by Colonel Doherty. They and the Stockport cavalry are now in readiness.

A communication has been made to Sir John Byng, the General of the District, to the above effect, requesting at the same time that a detachment of troops might be ordered to this place to remain here at least until all is quiet, as it is impossible for the civil power upon occasions like these to repress so numerous and tumultuous an assembly, which request we have to repeat to your Lordship.

P.S.—12 o'clock. Since writing the above, Mr. Garside's factory has been attacked, and the detachment of cavalry has been called upon to act, and the Riot Act read. The mob is dispersed, but they have broke many windows in the factory, and wounded one or two of the thirteenth.[1] (H.O.42/178).

(224). *X.Y.*[2] *to Major-General Sir John Byng*

Oldham, 16 *July,* 1818.

... The hatters met ultimately at Middleton, where they were joined by the craft from Ashton-under-Lyne, Denton, Manchester, Bury and Rochdale ... With respect to Manchester the dyers have returned to their work, having obtained their wished-for advance. The spinners are still out, and I have heard of a movement among the weavers there ... (H.O.42/178).

---

[1] Mr. Lloyd wrote to Henry Hobhouse at 2 a.m. on the 17th : '... I came in from the Sessions to-night and made immediate arrangements, and all have done their duty. We have taken about 20 prisoners and shall proceed to examination in the morning. Several of us are hurt, amongst the rest my son, but all is very peaceable now, and no fears.' (H.O.42/178).

[2] A secret agent. He considered that the leading Reformers were at the bottom of the tumults in Manchester. His report is enclosed in Sir John Byng's letter to the Home Office dated the 20th.

(225). *Major-General Sir John Byng to Henry Hobhouse*

Pontefract, 18 *July*, 1818. (*Confidential*).

. . . The Commanding Officer[1] sent a troop of dragoons, and they[2] have sent an earnest solicitation to me to give them a permanent force, but I am much averse to doing so on many accounts. From its locality Stockport is not a place for cavalry. If opposed with the least judgment, they would be rendered of no avail. . .

That no adjustment has taken place between the masters and the men has a bad appearance, for we learn from it that 20,000 men (the least number I have heard them estimated at) have continued somehow to subsist for a fortnight without work. The hatters, a numerous body in the vicinity of Manchester, have given notice that they will strike work on this day . . . (H.O.42/178).

(226). *J. Lloyd to Henry Hobhouse*

Stockport, 19 *July*, 1818.

. . . From the inquiries I have made I understand that the masters cannot afford to raise the wages of the power loom weavers. Indeed they ought not to do so by apparent compulsion. It is most pernicious for masters to yield to the intimidation of the ungrateful workmen. The boys were getting 15s. per week by the looms when they turned out, and those that have turned out have an idea that if they subdue Mr. Garside, the masters in general will be under the necessity of advancing to their terms. His factory and workpeople are well watched, and shall receive all the protection I can procure. His confidence is strengthened by the attention which has been latterly paid. I believe he had good cause to complain of the apathy and unwillingness of the respectable inhabitants and of the constables themselves in the first instance, who dared to dispute the policy of his conduct . . . (H.O.42/178).

(227). *Henry Hobhouse to Major-General Sir John Byng, Pontefract*

Whitehall, 20 *July*, 1818. (*Private*).

. . . The disputes between the masters and their journeymen *ought* to be matters only of individual concern ; and Lord Sidmouth thinks

---

[1] At Manchester.
[2] The Stockport magistrates.

that in good policy they ought still to be so treated until they give rise to a breach of the peace. He always treats them so as long as possible, and is pleased that you have acted upon the same principle. In short, he is very much gratified that the military force in the Northern District is confided to an officer of so much judgment, and whose views are so coincident with his own. (H.O.79/3/182-83).

(228). *Thomas Woodcock (Mayor of Wigan) to Viscount Sidmouth*

Wigan, 22 July, 1818.

. . . The peace of this town is threatened by meetings of the cotton spinners who refuse to work, and I have been requested by the mill-owners to petition for a troop of horse to be ordered here for their protection. (H.O.42/178).

(229). *J. Lloyd to Henry Hobhouse*

Stockport, 23 July, 1818.

. . . The determination of Mr. Garside to act firmly and rightly . . . has had the best effects upon the minds of the turned-out work-people, who have, since I last wrote, been applying to resume their servitude with Mr. Garside . . .

Ibid to Ibid., 25 July, 1818 . . . Mr. Garside's turn-outs have all been with him to-day—have begged his pardon, asked to return, and he accepts their services ! This is the triumph of firmness and perseverance . . . (H.O.42/178).

(230). *The Weavers' Address to the Gentlemen, Landholders and Leypayers of Oldham and its Vicinity*

[A printed handbill]

Oldham, 25 July, 1818.

. . . After the Peace of Amiens, during the years 1802 and 1803 our wages were from 3s. 3d. to 3s. 6d. per pound for 24 hanks weft, and a pound is considered a reasonable day's work for a man. After deducting 3d. per shilling for bobbin-winding, house-room and other incidental charges, the wages of a journeyman weaver would then amount to 2s. 7½d. per day or 15s. 9d. per week, and this was pretty near upon a par with the prices of other mechanics, and we maintained our rank in society with decent respectability without being reduced to a state of pauperism, wretchedness and want. We will now contrast our present situation with the past, and it will show pretty clearly the degraded state to which we are reduced.

During the *last two years* our wages have been reduced such a pitch that for the greatest part of the time we have received no more than from 1s. to 1s. 3d. per pound, which, after deducting as above stated, would bring the *journeyman's wages* to the price of 9d. or 10d. a day, or from 4s. 6d. to 5s. a week, and we appeal to your candour and good sense whether such a paltry sum be sufficient to keep soul and body together, as we have our provisions to purchase from the same market and at the same price as other people who have been earning *three times* the money . . .

We will now call your attention to the situation in which we should be placed by the *attainment* of the solicited advance of our wages, which is stated to be, to *one penny per hank* or *two shillings* per pound for 24 hanks weft. The wages of the journeyman weaver will then amount to 1s. 6d. per day or 9s. per week, and this advance we are convinced might be easily obtained if the MANUFACTURERS WOULD EXERT THEMSELVES AS A BODY for the relief of their suffering *workmen* . . .

From the extreme depression which took place in the *market* after the late Peace, we are persuaded that we cannot expect to receive such an advance all at once as may be considered *a fair compensation* for our labour, but from the late increased and increasing demand for goods we are convinced that the present solicited advance might be *easily obtained in the market*, and by a persevering attachment of the manufacturers and weavers to each other's interest, we might soon be replaced in the enviable situation from which we have fallen, enviable indeed when compared with our present sufferings . . . (H.O.42/178).

(231). *Sir John Byng to Henry Hobhouse*

26 *July*, 1818. (*Most private*).

. . . I do not at all like the aspect of affairs in Lancashire. The combination about wages has existed too long ; the peaceable demeanour of so many thousand unemployed men is not natural ; their regular meeting and again dispersing shows a system and organisation of their actions which has some appearance of *previous tuition*. The evil appears to extend from town to town, but not to decrease in any place . . . (H.O.42/178).

(232). *Colonel Fletcher to Henry Hobhouse*

Bolton, 26 July, 1818.

[The turn-out of the Manchester cotton spinners still continues. Two mills have been set on fire.] . . . That at Preston was got under without much damage, but in that at Bolton, Messrs. Ormrod and Hardcastle's loss is very considerable (about £30,000) . . .

Mr. Chippendale says that at the inn in Failsworth after the last public meeting of the seditious in the field was over, the orators publicly boasted of the *turn-out* being their work, and I think it cannot be doubted that these itinerant orators such as Johnson[1] and others will endeavour to avail themselves of every species of discontent to further their own revolutionary views. From whatever cause it originates, a somewhat similar spirit seems to be spreading amongst the weavers . . . In regard to the comparative ground of discontent in the two bodies of spinners and weavers, the weavers have undoubtedly the greatest . . . but unless the employers can vend their goods to a profit I do not see that any interference can have any good effect. If the demand for goods should exceed the means of supplying it, the wages would soon rise to the desired level, and one great source of discontent in the most numerous class of our manufacturing population would be done away with, and the promoters of sedition here would find very few followers. As to the adult spinners they have no reason to complain, their wages being double or even treble that of the weavers. The *non-adults* (who are not, however, the complainants) may have cause both on account of the length of time they are kept employed, and the disproportionately small wages allowed them compared with those of the adults . . . Some of the persons employed have been told that their allowances would be discontinued in the course of next week, and the others I intend to apprise the first opportunity afterwards . . .

[*Enclosure.*]

William Chippindale to Colonel Fletcher.

Oldham, 25 July, 1818.

. . . Their [the weavers] condition is so extremely depressed, and their conduct has hitherto been so proper and orderly, that the strongest

[1] Joseph Johnson, a brushmaker of Manchester, was a well-known Lancashire reformer. He was present at the 'Peterloo' meeting in Manchester on 16 August, 1819, was subsequently indicted for conspiracy and unlawful assembling, and was sentenced to twelve months' imprisonment.

sympathy is excited towards them in every feeling mind. Since I saw you in Church Lane, they have waited upon the manufacturers in the most orderly and respectful manner, but have not received any encouragement to hope for an amicable adjustment. A meeting has consequently been called to be held upon Oldham Edge on Monday, and I understand a turn-out is the expedient to be resorted to. The demand of the weavers is so moderate and reasonable that all people have been desirous of an accommodation. I am fully aware of the difficulty and delicacy of interfering betwixt them, but cannot approve of the conduct of the manufacturers towards the weavers. If the trade will not afford an advance, a very plausible case might have been made out by the manufacturers, and something should have been done by them to appease the irritation. Instead of this they have not used the smallest exertion, or as a body taken the least notice of the subject. When waited upon, most of them said they would advance if a certain manufacturer would agree to it first, knowing, it is supposed, that the determination of the person referred to was not to advance. Now this has much increased the irritation, as the inference drawn by the weavers is that they could afford to advance if they were disposed . . . (H.O.42/178).

(233). *Henry Hobhouse to the Rev. W. R. Hay, Manchester*

Whitehall, 28 July, 1818. (*Confidential*).
Understanding that you are now at Manchester, I take the opportunity of troubling you on the state of that town and neighbourhood.

It is remarkable that though the great body of cotton spinners have now been so long out of work, and it was necessary in one instance (as we learn from Sir John Byng) to call for military succour, yet Lord Sidmouth has *not once* heard from the magistrates of Manchester on the subject, and has received *only* one letter from the Boroughreeve and constables, which bears date so long ago as the 9th instant, before the military were called into action.

Whether this silence is to be ascribed to any umbrage taken by the persons alluded to, from some cause of which *we* have no conception, or whether they do not view the matter in a serious light, and deem it unconnected with political considerations, I know not, but from whatever cause the silence may have arisen, Lord Sidmouth is desirous that it should be broken, and would prefer that a communication should be voluntarily made to him (or appear so to be) than that it should be called for from hence. And if the cause be of the first kind, which I have suggested, as no offence has been intentionally given, everything which can with propriety be done for appeasing any irritation will be cheerfully done at this Office.

I am not aware of any reason to doubt that the present discontent arose exclusively from commercial causes, but there is strong ground to believe that the political malcontents have been endeavouring to convert them to their own wicked purposes, and it is of great importance to ascertain to what extent they have succeeded, and by what means so large a body of mechanics has been subsisted without any visible means of livelihood for so long a period . . (H.O.79/3/186-89).

(234). *James Norris, J.P., to Viscount Sidmouth*

Manchester, 29 July, 1818.

. . . About six weeks ago the bricksetters and their labourers together with the joiners and carpenters first turned out for an advance. The former got what they wanted ; the latter one-half of what they wanted. Just as the latter people obtained their object, the *dyers* turned out and were out for about a fortnight or three weeks. They adopted a practice for the first time here of parading two and two through the public streets almost every day — certainly conducting themselves with great order, but still the practice being novel, it tended to alarm. My brother magistrates and myself did not think it right on this account to interfere in their practice in order that the lower classes might see distinctly that we kept aloof from any question between them and their employers as to the advance of wages, and in order that they might pay a greater respect to any judgement which we might be called upon to pronounce in case the masters proceeded against any of them under the Combination Act. No case however was at any time brought before us, and the dyers, who, it was generally imagined by the public, had not been so well paid as many other classes, ultimately obtained their prices. About a week before the dyers returned to work the spinners almost throughout the whole of the town and neighbourhood on one day struck for an advance, having previously given their employers notice that they would do so a fortnight before, and thus a number of at least 10,000 hands were in one day turned loose on the town and created no small degree of alarm. This number has been continually augmenting, and the number now out in this branch of trade is, I believe, considerably more than the number I have stated. The spinners adopted the practice of assembling in large bodies of two and three thousand each and parading through some of the streets of the town almost daily, certainly still without committing any breach of the peace ; and the magistrates, therefore, for the reason above stated with respect to the dyers, did not think it judicious to interfere. The spinners, from their working in such large numbers together, have a much better opportunity of effectually fulfilling their objects of combinations, and have undoubtedly from the beginning carried on such a system of intimidation against those who are willing to work, that the masters have not been able to break through it, nor to bring any case before the magistrates. The difficulty the masters have is that of identity. Four or five hundred or perhaps one or two thousand assembling from different factories and at the hour of work, viz. 4 or 5 o'clock in the morning, go to a factory at the other end of the town where they are not known, and so carry off by force or intimidation, though without any violent breach of the peace, the hands who might be disposed to go to work — and the parties assembled being strangers, the masters have in no one instance that I have heard of been able to identify persons, so that no case can be made out under the Combination Act. This is certainly a most unfortunate circumstance, because a few strong examples might have the effect of encouraging those to go to work who are willing but who under these circumstances dare not.

The system of support from one trade to another is carried on to an amazing extent, and they regularly sent delegates out to the different towns who are in work to receive their subscriptions. There is no doubt however that, notwithstanding this support, they suffer considerably from privation, but still there is no appearance of their going in to work at the old prices, and the masters, I believe, are generally pertinacious, and with great reason, because the spinners, averaging them throughout the mills in Manchester, gain 30s. per week each hand ; and the larger [the] family a man has, the better for him, because he can employ his children. There can be little doubt but that the spinners have sent their emissaries to different towns in the country, so that all the towns in the neighbourhood are equally well acquainted with what the body of spinners are doing here, and at any day if they thought it conducive to their ends, the whole neighbourhood might be in the same condition. The example of turning out is from all these circumstances spreading most widely, and I believe the weavers (who certainly are the most suffering part of our labouring classes) have come to a determination to seek an advance, and committees are now forming amongst them for that purpose, and several large meetings near the neighbouring towns have been held with this view. I trust the masters will take their case into consideration, and if possible afford them the increase desired, in order that so very large a body as the weavers are in this County may not be added to the extensive number already idle.

In two instances since the spinners have been out we have had riots in this town, but I consider each of them to have been accidental and not premeditated. In the first instance it was an attack upon the beadles of the town, who had been dispatched on a duty near to one of the large factories, and the men, being at that time assembled, which was perhaps natural, considering they had nothing else to do, and the beadles of so large a town being, I had almost said, necessarily obnoxious to the lower classes, they were recognised and pelted and forced to take refuge in a house the windows of which were demolished, and myself and a troop of dragoons were obliged to go to the spot in order to release them. A body of special constables with the head constable went up to the place prior to my reaching it, and had secured twelve of the rioters, eight of whom are to take their trial tomorrow for the offence. It was not, however, without considerable difficulty that they succeeded in quelling the disturbance, themselves being assailed on all sides by brickbats, stones, &c., and the number assembled on this occasion were about 3,000 men.

The latter instance occurred on Monday evening last on the *accident* of a fire. A body of about 500 had got together evidently with a view to take advantage of the fire and breed a serious disturbance, but fortunately it did not succeed. The constables who attended at the fire to keep off the mob were rather overpowered and at all events kept in check, and the Boroughreeve very properly sent immediately for assistance to the Barracks; and for myself I [was] obliged, seeing the inflammatory state of this mob, to read the Riot Act, and as soon as the troops appeared, the mob dispersed, without anything serious happening as far [as] regards the military or their being called upon to act. The gentlemen of the town who attended to assist the civil power on this occasion were many of them much bruised and hurt by the number and size of the brickbats, &c. with which they were assailed, and there can be little doubt that this assemblage had got together for the avowed purpose of destruction and disturbance in every way in which they could produce it.

I am happy to inform your Lordship that the town and neighbourhood still remain quiet, and except in the two instances I have mentioned, no riots have taken place, but from the disposition manifested by the mob of Monday it is more than probable that the more desperate amongst them are meditating some disturbance beyond that which might possibly arise from the present dispute between the men and their masters. I have already stated to your Lordship that the men out of employ assemble in considerable bodies at the outskirts of the town, and are evidently acting much in concert and under very excellent organisation. Whether there may ultimately be anything political in their intentions and movements I am not able to state to your Lordship, but your Lordship will perceive how easy a matter it might be for the disaffected in this part, and of which I am sorry to say I think we have too many amongst the lower classes to throw politics into the way of these men and convert what at present appears but a turn-out into an engine for alarming the Government of the country and producing a new order of things under the stale idea of a reform, and to insinuate at this time into the minds of these men that this will be about the time for removing all their grievances, as they would term them, by means of a general rising.

I am sorry to inform your Lordship that from all I can learn, Messrs. Drummond, Baguley, Ogden, Knight,[1] and in short, all the men who disturbed the public peace last year, have been most active for several months past in disseminating amongst the lower orders at meetings convened for the purpose in the different lesser townships in the neighbourhood the most poisonous and alarming sentiments with respect to the government of the country, and have continually inculcated the idea of a general rising, and although I do

---

[1] They were all well-known Lancashire reformers. Samuel Drummond and John Baguley had organised the march of the 'Blanketeers' on 10 March, 1817, the purpose of which was to petition the Prince Regent against the Habeas Corpus Suspension Bill, and to intimidate the Government into making concessions to the Radicals. John Knight, the itinerant orator, was sentenced to two years' imprisonment for taking part in the Burnley meeting on 15 November, 1819, to protest against the action of the Manchester magistrates at 'Peterloo.' The Petitions to the House of Commons of Knight, Baguley and William Ogden (Canning's 'revered and ruptured Ogden'), who were imprisoned under the Habeas Corpus Suspension Act in 1817, are in *Parl. Deb.*, XXXVII. 191, 441, and 412, respectively.

not by any means think that the system of turning out in the different trades is connected with this idea, or that the sentiment itself has taken root in the minds of the mass of the population, yet I am disposed to think that this idea gains ground and that in consequence the working classes have become not only more pertinacious but more insolent in their demands and demeanour, particularly with reference to the spinners who have no reason on earth to ask an advance of their wages except they think that it is one way of coming at the property of their employers. Several inflammatory handbills have been addressed to the public from the press of Ogden . . . About ten days after its appearance, the spinners by their Committee had the address to renounce this handbill, which, as far as it went, was certainly well in them.

Baguley, I believe, is ascertained to be amongst them, and I have as little doubt that the rest of the celebrated orators of last year, so well known to your Lordship, are by no means idle at this important juncture. These gentlemen are not unskilful in contrivances, and I am sure they have no feeling of fear to contend with on their own parts, for they are certainly much bolder grown than they were last year, and if they can avail themselves of the present temper of the working people to throw this populous district into disorder, and I might, I think, truly add, rebellion, they certainly will attempt it. The opportunity is but too favourable, but I am not prepared to add that I think their plan is at all organised at present. The impression on the minds of a number of our most respectable merchants, &c. is that an attempt of this sort will certainly ultimately take place, and I trust whenever it does, we shall be prepared to meet it. Most undoubtedly, if these people continue to travel about the country and disseminate the principle alluded to, it must in the end gain considerable strength in the public mind and feeling.

I understand the minds of the working classes in many of the neighbouring towns are at this time perceived to be in a state of agitation, but their movements and conduct are well watched by intelligent men in their neighbourhood, and I have little doubt timely notice will be communicated to your Lordship through myself or others in the Commission of the Peace, should the thing at all appear to ripen. I certainly myself should not entertain any apprehension but for the circumstance of so many trades and in such numbers having turned out nearly about the same time and from the pertinacious manner in which so numerous a body as the spinners are enabled or emboldened to continue out, and which may

T

at all events very possibly lead to some serious riot and disturbance when the people begin to find they can no longer live upon their means without returning to their labour. I believe their weekly division of the money which they contrive to raise from the other trades is by no means considerable, and that in numbers of instances these deluded people have pawned their furniture &c. for support, so that undoubtedly they must be greatly suffering from privation . . (H.O.42/178).

(235). *Henry Hobhouse to the Rev. W. R. Hay*

Whitehall, 30 *July*, 1818. (*Draft*).

. . . It is hoped that the disputes between the masters and their journeymen will be adjusted without their giving rise to any tumultuous proceedings, and his Majesty's Ministers are satisfied that the good offices of the magistrates will be zealously and discreetly exercised for the attainment of this important object. But while so large a body of men are unemployed, are destitute of the ordinary means of subsistence, and are exposed to the influence of such doctrines as those to which you allude, it is impossible not to feel great anxiety for the issue, and if the peace shall be broken, as firm a reliance is placed in the resolution and vigour of the magistrates for the suppression of tumult as in their temper and forbearance before it breaks forth. They may be assured of the most strenuous support from the Crown, and orders are given for reinforcing Sir John Byng if he should unfortunately feel any doubt of the adequacy of the force now under his command . . . (H.O.42/178).

Ibid. to Ibid., Private . . . Even if the views of the unemployed workmen were originally unmixed with politics, it is too much to expect that they should remain so, when they are daily and nightly exposed to the harangues of such men as Drummond, Bagguley, &c. It would therefore be an important measure if the magistrates could find sufficient ground for taking those demagogues into custody.

I am sorry to find that the opinion of some intelligent persons in your country is that as between the weavers and their masters, the former have just cause of complaint, though with the spinners the fault is on the other side. If this opinion is just, it is too much to [be] desired that the master weavers should, before it is too late, be convinced of their error and correct it . . . (H.O.79/3/195-97).

(236). *The Rev. W. R. Hay to Henry Hobhouse*

Manchester, 30 *July,* 1818. (*Private and Confidential*).

... The difficulty of the situation of those who fill responsible situations here is great beyond anything I ever experienced, and as far as I can judge, likely to increase. I see everything expected from the civil power, and no exertions on the part of those whose interest it is to exert themselves and to act in concert ; and I have reason to think that the masters are ready to murmur at the magistrates and the police for not obtruding themselves in situations where they could not act legally and with permanent effect, while they themselves, with instances before them of which they could avail themselves, wholly decline to put the law into action. The magistrates here came to a determination on the question, not to put themselves forward in it — it was, in profession, one between servants and employers.[1] However they might have their suspicions, or perhaps convictions, of the mixed nature of the proceedings, it appeared to them that the first impression was that of combination — that they were the ultimate resort on this question, and that therefore, if for no other reason, they should be the last to stand forward, unless the peace were actually threatened or broken. Mr. Norris informed me and by letter consulted with me on the view the magistrates had taken, and I fully agreed as to them. The masters were advised to act with energy : to publish their declaration that they would protect those of their operatives who were disposed to come to their work, to watch those who obstructed their people from coming, and to offer rewards for the detection of those who should stop them. Nothing of this sort has been done — no declaration on the part of the masters has been put forth, and I think that I may say has been, if ever taken up, wholly abandoned. My impression is that they are collectively and individually frightened, and as fast as a suggestion is offered, they allege generally that it would not be wise to adopt it. They, who have the means, are ready to call upon the civil power for the responsibility, while they neither take or try any effectual means to cure or meet the evil. And in some instances it is easy to collect that they profess an opinion that the civil power

[1] He had written to Sidmouth on the 28th : '. . . With respect to the dispute between the masters and their men, the magistrates have not in the slightest degree interfered, their sole object being to preserve the public peace . . .' (H.O.42/178).

is not only inactive but highly culpable. I am well assured that this is not the case. Some of the masters have cases of combination, but they decline, in fact refuse to bring the cases forward. All this is lamentable, but so it is. I do not consider that the magistrates or officers of Manchester have ever considered the matter of light importance or unconnected with more important designs — but as I stated, they have had to judge without any other general information ; in truth, they have had little if anything else to transmit than that a large body of men were out of work, and many were active in preventing others from resorting to the factories. The thing has continued from day to day and from week to week in the same state. But I can assure you that as far as the question has proceeded, I think there would be little else to state than that from the neglect and backwardness of the masters, examples which might have been made, have not been made. Some few days ago a deputation came from the masters to the magistrates. We told them that we were desirous to be of use to them, but that they must avail themselves of the powers and opportunities they had. Various measures were suggested to them ; they were, as soon as suggested, declined. In truth, they told us that they felt it a duty to tell us how things were circumstanced, and that, having done so, they left the rest to us. It is said that a similar notice is to be given to-morrow to the police. Everything therefore shapes itself as uncomfortably as possible.

In the meantime I have the pleasure to tell you that to-day eight people have been tried for a riot and assault at Pollard's factory. Of these seven have been convicted and sentenced to six months' imprisonment in Lancaster Castle. I conceive that the jury acquitted the eighth because he was drunk. The ninth who was on the indictment, an Italian, pleaded guilty. It appeared that though present, he was accidentally so. He could not speak English and was wholly apart from any of the trades here. He was sentenced to pay a nominal fine. Mr. Cross[1] made for the prosecution a most judicious and impressive speech, which was well heard. In passing sentence, I took an opportunity of saying that any number of persons desirous of returning to their work, and informing the magistrates that they were likely to be prevented, should be assisted to it by the civil power and protected — and as far as may be it will be so — but what

---

[1] Sir John Cross (1766—1842). King's Serjeant, 1827 ; Attorney-General of the Duchy of Lancaster, 1827 ; knighted, 1831, and appointed Judge of the Bankruptcy Court.

signifies this if the masters, from fear of making themselves obnoxious, do not render them marked and ostensible assistance ? ...
(H.O.42/178).

(237). *J. Lloyd to Henry Hobhouse*

Stockport, 1 *August,* 1818.

... It would be in their [the masters'] own power to bring me proof
of the combination and the persons concerned in collecting subscriptions for the support of it, I have shewn them some information
I have obtained and I believe an indictment for conspiracy is likely
to be preferred at [the] next Lancaster Assizes by respectable
solicitors in Manchester, with the assistance of myself against some
of the parties.

I enclose copies of some of the manuscript papers which have fallen
into my hands, and others are actually printed.

The 'No.' means the factory, the 'F' the number of friends contributing within Stockport. I could very much wish to proceed in
the Exchequer to get possession of the funds under the Act above
alluded to : 39 and 40 of George III, c. 106 ...

[*Enclosure*].

Subscriptions, 25th and 27th July, 1818.

No.	F.	£	s.	d.	No.	F.	£	s.	d.	No.	F.	£	s.	d.
1	13		13	0	14	3		3	0	40	7		7	0
2	1		2	0	15	13		13	0	41	12		12	0
3	3		7	0	19	18		18	0	42	7		7	0
4	1		1	0	22	3		3	0	46	1		1	0
5	1		1	0	26	12		12	0	47	23	1	3	0
6	2		2	0	29	1		2	0	48	6		5	6
7	12		12	0	31	18½		18	6	49	2		4	0
10	32½	1	12	6	36	2		2	0	50	5		5	0
11	15		15	0	37	18		18	0	51	5		5	0
12	4		4	0	38	18		18	0	52	4		4	0
13	25	1	5	0	39	28	1	8	0	57	11		13	0
												16	16	6

Ten voluntary loans from the following distinguished philanthropic characters:

	£	s.	d.
		10	0
	1	5	0
	2	0	0
	1	0	0
	1	0	0
	1	0	0
	6	11	2
	2	0	0
	2	0	0
	1	0	0
	35	2	8

1818.	*Disbursements*		£	s.	d.
July 25th	To delegation by J.B.		1	0	0
	Present and last week casualty pay to J.B. ...			12	0
	Clerk, office, &c., T.B.			10	0
	President and Solicitor's time, &c., W.B.			8	0
	Paid back to M.D.		5	0	0
27th	Returns printing			5	0
	Writing paper			1	2
	Postage of two Wigan letters			1	3
	Paid to Mr. J.W.		1	0	0
	Paid to Mr. T.H.		1	0	0
	Paid for two delegates foreign, T.F. and T.R., meat, drink and lodging two days			7	4
	Paid back to Mr. W.B.		2	0	0
	Paid back to Mr. J.F.		1	0	0
28th	Country friends by S.W.		15	0	0
29th	To 21 men and women at 7s. each, deducting for debts, loan and labour, 9s. 1d.		6	17	11
			35	2	8

Subscriptions, 6th July, 1818

No.	F.	£	s.	d.	No.	F.	£	s.	d.	No.	F.	£	s.	d.
1	18		18	0	19	18		18	0	40	5		5	0
2	10		13	0	22	10		17	0	41	19	1	1	0
4	7		7	0	24	8		15	6	46	1		1	3
5	7		7	0	25	4		7	6	47	23	2	4	6
7	20		13	6	26	12		12	0	48	10		13	0
10	32	1	12	0	29	15	1	17	6	50	5		7	6
11	49	2	9	6	30	—		6	0	51	5		5	0
(supposed)														
13	17	1	5	6	31	21	1	8	9	52	4		5	6
14	1		1	6	34	1		1	0	53	1		1	6
15	13		13	0	38	21	1	9	6	58	2		3	6
18	4		5	9	39	33	2	2	0			25	8	3

	Disbursements	£	s.	d.
July 4th	To two men for the audit of all preceding accounts...		9	0
	To the clerk for one day office ...		2	6
	To one man for 6 days' presidency ...		18	0
	To one man for a future expedition on trade investi-			
	gation ...		10	0
	To one quire of paper and ink ...			9½
	To great architect Juvenile Hiram, in re-expedition...		1	6
July 6th	Paid for liquor, had by the old committee ...	1	0	10
	To the clerk ...		2	6
	To one man unpaid by the old committee (E.B.) ...		7	0
July 7th	Paid for printing and paper, had by the old committee		2	9
	Paid to 73 men and women at 5s. each ...	18	5	0
		21	19	10½
	Balance in hand	3	8	4½

(H.O.42/179).

(238). *James Norris to Viscount Sidmouth*

Manchester, 2 August, 1818.

... I fear I may have been considered remiss in not having before written to your Lordship on the state of this neighbourhood, but considering it as a mere question between the workmen and their employers as to the price of wages, I did not think it requisite to trouble the Government upon a subject which I had not any reason to suppose would continue so long in discussion, or that it would have broken in upon the public peace in the way in which it has latterly appeared to do. That the soi-disant reformers should lay hold of this, as they always will (till put down) of any occurrences that may happen for the time to agitate the public mind and make it the instrument of their own designs upon the Government and peace of the country, I have always been prepared to expect ...

... In order to protect the hands who are willing to work, of which it is supposed there is a considerable number, a handbill which I enclose your Lordship has been placarded or published on the walls to give encouragement to such persons to resume their employment and to assure them of the protection of the civil power. The effect of this measure will be tried tomorrow morning. All the mills will be opened and in case at any one the hands should be obstructed, the civil power will be ready to assist, and in case of still further need the military will be in readiness. I trust the well-disposed workmen will avail themselves of this opportunity, if not tomorrow, in a few days, and I have no reason to apprehend that it will lead to any breach of the peace, but of course in the present temper of the lower classes, reduced as they now are in the means of subsistence, there can be no answering decidedly for the entire preservation of the public peace . . .

I am sorry I have it not in my power to inform your Lordship that the manufacturers have granted to the weavers their demand of increase of wages. The public feeling is certainly in favour of the men — they are the most suffering class. I still hope the question between these parties will be settled without any ill blood. The men have been very temperate in their manner of asking for the increase, and avow, I understand, that they will have nothing to do with any other question — alluding to that of reform — all that they affect to want or ask being an advance of wages . . . (H.O.42/179).

(239). *Henry Hobhouse to James Norris*

Whitehall, 4 August, 1818. *Private.*
. . . You cannot be more fully impressed than Lord Sidmouth is, with the propriety of the magistrate forbearing to interfere in questions between master and servant so long as the peace is unbroken, but it is impossible for the Secretary of State to contemplate with indifference the danger likely to result to the public weal from the existence, in such a population as that of the south-eastern part of Lancashire, of large bodies of men without the visible means of subsistence, and exposed to the harangues of the disaffected demagogues, who are known to be ever alive to the means of doing mischief in that quarter of England. And of course, when such a state of things exists, Lord Sidmouth is anxious to obtain frequent and authentic information of what passes, although the magistrates may not have been called into action . . . (H.O.79/3/208-10).

(240). *James Norris to Viscount Sidmouth*

Manchester, 5 August, 1818.
. . . Two or three factories have been at work and no interruption offered to the hands going in, but I fear very few hands have availed themselves of the factories being open . . . There is undoubtedly great misery amongst those connected with the factories (women and children) but who are not really turn-out spinners. I heard this day at least 100 cases of this sort, being appeals to the magistrate from

the determination of the churchwardens; but I have in very few instances granted any relief ... (H.O.42/179).

(241), *James Norris to Henry Hobhouse*

Manchester, 7 August, 1818.

... The plan which the operatives now threaten to adopt is to take the names and addresses of the individuals who work, and prevent their leaving their own houses. This however will be attended with considerable difficulty and cannot long (if at all) be carried into execution ...

To-day two persons have given bail for an assault, upon the mother of a child carrying breakfast to it at Mr. Houldsworth's[1] mill, and a case of combination against two others at the same mill has been remanded till tomorrow ... Other warrants have also been applied for and granted, and all this manifests a degree of activity on the part of the masters from which I hope for the most favourable results ...

The hands are certainly pursuing all possible means of obtaining money — by subscription from other trades, borrowing from the publicans and shopkeepers, and begging in every shape. This system of course can last but a short time longer. I understand, in order to oblige the hands to assemble and parade, no individual is allowed to participate in the weekly division who does not assemble and parade ... (H.O.42/179).

(242). *J. Lloyd to Henry Hobhouse*

Stockport, 8 August, 1818.

... Owing to the determination of the masters who have been influenced by a proper example, and owing to the want of funds to support them in idleness, they are applying to be taken in, and many have actually been taken into their employment again at the different factories here which the steam-loom weavers deserted just one month ago. No advance!

I learnt that they had a fund at a certain public house in this town. I yesterday went myself and surprised them at the Exchequer — took all their names down and have just now had them answering under summons by authority of the Combination Act the landlord as well as the Committee who have all rendered themselves liable to commitments, but the case is postponed for a meeting on Monday.

[1] M.P. for Pontefract.

I am happy to find that the means is too contemptible to render the combination a matter of any serious consideration to the masters here, but from the principle being so very pernicious the offenders shall not wholly escape — that the public may know a little of the law . . .

The out-door weavers and I are upon very good terms, and I have no apprehension whatever of them as a body doing anything wrong. (H.O.42/179).

(243). *Colonel Fletcher to Henry Hobhouse*

Bolton-le-Moors, 8 August, 1818.

. . . The spinners in the neighbourhood of Wigan have, as I understand, *struck* in imitation of those of Manchester . . . An advance, however, in the weavers' wages of about 10% which has taken place in this neighbourhood, and which will, I trust, become general, will probably prevent that numerous part of our population from becoming the dupes of wicked and designing agitators, and thereby defeat the expectations of the disaffected. (H.O.42/179).

(244). *James Norris to Henry Hobhouse*

Manchester, 8 August, 1818.

. . . A *considerable* number were collected today in Oxford Road in the neighbourhood of the factories in different groups supposed to be for the purpose of dividing money — but it is at present quite impossible to get amongst them so as to ascertain what they do. I believe they get considerable sums of money from the different trades for a considerable distance from this place, and so long as they continue to get thus supplied, there is but little chance of their going in to work . . .

I am sorry to say that in a case of combination which should have been heard this day, the case was obliged to be remanded in consequence of the absence of the boy who was ill-used, and he has either been bribed or carried away by force . . .[1] (H.O.42/179).

[1] Henry Hobhouse wrote to Norris on the 10th : '. . . It will be highly satisfactory to Lord Sidmouth to learn from them [*i.e.,* from Norris's letters of the 7th and 8th] that the masters appear to be coming forward to enforce the law against the delinquent journeymen ; more good is to be anticipated from this proceeding than from any other measure. The backwardness of the masters in this respect has always appeared to his Lordship the most formidable symptom attending the recent state of circumstances in Lancashire.' (H.O.41/4/148).

(245). *The Rev. W. R. Hay to Henry Hobhouse*

Ackworth, 9 August, 1818.

. . . In respect of the weavers I was sorry to find on my return through Manchester that little if anything had been done. There seems a general acknowledgment that their masters might raise their wages considerably with their own profits, and it is expected that they will be raised. Still however nothing was done.

The division to the spinners on Tuesday last was 10d. per head. Whether or no this included the female spinners I cannot tell. The masters have within the last week taken more courage ; whether or no this has arisen from the less encouraging prospects of the operatives I know not. Had the masters exerted themselves earlier, things would have been brought to a settlement before now. I cannot help feeling that the question of wages will be settled now without riot . . . (P.R.O., H.O.42/179).

(246). *Henry Hobhouse to James Norris*

Whitehall, 9 August 1818. *Private.*

. . . I should derive great satisfaction from hearing that a case can be made under the Combination Act against Bagguley, Drummond and Johnston. Their conviction would have a doubly good effect since it would remove them for a while from the scene of action, and would expose to the world the leaders of the conspiracy.

It is much to be wished that the masters in general would follow the example of Mr. Houldsworth. Greater good would be effected by proving that the law when put in force is capable of repressing the mischief than by any other means. This doctrine Lord Sidmouth is very anxious to see inculcated in every shape . . . (H.O.79/3/221-22).

(247). *James Norris to Henry Hobhouse*

Manchester, 10 August, 1818. 10 *p.m.*

. . . I believe the spinners get very considerable relief from the trades *in London* where a delegation is within a day or two gone up for the purpose of collecting. I understand and believe that the tailors have contributed very considerably — as much as £600 at one time — whether the amount be correct or not I cannot answer . . . (H.O.42/179).

(248). *Henry Hobhouse to the Rev. W. R. Hay, Ackworth, Pontefract*

Whitehall, 11 *August*, 1818. *Private*.
. . . Everybody here concurs with you in feeling the injury which has been done at Manchester by the backwardness of the masters. How is it possible for any Government to protect men who will not protect themselves ? This is the text which ought to be preached on at Manchester for the next three months . . . (H.O.79/3/229-30).

(249). *James Norris to Henry Hobhouse*

Manchester, 11 *August*, 1818.
. . . I believe that one main support of the spinners has been the shopkeepers who have permitted them to have credit to a considerable extent, but this must necessarily have an end, and I take it has already pretty nearly exhausted itself . . . (H.O.42/179).

(250). *Henry Hobhouse to James Norris*

Whitehall, 12 *August*, 1818.
I much regret that you have not been able to bring justice home to the men who were in custody for ill-using Mr. Houldsworth's spinner, because it gives to the criminal a triumph over the law which in the present state of your town is the most pernicious event that can happen. I am happy to find that at Stockport several convictions have taken place under the Combination Act, and their good effect is apparent . . . (H.O.79/3/230-31).

(251). *James Norris to Henry Hobhouse*

Manchester, 12 *August*, 1818. *Private*.
. . . One *small* huckster near the factories has given credit to the men to the amount of £250. This instance enables one to judge of the means they have had of holding out, added to which, no doubt, they have received considerable supplies from London and other large towns . . . (H.O.42/179).

(252). *William Shepherd Kinnersly, M.P., to Viscount Sidmouth*

Newcastle, Staffordshire, 12 *August* 1818.
. . . The associated journeymen-hatters in this place have held a

meeting for the purpose of subscribing towards the support of the workmen in Manchester who are holding out against their employers. Some money was subscribed and sent with a promise of a further sum in a fortnight. The sum was trifling, being only £5 from five or six hundred men, but important as shewing the system. (H.O.42/179).

(253). *James Norris to Henry Hobhouse*

Manchester, 13 August, 1818.

. . . Money. . . has been divided, amounting to 9d. per head.

The case against the two spinners for obstructing and otherwise ill-treating one of Mr. Houldsworth's hands has been heard today by Mr. Wright, Mr. Marriott and myself, and a very complete case made out. The men were sentenced to three months in Lancaster Castle, and immediately gave notice of appeal and entered into the recognisance required by the Act, viz. £10 for the principals and £5 for the sureties — thus rendering all that has been done a perfect nullity, and it does appear from this case that the Combination Act is of very little if of any use. The case could not be made out against them as for a conspiracy. The power of appeal should in my humble opinion be taken away . . .

I learn from good authority today that the average of earnings per week for the last six months, taking 40 principal mills, is 31/10d. for every adult male spinner, and 18s. for women and boys of 16 or 18 years old. The statement therefore put forth by the operatives is entirely untrue . . .[1]

---

[1] The cotton-spinners' Address to the Public is in *Annual Register*, 1818, Chronicle, pp. 100-102. '. . . In 1816 the average clear wages of the spinners in Manchester was about 24s.; they were then reduced from 20 to 25%, and have ever since laboured under that reduction. And it is to be remarked that spinners relieve their own sick, as well as subscribe to other casualties ; therefore, when their hours of labour, which are from 5 in the morning until 7 in the evening (and in some mills longer) of unremitting toil, in rooms heated from 70 to 90 degrees, are taken into consideration, we believe the public will say with us that no body of workmen receive so inadequate a compensation for their labour . . .' Henry Hobhouse thus referred to this Address in a letter to Mr. Norris, dated 6 August : '. . . The worst symptom about their Address is the style in which some parts of it are drawn up, which evidently shew that recourse has been had to some person of superior education to themselves.' He added : 'I trust that the arrangements for protecting the hands who may be disposed to go to work will be successful.' (H.O.41/4/145).

The frequency of the turnouts in the various trades is now become such that they will ultimately get well organised and too powerful to be put down. As it is, all the manufacturing districts throughout the kingdom have their delegates or other means of communication in cases of extensive turnouts . . . (H.O.42/179).

(254). *Henry Hobhouse to James Norris*

Whitehall, 13 August, 1818.
. . . I am sorry to learn that many of the manufacturers do not think fit to keep their workshops open.

This conduct scarcely allows a fair chance to the journeymen who may choose to return to their work, and is therefore much to be reprobated. Not less so is that of the shopkeepers who have aided the turn-outs in their combination by giving them credit.

Your account of the weavers is more satisfactory, but it is not agreeable to hear that the motions of the spinners are unknown, for if they are secret they cannot be very laudable . . .

Ibid. to Ibid., 14 *August* 1818. *Private and confidential :*—I am sorry to observe by your letter of the 12th that a want of unremitted resolution continues to prevail among the masters.

If they shut their manufactories, how can they expect the journeymen to return to them ? And how can any authority either civil or military drive them back ? Not that authority can be legitimately applied to such an object. Your statements have led to no favourable opinion of the masters, and if they yield at after last, having resisted so long to the imminent hazard of the public peace, that opinion will be still lowered . . . (H.O.79/3/234-36).

(255). *Henry Hobhouse to Major-General Sir John Byng*

Whitehall, 14 August, 1818. Private and confidential.
. . . Matters have certainly been better managed at Stockport than at Manchester. The masters have been more firm, and the convictions under the Combination Act have done great service. The doctrine I have inculcated is that the first object is to shew to the workmen that the law is strong enough, if it be but properly enforced, but this principle has not been acted upon in Manchester, where the manufacturer seems to rely more on your sword than on any other weapon . . . (H.O.79/3/239-40).

(256). *Henry Hobhouse to William Shepherd Kinnersly, M.P.*

Whitehall, 15 *August,* 1818.

I am directed by Lord Sidmouth to acknowledge and thank you for your letter[1] of the 12th inst., acquainting his Lordship that the associated journeymen hatters in the town of Newcastle-under-Lyne have held a meeting for the purpose of subscribing towards the support of the workmen in Manchester who are holding out against their employers. If the case can be made out to come within the Combination Act, and the circumstances can be proved by competent evidence, Lord Sidmouth thinks it extremely material that a prosecution should be instituted against the offending parties. (H.O.41/4/149-50).

(257). *William Marriott, J.P., to Henry Hobhouse*

Prestwich, 17 *August* 1818.

. . . The weavers . . . some years ago were so extravagantly paid that by working three or four days in the week they could maintain themselves in a comparative state of luxury. They then spent a great portion of their time and money in alehouses, and at home had their tea-tables twice a day provided with a rum bottle and the finest wheaten bread and butter. When the change took place, and it became necessary they should lend themselves to habits of increased industry and frugality, some discontent arose. Still, had they not been wrought upon by the machinations of demagogues and disappointed reformers, I firmly believe they would have conducted themselves with decency and order. During the years 1816 and 1817, being the only magistrate on this populous side of the country, I had a great intercourse with the distressed weavers, and really can with truth say I found them extremely well behaved and always thankful for a very moderate pittance of parochial relief . . . (H.O.42/179).

(258). *Henry Hobhouse to James Norris*

Whitehall, 19 *August,* 1818.

Having submitted for the consideration of the Solicitor-General (the Attorney-General being absent from London) the points mentioned in your letter of the 14th inst. as to the right of the

[1] No. 252.

magistrates to disperse the persons assembled about the mills in the manner therein described, and also as to their right to disperse persons assembled at meetings such as that lately held on Kersall Moor, I have now the honour to acquaint you that it is the Solicitor-General's opinion that if the persons assembled about the mills or on Kersall Moor conduct themselves peaceably and quietly, and there are no circumstances attending the meetings of actual force or violence, or having an apparent tendency thereto, the magistrates will not be justified in interfering to disperse them. (H.O.41/4/150-51).

(259). *Henry Hobhouse to William Marriott*

Whitehall, 19 August 1818. *Private.*

. . . On the present occasion the master spinners appear to have acted with very little discretion towards their men. I can of course form no judgment whether the claims of the men are either wholly or partially reasonable. But when they were first preferred, or indeed before, the masters ought to have taken that point into their un-biassed consideration, and have taken their resolution as to the line which it became them to adopt. From a resolution so formed, they ought not to recede. But I fear none such has ever been formed, but the men have been set at defiance without considering the justice of their pretensions. After they have been so long resisted, it would be mischievous that they should finally succeed. Government and the magistracy must ever discountenance combination, but they have much to complain of those who give rise to the combination by relying on the support of the law instead of considering the justice of the demands made on them. (H.O.79/3/254-56).

(260). [The following is a copy of a printed handbill].

Manchester, August 19*th*, 1818.

At a *meeting of Deputies* from the under-mentioned TRADES from Manchester, Stockport, Ashton-under-Lyne, Oldham, Bury, &c., &c., &c.

Calico printers, dyers and dressers, hatters, blacksmiths, jenny spinners, cotton weavers, bricklayers, fustian cutters, colliers sawyers, shoemakers, slubbers, mule spinners, machine makers, &c

The following Address and Resolutions were unanimously agreed to

At a general meeting of trades convened to take into consider-ation the distressed state and privations to which the working class of society are reduced by their avaricious employers reducing wages to less than sufficient to support nature or purchase the bare necessaries for our existence, with great economy and hard labour ; therefore, to render redress in such cases of distress to any body or party reduced as aforesaid,

RESOLUTIONS

First — That there be a Union of all Trades called the PHILANTHROPIC SOCIETY, to be held in Manchester on the second Monday in every month, when all TRADES shall send a *delegate* with proper credentials for admission.

Second — That every trade be recommended to raise a FUND amongst themselves for the general benefit of all trades joined in this Union, and in particular any trade that may be engaged in resisting oppression, or to alleviate distress, and to enable the labouring part of the community to live in comfort and decency.

Third — That any trade feeling the necessity of an advance of wages, that trade shall be bound to give notice to a meeting of delegates convened for that purpose ; and their concurrence being obtained, all other trades will support them.

Fourth — That if any trade be under the necessity of leaving their employ through the oppression of their employers, they shall first call the general representatives together and inform them, provided that such representatives be not overpowered with too much business at one time, that they may be prepared for supporting the cause and provide for the same ; in short, no trade shall leave their employ without first calling the other trades together, and then act by and with their consent in taking the most favourable time for resistance.

Fifth — That any body of workmen being oppressed or illegally used, this Society will support them in obtaining legal redress.

Sixth — That all printing of notices, &c. with all delegations, or any other necessary expenses, shall be paid out of their separate funds.

Seventh — That a Committee of eleven persons be chosen by ballot, out of the different trades who form this Society, and shall be regularly enrolled on the list kept for that purpose. The Committee to go out by regular rotation every month, so that the whole may be changed every three months.

Eighth — That in order to preserve decorum in this Society or meeting of representatives, no person shall be allowed to advance

U

any political or religious argument, under a forfeit of 3d. for the first offence, and 6d. for the second, which must be paid the night it is forfeited.

Ninth — That there shall be an Auxiliary Society of the different trades in each town ; that each trade shall have its own by-laws, and each auxiliary to act in conjunction with the Resolutions of the central Philanthropic Society.

Tenth — That the representatives be empowered to alter or amend, add or diminish any Rule or Rules for the benefit of this Society, provided it does not infringe upon or act against any trade or division belonging to the general Philanthropic Society.

G. Cave, Printer, Exchange Buildings, Manchester.[1]

(H.O.42/179 and 181).

(261). *Henry Hobhouse to the Rev. C. W. Ethelston, J.P.*

Whitehall, 20 August, 1818. *Private.*
. . . It is a very curious problem from whence the great supply of money has been made to the workmen who have thrown themselves out of work, and any light will be valuable that can be thrown on that question . . . (H.O.73/3/260).

(262). *Henry Hobhouse to J. Lloyd*

Whitehall, 21 *August* 1818. *Private.*
. . . You cannot please me better than by turning your attention to the Friendly Societies, by which I have no doubt the sytem which is the bane of your country is in a great degree supported . . . (H.O.73/3/261).

[1] This handbill, of which there are several copies in the Home Office papers (the date is omitted from the one in H.O.42/181, and the first sentence from the one in H.O.42/179) was sent by the Home Secretary to the Solicitor of the Treasury on 18 October, 1818, with a direction to submit it to the Law Officers of the Crown. Lord Sidmouth asked for their opinion 'As to how far it is a fit subject for a criminal prosecution ?' Sir Samuel Shepherd (Attorney-General) and Sir Robert Gifford (Solicitor-General) replied, on 19 October, 1818 : 'We have considered the accompanying paper and we are of opinion it would not be advisable to institute any prosecution for the publication of it. Indeed, we very much doubt whether it could be made the subject of prosecution, and as the spirit of combination amongst the workmen in this part of the country has in some degree apparently subsided, a prosecution now instituted (and particularly if it failed) might rather tend to revive than extinguish it.

(263). *Henry Hobhouse to Thomas Scholes Withington*

Whitehall, 21 August 1818. *Private.*
I thank you for your information. I am sorry there should be any defection amongst the masters, but it is better that it should be confined to me than spread further. It would be unpardonable in them to yield the point after they have so long endangered the peace of the county by resisting the illegal combination.

I am happy to learn that an indictment for a conspiracy has been found on the prosecution of a master spinner at Heaton Norris, I wish there had been a few more such prosecutions. I am sure that they would have greatly tended to the dissolution of the conspiracy. *Ibid. to Ibid., Whitehall, 24 August* 1818. *Private* . . . . Mr. Marriott has sent me a paper[1] containing a plan for a general combination among all trades, and I have information from other quarters of a similar tendency. This is a serious subject, on which all the intelligence you can collect will be valuable. There is certainly a great indisposition among the masters to use the engine which the Legislature has put into their hands for their self-preservation, and no means should be untried of stimulating them to put the law in force . . . (H.O.79/3/261-62, 266-67).

(264). *Henry Hobhouse to J. Lloyd*

Whitehall, 24 August, 1818. *Private.*
. . . All the information I receive tends to shew a serious intention to creating [*sic*] a combination among the journeymen in all trades, and it is very important to procure evidence on this subject, as a prosecution must be resorted to if possible. I have seen a paper[1] printed by Wilson of Manchester, expressly owning this object . . . (H.O.79/3/264-65).

(265). *Henry Hobhouse to William Marriott*

Whitehall, 24 August 1818. *Private.*
I have to thank you for your letter of the 22nd containing a very important paper[1] purporting to promulgate the Resolutions taken for the union of all trades into a general combination of the journeymen against their masters.

Probably no such meeting was held as is expressed in this paper,

[1] No. 260.

but I have from several quarters intelligence tending to show that such a general combination is in progress.

The great thing wanting in your town and neighbourhood is that the masters should bring forward evidence (of which they must possess abundance) to enable the magistrates to put in force the Combination Act. I am glad to hear that there was one indictment for a conspiracy found at the Assizes. If there had been ten instead of one, it might have gone a good way to settle the business (H.O.79/3/268-69).

(266). *Henry Hobhouse to the Rev. C. W. Ethelston*

Whitehall, 24 August 1818. *Confidential.*
. . . The grand desideratum in your country at present seems to be a want of spirit in the master manufacturers to make use of the means which the law affords them in the Combination Act for the suppression of the conspiracy which has existed for so many weeks, and appears to be gradually spreading.

If the law had been early and spiritedly enforced, there can be no doubt that great good would have resulted from it. Even yet, much benefit would arise from resorting to the Act, and I regret to see it almost a dead letter while conspiracy is increasing on every side. No means should be spared of exhorting the masters to their duty in this respect. It is impossible to doubt that they are in possession of abundant proofs if they would but bring them forward. (H.O.79/3/269-70).

(267). *The Rev. C. W. Ethelston to Viscount Sidmouth*

Longsight, Manchester, 24 August 1818.
. . . If they [the colliers] 'turn out,' the cotton spinners, who work by steam, cannot turn in if they were so inclined. The machinery of the mills must stop without fuel . . . (H.O.42/179).

(268). *Henry Hobhouse to the Chief Justice of Chester*

Whitehall, 25 August, 1818. *Private.*
I am persuaded you will forgive me for offering a suggestion which would be quite unnecessary if you had the same means of information which I have.

The system of combination among the journeymen in the vicinity of Manchester, including Stockport and the adjacent parts of Cheshire, has gone to a length of which you have no idea. It extends not merely to a conspiracy in each trade of the journeymen against their masters, but a scheme is actually in progress for forming a combination among the mechanics in *all* trades to afford reciprocal aid to each other. Whether you will have any indictments for a conspiracy or not, I cannot tell; but I am persuaded that a luminous exposition of the law on that subject, such as would come with effect from you, could not fail to be useful to the public; and if you should feel it right to add a word or two on the duty of detecting and counteracting such conspiracies, they would be well applied to the existing circumstances; for the magistrates are placed under the greatest difficulty in acting, for want of evidence being brought before them through the timidity of the masters . . . (H.O.79/3/275-76).

(269). *J. Lloyd to Henry Hobhouse*

Stockport, 25 August, 1818.

. . . Mr. Cross and I had some conversation about Manchester, and we agree that the cotton spinners who have voluntarily placed themselves out of employment and paraded the streets, to the disgrace of the police, are to all intents *rogues and vagabonds*, and liable to be committed — their cases coming completely within the meaning of the Act of 17 George II, c. 5. 'All persons not having wherewith to maintain themselves, live idle without employment, and *refuse to work for the usual and common wages given to* other labourers in like work, &c.'[1] . . . (H.O.42/179).

(270). *James Norris to Henry Hobhouse*

Manchester, 26 August, 1818.

. . . Many of the master spinners have again opened their factories with a determination to defend the hands going to work, &c., but the result is a continual call upon the constables to assist at different factories to protect the hands at the same time, and the town is thereby kept in constant commotion . . . The spinners have wished

---

[1] The letter was endorsed by Hobhouse: 'There must be proof of poverty and of refusal to work.'

that the military should be employed to escort hands, but this I have of course peremptorily denied coûte que coûte, unless orders from the Home Office should come for that purpose, and in short I do not allow them to be called out unless in case of *urgent necessity* . . .

I cannot think that the trades are at all organised for a general turnout, as no doubt calculated upon by the secret movers of these disturbances, but the idea necessarily acquires strength amongst the lower classes, and will shape itself better every week and indeed every day, and *some* no doubt are ripe for it at this moment.

. . . A principal delegate who is said to have had £160 to divide amongst the people today, and for which they were assembled in Oxford Road at 4 o'clock, has *absconded* with the money and left the turn-outs in the lurch. This has occasioned, as you may suppose, considerable consternation amongst them, and they even got one of the beadles who happened to be in the neighbourhood to go and look after him, but he was not to be found . . . (H.O.42/179).

(271). *Colonel Fletcher to Henry Hobhouse*

Bolton-le-Moors, 26 August, 1818.

. . . In regard to the combination of the workmen in the different trades, I think it is incumbent on those concerned to resort to the laws in force when any trangression of these laws has occurred. As a *collier* I have met with such trangressor, and have brought my complaint before *two* disinterested magistrates this day, who have convicted them of *combination*, and sentenced them to *three* months' imprisonment in our *county gaol*. I have recommended to all other masters to exert themselves, and not *inertly* rely on the exertions of the police or others, and several have this day applied for and obtained warrants to apprehend their respective workmen for breach of *contract*. (H.O.42/179).

(272). *William Chippindale to Henry Hobhouse*

Oldham, 27 August, 1818.

. . . I understand there was a small disturbance at Manchester yesterday amongst the spinners, but I have not heard any particulars. I fear something serious will occur if the misunderstanding is not speedily settled. One of the persons with whom I am in the habit of communicating met with one of their emissaries to-day, sent out to collect subscriptions and spread mischief, and he told him in confidence he need not be surprised if he heard *very soon* of some of the masters being *popped off*.

There is at present great uneasiness amongst the weavers, which is drawing fast to a crisis. It is confined chiefly to the weavers of muslins and other thin fabrics. The weavers of fustians (which is the manufactory of this town and neighbourhood) have experienced a considerable advance lately and are much appeased. The muslin weavers are a numerous body. They chiefly inhabit Manchester, Bolton, Stockport, Ashton-under-Lyne, &c. They hold a meeting on Monday next to receive the final answer of the manufacturers to their proposals, and if they are not agreed to, they turn out the day following. They ask an advance of 7s. in the pound — viz. for the work which they used to receive 20s. they now demand 27s. All the best informed manufacturers say it is excessive and cannot be complied with. I have great reason for believing that an agreement is not desired by many of the weavers' Committees, which is the reason of the advance being so exorbitant.

The turn-out amongst the colliers has doubtless been communicated to you from different quarters . . On Tuesday I transmitted him [Colonel Fletcher] some information which I consider of considerable importance, as it establishes the fact of the interference of the Jacobins. Since that, I have found that the notorious Dr. Healey[1] has been tampering with the workmen of the Alkrington Colliery, a concern of which I have the management . . . It is not at all improbable that on Tuesday next there may be a turn-out of the coalminers, spinners and muslin weavers[2] — the spinners partial, being chiefly confined to Manchester, the two others general. Altogether, they will certainly form a numerous body. Their discontents are secretly fomented by that spirit which has so long disturbed the quiet of the country, and which would urge them on to violence if an opportunity should present itself for making an impression . . . (H.O.42/179).

---

[1] Joseph Healey, with Samuel Bamford, was arrested under a warrant of the Secretary of State in March, 1817, following the suspension of the Habeas Corpus Act. He was one of the organisers of the Manchester meeting at 'Peterloo' on 16 August, 1819, and was subsequently sentenced to twelve months' imprisonment for seditious conduct on that occasion. After working as a weaver in Bolton he became a quack doctor.

[2] In that neighbourhood.

(273). *Henry Hobhouse to J. Lloyd*

Whitehall, 27 August, 1818.

. . . I agree with Mr. Cross and you in your construction of the 17 George II, but in carrying it into execution you will probably find difficulty in proving two of the requisites, viz., that a man has not wherewith to maintain himself, and that he refuses to work for the usual wages. The first will scarcely be proved unless either by the man's declarations or by his having applied to the overseer ; and to prove the second there must be a tender of work, But the law is a salutary one, and I don't mean to discourage you from enforcing it whenever you can. (H.O.41/4/151-52).

(274). *J. Lloyd to Henry Hobhouse*

Stockport, 29 August, 1818.

. . . Their [the Spinners'] Committee has been surprised to-day and their fund broken up. The landlord of the public house where they were met at Manchester gave information to the police, and the Committee, five, namely, John Ollis, Cuthbert Hutchinson, John Fowler, Edward Johnson and John Hague are all now in custody. I have been at their examination this afternoon. The magistrates have ordered them to find bail, two sureties £200 each and selves in £200, to answer for conspiracy. The Treasurer, John Medcalfe, had run away with £150. (H.O.42/179).

(275). *An Advertisement in the Manchester Observer*
29 *August,* 1818.

COTTON SPINNERS.

WANTED, TWELVE GOOD MULE SPINNERS at our Factory, Mill-street, Ancoats — on the same terms as those late in our employment previous to the turn-out. To save trouble, none need apply but men of steady habits and good character ; to such, constant employment will be given. The hours of work are 12½ each day, and the average wages of the 12 men for the last four weeks previously to their turn-out, were 35s. per week each man, clear of all disbursements whatever ; and the same can now be earned regularly by those we may employ.

Moore & Welch.

Manchester, 28 August, 1818.

(276). *J. Norris to Robert Henry Clive*[1]

Manchester, 31 August, 1818.

... Today ... was the day fixed by the weavers in this populous district for a general turn-out for an advance of wages, and in consequence some thousands ... of that body came into town from the neighbouring districts in pursuance of their public notice, to solicit from the masters an advance of 7s. in the £ ...

Many of the masters, say about thirty, have agreed to the full advance — others have consented to an advance of 5s., others 3s. and 3s. 6d., and some have told them that they will call in their work and for the present issue no more. This of course has mainly depended on the particular wants of the respective masters — some having large stocks on hand whilst others have less ... (H.O.42/179),

(277). *Henry Hobhouse to Messrs. Spode and Copeland, of Portugal Street, Lincoln's Inn Fields*

Whitehall, 31 August, 1818. Private.

I am directed by Lord Sidmouth to acquaint you that information has been received at this Office that three persons have been travelling through the Potteries for the purpose of collecting money from the lower orders of potters in aid of the turn-out mechanics at and near Manchester. His Lordship is confident that if any fact of this kind comes to your knowledge, you will not fail to bring the parties to punishment under the Combination Act. (H.O.79/3/300-1).

(278). *J. Jones of Oldham to William Shepherd Kinnersly, M.P.*

Oldham, 1 September, 1818. (Copy).[2]

[Several mines in the district are not at work] ... Mr. William Lee's colliery near Ashton is standing, and the colliers refusing to get coal to supply the engine lifting the water from the mines, it was this morning not at work, and the mine water rising. At the colliers' meeting at Manchester on Saturday last, the following memorandums are communicated to me. Though there was about 120

---

[1] He had recently succeeded John Hiley Addington (deceased) as Under-Secretary of State. He was the second son of the first Earl of Powis, and was M.P. for Ludlow (1789-1854).

[2] Enclosed in Kinnersly's letter to Lord Sidmouth, London, 4 September, 1818. The letter may not have been quite accurately copied. Kinnersly said that the information received was to be relied upon.

colliers present, they resolved not to work any more till the prices and measure was agreed to . . . When Colonel Fletcher's colliers gave in their proposals, he called it a combination, and sent four to Lancaster, when some colliers said they were to bring him down on his bare knees for this . . . The company was so numerous, it was thought best in future for one collier to represent one colliery if it can be so arranged ; if not, two must come . . .

There was a very considerable meeting of weavers met in Market Place, Ashton, yesterday, when very strong language was expressed, such as there was men who would lead them on with swords and arms — when many voices called out they were ready to join — that it was not very material whether their masters gave them 2s. or 7s. (7s. is what the weavers ask as increase on every 20s. heretofore paid) for it would not be long before some great events were to take place . . . (H.O.42/180).

(279). *Thomas Sparrow (Town Clerk) to Viscount Sidmouth*

Newcastle, Staffordshire, 1 September, 1818.
Two men were taken up here by order of the magistrates and are now in custody, pretending to collect money for the weavers in Manchester . . . They say there are men collecting in different parts of the kingdom, and this district, Shropshire and Gloucestershire were allotted to them . . . (H.O.42/180).

(280). *James Norris to Robert Henry Clive*

Manchester, 1 September, 1818.
This day has passed away without any disturbance of the public peace, &c. At one mill two persons were apprehended by the proprietor (Ewart and Co.) and committed for a conspiracy, &c. John Brough, the captain of the pickets, has also been apprehended and committed. This is an important character. The Court was full of spinners to hear these cases. Mr. Wright and Mr. Marriott assisted me in the Court to-day in this business . . .

We had this morning a procession of *upwards* of 2,000 men — supposed to be principally weavers, but having some *cotton spinners* amongst them. They marched through the principal streets and where there were warehouses. It is understood that they have left delegates in the town who are to collect the sense of the masters, &c. and report to them on Thursday. Similar proceedings have taken

place at Stockport, Blackburn, &c. There appears indeed a simultaneous movement throughout the manufacturing district, and
it creates naturally considerable alarm . . .

In one or two instances I have heard of taking away the shuttles
but I think they have not at present ventured on this practice, and
as I think the weavers are not upon the whole disposed to join the
reformers, I hope the day of insurrection is not so near as Mr.
Baguley wishes, and as far as respects the mere question of wages,
however important, it is not so much so as that of a general insurrection which is so much sought after by the reformers . . .
Ibid. to Ibid., Manchester, 2 September, 1818. Private :— . . . The
morning until about eleven was perfectly peaceable — no collecting
about the mills, nor any military required. At eleven a committee
of gentlemen of the town was assembled for the purpose of discussing
the best means of securing the peace, &c., and particularly of
requesting the magistrates to put in force the Watch and Ward Act.[1]
During this meeting a report came down that several thousand
weavers were on the road from Stockport and the adjacent country
with two colours and music. The weavers of our own neighbourhood
were also assembling in St. George's Fields close to the town. About
the same time, and whilst the committee were sitting, various
messengers were sent to state that the mill of Mr. Gray was attacked
by a very large body of men and that the hands in the mill were
firing on the mob who had demolished the greater part of the
windows in the mill and had attempted the gates, and that five
or six persons had been wounded, *and one mortally* . . .

The turn-out of the weavers in such large bodies has encouraged
the spinners, and the whole contest seems warmly renewed, and with
considerable danger. I now think that the turn-out of the weavers
has become alarmingly extensive, and in short, I know not where
it may end. There are delegates out in various directions for the
purpose of encouraging other large towns to do the same, and a
determined hostility seems set afoot. The Government cannot in my
opinion be too active nor afford too great succour at this momentous
crisis to this populous neighbourhood. I think the combination *very*
extensive and truly dangerous, and I consider the mob much
governed by Baguley, Drummond and Co., whose speeches yesterday
all tended to impress on the minds of their auditors, as I understand,

---

[1] The Manchester and Salford Police Act of 1792, 'an Act for cleansing,
lighting, watching and regulating the streets . . . of Manchester and Salford'
(32 George III, c. 69).

'Death or Liberty,' and that now was the time. What has become of the weavers I cannot tell — but I fully expect to hear of attacks on the mills in the course of the night or by four in the morning. It is said that the weavers are to assemble at Stockport in large numbers tomorrow, but from all I can hear, Manchester is the great theatre of rendezvous and attack ; and it appears so. I think two or three pieces of artillery in this place at this time would have considerable effect . . . If the thing continue a day longer it will be necessary to put every mill on its defence, and many lives will be lost. In short I do look to some bloodshed in this affair, and perhaps it may be for the best. We are in this place at present almost in a state of military law. I hope the events of tomorrow will enable me to send you more favourable accounts, but I have very considerable fears on that point. The species of warfare carried on by the mob is the guerilla, and as you may suppose, most harassing. They assemble and execute their mischievous purpose, after which on the least intimation of the military coming they are dispersed, and there is nothing to be done. No doubt the appearance of the weavers this morning encouraged the spinners and led to the unpleasant service in which the civil and military have been engaged ; and as the weavers are likely to increase rather than decrease when both parties become desperate and the reformers urge them on, which they declare they are ready to do, we must expect some very severe and dangerous proceedings. In the forlorn hope that I may have more favourable news to communicate tomorrow, I am, Sir, [&c.] (H.O.42/180).

(281). *Robert Henry Clive to James Norris*

Whitehall, 2 September, 1818.
. . . Lord Sidmouth, who is returned to town, has directed me to express his extreme regret that the master weavers should have been brought to a concession no less delusive in its probable consequences than dangerous in point of immediate example. However reasonable the claims of the weavers might originally have been, it is most unfortunate in Lord Sidmouth's opinion that they should have proved successful at the time when those by whom they were preferred were engaged in an unlawful combination to enforce them.

His Lordship earnestly hopes that the dissolution of the other combinations which unhappily still continue, will not be attempted by similar concessions . . . (HO.79/3/304-5).

(282). *J. Lloyd to Henry Hobhouse*

Chester, 3 September, 1818.

. . . I have got an indictment against five spinners for a conspiracy to raise wages, &c , and have one, the Treasury [*sic*], in custody in the Castle ; Bench warrants against the rest . . . (H.O.42/180).

(283). *James Norris to Robert Henry Clive*

Manchester, 3 September, 1818.

I am happy to say that this day has passed more quietly than I had expected. The patrols in the morning found everything peaceable, and no assemblages about the mills. At ten a body of about 1,500 persons marched from a general rendezvous in Newton Lane to Stockport, having a number of colours flying with the words 'seven shillings or nothing' inserted on them. They marched peaceably towards Stockport to the music of a fife. This body returned about six o'clock, and it is understood they mean to assemble again tomorrow and proceed to Ashton-under-Lyne. About eleven, information came to the Police Office that numbers of spinners were assembled in Oxford Road, with a view to attack some of the mills. Mr. Birley's was in fact first attacked with a volley of stones. The mob then assembled round Mr. Ewart's mill and broke a considerable quantity of glass . . .[1]

These are the principal attacks that have been made today, but their harassing nature is such that it impedes the inclination of the hands to go to work and has rather an unfortunate effect upon the master spinners, who are thereby deterred from being so active as might be wished in opening the mills, &c. Three or four considerable mills have however got armed men in them, and if an attack be made upon them we may expect serious work . . . This state of things has become extremely harassing as well to the civil as military power, and the magistrates have come to a determination to issue a public caution against all public assemblies and processions whatever, which they are determined to put down, &c. as dangerous to the public peace . . . (H.O.42/180).

[1] Attacks on other mills followed.

(284). *Robert Henry Clive to Thomas Sparrow*

Whitehall, 3 September, 1818.

I am directed by Lord Sidmouth to acknowledge and thank you for your letter of the 1st instant on the subject of the subscriptions for the manufacturers who have thrown themselves out of employ at Manchester, and stating that two men have been taken up in your town who were collecting money for this purpose.

Lord Sidmouth entirely approves of the communication you have thought it right to make to the Borough Reeve of Manchester on this subject, and it is his Lordship's opinion and advice that the magistrates of Newcastle [Staffordshire] should act upon this occasion in concert with the civil authorities of the former place.

P.S. You are doubtless aware that the offence for which you have apprehended the two men comes within the fourth section of the 39 and 40 George III, c. 106, and therefore this punishment might be immediate. (H.O.41/4/153-54).

(285). *Colonel Fletcher to Henry Hobhouse*

Bolton-le-Moors, 4 September, 1818.

. . . The danger of a committee dictating what wages must be paid, is manifest, and if [it] should be submitted to, a worse than universal suffrage would succeed. It would introduce a mob oligarchy, bearing down all the better orders of society, and would quickly be succeeded by universal anarchy . . .

Most of the colliers in this immediate neighbourhood have returned or are returning to their employment, but I apprehend, in some instances, under a compliance of their masters with some part of their demands, for want of a due firmness on the part of such masters (resulting in some instances from fear and in others from a criminal apathy) which is much to be lamented. About Oldham the colliers are universally *out*. Mr. Chippindale writes that the masters have not courage to proceed against them either for combination or neglect, although the workmen's organised committee sits on stated days at a public house in Manchester, as if on legal business.

The master manufacturers of this town on Monday last agreed almost unanimously to advance their weavers' wages 3d. 6d. in the pound, which some of the more sensible and honest among the weavers openly say ought to be gratefully accepted . . .(H.O.42/180).

(286). *The Rev. C. W. Ethelston to Viscount Sidmouth*

Manchester, 4 September, 1818.

. . . I am convinced from what I see and hear in every direction that the lower classes here are radically corrupted. An advance of wages or prices for work done, as I have before intimated, is a mere stalking horse. In this idea I am confirmed not only by the public statement of the master spinners, but by the undisguised and open avowal of some of those whom they employ. Their aim is revolution, and to effect their object they have established a regular chain of connection not merely amongst their own description of people but amongst all classes in a subordinate situation. The master key of communication is known only to themselves, and it is astonishing with what Masonic secrecy it is kept. The Resolutions of a committee, which has strong common sense, though not cultivated education for its basis, are divulged only at the precise moment when they are to be acted upon. What is done is done viva voce by special messengers, who, if apprehended, can be convicted by no written document. If they are ordered to assemble numbers at a given time and at a given place, they themselves retire into their shells, and the uniformed mass (as far as respects their real views) are fired upon by the military or imprisoned by the magistrates. It is perfectly well known that Baguley, Drummond and Johnson are at the bottom of all this mischief . . . (H.O.42/180).

(287). *James Norris to Robert Henry Clive*

Manchester, 4 September, 1818.

. . . A number of mills are now well armed, which the spinners, &c. well know, and this will prevent any attack upon the mills. They now determine again on annoying the workmen at *their own homes*. I trust this will not last long, but that the spinners will go in. (H.O.42/180).

(288). *Colonel Fletcher to Robert Henry Clive*

Bolton-le-Moor, 4 September, 1818.

. . . The multitude of unemployed persons thus organised and attempting a general union or combination of trades under such leaders as Baguley, Pilkington,[1] &c., &c., must needs be dangerous to the public peace . . .

The danger of a committee dictating what wages must be paid, is manifest, and if [it] should be submitted to, a worse than universal suffrage would succeed. It would introduce a mob oligarchy, bearing down all the better orders of society, and would quickly be succeeded by universal anarchy . . .

Most of the colliers in this immediate neighbourhood have returned or are returning to their employment, but I apprehend, in some instances, under a compliance of their masters with some part of their demands, for want of a due firmness on the part of such masters (resulting in some instances from fear and in others from a criminal apathy) which is much to be lamented. About Oldham the colliers are universally *out*. Mr. Chippindale writes that the masters have not courage to proceed against them either for combination or neglect, although the workmen's organised committee sits on stated days at a public house in Manchester as if on legal business.

The master manufacturers of this town on Monday last agreed almost unanimously to advance their weavers' wages three shillings in the pound, which some of the more sensible and honest amongst the weavers openly say ought to be gratefully accepted. This difference of opinion may serve to divide the body and so far tend to good ; but the temper of the lower orders in general has been so soured by the vicious publications which the Press of late years hath teemed forth, continually inflating the people with high notions of their rights, but concealing from them the knowledge of their duties, that sooner or later it is to be feared that some ebullition of popular fury will break forth, requiring not only legal but military execution . . . (H.O.42/180).

(289). *James Norris to Viscount Sidmouth*

Manchester, 5 September, 1818. *Private*

. . . The conduct adopted by the magistracy, and the valuable assistance of Sir J. Byng yesterday in pursuing and dispersing by gentle means the body of men from this place who had set out for Ashton, has much contributed, I think, to dispose the main body of weavers into a right understanding of their true interests, and the folly of imposing an arbitrary price of wages on their masters by

---

[1] Robert Pilkington, of Bury, was one of the Reformers arrested in 1817, and imprisoned without trial, following the suspension of the Habeas Corpus Act. His Petition to the House of Commons is in *Parl. Deb.*, XXXVII, 677.

means of combination, &c. The main body of weavers, I have reason to suppose, have only what they conceive a fair advance of their wages in view, and are therefore now disposed to go to their work upon such advance as their masters are disposed to give — but as in all classes there are many evil disposed, so in this class there are many who will not permit this strong good sense to have effect on the industrious and worthy weaver. This has been evinced today by many attempts having been made by small gangs of eight or ten assembling in the outlets of the town and violently obstructing the weaver in coming into the town with his work. The moment this line of conduct was ascertained, a strong party of constables, accompanied by two magistrates (Mr. Wright and Mr. Marriott) and a Company of the 95th, went to the roads in question and remained there a considerable time to assure the individuals by their presence that they should be protected. This had the desired effect — the deliquents retired on the approach of this civil and military body from the scene of action . . .

Today a deputation from Mr. Holt's spinners waited on him to offer to go to work, and I hope this will be the case on Monday. This example will have great effect, and I should not, I confess, be much surprised if many more hands were so disposed and will take the same course on the same day, or Tuesday. Their spirit though not their obstinacy appears broken. They have carried on their opposition as long as they can ; assistance from other trades seems at a stand, and in short they are in confusion at their meetings and uncertain what to do. Monday will be a day of trial, and I trust will produce the most fortunate results, so far at least as respects the spinners. All the mills are to be opened on that day. The military have four or five different barracks assigned them near the principal seats of the factories, &c.; the civil authorities will be in readiness, and if under these appearances the mills get pretty fully to work in a day or two, all will be well. I trust the whole will be a lesson both to the masters and the men, from which they may each learn instruction with respect to their future conduct on like occasions. Mr. Holt's hands on an average netted 34s. per week clear per head.

The colliers, I am happy to inform your Lordship, will most likely all be in on Monday. Indeed, some of those don't understand at this moment why they turned out. I could tell them — an advertisement in the papers inserted by characters who wanted a political or insurrectionary movement . . .

With respect to the weavers, the main body of them, I believe,

V

are well disposed. They naturally jump at 7s. in the £, but would be perfectly contented with two or three shillings. This has certainly been offered by many masters, a little perhaps through fear, and on this subject I perfectly coincide with your Lordship in opinion, most unfortunately for the general interests of commerce and the community — but as the weavers have been working hard for small wages for some few years, if any description of labourer in this district be entitled to indulgence in this respect, it is the weaver . . .

. . . I have not heard of any projected turnout of any other class of workmen. All the other trades seem perfectly content and at work. (H.O.42/180).

[The following advertisement was published in *Cowdroy's Manchester Gazette and Weekly Advertiser* on Saturday, 5 September, 1818 :]

(290). *Employment for Mule Spinners*

A number of steady industrious men, who are acquainted with fine spinning, and can bring respectable characters, may have immediate employment and full work at the spinning factory of David Holt, Temple Street, Chorlton-row.

The spinners who turned out from my factory, and have since associated themselves with the existing illegal combination, publicly declared they had nothing of which to complain, having each of them received a weekly amount, clear of all deductions, of upwards of 32s. for the last six months ; but that they were, by the *alarming threats of the promoters of the existing combination, compelled to leave their employment.*

Commiserating the distress into which many innocent families have been thrown by this inordinate and unwarrantable exercise of undue authority, I hereby give this PUBLIC NOTICE that ample protection will be afforded to the well-disposed who avail themselves of this invitation ; and that, in this way, themselves and their families may be sustained in comfort and credit, and the evil of which the present turn-outs complained, be avoided.

Chorlton New Mills, August 29, 1818.　　　　　　　　David Holt.

(291). *William Chippindale to Viscount Sidmouth*

Oldham, 6 September, 1818.

. . . A meeting of weavers' delegates was appointed to be held at Bury yesterday, the principal object of which was of the highest importance, it being to decide whether the whole weaving body of this county, together with that of the manufacturing districts of Cheshire and Derbyshire, should turn out or return forthwith peaceably to their employment . . . They decided in favour of the latter, but not without a struggle of uncommon severity for several hours. A person of the name of Ellison, of Bolton, was the chairman, and he conducted himself with great moderation and propriety. Fortunately, he was peaceably disposed. The advocates for the turn-out were Pilkington of Bury (a man whose character is made up of everything that is bad) together with the delegates from Manchester and Stockport and some others, whose names my informant did not know. The meeting consisted of 52 *delegates*, a number unusually large. On the question being decided in favour of peace and good order, the advocates for the other side manifested the strongest marks of chagrin and disappointment, and my informant represents their countenance as beggaring all description. The greatest efforts were made by them and by Pilkington in particular, to effect the turn-out. The various stratagems he put in practice for that purpose caused so great an interruption to the progress of business that it was long after midnight before the meeting was dissolved. Pilkington paraded for several days the last week at the head of the weavers of Bury, both in that town and in Bolton, in a very menacing way. The whole of the movements in the three trades of spinner, weaver and collier have been effected by the agency of the old disaffected leaders, so well known to your Lordship . . .

With respect to the colliers of this district, who have been so great an object of terror whilst out of employment, your Lordship will be pleased to know that the proprietors have arranged their differences with them, and they will nearly all return to their work tomorrow. There is not the *smallest cause* to apprehend any danger to the public peace from them . . . (H.O.42/180).

(292). *James Norris to Viscount Sidmouth*

Manchester, 6 September, 1818. 11-30 p.m.
. . . All the mills are to be opened tomorrow at the usual hour. The military will be in attendance to assist the civil authority . .
Ibid. to Ibid., Manchester, 7 September, 1818 :— . . . It has been the constant wish of the civil authority here . . . never to call in the aid of the military except on some urgent occasion, and I cannot

but think and hope that this line of conduct has been advantageous upon the general question, and of considerable consequence in a political point of view. The labourer has had a fair chance with the master and must see of necessity that he is in the wrong, and will therefore submit with the better grace. I have no doubt that all this will have its due effect on the labouring classes in all trades, and prevent the recurrence of combination for some time.

I have infinite pleasure in informing your Lordship that everything looks much brighter today than it did last week. The breaking up of the *committee* of the spinners, the difficulty in consequence of getting new ones to act with vigour, the loss of support from other trades who will no longer contribute whilst the funds are misapplied or stolen, the want of confidence in each other, the miserable state to which the operatives are reduced by their neglect of work, the determination on all hands to protect by all and every means those who are willing to go to work — all these circumstances and others which I need not enumerate, have contributed to place us today in a situation which leads me to hope with confidence that this serious combination is now broken. The mills this morning have generally been opened and many of them nearly filled. All Mr. Holt's hands are returned to work, and most of the other mills are filled to the amount of one third at the least. Instead of having general meetings, each mill has sent a deputation to the master to endeavour to come in upon terms which have been uniformly rejected ; and the general hope and feeling is that in fact the hands will now be glad to go to work without any stipulation whatever, Many are gone in today, and tomorrow and Wednesday will, I think, see all the mills, or nearly so, at work. The main body of the weavers have also agreed to go to work at such advance as the masters may consent to give. Some are still outstanding and some bad characters amongst them are still endeavouring to prevent by advertisements, &c. this labouring class from going to work ; I trust, however, without effect. They are narrowly watched, and examples will immediately be made of such as may be found offending against the laws. Some of the ringleaders amongst the weavers are already marked, and I trust justice will overtake them because I think their *motive* is bad . . .

If the weavers go back to work, all is settled. The colliers are at work, and the spinners must submit. Your Lordship does not more seriously deprecate concessions upon these occasions than I do. The weavers will only gain two or at the most three shillings by this urn-out, and if any labourer be more entitled than another to a avourable hearing, I am of opinion it is the weaver. Still, the principle of concession upon these occasions of combination is truly erious, and if in future complied with, must have the most detrimental effect upon the manufactures of this country. I hope the .ase will not again speedily recur, and the danger of them will be till less if we can keep ourselves free from that pest of our happiness and freedom — the itinerant radical reformer. (H.O.42/180).

(293). *The Rev. C. W. Ethelston to Viscount Sidmouth*

Macclesfield, 7 September, 1818.

. . I shall be able to prove that Baguley was in my neighbourhood on Friday last exciting the weavers to conspiracy against their masters. At his instigation vitriol was thrown into the warps of the weavers who were not in the combination for an increase of pay. The same was done at Middleton and at Ashton on the evening of the day Sir John Byng dispersed the mob. Of this I am assured by Mr. Chetwode, a magistrate for the Ashton district. (H.O.42/180).

(294). *James Norris to Viscount Sidmouth*

Manchester, 8 *September,* 1818.

. . . The spinners have this day continued to go into work, many of the large mills being completely filled, and the rest filling as fast as can be reasonably expected . . . Mr. Houldsworth, the new member for Pontefract, entirely filled his mills this morning, and so much at ease does he feel now, that he immediately set out for Pontefract to attend the Races which commence to-day . . .

The master spinners have, I believe, also today (being then assembled on other important business) taken into consideration the question respecting the hours of work, and have come to a resolution to restrict them to twelve working hours per day. This may prevent any further discussion on this point in Parliament,[1] but it is not at present to be proposed as it might seem to be a

---

[1] The first Sir Robert Peel presented to the House of Commons on 10 February, 1818, a Petition from the cotton spinners of Manchester praying for a shorter working day, even though it would mean a reduction in wages (*Parl. Deb.*, XXXVII, 264). On the 19th he introduced his Cotton Factories Bill to limit to 12½ hours (including 1½ hours for meals) the working day of children in cotton mills. (*Ibid.*, XXXVII, 559).

giving way to the men, who do not appear to have deserved it
The resolution however is passed at the General Meeting . . .

The shopkeepers and publicans near the factories will be great
sufferers by the turn-out. They have no doubt supported the men
under it who are much indebted to them but who will most likely
never pay. I am not at all sorry for this. Had it not been for this
support the contest would have much sooner ended.

The minds of the operative spinners, as your Lordship may
suppose, are greatly dissatisfied at this result of things, but still on
the whole, from all I can learn, the majority are not sorry to go to
work. I trust and hope that by this contest a great check has been
given to the system of combination, and that so serious a one will
not speedily occur again.

Ibid. to Ibid., Manchester, 10 *September*, 1818 :—. . . The spinners
have gone to work *in general* I believe with the best intentions —
tired of their obstinacy and *really happy* to get to work. In one
instance only I have heard of its having been accompanied with a
threat of a future turn-out when the county at large shall be prepared for that purpose. I hope however this is merely a threat from
dissatisfied individuals, and that the feeling does not pervade the
body. No concessions whatever have been made on the part of the
masters, and in many instances the operatives have been called
upon to sign a written declaration that they will not in future be
concerned in any combination which they have signed.

I am sorry, however, to be obliged to state to your Lordship that
the weavers do not appear to be settled — some are content with
the advance proposed, others not, and there are not wanting
amongst this body many persons whose sole object is to get the
weavers out, and turn the circumstances to other and political
purposes. The heads of their committee of combination *are well
watched*, and will, I have reason to believe, be shortly brought to
justice. The merchants and manufacturers seem fully determined
to put down this combination by the most active exertions.

Enclosed I send you a printed form of petition from the weavers
for relief.[1] You will be surprised at the method &c. which it pursues.
The magistrates, however, have thought it their duty to issue a
printed notice that such subscriptions are illegal, &c., and in the
meantime the merchants of this place have had a meeting for the
purpose of considering the best means of subduing this confederacy.

---

[1] See illustration opposite.

They will *continue* to meet for this purpose, and the most fortunate result may be expected from their exertions. The weavers' district is *a very* extensive one, and will require great exertion to keep it tranquil . . . (H.O.42/180).

(295). *Robert Henry Clive to James Norris*

Whitehall, 10 *September,* 1818. *Private.*
. . . His Lordship is decidedly of opinion that the resolution of the masters to restrict the spinners to twelve working hours per day should not be disclosed at present. The resolution itself Lord Sidmouth considers judicious, but the disclosure of it at this moment would have an appearance calculated to produce very injurious effects. (H.O.79/3/319).

(296). *J. Lloyd to Henry Hobhouse*

Stockport, 10 *September,* 1818.
. . . The weavers have adopted a system here of billeting the turn-out weavers, which I shall inquire into tomorrow with a view to some legal steps to prevent it getting to something else of a more serious nature . . . (H.O.42/180).

(297). *Viscount Sidmouth to Colonel Fletcher*

Whitehall, 10 *September,* 1818.
. . . Appearances are unquestionably improved at Manchester, Stockport and Bury, and I trust that a favourable change has also taken place at Bolton and Blackburn and other towns which have recently been the scenes of discontent and agitation. It is, however, to be much regretted that any compromise whatever should have taken place with persons who were pursuing their object by illegal means ; and the period is too probably not distant when the effect of concession will be severely felt . . . (H.O.41/4/168-69).

(298). *James Norris to Viscount Sidmouth*

Manchester, 11 *September,* 1818.
. . . The spinners are at work — the weavers in this immediate neighbourhood are also gone and going in, but in the more distant districts such as Blackburn, Burnley, &c. they are still out, and this

body, generally speaking, is not at rest. We have been at pains to come at the weavers' committee which sat at Bury *last Saturday*, and I think we shall be able to lay hold of half a dozen in the course of a day or two.

Enclosed I send you a public notice which we have issued here to prevent the effect of the weavers' petition for assistance which I sent you last night.

I am sorry to be under the necessity of informing your Lordship that there is reason to apprehend that the system proposed for a general turn-out amongst the trades is by no means at an end. We have now here delegates from Birmingham and Nottingham who are stated to have a considerable sum with them for the purpose of relieving the spinners, but they came too late. A committee, however, still sits for the purpose of organising the system promulgated by the advertisement (Cave — printer) sent to the Home Office about a fortnight ago[1] . . . I have little doubt it will be attempted to be carried into effect, and *in this quarter at least every exertion will be made to check it*. If this system however be obstinately pursued, it will require the united efforts of all to counteract it. Our attention at present is directed to the proceedings of this committee of general union, and your Lordship may rely on being constantly informed of all that can be learnt respecting their motions and intentions. I do consider it certainly of great importance to the country, and the more so because it is a system so well calculated to draw in a great majority of the labouring classes of the community. The spinners who are gone in are evidently at work with great alacrity and cheerfulness, but on the whole it is observed that they are in greater spirits than is natural considering their situation under the circumstances of the turn-out, and this is attributed to the confidence they feel in the general turn-out to which I allude. This idea is certainly strongly held out and even publicly talked of amongst the operative spinners who are gone in, notwithstanding which they have in several instances signed agreements never again to be concerned in combinations or in contributing to their support. They have apparently come in, in the most humble and submissive manner and without the slightest concession on the part of the masters, and of course upon the old prices and upon their own SOLICITATION . . .

Ibid. to Ibid., Manchester, 12 *September*, 1818 :—. . . This town and

[1] No. 260.

the immediate neighbourhood continues perfectly quiet, and I have not heard today if any instance of weavers being molested in bringing in their work, which occurred to some extent last Saturday, being a day on which weavers most frequently bring in their work. I am sorry, however, to hear that the neighbourhood of Blackburn is still disturbed and the weavers remain out, and I fear that in other parts they are not settled at their work but are still looking forward to the 7s. in the £ which they set out with demanding . . . The general union amongst the trades is still much talked of . . .

With respect to the question of reducing the hours being a *concession* to the spinners, I fear I have misinformed your Lordship and I am convinced if the master spinners thought it would be so taken, they would not for one moment think of acting upon it, as their great object is to avoid even all *appearance* of concession at this time. I have had an interview with Messrs. Douglas and Birley, very considerable spinners, upon this subject today, and the result of their information is this. They say the shortening of time to 72 hours per week cannot be construed into any concession on the part of the masters, the best journeymen spinners having generally preferred those mills where they were allowed to work the greatest number of hours in a day ; the working spinner being paid according to the quantity of work done, his earnings must necessarily be reduced in proportion to the diminished time. The other hands who are paid *by the day* will be subject to no variation in their wages in consequence of the lessened time. The present moment they allege is the most favourable season of the year for putting the variation of time in force on account of its being the usual period for lighting up the mills. It is not intended to make any public annunciation of the change of time but to act upon it *silently*. The reduction of time will vary from two to five hours per week. The masters say they feel perfectly satisfied that this variation of time will not only not be in point of fact a concession to the operative spinners, but that it will not be so considered by them, for they have never expressed a wish to work a shorter time. Perhaps under these circumstances your Lordship may alter your judgment upon this point ; at the same time I beg to assure your Lordship that the master spinners will defer to your judgment if still against their intentions upon this subject.

With regard to the advertisement of a reward and pardon, &c. for the apprehension of persons concerned in the attack on Gray's mill, the master spinners are extremely anxious that this should go forward for this reason. They say they are convinced the attack was preconcerted and by the *worst people* amongst the turn-outs. There are about a hundred hands of this description who will never be received again into any mill, and as these hands under their situation may be influenced to do all the mischief they can, the masters conceive that this advertisement will be the means of keeping them quiet and in all probability, of driving them from this part of the country. They seem *extremely sanguine* on this point . . . *Ibid. to Ibid., Manchester, 14 September, 1818* :— . . . From all I can learn, the operative spinner has been sincerely happy to resume his employment, and I hope it will eventually appear without any intention to turn out again for some time. The weavers I trust are in the same mind and content with the advance which they have obtained. If they attempt to turn out again for the remainder of the seven shillings which they demanded, they will in all probability lose the advance they have now pretty generally obtained in this immediate neighbourhood. I have no doubt the majority will be content if the ringleaders and delegates will permit them. Of the latter who met at Bury about nine miles hence on Saturday, 5 September, for the purpose of framing resolutions (which are printed and circulated) to turn out again on the 1st October for the remainder of the seven shillings, I hope either today or tomorrow we shall have three or four of them in custody to answer for this combination and conspiracy, and I have great reliance on this having considerable effect throughout the country . . .

It is very agreeable to find in what an odious estimation the reformers are held,[1] who I shall always think were at the bottom of this turn-out with a view to the establishment of the general union, &c. . . . This committee will still be pursued till it is destroyed effectually.

The master spinners are much hurt and annoyed at the reasoning which appears in the *Star* paper *daily*, and at the correspondence therein from this place, which can only be dictated by the *worst motives*, and is most untrue as well as impolitic at this time. I hope they will write up to contradict it.[2] (H.O.42/180).

---

[1] So it was reported by a secret agent employed by the Borough Reeve of Manchester.

[2] 'The masters in every line of manufacture have the power of combining, and too often do combine, against their workmen, and . . . in such cases their proceedings are always conducted in private. Holding the purse, they never

[*Continued on p. 299*]

(299). *Robert Henry Clive to James Norris*

Whitehall, 14 *September*, 1818.

. . . It is most satisfactory to his Lordship that the spinners have returned to their work without concession or compromise, and he feels confident that the spirited and judicious conduct of the merchants and manufacturers, combined with the vigilance and exertions of the magistrates, will ultimately succeed in destroying all that remains of the late very formidable conspiracy ; and it is only by complete success in accomplishing this object, that the danger of a renewed and more extensive combination can be averted.

The apprehension and conviction of the heads of the weavers' Committee would most materially contribute to the re-establishment of permanent tranquillity . . . (H.O.41/4/169-71).

(300). *James Norris to Viscount Sidmouth*

Manchester, 16 *September*, 1818.

. . . Blackburn, Burnley, Padiham, Preston, &c. are in a serious state of agitation from the weavers remaining out and manifesting very turbulent symptoms . . .

Pilkington (a prisoner of your Lordship's last year), Ellison and Kay were this day committed for a conspiracy at Bury on 5 September, upon which they issued the handbill of that date, now in your Lordship's possession. One of them has already tendered bail which was for *each*, two sureties of £100. I hope this committal will have a good effect, particularly in the neighbourhood of *Bury and Bolton* . . . (H.O.42/180).

[*Continued from p. 298*]

need to parade the public streets in bodies, or to expose themselves openly to the censure of the community ; and, on every slackness of demand, they set the workmen in competition against each other, on the *descending scale* of prices, in such a manner as to be guilty of acts of great injustice, not only to the workmen, but to every member of the community . . .' (5 September, 1818). This was a typical comment. The paper approved of the conduct of the Manchester magistrates, praising their 'unceasing labours, constant perseverance and considerate attention' (11 September). 'We learn by some of our private letters that, great as have been the sufferings of the workmen, absolute want of means to subsist any longer has not been the cause of their return to employment. They have had no less a sum than *four thousand five hundred pounds* transmitted to them from various societies of workmen throughout the kingdom ! . . .' (*Ibid.*)

(301). *H. Enfield to Robert Henry Clive*

Nottingham, 16 September, 1818.

I have the honour to acknowledge the receipt of your favour of the 14th instant, communicating, by direction of Lord Sidmouth, information of two persons, one from Nottingham and the other from Birmingham, having been to Manchester as deligates for the purpose of promoting an Union of Trades, the object of which is to dictate the wages and allowances to be paid by master manufacturers to their journeymen, &c., &c.

This information I have communicated to several of the manufacturers here . . . (H.O.42/180).

(302). *Dr. T. D. Whitaker, J.P. to Viscount Sidmouth*

Holme, near Burnley, Lancs., 17 *September,* 1818.

. . . The Hundred of Blackburn is in a state approaching to that of a general insurrection in consequence of a dispute betwixt the weavers and their employers on the subject of wages . . . We have in consequence been compelled hitherto to use conciliation, which has only had the effect of emboldening the mob and encouraging them to acts of greater outrage.[1] The ringleaders which had been apprehended have been liberated by violence . . . The houses of the weavers who are willing to work are visited, their looms and work marked, and themselves inhibited from proceeding, by threats of fire or other mischief.

In the meantime, and during the general suspension of labour which these outrages occasion, the funds of the Benefit Societies are openly applied to the support of the obstinately idle, and no obscure hints are thrown out that when these resources are exhausted, and in the event of parochial relief being refused, other and forcible methods of obtaining subsistance without labour will finally be resorted to . . .

Ibid. to Ibid., 18 *September,* 1818 :— . . . The plunder of the funds belonging to the Benefit Societies has become so general as to call for the intervention of the Legislature . . . (H.O.42/180).

---

[1] The magistrates had only a single troop of horse for a district of more than 200 square miles.

(303). *James Norris to Viscount Sidmouth*

Manchester, 19 September, 1818.

... The weavers at Blackburn are going in, and I trust their conduct will operate as an example to the district at large in that neighbourhood ...

Part of the delegates at Bury ... have been bound over to answer to a charge of conspiracy at the next Sessions. The sureties were fixed at £100 each, which each of the defendants has found, and *Pilkington* even is now on bail, which, considering his character, I am a little surprised at. It is intended immediately to look after some of the other delegates in order that they may be held to bail on the same charge ...

I am happy to find that the editor of the *Star* is coming round, and from a *particular* communication to him from this place his information is much more correct, *of which he is, I believe, fully aware.* A paragraph has appeared in that paper and some others, insinuating that American agents have been busy here *lately* to seduce the spinners abroad, &c.[1] There is *no truth whatever* in this statement, and if it were so I am informed by Mr. Douglas and Mr. Birley there is no occasion for the slightest alarm, as, if all the hands now out [of] employ were to be shipped for America, they could not do an atom of injury to the trade of this place, as they are not any of them of the class of mechanics (strictly so called), but spinners only, who might be replaced here immediately, and who cannot carry any secrets abroad, &c. The masters seem determined not to give employment to any of these men — they were the most refractory with the least occasion, most of them earning from two to three pounds clear weekly.

Ibid. to Ibid., 22 September, 1818 :— ... Burnley and the immediate neighbourhood is restored to perfect peace and quiet, and the weavers have resumed their employment since Friday last, the day after the Manchester Yeomanry made its appearance in that town. Padiham ... is not so quiet, but there is little doubt they will follow the example set them at Burnley ... Blackburn and Bolton are also at work, and I trust the weavers generally throughout the county will remain satisfied with the advance they have obtained and not attempt to move again for the remainder of the seven shillings, as if they do there is little doubt they will run much risk of losing what they have got ... (H.O.42/180).

[1] Not until 1824 were the laws repealed which made it a crime for an artisan to attempt to emigrate.

(304). *Colonel Fletcher to Viscount Sidmouth*

Bolton-le-Moors, 22 September, 1818.

. . . For more than a week past, the weavers of this town and neighbourhood had, for the most part, returned to their employment, but
I fear under some concessions on the part of the masters, either expressed or implied. Their leaders endeavoured to prevent their
return, by various falsehoods, but finding their inability to dupe
them much longer, they made a virtue of necessity, and published
a sort of permission for the resumption of their work, thereby the
better to keep up an opinion of their consequence amongst the
working classes, and, no doubt, also, with the view of continuing in
the direction of their affairs and deriving therefrom a maintenance
without manual labour . . .

Another turn-out of this body [the Bolton weavers] was con-
templated, probably with the view of supporting the weavers of
Preston, Blackburn, Burnley, &c.; but the design is for the present
laid aside . . .

The turn-out of the weavers has afforded to the designing Jacobins
the means of organising that great portion of our Lancashire population. Under the alluring pretext of procuring an advance of wages,
an ascendancy in their proceedings has been obtained by the
leaders that will, I fear, be used to the worst of purposes . . .

The miners have all returned to their employment, but in most
instances with an understanding that their wages were to be advanced. My own colliers that had turned out have returned to their
work without any promise of advance, and the *four* who had been
committed to the Castle at Lancaster for three months for combination, have humbly signified their wish to return to their work,
and solicited my interposition to endeavour to procure his Majesty's
pardon.

Thinking that the confinement of these men has had a salutary
effect in checking the further spread of collier turn-outs, and that
their return to their homes and employments will be as efficacious
to prevent a recurrence of such combinations as a continuance in
prison to the term of their commitment, I humbly presume to request that his Majesty's pardon may be extended to Thomas
Haworth, William Greenhalgh, James Taylor and Robert Norris,
who were committed on the 26th of August last for the term of three
months, by James Watkins and Joseph Watkins, Esquires . .
(H.O.42/180).

(305). *Joseph Forster (Mayor) to Viscount Sidmouth*

Newcastle-on-Tyne, 6 October, 1818.

. . . A few days ago the sailors at Shields, collected in some numbers in consequence of unfavourable winds which detained their ships in port, had begun to complain of the smallness of their wages, and threatened a suspension of work if they were not increased. The owners of the vessels were led to give an advance by agreeing to pay £4 instead of £3 a voyage, and the wind at the same time becoming favourable, the seaman agreed to go to sea with that advance, and the disturbance which might have been apprehended has been prevented. As, however, these compliances on the part of the owners often led to further demands on the part of the men, and as their return to port will again assemble them in numbers, it may be as well to guard against the dissatisfaction being revived.

About the same time I received information that the miners in Weardale in the county of Durham, about twenty miles from this place, had stopped work, and had demanded an increase of their wages from their employer Colonel Beaumont. This not being complied with, the men have formed themselves into a large body controlled by what they call a committee, and after having published some inflammatory placards exciting to tumult, have threatened not only to desert their engagements and their work, but to do damage to the mines and to the works if their demands be not complied with.

At present their committee, or a delegation from the whole body, are applying to the agents of their employer by petition in the nature of a menace, and the result is not known nor perhaps can be known for some days ; but being formidable in number it may also be prudent to guard against their being excited to mischief . . .
(H.O.42/181).

(306). *J. Lloyd to Robert Henry Clive*

Stockport, 10 October, 1818.

. . . The colliers in our neighbourhood have been for seven weeks in disorder and [there have been] many turn-outs. Some gentlemen of my acquaintance in Manchester having a considerable concern in Cheshire, some miles westward of this, employed me to go up amongst them on account of some violence and threats to new hands they were employing, and I yesterday morning at 3 o'clock, had a ringleader apprehended and had put another in custody before [*sic*] whilst they were assembling in numbers, and have the satisfaction to find the men have made overtures to return to their duty, and the matter is thus happily settled . . . (H.O.42/181).

(307). *Major-General Sir John Byng to Viscount Sidmouth*

Pontefract, 10 *October,* 1818.

I was prepared to set off for town this morning, but having received a report that the miners in the county of Durham have turned out for an increase of wages,[1] and further, that there is some fresh alarm in the weaving district of Lancashire, attaching but little importance to either account, I have nevertheless . . . thought that you would most approve if I remained here till the 16th or 17th. . . (H.O.42/181).

(308). *James Norris to Viscount Sidmouth*

Manchester, 11 *October,* 1818

. . . I wished to acquire what information I could respecting the General Union of Trades before I again troubled your Lordship. I am happy now to be able to inform you that from all the inform- ation I can acquire, the General Union, so far at least as respects this district, is broken up. Delegates from Nottingham, Birmingham and Liverpool were here about a month ago, but they came after the spinners had gone in, and found the latter, I believe, so happy in being again employed, that it broke their own spirit and they left here in disgust. How far the principle of the Union pervades the kingdom, your Lordship has much more extensive means of judging than I can possibly have, but so long as delegates are permitted to go from place to place to obtain subscriptions, &c., the principle will not only be kept alive, but must ultimately approach perfection and endanger the public peace and welfare, however for a time it may seem to be at rest. Some legislative measure alone will, I fear, be able to counteract it.

The last meeting of delegates that I have any account of was held at Todmorden about twenty miles from this place on Monday the 21st September. There were delegates from the weavers at Somerset, printers and crofters from Bury ; weavers from various other parts,

---

[1] He confirmed this the next day, adding, 'I hear not of any tendency to ill conduct.' (H.O.42/181).

amounting in all to about twenty-four. The proposal was for each person to pay in 3d. per week, but in consequence of the great distrust each had of the other, the spinners having gone in, and the headmen of the spinners and weavers being in custody, they were alarmed, and the *clerks* (for such I believe they had) of the different divisions and townships who collected the different contributions, were directed to divide the funds and return the money, amounting to about £40.

I am informed that the plan of the General Union *certainly* originated at *Nottingham*, and Todmorden was to have been a great centre of the Union, as laying [*sic*] out of view — it lays in a central situation between Manchester, Halifax, Blackburn and Bolton, and is a very retired situation. Shoemakers, tailors and other trades had joined in the Union, but I believe for the present at least it is broken up. The spinners' submission, with the imprisonment of Baguley, &c., have mainly contributed to this happy event, and if the different Committees, who are to take their trial at the next Sessions, be found guilty, I think it will not only have a good effect but may possibly for some time at least effectually destroy this Union.

The rejected spinners have been in a state of continual agitation and resentment since the trade went in ; they find now that they have lost irrecoverably a substantial and valuable source of livelihood such as they cannot again obtain. They have in consequence threatened those who are gone in to take their wheels from them the very first opportunity that offers of a new turn-out unless they contribute to their support, which I understand is done very scantily if at all. They have gone to Mr. Houldsworth offering to disclose all they know of the late tumult, &c., and have even offered to work for a lower price considerably than that at which they went out if they may be again taken in. Whether these offers are to be acceded to ultimately I know not, but certainly, I understand, not at present, nor will their information be received unless it be perfectly voluntary and unclogged with any condition as to being again employed, &c.

I forgot to say that at the meeting at Todmorden the people seemed aware that the promoters of the Union kept the scheme afloat merely for their own support, and that they had pocketed a deal of the contributions.

With respect to the spinners I hope there is no fear of their turning out again for some time to come, perhaps for years — and

W

this is the general opinion amongst the masters. With respect to the weavers, I don't think they have any idea of again turning out for the additional three or four shillings ; they will, on the contrary, consider themselves well off if they can retain what they have got, which latter indeed I much fear, as the manufacturing is not so brisk, as it was, and rather than manufacture at a high price and without demand, the masters will stop their looms, and this, I understand, is now much dreaded by the *weavers* in many parts. At Preston I am CREDIBLY informed, the weavers are *all* at work without any advance or very little, and so they are, I believe, in all other parts notwithstanding the infamous accounts to the contrary which are daily issued by the *Star* newspaper. It is quite evident from what daily appears in that paper that we have some very bad spirits amongst us in this County who seem anxious to throw us again into commotion if possible. Almost the *whole* of the accounts published in the *Star* are untrue. They however get copied into most of the other papers, become widely circulated and are thus calculated to bring about the most mischievous consequences. I am not aware that there is any place in the County where the weavers are still out, and in many places I believe they are not even discontented ; but they may very soon be rendered so by such accounts as appear in the *Star* paper. I have no doubt whatever but the correspondent of the *Star* will turn out to be someone politically connected with that class who have so long and so seriously endangered the peace of this County . . . (H.O.42/181).

(309). *Robert Henry Clive to James Norris*

Whitehall, 14 October, 1818.
. . . The project of effecting a Union of Trades, though possibly relinquished at present as hopeless at Manchester and some other places, is not entirely abandoned. In the metropolis it is still persisted in, though with evident languor. The meetings for the purpose of promoting it, are not numerously attended, and the subscriptions are inconsiderable in their amount. The connection with Manchester and other manufacturing places is frequently asserted at those meetings, but no proof of it has been afforded since the departure from town of the Manchester delegates.

The master manufacturers appear to Lord Sidmouth to have acted most judiciously in refusing to receive into their employ, for the present at least, such of the spinners as took the most prominent parts in the late combination ; and the attempt to excite public sympathy for persons of this description is unwarrantable and highly mischievous ... (H.O.41/4/204-6).

(310). *Joseph Forster (Mayor) to Viscount Sidmouth*

Newcastle-upon-Tyne, 16 *October*, 1818.
... The miners returned to their employments and their employer has furnished them with the subsistence money which has been usually paid at stated intervals notwithstanding the interruption that had taken place in their work. And the bargains with them, which are generally made for three months, being now expired, the agents are empowered to renew them on an advance of one half of what the miners had peremptorily demanded. The motives which have led to this partial compliance I have no doubt were good, and it was stated to them to be founded on their return to their work, and on an increase of the price of lead. It remains to be seen whether the new contracts will take place ; if they should not, there will be much reason to apprehend that the disturbances will be renewed. I should inform your Lordship that the terms of the contracts with the miners frequently vary as by long usage in the Weardale and most other leadmining districts, they are proportioned in some degree to the price of lead, than which nothing can be more fluctuating ...

With respect to the seamen, all has remained quiet in this port, and indeed they have not yet returned from their voyage. (H.O.42/181).

(311). *James Norris to Viscount Sidmouth*

Manchester, 20 *October*, 1818.
.. The cotton spinners I really think will be quiet for some months if not longer, but with respect to the weavers it is certainly more doubtful. The masters are obliged on account of the slackness of the demand, to reduce the prices again in some instances or to call in their work, and the weavers have met in SMALL numbers once or twice in the neighbourhood. I fear that the approach of winter will continue to reduce the demand and consequently the price, and that we may consequently have more dissatisfaction. I really hope and believe however, that the masters will entertain every consideration possible for the men and give them all they can afford and perhaps in consequence the evil may be averted ... (H.O.42/181)

(312). *Colonel Fletcher to Viscount Sidmouth*

Bolton, 20 October, 1818.

Permit me to return to your Lordship my grateful acknowledgements for the pardon which his Royal Highness the Prince Regent
has been pleased to grant to the four colliers of mine who had been
committed to Lancaster Castle for combination, for the procuring
of which pardon they are doubtless indebted to your Lordship for
your interposition in their favour.

. . . There have been some partial attempts amongst the working
bleachers to *turn out*, but their employers immediately complaining
to the magistrates of this Bench, five were yesterday committed for
neglect of work, which prompt procedure will, it is expected, crush
in the bud this dangerous spirit amongst the workmen in that
branch.

A meeting of weavers is said to be intended at Leigh (about eight
miles from hence) but I hope it will neither lead to violence nor to
any fresh turn-out. Battersby is the notorious leader of these sort of
movements in that neighbourhood, a person who, about two years
ago received parochial relief, but who now has abundance of the
necessaries of life, which he has derived principally from the contributions of the deluded weavers. Our informants will communicate
the proceedings, should any take place. (H.O.42/181).

(313). *J. Lloyd to Robert Henry Clive*

Stockport, 28 October, 1818.

The weavers have this day applied to our magistrate for *permission*
to hold another meeting about trade. He tells me he was very angry
with them.

It appears, by enquiries at Manchester today (having been
attending the Sessions there), that the masters are *lowering* wages
again. This is disapproved of by the generality of masters, who say
it is a mere temporary depression . . . (H.O.42/181).

(314). *Robert Henry Clive to James Norris*

Whitehall, 6 November, 1818. Private.

I have been informed that a person representing himself to be a
delegate from the cotton spinners in Manchester, has lately arrived
in London for the purpose of raising collections in their favour. His

name is James Hughes, and his residence in Manchester was 45, Blossom Street. I shall be obliged by your making inquiry about this man, and informing Lord Sidmouth of the result with as little delay as the circumstances will permit. (H.O.79/3/329).

(315). *James Norris to Viscount Sidmouth*

Manchester, 18 *November*, 1818.

[James Hughes] . . . came originally from Chester, where he was brought up a shoemaker. He left Chester many years ago and came to this town where he learnt to spin, and followed that business for some time. About two years ago he was turned away from Mr. Murray's factory (a very considerable one in this town) for drunkenness, since which he has done no work but followed the occupation of a delegate and was very busy in the late turn-outs. I learn also that he is now in London, most likely in his *trade* of delegate, but under what instructions or on what account I have yet to learn, which I hope to do in a very few days, when I will not fail to inform your Lordship. When delegates are really employed on any mission, they are allowed one guinea per week ; and the occupation not being very laborious, when once a man gets appointed to that office I presume he is not willing to resign it but is rather anxious to continue the employment on any pretence ; and no doubt the delegate takes care to reap other advantages from his situation besides his mere pay. The system of delegation is in every point of view so pregnant with danger and mischief that so long as it is unchecked by the *strong* arm of the law, the system of general turn-outs will be kept alive, and *may* by such means become more formidable and extensive than they have hitherto been. Perhaps if being a delegate were to be made a felony or to subject the party to a long imprisonment, the evil might be subdued . . .

We appear to be in perfect peace and tranquillity in this town and neighbourhood. All trades are at work and as contented (except perhaps the weavers), as recent circumstances can possibly be supposed to admit. This observation peculiarly applies to the spinners who seem, I learn from many quarters, to be cheerfully at their work and happy. I hear from a respectable mill [*sic*] and one of the most forward in the late turn-out that there is a schism amongst the late turn-outs themselves ; one party will not speak to another in the same mill. This difference is supposed to be between the leaders of the late turn-out and those who were *forced* to remain out, which latter would at least amount to ⅘ths of the whole. They certainly suffered much and *are still* greatly in debt, which naturally makes them discontented with the authors of their distress. With respect to the grand union I have reason to believe that it is not making any great progress here at present. About a fortnight or three weeks ago a person who has always afforded very accurate and good information, had a conversation with Swindells, who your Lordship will remember was the delegate in London, and Swindells said that the union was not going on so well here as he could wish, but it was in a promising way in the country, and particularly at Nottingham, where, from all I can learn, there is little doubt the system of the grand union originated.

I have indeed learnt from one quarter that a subscription is on foot both amongst the weavers and spinners, but for what purpose my informant could not say. He is a respectable manufacturer and has promised to produce all the information for me which he can on this subject. He had heard that the spinners' fund amounted to £600, but I much doubt this, as I think this class will not lend themselves to another turn-out hastily, and I think they are too much in debt to spare much for any purpose of the sort alluded to. Were their situation otherwise, I know not any body of men so able to raise a considerable fund. The women in one factory have been observed to be rather surly towards their employers, which is attributed to the circumstance of the females in very many instances having been driven by the turn-out to the melancholy necessity of going upon the town for support . . . (H.O.42/182).

(316). *Henry Hobhouse to Lewis Allsopp*

Whitehall, 23 November, 1818. *Private.*
Lord Sidmouth desires me to communicate to you that he has recently obtained additional ground for thinking that the Grand Union of Trades originated at Nottingham, where it is represented to flourish and thrive much more than in any other quarter. He therefore wishes it to be well watched. (H.O.79/3/333).

(317). AN ADDRESS TO THE
GENERAL BODY OF MECHANICS

Brother Mechanics,

The rapid and extensive strides of despotism and oppression, which have followed in regular succession for these last 25 years, has in proportion to its advance added ingenuity and deception in its train, backed by a legislative enactment of a most partial and despotic law, under the name of 'the Combination Act,' which, while it imposes on the working mechanic the obligation of disposing of the only species of property he has in possession, viz., his labour and talent, at a price far below the necessary demands of subsistence, leaves the masters at liberty to make what demand they may think proper on their several manufactured articles, having nothing but a competition of the market to contend with.

Brother mechanics, the sun of your independence and respectability have long passed the zenith of its splendour — the wretchedness of yourselves and your families, through the scantiness of your remunerations for your labour and talent, have left you weak and destitute ! The spirit of your fathers is fled — the hand of poverty has, in conjunction with methodistical cant and chicanery, benumbed youɪ mental and physical exertions ; the broad and malignant grasps of aristocracy, extended out by a cruel and overbearing number of employers, have acted as an opaque body over the sun of your rights and independence — have intercepted all the cheering rays of social and domestic happiness, leaving you nothing but the winter of poverty and oppression to travel through to your very graves.

But, cheer up, brother mechanics, the remedy is within your own body ; a few embers of that fire which was kindled by our forefathers is still alive, and only wants to be nourished to maturity to light all around ; the blaze of which will soon decompose the opaque body of oppression and tyranny which has so long intervened between you and your rights.

Useful and industrious mechanics ! Come out from among the mean and servile tools of oppression — leave them to their fate, and consider yourselves members of society — set a proper value on your merits as men, and let your actions be such as to extort, even from your masters and the servile crew under them, the approbation of your conduct. Unite in one bond of sociable friendship, and provide the necessary means of protection for those whose just and

fair demands of remuneration have been only met by the dis
pleasure of a cruel and tyrannical master. Your means of protectio
is in your own power — a subscription of only ONE PENNY pe
week, from as many mechanics of all branches as may think prope
to subscribe, would, in a short time, give you sufficient means t
procure every legal and constitutional plan for the redress of th
manifold grievances the several mechanical bodies labour unde
which subscription, with every other matter, will be regulated by
Committee consisting of a Deputy from each trade, subject to rule
and regulations agreed upon by a joint meeting of the sever
Deputies belonging to the mechanical body, when organised, will b
submitted to your consideration.

London, November 1818.

W. C. Mantz, Printer, 159, Brick Lane, Spitalfields.

(H.O.42/182.) [A printed handbill

VIII. 1819. A YEAR OF WIDESPREAD TROUBLES

Trials of Union leaders in Lancashire.
The St. Helens colliers.
The journeymen hatters at Ashton-under-Lyne.
The colliers' turn-out in Lancashire.
The Nottinghamshire framework-knitters.
The Coventry ribbon weavers.
The lightermen, seamen and colliers on Tyneside.
The colliers in the Leeds district, and in Flintshire.

(318). *Henry Hobhouse to James Norris*

Whitehall, 1 *January*, 1819. *Private*.

. . . Lord Sidmouth has learnt from Nottingham that the persons who went from thence to abet the General Union of Trades at Manchester, were one Richards, a resident in Nottingham, and James Retchford, formerly a shoemaker of Leicester, but latterly a hawker of pamphlets at Nottingham. His Lordship deems it right that you should be apprised of this, in case either of these men should fall under your cognisance. (H.O.79/3/340-41).

(319). *James Norris to Viscount Sidmouth*

Manchester, 16 *January*, 1819. (*Private*).

. . . All the trades of this place are pretty fully at work, and I believe contented, nor do I hear anything of the general union of trades, although I have little doubt the system will continue to be carried on by the delegates and those who live in idleness, preferring it to labour.

I hear very favourable reports from the mills of the conduct and peaceable demeanour of the spinners, whose prices in some instances have been recently a *little* raised. Great, and I think *not unfounded* apprehension of some mischief again occurring is entertained by the master spinners from the manner in which Mr. Gould is again moving amongst the operatives the question of time, &c. They believe that this was the main origin of the late turn-out, and that if again agitated, the same result is SURE to follow : this is a *uniform* opinion amongst them. Our population is most rapidly increasing, and in consequence all trades, particularly weavers and spinners are *overstocked*, and this competition of necessity reduces the prices, particularly of the *weavers*, which are as low as they have ever been. The evil, therefore, of preaching sedition, &c. to the multitude under such circumstances is alarmingly increased . . .

Ibid. to Ibid., Manchester, 29 January, 1819 :— Pilkington, Kaye and Ellison, three of the committee of weavers sitting at Bury on 5 September last for the purpose of raising the price of wages and deterring others from working under a certain advance, were this morning tried at the Quarter Sessions and found guilty. The two former were sentenced to two years' imprisonment in Lancaster Castle and the latter to one year.

John Doherty[1] was also indicted for conspiring with others to intimidate persons from working at Messrs. Ewart and Co.'s cotton factory, &c. and found guilty. Sentence — two years in Lancaster Castle . . . (H.O.42/183).

(320). *Henry Hobhouse to James Norris*

Whitehall, 6 February, 1819.

. . . With regard to the indictment against the cotton spinners' committee, Lord Sidmouth would not recommend any measure which might by possibility weaken the effect of the late verdicts, but he doubts whether that prosecution should be abandoned upon any terms short of the defendants suffering judgment by default. It will then be an act of mercy in the prosecutors not to bring the defendants up for sentence . . . (H.O.79/3/346).

(321). *James Norris to Viscount Sidmouth*

Manchester, 3 February, 1819.

I am happy in having it in my power so early to confirm your Lordship's opinion respecting the good result of the late trials at our Quarter Sessions. The cotton spinners' committee, nine in number, had during the Sessions removed their trial into the King's Bench, being so advised, I believed, by their Attorney. Since the trial, however, of Pilkington, &c., they have been with Mr. Milne, the prosecutors' Attorney, earnestly entreating he will put them in

---

[1] Doherty was the famous leader of the Lancashire cotton spinners.

the way of submitting and pleading guilty, which they are most anxious to do. He informed them of course that they themselves having removed the indictment, had put it out of their own power to do it except by going up to town or waiting until the Assizes. They are extremely low and distressed upon the subject, and on Monday, two of them waited on me with a paper signed by seven of the number, testifying their submission, &c. and requesting my aid and advice. I necessarily informed them that it was quite out of my power and province, &c., at the same time intimating that with a view to their present submission, &c. they could not be in better hands than Mr. Milne, who would fairly state their conduct, &c. to the prosecutors, who I thought had no vindictive feelings towards them, but were solely actuated by a feeling for the public good on future occasions of this kind. In truth, I understand the prosecutors are much disposed to be as favourable as possible with these men, upon their making a proper submission, &c., and from which now all the good will result, and perhaps more, that might be expected from their trial and conviction . . .

As far as I can learn, all the trades are now quietly and steadily at work except the weavers, who are (perhaps naturally), discontented . . . (H.O.42/184).

(322). *The Earl of Derby to Viscount Sidmouth*

The Oaks 19 *February*, 1819

Although I have no doubt your Lordship has before this time been fully informed of all particulars relative to the disturbance which has taken place amongst the colliers near St. Helens, I conceive it to be not only my duty (but to be the wish of the magistrates who have acted upon this occasion), that I should lay before your Lordship their statement of the transaction, and the present state of that part of the country. I flatter myself the measures which have been taken by the magistrates will preserve the future peace of the country and put a stop to these illegal combinations . . .

[Enclosure]

Michael Hughes and George Williams to the Earl of Derby

Raven Inn, St. Helens, 17 *February*, 1819.

. . . It is now some weeks (six or seven) since the colliers of this district indicated disturbance ; that of 13 collieries within this district, the majority of the workmen from seven have withdrawn themselves to the amount of about 250, whose proceeding has thrown out of work between 300 and 400 others connected with the coal getters.

The discontent arises from a reduction of wages having taken place about three years ago, and to which no opposition was then made, the return to which rate of wages is what they now demand of the proprietors, who on the other side state that they have been employing one-fourth more of coal getters during a depression of trade for those three years more than prudence would justify actually to keep the whole of their men in work ; the coal getters obtaining as wages during that time (at the reduced rate) upon a general average of collieries and weeks about a guinea each man per week.

The discontent however is stated to be the insufficiency of wages, and all calculations and reasonings upon the subject we have found utterly unavailing to induce them to return quietly to their employment.

On the 12th instant, being here for this purpose of taking examinations and of pacifying them, we were obliged to commit one of the conspirators for administering an unlawful oath, which threw them into such a state of exasperation that *our* safety was put to hazard, and on the 13th we thought it advisable to obtain a military force from Warrington of 80 rank-and-file. A company was also marched hither from Liverpool composed of 40 rank-and-file. On the 13th, as some outrages had taken place and more were threatened, we thought it advisable to send to Manchester for a detachment of the 7th Hussars, which arrived this forenoon, consisting of 34 horses, officers and men, commanded by the Earl of Uxbridge . . . (H.O.42/184).

(323). *James Norris to Viscount Sidmouth*

Manchester, 20 February, 1819. (*Private*)
. . . The wages of weaving are at present *extremely low*, and if the principles held out on these occasions[1] are pursued, it can have but one conclusion, viz., some serious public disturbances throughout the County. I fear that the present question before Parliament respecting the cotton mills may have the same tendency, inasmuch as if the time of working be curtailed, the wages will of necessity be so

---

[1] Large public meetings, such as that at Stockport on the 15th.

by the masters, and it is in fact, I fear, but legislating about the price of labour, and if the wages decrease, may not another turn-out be expected ?[1] I mention this independent of the great leading question by the supporters of the Bill as to the propriety or humanity of working children under a certain age more than a certain number of hours per day. This may be well worth the attention of the Legislature, but ought it not to come forward in the shape of a general Act for the whole country in all trades, as suggested by the Lord Chancellor ?[2]

I much fear we shall have a similar summer to the last, but much will also depend on the issue of the trial of Baguley and Co. If they be convicted, it will, I have little doubt, have a wonderful effect in silencing the remaining desperate demagogues of the day, and in that event much less may be apprehended from the system of the turn-outs. Washington[3] has been in this part for two months back, but about ten days ago I learnt from good authority that he had decamped with £50 or £60 of subscription money for the use of the general union. If he makes his appearance the warrant in the Constables' Office here will be put in force against him. (H.O.42/184).

(324). *Henry Hobhouse to James Norris*

Whitehall, 24 *February*, 1819. (*Private*).
. . . Any depression in the rate of weavers' wages is greatly to be lamented, because it administers fuel to the latent sparks of discontent ; but it is a subject upon which you are well aware that no relief can be afforded either by the executive or the legislative branches of the Government.

Lord Sidmouth is well aware that you are not singular in the opinion that the renewal of the discussion in Parliament of the question respecting the cotton mills is likely to revive the turbulent spirit of the last year. But it is a subject upon which the best intentioned members of both houses and of all parties are so divided

---

[1] The Cotton Factories Bill, introduced in 1818, was passed in 1819.

[2] Lord Eldon made several speeches on the Bill. On 25 February, he said, 'A general law ought to be passed, if necessary, for the regulation of manufacturers of all kinds, but it might happen that a particular law, applicable only to children in one trade, might expose them to greater evils than those from which it was intended to protect them' (*Parl. Deb.*, xxxix, 654).

[3] One of the leading Lancashire Luddites.

in their sentiments that it is impossible to exclude it from consideration ; and his Lordship trusts that the vigilance of yourself and your brother magistrates, assisted by the experience you acquired in the last year, and by the effect of the recent conviction of some of the conspirators of that day, will prevent the ill effect you anticipate from the agitation of so delicate a question. . . (H.O.41/4/253-54).

(325). *Michael Hughes to the Earl of Derby*

Prescot, 2 March, 1819.[1]
... The most complete tranquillity has been restored to this neighbourhood, the colliers having very generally returned to their work as usual, without the smallest injury having been done to the person or property of any individual. (H.O.42/185).

(326). *James Norris to Viscount Sidmouth*

Manchester, 8 March, 1819. (*Private*).
... I have the satisfaction to inform your Lordship that the cotton spinners' committee, nine in number, entered into their recognizance this evening before me in the sum of £100 each to attend at Westminster to receive sentence on their plea of guilty whenever called upon, &c. — and they all expressed themselves *extremely thankful* for the lenity which had been shown to them, and *appeared* very penitent, promising never to offend in like manner again, &c., &c. (H.O.42/185).

(327). *The Rev. C. W. Ethelston to Viscount Sidmouth*

Longsight, Manchester, 28 June, 1819. 11 *p.m.*
I am this instant returned from Ashton-under-Lyne where I have been in my magisterial capacity for the purpose of hearing a very aggravated case of combination amongst workmen. The whole town and neighbourhood are in a ferment and the journeymen hatters have 'turn'd out' in great numbers. (H.O.42/188).

---

[1] In Lord Derby's letter to Lord Sidmouth, 4 March, 1819, in which he says 'the late disturbance at St. Helens has happily subsided.'

(328). *James Norris to Viscount Sidmouth*

Manchester, 30 June, 1819. (*Private*).

. . . The distresses of the labouring classes are great beyond all expression. The merchants and manufacturers themselves are somewhat depressed from the extraordinary stagnation of commerce, and cannot employ the hands as they could wish, in consequence of which numbers are out of employ, and in this situation all the working classes are beset by the Reformers, who, by the licentiousness of the Press and of their speeches are inculcating every species of dissatisfaction and even insurrection and rebellion . . .[1]

Mr. Ethelston attended on Monday at Ashton to assist Mr. Chetwode (who married a sister of Mr. Littleton,[2] the member for Staffordshire) in his magistrate's duty. A case of combination amongst the workpeople of a Mr. Whitehead came before them, and it had excited such an interest that Mr. Ethelston states upwards of 2,000 had assembled in the town, and this notwithstanding the meeting at Stockport. The mob conducted itself very indecorously — retired at one time to a moss close to the town as if to deliberate, and were repeatedly heard to shout as if to intimidate the magistrates. The case was adjourned for some reason unconnected with the mob, but Mr. Ethelston says that had the magistrates then decided it against the workmen he conceives it would have been dangerous for him to have returned home . . . (H.O.42/188).

(329). *William Shepherd Kinnersly to Lord Dartmouth*

Newcastle, Staffordshire,[3] 15 *July,* 1819.

. . . For a few days past there has been certain appearances of a connection between the disaffected in this neighbourhood with those

---

[1] Mr. Lloyd had written to Henry Hobhouse on the 15th : ' . . . Further reductions having lately taken place . . . it is quite impossible the weavers can live upon their earnings. These men conduct themselves in a very respectful manner, and the whole body are peaceably disposed. Everything that can be done will be done for them so far as we are concerned. There is a meeting of Justices tomorrow, and I have privately invited the principal manufacturers to attend the magistrates, to consult upon some plan for the relief of the weavers.' (H.O.42/188).

[2] Edward John Walhouse assumed the surname of Littleton, and was created Baron Hatherton in 1835 (1791-1863). His sister, Charlotte Anne Walhouse (d. 1837), married the Rev. George Chetwode in 1818.

[3] Enclosed in Kinnersly's letter of the same date to Lord Sidmouth. The copy is in his own hand.

in Manchester. A regular correspondence is established . . . A Club
of journeymen potters is established under the pretence of keeping
up the prices of wages and of supporting any men who are out of
employ. From this Club being established at the present moment, I
have no doubt it is done with political views, and that the declared
intention is merely a cover. In some parts of the Potteries a spirit of
disaffection has showed itself in a very open manner. I feel satisfied
that the connection has been of very short duration and that it is
not become general . . . (H.O.42/189).

(330). *Lewis Allsopp to Viscount Sidmouth*

Nottingham, 12 August, 1819.
. . . The workmen have struck here the same as in Leicestershire —
about 3,000 from Arnold and the adjoining villages paraded the
streets yesterday, marching with great order and regularity . . .
(H.O.42/191).

(331). *H. Enfield to Viscount Sidmouth*

Nottingham, 13 August, 1819.
The magistrates of this town direct me to inform you that considerable numbers of the workmen in the framework-knitting manufacture of Nottingham and its vicinity have turned out, refusing to
work at the present prices.

About 3,000 of them entered the town on the 11th inst. at one
o'clock in the afternoon and paroded several of the streets, having
previously assembled at a public meeting on the Forest within the
limits of the town, pursuant to notices placarded the day before.
Many of these persons appeared to be from the adjacent villages.
They proceeded in a peaceful and orderly manner, exhibiting every
appearance of poverty and distress — and dispersed quietly, first
calling over a list of names. Yesterday a similar procession took
place of about 300. These persons were principally men of the town,
and it has been reported to the magistrates that they have represented this meeting to be far more numerous than the meeting of the
day before.

The magistrates have learnt that at the meeting held yesterday
upon the Forest, which principally consisted of workmen in the
town, that the country hands who had already struck were traversing
the country to induce all to turn out— and that they had

appointed a Treasurer and persons to collect subscriptions for their support from tradespeople and others.

Their plan of assembling is first to meet in districts or sections, each section having a Leader whom they call Captain, who has a list of their names, and having mustered them at the appointed time they repair in a body to the General Meeting at the Forest, and when they disperse after parading the town, they are called over in a similar manner, again meeting in their sections in the afternoon when they are again called over. This is done to ascertain that they are not at work. (H.O.42/192).

(332). *Henry Hobhouse to H. Enfield*

Whitehall, 14 *August,* 1819.

. . . I know the regret he [Lord Sidmouth, who had gone out of town for some days] will experience at the receipt of your intelligence, and particularly at that part of it which represents the state of organisation observable among the men who have thrown themselves out of work. We know that where the magistrates can interfere they will do so with intelligence and effect. But it is to be hoped that the differences between the masters and workmen will be adjusted without the intervention of authority . . . (H.O.41/4/469).

(333). *The Postmaster, Coventry, to Francis Freeling*

Coventry Post Office, 20 *August,* 1819. (*Copy*).

. . . This city is a loyal city as [*sic*] any place in this kingdom. Politics have nothing to do with the present question. The men in my opinion have been very ill-treated by some of their masters. It is only a turn-out for the men not to work any longer at the reduced prices, while a number of masters are paying £10 per week more wages for the same work. Many thousands have gone through the city with an ass, and have done what they call a little justice — but they were stopped with perfect ease, and have promised not to give the least offence . . .

[*Enclosure* : *A printed handbill.*]

RIBBON TRADE

At a meeting of the Ribbon Weavers, held in the Windmill Field, on the 18th of August, 1819, the following Resolutions were unanimously adopted :

X

Resolved — That this meeting feel much pleasure in knowing from the result of the conference of the Masters last night, at the Castle Inn, that nothing is wanting but a simultaneous operation throughout the trade, to enable the weavers to live by the labour of their own hands.

Resolved — That the thanks of the meeting are due to the kind attention of the magistrates to the peaceable and firm application of the weavers for an advance of wages, and particularly for their requisition to the masters to take the case into their immediate consideration.

Resolved — That the thanks of the meeting are also due to those masters who so promptly complied with the requisition of the magistrates, and particularly for their readiness to adopt the list of prices agreed to in September, 1816.

Resolved — That seven respectable persons (not in the trade) be requested to wait on the inhabitants generally for the purpose of soliciting pecuniary contributions towards the relief of the most needy of those persons who have not been able to attend to their work in consequence of the present stagnation of employment and particularly those persons who are entirely destitute of work.

Resolved — That Charles Lilly, Esq., be requested to hold the office of Treasurer, and receive the money when collected for that purpose, and that a Committee be appointed from the present meeting, to whom all persons claiming relief from the Fund shall be referred ; and the said Committee shall recommend such persons as they may conceive proper objects for participation, by a note signed by the Chairman, addressed to the Treasurer, stating what sum will be necessary for his immediate relief.

Resolved — That this meeting are firmly persuaded that to the system of half-pay apprenticeships may justly be ascribed the greater part of the distress which has been so long felt among the weavers, and that from henceforth they will denounce with their *most public disapprobation* and *censure* all persons who shall hereafter take any apprentice under any other engagement than that of wholly maintaining, clothing and lodging such apprentice, under an Indenture duly stamped ; as also those persons who practice taking one-third or half of the journeyman's wages for the use of the looms.

Coventry, 18 *August*, 1819.   (H.O.42/192).

(334). *Messrs. King and Sculthorpe to Viscount Sidmouth*

Hinckley, 23 August, 1819.

Mr. John Sills, one of the principal manufacturers of hosiery in this town, has lately received an anonymous threatening letter . . .[1]

Some weeks ago the framework-knitters of Hinckley, in common with those of other parts of the County, resolved not to work for less than certain prices which were agreed upon in 1817, and the inhabitants at large, considering their demands reasonable, agreed to support them by parochial relief altogether rather than compel them to work for reduced prices, and then make up what they might require out of the poor rates.

The hosiers made no objection to a general advance of wages, but, as a partial advance would operate to the prejudice of individuals, they would not give the higher prices till all the hosiers of the County agreed to do the same.

Mr. Sills is principally concerned in manufacturing cotton hose, and, the Leicestershire manufacture being worsted hose, he said that, as to worsted goods, he would adopt the regulations of the Leicester hosiers, but that as to cotton goods he would not, because if he did he should not be able to bring his goods into the market in competition with the manufacturers of cotton hosiery in Nottinghamshire and Derbyshire. It is supposed that this determination of Mr. Sills may have gained him enemies amongst the framework-knitters, who do not consider the peculiar injury which he would sustain by acceding to their demands . . . (H.O.42/193).

(335). *The Duke of Newcastle to Viscount Sidmouth*

Clumber, 29 August, 1819.

The stockingers in this County have in a body struck work. They have hitherto subsisted on a subscription fund, but that is now exhausted, and they have tried me for money, which I have declined. Their wretchedness is extreme. Their Treasurer told me two days ago that the fund had amounted to £250, from which 600 men have been supported for a fortnight. They were earning, the lowest say, 5s., the highest 9s. a week before they struck, by working 12 hours

---

[1] 'Be careful or you shal hav a bit of cold led.' A reward of £100 was offered for the apprehension of the writer.

a day. This honest maintenance, though low, they have exchanged for their present miserable pittance, which is, from this fund, 3s. a man per week, if with a wife, 1s., and for as many children as he may have, 3d. a head. Hitherto all has been peaceably conducted, but the men parade in very large bodies, and make a display of their poverty. It is also said that they have drilled. They certainly *always* parade in parties of threes or fives, keeping step and under command, and they have *hinted* to me that it will be well to afford them means of subsistence, as hungry men know no law, and they cannot answer for what may be the consequence when their fund is exhausted, and they pinched with want.

I enclose for your Lordship's information their Address to me and my answer. I shall be sorry to irritate, but, at the same time, no encouragement must be given. The storm will break sooner or later, therefore, if it is to be, better now than later. At the same time I will endeavour to act with moderation and prudence mixed with determined firmness.,

I find I can learn no truth here, therefore tomorrow I go to Nottingham and shall make a thorough private investigation of everything. I shall then, I hope, be able to form some judgement and to act upon some plan ; first of all I must look to security which at present, I am told, is very defective . . .

P.S. I have been told to-day that to-morrow is to be a grand day with the stockingers at Nottingham, as they mean in a body to return their frames to the hosiers. Your Lordship must not be surprised if his Majesty's Lieutenant returns with a broken head.

[Enclosures.]

To his Grace the Duke of Newcastle (Lord Lieutenant),
the Nobility, Gentry and Clergy of the County of Nottingham
The humble Address and Petition
of the Two-needle Framework-knitters

We think we should be wanting in duty to ourselves and families, were we not, with all due respect and humility, to call your serious attention to those heart-rending woes and severe privations under which ourselves and families are now groaning, and to justify ourselves in sending forth the present Address, we beg leave to state that from the various and low prices given by our employers, we have not, after working from 14 to 16 hours per day, been able to earn more than from 4s. to 7s. per week to maintain our wives and families upon, to pay *taxes, house-rent, &c.*, which has driven us to the necessity of applying for *parochial aid*, which after all, has not in many instances left us sufficient to supply the calls of Nature, even with the most parsimonious economy ; and though we have substituted meal and water, or potatoes and salt, for that more wholesome food an Englishman's table used to abound with, we have repeatedly retired after a hard day's labour, and been under the necessity of putting our children supperless to bed, to stifle the cries of *hunger ;* nor think we would give this picture too high a colouring, when we can most solemnly declare that for the last eighteen months we have scarcely known what it was to be free from the pangs of hunger.

Think what must be our feelings when our little ones cling around our knees for bread, which we are unable to give them ! Our partners in life, the poignancy of whose grief may be conceived, but cannot be described, looking on the pale and meagre form of her husband ; her child, perhaps, at her breast, feebly sucking for that nourishment which Nature almost refuses to bestow ! ! This is a state of misery, wretchedness itself cannot depict ; we hope, then, it will not be deemed too much to require from our employers a reasonable regulation and advancement in our prices, which they acknowledge they are willing to give, could it be adopted generally : all we ask and desire of them is an adequate remuneration for our labour.

We trust and hope we live amongst a Christian people not forgetful of that glorious precept of our Divine Master, 'to love one another, to feed the hungry, clothe the naked, to pour in oil and wine, and bind up the wounds' of those lacerated hearts with feelings of sympathy ; and we confidently rely on the generous, humane, and benevolent exertions which, in your wisdom, you may think proper to adopt, for the extricating of us from that climax of human misery in which we are at present involved.

Sincerely hoping this well-meant call will not remain unanswered, but that we may live in the most grateful remembrance of your assistance, we subscribe ourselves on behalf of the trade.

Walter Miller,
Thomas Sands,
Samuel Brentnall.

Committee Room, Ball, Coal-Pit Lane.

The Duke of Newcastle's reply to the Address

Clumber, 25 *August*, 1819.

I have received your letter and Address. For the present I will only assure you that your case shall be attentively examined by me, and that it shall occupy my most serious consideration.

You have been so good as to look upon me as a friend ; believe me I am and will be your real friend ; and if in this character I can have any influence with you, let me exhort you to be patient under misfortunes — to be peaceable, orderly and obedient to the laws. Let me beg of you to bear up manfully, and make the best of even what you may consider an indifferent lot. The evil must be merely temporary : let us look forward to better times, and *pray remember this, that nothing will more speedily contribute to restore prosperity than confidence amongst all classes, arising from a consciousness of perfect security.*

Believe me to be your well wisher and true friend.

(H.O.42/193).

(336). *The Duke of Newcastle to Viscount Sidmouth*

Clumber, 31 *August*, 1819,

I am just returned from Nottingham, and I have the pleasure to inform your Lordship that the result of my visit has been more satisfactory than I had previously any reason to expect.

The people are orderly, peaceable, and I must say reasonable, but still they have entered into a conspiracy, and therefore cannot be entitled to any legal assistance. I have, I hope, been able to effect some good by going to Nottingham. After a long and patient investigation I have been enabled to arrive at the following conclusions.

That the workmen should receive from me the answer of which I enclose a copy, and that I should advise the hosiers to give the full price to their workmen whenever they employ them. I feel much gratification in having been enabled to effect this latter measure, as it is one which I think they will never regret to have adopted, and which I expect will ultimately be the means of placing the trade on that respectable footing which will amply repay them for their present good spirit and manly concession.

I have every reason to believe that all will remain quiet. If unfortunately it should be otherwise, the proper preparations are made to repress outrage or violation of the public peace.[1]

[Enclosure.]

The Duke of Newcastle cannot leave Nottingham without expressing his great regret at being unable to devise any legal means of adjusting the differences now existing between the workmen and their employers in the hosiery business, but having received applications which make it appear that colonisation at the Cape of Good Hope would prove a desirable object to many, the Duke wishes to acquaint the workmen that he would afford the measure every facility in his power either by giving them personal information or by convening the County to take the subject into consideration upon receiving a proper application for that purpose. (H.O.42/193).

(337). *H. Enfield to Viscount Sidmouth*

Nottingham, 1 September, 1819.

The magistrates direct me to report to your Lordship that yesterday the framework-knitters brought in many of the stocking frames and deposited them in the streets at the doors of their masters. Men harnessed together in ropes drew the frames upon drags, Great crowds being collected by these proceedings, evidently tending to endanger the public peace, the magistrates, who were all in attendance throughout the day at the Police Office, issued a handbill prohibiting all persons from joining therein. The magistrates hope that this admonition will preserve quiet — if not, they are prepared to enforce the observance of good order.

The behaviour of the workmen themselves is, with the exception of this outrageous furtherance of their combination, peaceable. Whether it will continue so, or what will be the termination of this distressing state of things, remains to be known. Many of the manufacturers have '*come in*' to the prices asked . . .

[1] The Duke wrote to Lord Sidmouth on 14 December : ' . . . By calculation it comes out that from four to six thousand must be the *outside* of the effective population of the manufacturing district of this county : and supposing them *all* to be disaffected, in their isolated situation they are not much to be dreaded. Besides this numerical fact it is well ascertained that great disunion prevails, and that the attention and kindness which has been shown to the lower by the higher orders here, has made a great impression on the minds of the former, adverse to violent measures, and the Nottingham people are complained of by the northern delegates for their slackness in the cause.' (H.O.42/201).

I am afraid that I am intruding upon your Lordship by thus lengthening my letter, but the miserable situation of the poor creatures around us will, I am sure, secure me your Lordship's forgiveness, if I be somewhat out of official course. The prospect is fearful unless some immediate supplies for the necessary wants of the workpeople, and some employment for them *out* of their present over-charged trade, can be furnished.

Ibid. to Ibid., Nottingham, 2 September, 1819 :— Yesterday . . . the framework-knitters continued to deliver their frames throughout the day — but quietly, and without any disturbance of the public peace.[1] (H.O.42/194).

(338). *Joseph Forster* (*Mayor of Newcastle*) *to Viscount Sidmouth*

Newcastle-upon-Tyne, 28 *September,* 1819.

It gives me much concern to have occasion to apprise your Lordship that in the course of yesterday a strong body of the lightermen employed on this river assembled and proceeded to prevent by force the navigation of the keels or barges carrying coals from the staiths to the ships.

They have, however, since sent a respectful petition to their employers stating the cause of their dissatisfaction ; and as the gentlemen interested in the coal trade have appointed a general meeting to be held on Friday, first for the purpose of taking that petition into consideration, I entertain the hope that they will soon return to their duty.

I have not, my Lord, any reason at present to suspect the influence of any kind of political notions amongst them, but I cannot help feeling apprehensive that much industry may be used by ill-disposed persons to inflame them to mischief.

I beg leave to represent to your Lordship that the military and naval force now here is small, consisting I believe of only two weak troops of cavalry and two revenue cutters.[2] (H.O.42/195).

---

[1] To these two letters, Henry Hobhouse replied, on the 3rd : ' . . . Lord Sidmouth . . . trusts that some arrangement will take place between the masters and the workmen which may lead to the return to their work without any breach of the peace.' (H.O.41/5/10-11).

[2] The letter was endorsed by Henry Hobhouse : 'Directions have been given by the Admiralty for a sloop of war to proceed to the Tyne from the Firth of Forth.'

(339). *Joseph Bulmer to Viscount Sidmouth*

South Shields, 28 September, 1819.

As the spirit of discontent is beginning to show itself in this district, I deem it my duty to give your Lordship early information. The keelmen, from real or pretended grievances yesterday struck off work, and this morning I have seen many of them in boats on the river preventing keels going with coals to the ships. I understand the men allege that their employers load the keels with more than the usual quantity of eight chaldrons (which over-quantity the coalminers give to the shipowners instead of reducing the price) and only pay the same wages. This is not a time, my Lord, for masters to do anything that looks like oppressing their labourers, and therefore I think the Mayor and magistrates of Newcastle should lose no time in getting those differences adjusted, for I fear if the keelmen remain long in this state, the sailors will begin to feel uneasiness, and those two great bodies of men may join. 'Tis certain the reformists will endeavour to promote discord as much as they can. We have some of them here, but 'tis only among the labouring class. I have learnt they intend to hold a meeting to-night[1] . . . (H.O.42/195).

(340). *Samuel W. Sweet to Viscount Sidmouth*

[Illegible] Street, 30 September, 1819.

I am anxious to bring to your Lordship's recollection the memorials presented to your Lordship in 1814 and 1816 by the master manufacturers of Lancashire on the subject of the combinations of workmen, and the solicitation then made for an alteration in the Combination Laws. I had the honour of attending your Lordship with some of the most respectable manufacturers in the County, and the alarming events that have recently taken place were anticipated and pointed out to your Lordship as likely to result from the adoption of what was then a new plan of combination — namely, a combination among the heads of combinations of different trades. Your Lordship was impressed with the necessity of an alteration in the general law of combinations, but ultimately referred the deputation to the Law Officers of the Crown, and we were allowed to attend a consultation with the then Attorney and Solicitor

---

[1] He was an Acting Magistrate.

General, at which they declared their opinions that the laws were sufficient for the punishment of the conspirators, and that they could advise no application to Parliament for an extension of the laws or for the indemnity and protection of prosecutors and witnesses. The protection of the property and persons of manufacturers and witnesses who might give information or evidence or prosecute was strongly urged, but without effect, and the consequences of not enacting more efficient laws to give this protection and for seizing papers and the discovery and punishment of offenders, are too striking to need any comment.

Allow me, my Lord, at the present crisis, not only to request your Lordship's attention to the memorials alluded to but to the detailed suggestions made to your Lordship as well by the master manufacturers as by the London Committee, for in these may be found some hints from practical men which may be useful in the proposition of any new law, should such be in the contemplation of Government, but unless an indemnity to prosecutors, witnesses and persons assisting Government be provided for, there will be no inducement for exertion. On the contrary — loyal and well-disposed persons hold back on account of the exposure to loss and injury to which their property, persons and families are subjected. Indeed, my Lord, I think it right to add that the lukewarmness of the loyal and well-disposed is, according to the generally expressed opinion, to be attributed to the want of protection and support from Government in case of injury or loss . . .[1] (H.O.42/195).

(341). *Michael Fairles, J.P., to Viscount Sidmouth*

South Shields, 30 September, 1819.

. . . The whole of the keelmen upon the river Tyne have stopped work. They complain of short employment and of being obliged to convey a larger quantity of coals in their craft than usual, without any additional pay ; also require that no vessel above the burthen of 96 chaldrons of coals shall be allowed to load at the spouts. Your Lordship will observe that at these spouts vessels of large burthen are laden without the employment of craft, and it is doubtful in case this stop continues, the pitmen, who are a numerous and ignorant race, may join them. Some Radicals have appeared amongst them. Added to this, we have a very large fleet in port, and conse-

[1] Endorsed, 'Nil.'

quently the seamen unemployed, and unfortunately no ship of war with us. The *Alert* left about ten days ago for Sheerness, and report says she is not to return. As I have stated before to your Lordship, Shields harbour never should be without a ship of war. Had we had one with us I think it likely this matter might have been prevented. My advice this morning is that a meeting of the coalowners and a deputation from the keelmen will be held at Newcastle on Saturday, and that some of their demands are likely to be acceded to, but that of the spouts will not. I am of opinion we should be provided against the worst.[1]   (H.O.42/195).

(342). *The Duke of Northumberland to Viscount Sidmouth*

Alnwick Castle, 1 *October,* 1819.
'. . . The keelmen of the Tyne have lately shown an inclination to riot and have obstructed the keels in navigating the river.

I have great satisfaction, however, in acquainting your Lordship that the disturbance has originated solely in a dispute about additional wages, and is, I believe, totally unconnected with politics. I trust that in two or three days this dispute will be amicably adjusted, and tranquillity will again be restored . . . (H.O.42/196).

(343). *Robert Wheldon[2] to Viscount Sidmouth*

North Shields, 2 *October,* 1819.
. . . There are now in the harbour of Shields about 300 sail of ships, and in consequence of the keelmen having for the present refused to do their duty and preventing any coals being sent down to the ships, the pitmen and the seamen who are both numerous bodies, are laid idle. For the present they are quiet, but should they become tumultuous, we are without any military or ships of war to assist the civil power in case of need. (H.O.42/196).

(344). *M. Fairles to Viscount Sidmouth*

South Shields, 3 *October,* 1819.
As the keelmen and coalowners have not come to an amicable understanding, I enclose for your Lordship's information the

---

[1] Henry Hobhouse endorsed the letter: 'Regret at the disturbance. Hope it will be adjusted. Sloop of war ordered.'
[2] For Richard Barker, Clerk to the magistrates.

keelmen's petition, the coalowners' reply, with a letter from Mr. Thompson (a coalowner) upon the subject.

I yet doubt the pitmen, &c. may join the keelmen. The day I last wrote your Lordship I experienced much insult and contempt from about 200 ballast keelmen who attempted to prevent any ballast being landed from ships at the wharves . . .

[*Enclosures.*]

To the Gentlemen, Coalowners and Fitters on the River Tyne.

The Petition of the Keelmen employed on the river Tyne, humbly showeth,

That your petitioners have suffered very great privations from want of employment, chiefly owing to the vend by spout having increased so much of late.

Your petitioners humbly beg that no ship be allowed to take in more of her cargo or loading at any spout than *six keels*.

Your petitioners humbly beg that no keel be permitted to carry more than *eight chaldrons ;* the danger being very great in stormy weather or strong tides, if the keels carry more than that quantity.

Your petitioners humbly hope that the keelman's Fund will not be forgot at this time — an institution, they believe, all the gentlemen in the trade are friendly to, and without whose assistance it cannot continue. Your petitioners humbly beg that *one penny* per chaldron, for every chaldron vended by spout, be allowed to relieve the funds of that Institution.

28 September, 1819.

At a general meeting of the coalowners of this port, held at Newcastle on Saturday the 2nd October, 1819, the following Resolutions were passed unanimously.

It appearing to the meeting that the Keelmen's Fund has fallen into arrear to the amount of £161, owing to the number of claimants upon it, and to the difficulties of the coal trade ; and this meeting, wishing to encourage the same and to assist it with subscriptions, *it is ordered* that the sum of £300 be raised by a voluntary subscription of the coalowners, and paid into the bank of Messrs. Ridley & Co. to be placed to the credit of the Guardians of the Keelmen's Fund.

That no keel be allowed to carry more than eight chaldrons, and that in order to prevent the violation of this order, the Secretary of the coalowners be directed to call upon the off-putter at each staith, to take the oath prescribed by the Act for establishing the Keelmen's Fund ; and that any off-putter, neglecting or refusing to take such oath within one week, shall be discharged from his employment.

That the request of the keelmen to put any limitation or restraint on ships loading at the spouts, or to impose any duty or charge upon coals vended by spout, is illegal and therefore impracticable : and that an attempt to do so would be a violation of private property and of the principles on which all trade is carried on.

That the contribution of £300 be paid as above directed, as soon as the keelmen shall return to their respective employments.

And lastly, that these Resolutions be printed, and a copy sent to the Stewards of each Work, and to each Fitting Office.

Matthew Bell, Chairman.

An Abstract account of the State of the Funds of the Keelmen's Society.

	1815			1816			1817			1818		
	£	s.	d.	£	s.	d.	£	s.	d.	£	s.	d.
Collected from Fitters' Offices	1777	15	9	1772	15	4	1613	19	11	1812	2	10
Collected at 6d. per week	286	16	6	276	5	10	268	2	5	244	15	8
Collected Bye Tides	123	13	9	87	12	5	83	1	10	83	6	7
	2188	6	0	2136	13	7	1965	4	2	2140	5	1
Paid sick keelmen, superannuated members, widows and orphans	2235	19	0	2234	15	0	2127	4	0	2241	7	6

Balance against the Fund :

	47	13	0	98	1	5	161	19	10	101	2	5

Upon the Fund at present, 138 superannuated members ; 182 widows ; 6 orphans, and 22 sick keelmen, making a total of 348. (H.O.42/196).

(345). *Archibald Read (Mayor of Newcastle) to Viscount Sidmouth*

Newcastle, 5 October, 1819.

In consequence of the keelmen having yesterday evinced a disposition to mischief, I deemed it my duty as Chief Magistrate (having been elected yesterday) to proceed at an early hour this morning upon the river, the principal assemblage being about four miles from hence. Upon my appearance the men dispersed, but as I was anxious to have an interview, I quitted the steam packet, attended by three gentlemen, and obtained a full meeting about half a mile from the river . . . It proved more satisfactory than I expected, and having convinced the men of the illegality of their proceedings and the impossibility of my receiving their petition or attending to their complaints until they returned to work, they expressed their conviction that the whole of them would comply with my advice . . .

Ibid. to Ibid., Newcastle, 6 October, 1819.
. . . At a meeting held this morning by the keelmen they have come to the resolution of continuing off work . . . I greatly fear we shall towards the latter end of the week have the pitmen and sailors in a state of insubordination . . .

Ibid. to Ibid., Newcastle, 7 October, 1819. . . . The keelmen are in the same state as when I wrote yesterday. . . . My brother magistrate, Mr. Clennell, had an interview with about 300 of the keelmen yesterday evening which is likely to produce good effects. (H.O.42/196).

(346). *Joseph Bulmer to Viscount Sidmouth*

South Shields, 8 *October,* 1819.
. . . The keelmen are living by plunder, taking turnips and potatoes from the farmers in open day, and they declare, whatever offers their employers may make, they will not go to work till after Monday.[1] The shipwrights of South Shields (who are a numerous body) say no work shall be done on Monday, so that *all* may attempt the meeting . . . (H.O.42/196).

(347). *Archibald Read (Mayor) to Viscount Sidmouth*

Newcastle, 9 *October,* 1819.
. . . The shipowners have agreed to advance the wages of the men from £3 to £4 per voyage, which appears to give content. (H.O.42/196).

---

[1] When a mass meeting of Reformers was to be held at Newcastle.

(348). *Michael Fairles to Viscount Sidmouth*

South Shields, 12 October, 1819.
. . . From the peaceable termination of a public meeting of Reformers
held yesterday in the neighbourhood of Newcastle, and the little
interest which both keelmen and pitmen took in the business, I
augur that they will return to their employment about Monday first.
Their poverty, and the advice given them by their employers I trust
will have the desired effect. Should this fail, I see no other line but
to apprehend some of them by warrant. Two sloops of war are
arrived in the Tyne. (H.O.42/196).

(349). *Dr. Robert Gray to Viscount Sidmouth*

Bishop Wearmouth, 14 October, 1819.
As I think it probable that your Lordship may hear that a combination has taken place within a few days among the sailors of the
Port of Sunderland, I wish to assure you that there is good reason
to hope that an amicable arrangement will soon be made with their
employers who are disposed to raise the wages. The men do not
appear to have any connection with the Reformers. (H.O.42/196).

(350). *Archibald Read (Mayor) to Viscount Sidmouth*

Newcastle-upon-Tyne, 14 October, 1819, Thursday night, 10 o'clock.
I am sorry to inform your Lordship that an attempt to open the
navigation of the river Tyne (which has been interrupted . . . by a
riotous combination of the keelmen) has been attended with the
most alarming consequences. A furious attack was this afternoon
made by the mob at the mouth of the harbour on myself and the
civil power, and on the boats of his Majesty's ships stationed here.
Some shots were fired by the boats' crews in their own defence, but
as far as I have yet been able to ascertain, only with blank cartridges.

I take the liberty of urging most earnestly on your Lordship the
necessity of sending to this port without loss of time an adequate
force of ships of war and marines, and also of increasing the military
force in this neighbourhood. (H.O.42/196).

(351). *Joseph Bulmer to Viscount Sidmouth*

South Shields, 15 *October*, 1819.

. . . About six o'clock yesterday evening a few keels (four or five) came down the river, loaded with coals, protected by eight of his Majesty's boats ; the keelmen came to North Shields in great numbers, and from the wharf annoyed the men so much, who were casting the coals into the ships, that they were obliged to desist. The harbour master accompanied the men-of-war boats, and when he and his officers attempted to land on the Duke of Northumberland's quay (which is a very spacious place), they were assailed with brickbats, &c., &c. and obliged to retire. I am informed that the Mayor of Newcastle (who had also come down) at last effected a landing ; the marines being stoned most dreadfully by the mob (and I understand several of them wounded) at length *fired* over their heads, but this only had the effect of causing greater violence. At length the marines fired amongst them and *killed* one man and wounded others. The mob became very furious and demolished all the windows of the principal inn (kept by one Mrs. Carr, a widow) because several special constables had gone there for safety. The mob at length dispersed but threatened to assemble again this morning . . .

The keelmen were joined by a great number of the Radicals of North Shields, and the circumstances seemed greatly to interest those of South Shields, but we remain quiet. I believe, my Lord, that the lower orders here are ripe for anything. (H.O.42/196).

(352). *The Earl of Darlington to Viscount Sidmouth*

Raby Castle, 15 *October*, 1819.

. . . The refractory keelmen and the Radical Reformers are, I trust, perfectly separate, although very inflammatory language and seditious writings are diffused amongst the former, who formed, I suppose, a part of that large assemblage of people who met on Newcastle Moor on Monday, but who appear to have quietly dispersed.[1] (H.O.42/196).

---

[1] The Mayor of Newcastle sent Lord Sidmouth on the 17th an account of the riots, and added, 'I am happy to say I have every reason to believe the business between the keelmen and owners will be settled tomorrow, but this will not render us secure. The Reformers are now in a state of almost rebellion . . .'

(353). *Archibald Read (Mayor) to Viscount Sidmouth*

Newcastle, 19 October, 1819.

The keelmen refused to accept of the terms offered yesterday by the coalowners. I am in hopes of giving these men satisfaction to-day, as their only wish is now that for 100 to 140 of them, who have not employment may be found work, and I have summoned the Common Council to attend within an hour for the purpose of proposing that the Corporation employ the men who have not work, in dredging the river . . . (H.O.42/197).

(354). *The Duke of Northumberland to Viscount Sidmouth*

Alnwick Castle, 20 October, 1819.

. . . I have just seen Mr. Clennel, one of the most active magistrates in this County, and to whose decision the keelmen had referred the arrangement of their grievances.

After much difficulty his efforts have been attended with success, almost to the entire satisfaction of the keelmen. They have now, I understand, returned to work again in a cheerful and satisfactory manner, and the Corporation have determined to find work for all those keelmen who have been for some time out of employ . . . (H.O.42/197).

(355). *Archibald Read (Mayor of Newcastle) to Viscount Sidmouth*

Newcastle, 20 October, 1819.

. . . The keelmen have not returned to work ; they are now holding a meeting in a body about a mile from this town, and a deputation is to meet me this morning, but I much fear the result. The coalowners have acted most liberally, and the Corporation of this town offered to employ every keelman who has not work.

I received a letter from Sir John Byng urging the return of the 40th to Sunderland barracks. I have only to assure your Lordship that a diminution of force at this place will probably be attended with the most fatal results, and I most earnestly entreat your Lordship's attention to the inadequate force which we have, both military and marine.

We have the most formidable set of men to contend with, consisting of sailors, lightermen, pitmen, and I am truly sorry to add of Radical Reformers. I stated to your Lordship the immense value of

Y

the shipping now lying in the river, the inadequacy of the naval force and military to protect Shields, Newcastle and populous surrounding country . . .

Ibid. to Ibid., Newcastle, 21 October, 1819 :— . . . The differences between the coalowners and keelmen are satisfactorily arranged, and the men will go to work to-morrow. They would have done so this morning, but had not money to furnish their baskets ; their employers agree to advance on account of wages . . .

Ibid. to Ibid., Newcastle, 22 October, 1819 :—The keelmen, with the exception of two collieries, returned to work this morning, but I greatly fear that if the owners above alluded to do not accede to the terms granted by the other collieries, that the whole body of keelmen will be off work to-morrow, and I cannot contemplate such an event without the utmost dread of the consequences . . .

Ibid. to Ibid., Newcastle, 23 October, 1819 :—. . . As it was of the utmost importance to the country to keep the keelmen at work, I agreed to advance the men 20s. each, upon condition, that if the owners of Bewicke and Craisters did not repay me, the coalowners would do so. I named to your Lordship that the owners of the above colliery refused to complete the conditions which the others had agreed to, and I am to meet them this morning, and hope to convince them of the policy, if not the absolute necessity, of their complying. The advance made had the effect of setting all the keelmen upon the river to work . . .

Ibid. to Ibid., Newcastle, 24 October, 1819 :— . . . The state of this part of the kingdom continues as alarming as I represented it to be The pitmen are not only disaffected but extremely dissatisfied, many of their employers can only give them half work. A very large body of them from one of the collieries assembled on Friday last for the purpose of stopping the other collieries, but were prevailed upon to go to work that day, but there is the strongest reason to believe that this is only a temporary abandonment of their design, and that they will ultimately refuse to work . . .

Ibid. to Ibid., Newcastle, 27 October, 1819 :— . . . The keelmen are at work, and perfectly satisfied, but the dissatisfaction, and I most *truly lament to add, the disaffection* of the pitmen rapidly increases. At one colliery (Mount Moor) near to Gateshead Fell, all the pitmen except five have joined the Radicals, and almost the entire body of the pitmen entertain the same mischievous and abominable principles . . .

The number of pitmen upon the Tyne and the Wear, including boys, employed, are about 15,000 . . . (H.O.42/197).

(356). *An Advertisement in the Manchester Observer*

30 October, 1819.

We, the undersigned, the Committee appointed by the journeymen hatters of Oldham, feel it a duty incumbent upon us to return our most grateful acknowledgements for the attention paid to the body which we represent, by those masters who have kindly come forward and attended the different meetings which have been held at the White Bear Inn, opposite the Infirmary in Manchester, and at the same time they beg to solicit their further attendance on Wednesday next, at 10 o'clock in the forenoon at the said place.

They think proper also to enjoin those masters who have not yet attended, to favour them with their company, at the said time and place. It is the opinion of our body that the reduction of wages by those masters who advocate the same, must be from a mistaken idea, for if a higher price is given by the master to his workmen, it compels him necessarily to advance the price of his goods, and the merchants must buy the article of him (when wanted) whatever the market price may be. Regard ought also to be had to the disunion it may create in the trade, and even in the same family. Indeed, the evil consequences are so evident, and the mischief so pregnant to us, that to appease the feelings of the majority of the journeymen, the names of those masters who do not attend the next meeting aforementioned, must necessarily come before the public, but we trust no one will compel us to so disagreeable an alternative, but liberally come forward in so laudable a cause.

By order of the Committee :

Joseph Taylor, John Barlow, John Elson, John Lingard, John Holden, John Whitehead, James Hardy.

Oldham, 28 October, 1819.

(357). *Archibald Read (Mayor) to Viscount Sidmouth*

Newcastle, 2 November, 1819.

. . . I am most anxiously waiting [for] accounts from Shields. The wind is favourable for the sailing of the colliers, and a very short period must decide whether the unemployed and disaffected sailors will attempt to stop their proceeding to sea. It is of the most vital importance that they should sail. The Corporation of this town have subscribed for the benefit of the sailors' wives and families. Their

example has been followed by many gentlemen, which has produced
a favourable impression upon many of the sailors whose families
were in great distress in consequence of the large vessels having
been six weeks detained first by the keelmen not loading them ;
after, by contrary winds . . .

Ibid. to Ibid., Newcastle, 3 November, 1819 :— . . . Upwards of 90
colliers sailed last night, and I have no doubt of double that number
having taken their departure by this morning's tide. Thus we are
relieved from a most formidable force of upwards of 3,000 sailors . . .

Ibid. to Ibid., Newcastle, 4 November, 1819 :— I most deeply lament
to inform your Lordship that Messrs. Lamb, &c., owners of the
Bewicke and Craisters, Wallsend, having refused to comply with the
conditions agreed upon between the coalowners and keelmen, the
others have this day refused to work, and the whole body of keelmen will be off work tomorrow.

Ibid. to Ibid., Newcastle, 6 November, 1819 :— . . . All the keelmen are
off work. A deputation from them is to be with me, and the coalowners meet this morning, and I hope the differences may be adjusted. I however have fears upon that subject.

Ibid. to Ibid., Newcastle, 7 November, 1819 :— . . . A large majority of
the coalowners settled with the keelmen yesterday, and I hope the
greater part will return to work to-morrow . . .

Ibid. to Ibid., Newcastle, 8 November, 1819 :— Such of the keelmen
as were settled with on Saturday are at work this morning. There
are six collieries whose men are off, but I trust the whole will be
adjusted to-day . . .

Ibid. to Ibid., Newcastle, 9 November, 1819 :— . . . All the keelmen
are at work with the exception of one colliery, and the men and
agent are at this moment with Mr. Clennell and myself, and we
have no doubt of settling their differences . . . (H.O.42/198).

(358). *The Mayor of Leeds to Viscount Sidmouth*

Leeds, 25 November, 1819.
. . . The colliers in the neighbourhood of Leeds and its vicinity have
pretty generally struck for an advance of wages (as they term it),
or, to speak more intelligibly, have given over working — with the
intention of compelling their masters to comply with their demands.

The increase expected by the men who are working in the colliery
from which this town is chiefly supplied is no less than 2s. upon

every 3s. they earned before, and which hitherto has been about the average of the general daily earnings of the common men.

There has been a very general meeting of these and the neighbouring men held to-day at Dewsbury within a few miles of this place — for the purpose, as it is supposed, of arranging the terms to be proposed to their respective masters. Since that meeting, a number of them to the amount of 2,500 or 3,000 men have been in this town parading through the streets, attended by several different bands of music — but it does not appear that they have had any view at present beyond showing their numbers arrayed in some degree of military order — as they are all quietly dispersed. (H.O.42/199).

(359). *Henry Hobhouse to the Mayor of Leeds*

Whitehall, 27 November, 1819.

. . . It is with regret that Lord Sidmouth has read this intelligence, but he has the utmost reliance that by the steady resolution of the masters in resisting a demand which it is attempted to enforce by unlawful means, by the firmness of the magistrates in administering the law in all cases of combination which may be brought before them, by their vigilant endeavours to prevent any breach of the peace from being committed, and by their prompt and energetic determination to quell any disturbances which may unfortunately arise, the danger which is to be apprehended from this conspiracy will be speedily averted. But it is his Lordship's decided opinion that it could not fail to be most seriously aggravated by concession. (H.O.41/5/298-99).

(360). *The Rev. Henry Parry to Viscount Sidmouth*

Llanasa Vicarage, 7 December, 1819.

I think it necessary to trouble your Lordship with a short account of a disturbance that took place in the parish of Holywell (Flintshire) on Friday last and the following days, amongst the colliers employed in that neighbourhood. The dispute originally arose about an alteration in working a certain colliery in Bagillt in that parish, where a few colliers from the neighbourhood of Wrexham were introduced to teach the men the new mode of working the coal. This gave such dissatisfaction to the old workmen that they turned out to a man. On Friday, being the market day, they came to the town of Holywell and behaved in a very riotous manner, but being persuaded by the magistrates then present, they returned to their homes, but not before they put the inhabitants of that town to great fear. On the following day a more formidable combination took place, but they did not proceed to any riotous Act, threatening, however, to come to Holywell on Monday and have everything their own way, in consequence of which, a requisition was made to the magistrates by the inhabitants of that town, who sent to the commander of the troops to Chester for military aid, and consequently, part of two companies of the 71st arrived there early on Monday morning, and likewise two troops of the Hawarden cavalry, but happily there was no occasion for them, for the greater part of the colliers returned to their work on Monday, and in the course of this evening a reconciliation took place between the remainder of the colliers that stood out, and their employers, so I have it in my power now to inform your Lordship that tranquillity is perfectly restored.[1] (H.O.42/200).

---

[1] The Radical agitation for parliamentary reform which had culminated in the 'Manchester Massacre' on 16 August, 1819, was now being driven underground by coercive measures : the famous 'Six Acts' were being debated in Parliament. Lord Derby wrote to the Home Secretary on 13 December: '. . . The distress of the poorer class of people is becoming greater every day, and unless some measure can be devised to afford them an essential and permanent relief, it is but too probable that despair may drive them to such excesses as must not only lead to their own ruin but be productive of the greatest danger to the peace and safety of the country.' (H.O.42/201).

IX. THE LAST YEARS OF THE COMBINATION ACTS

1820. The Dewsbury blanket manufacturers.
      The weavers' strike in Glasgow.
      The copper-smelters and colliers of Swansea.
      The Lancashire cotton-spinners and weavers.
1821. The colliers of Wellington, Salop.
      The framework-knitters.
      The journeymen-hatters.
      The journeymen-coopers in London.
1822. The cloth-weavers of Somersetshire.
      The colliers in South Wales, at Bilston and Walsall.
      The lightermen and seamen on Tyneside.
1823. The cotton-spinners of Bolton and Glasgow.
      The spinners of Dundee.
      The weavers of Frome.
1824. The shipwrights of Sunderland.
      The silk-weavers of Macclesfield.
      The carpenters of Sunderland.
      The framework-knitters.
      Combinations in Birmingham.
1825. The Lancashire cotton-spinners and weavers.
      The colliers in Lancashire and in the Potteries.
      The Manchester dyers, farriers and shoe-makers.
      The seamen of Sunderland and Scarborough.
      The cotton-spinners of Glasgow.
      The shipwrights of London.
      The drafting of the Amending Act of 1825.

(361). *Jonathan Hopkinson to Viscount Sidmouth*

Dewsbury, 28 February, 1820.

Being selected as the professional adviser of those merchants and manufacturers in this place, who have been induced to step forward on the present awful aspect of affairs to endeavour to preserve the peace of this part of the north of England, I have been favoured with the perusal of the reply which your Lordship was pleased to direct to be made to the communication transmitted to your Lordship from Dewsbury on the 24th ult. respecting the disturbances which have recently taken place in this town and its vicinity . . . Although in an abstracted point of view the mischiefs complained of to your Lordship have 'been enhanced by the concession which the masters in the first instance made to the illegal combinations of the journeymen,' yet, it is most confidently anticipated that, when your Lordship is assured, as the fact is, that with the exception of two very respectable houses engaged in the manufacturing of blankets and other coarse woollen goods, viz. Messrs. Hagues and Cook and Messrs. Halliley Sons and Brooke, all the other persons following those branches of trade possess only small capitals which are chiefly embarked in such trade with a view to the employment (certainly with some exceptions) of their own families, it will naturally impress on your Lordship's mind the conviction that it has been morally impossible for those parties to act in concert together, because it is evident that the interests of the smaller capitalists would be promoted in the largest and most beneficial manner by *secretly* encouraging what has been termed 'The Union,' and the standing out of the workmen for an increase of wages, because if that object was attained, they and their families would be greatly benefited in the ultimate disposal of their goods.

Your Lordship therefore will at once perceive that there could not possibly be such a coalition between the merchants and manufacturers, as circumstances required *effectually* to check the combination of their workmen, for it may fairly be said that the great and smaller capitalists were divided against each other . . . The gentlemen whom I have particularly named have always remained firm in their resolution not to comply with the demands of their workmen, being impressed with the conviction that their so doing would have the effect of bringing those deluded men to a due sense of the impropriety of their conduct and of the necessity for their returning to their work, as the only amends they could offer for so flagrant a breach of their duty. This with many had the desired effect, and these are the persons who (as has been represented to your Lordship) are in consequence of their abandoning the Union, called '*Blackmen.*' It may not be amiss to inform your Lordship that with a view to encourage that line of conduct, a considerable advance of wages was spontaneously given to all who returned to their work, and yet it was not until after violent outrages had been committed in this town only a few individuals were bold enough

344

to step forward and complain of the same, and threats are openly made of vengeance against those individuals amongst whom I happen to be ranked as a marked man . . .

P.S. I have just now been informed by Messrs. Halliley Sons and Brooke that a number of men have applied to them for employment, expressing their willingness to abandon the Union and begin again to work, but declaring at the same time their conviction that at present they dare not do so for fear of being on that account rendered objects of the vengeance of those persons who still persevere in their injurious delusion . . . (H.O.40/11).

(362). *Colonel Fletcher to Viscount Sidmouth*

Bolton-le-Moors, 4 April, 1820.

. . . The weavers in many parts about Glasgow had struck or given over working. Many Radical weavers in Bolton on Friday last declared that they would weave no more. Probably in both places these resolutions will be broken, but the making of such declaration at places so distant, combined with the other circumstances of nocturnal meetings, manifests a directing hand somewhere, whose beck the Radicals follow.[1] (H.O.40/12/32).

(363). *Colonel Campbell to Major-General Sir John Byng*

Leeds, 17 *April,* 1820.

. . . The committee[2] here are busy forwarding subscriptions, and using their influence to induce all classes to *bury the trade,* as they term it — that is, to strike. I should imagine they would not easily persuade persons in regular and permanent employ to throw it up on any visionary scheme of ideal benefit . . . (H.O.40/12/7a).

---

[1] Popular meetings could no longer be held, but it was said that the Radicals in different parts of the country continued to keep up a regular communication with each other, and the itinerant delegates had their expenses paid out of a common fund. The presence of a large military force prevented further disturbances in Lancashire and Yorkshire, but Glasgow was in a state of unrest in March, 1820, and there was practically a general strike in that district at the beginning of April. The *Leeds Mercury,* 22 April, 1820, gave an account of the weavers' strike in Yorkshire.

[2] Possibly the committee of the Weavers' Union.

(364). *George Wyatt to Francis Freeling*

Post Office, Shiffnal, 20 *June,* 1820.

. . . The difference which has some days subsisted between the ironmasters and their colliers in this neighbourhood has now subsided by their masters having yesterday consented to employ them on the former terms . . . (H.O.40/13/108).

(365). *Sir R. Kemeys and four other J.Ps. to Viscount Sidmouth*

Swansea, 29 *August,* 1820.

Information on oath having been laid before us, the undersigned magistrates, that an illegal combination had taken place among the workmen of Messrs. Grenfell and Co., copper smelters, in this neighbourhood, thirteen of those persons were, after due examination, committed to prison under the Statute of the 39th and 40th of George III. A number of fellow workmen assembled and violently prevented the said thirteen persons from being lodged in prison. Three of the said persons were subsequently apprehended and taken to the gaol in the town of Swansea, but upwards of one hundred men armed with bludgeons marched into the town, in open defiance of the law, and proceeded to the gaol, the doors of which they broke open and rescued the prisoners. It is the determination of the magistrates to enforce, without delay, the operation of the law, but from information on which we can depend, we believe that there is a confederate spirit among the workmen of the various manufactories and collieries in this neighbourhood to resist the magisterial authority . . .[1] (H.O.40/14/125).

(366). *James Norris to Viscount Sidmouth*

Manchester, 29 *October,* 1820. *Private.*

In consequence of the receipt of Mr. Hobhouse's letter of the 26th inst. respecting our intended meeting this evening at Stayleybridge for seditious purposes, I obtained an interview with the person who has before given me information from that quarter, and I learn from him that he does not think any political meetings are now held in that neighbourhood. The working class, and particularly the weaver, is too well off now to trouble his mind much about politics . . . My informant says that he thinks the meeting alluded

---

[1] He asked for the assistance of a military force.

to, if any take place, will be among the spinners who are meditating a turn-out, and have already held several meetings on this subject. . .

I understand from Mr. Sharp that there is some talk in this town of a turn-out amongst the spinners, and which will be, he believes, decided upon to-morrow. Perhaps the meeting at Stayley may have relation to this movement. The general opinion is that they will not venture to turn out, as the spinning branch of trade is much the worst now going. All others are good. (H.O.40/14/93).

(367). *Cecil Weld Forester to Viscount Sidmouth*

Willey Park, 2 February, 1821.

. . . The magistrates of Wellington and Much Wenlock have requested me to state that the colliers in the neighbourhood of Wellington and Donnington Wood have struck for wages, and during the two last days have risen and gone about to the different works, and by force have taken the peaceable men who would have worked, and made them join them, so that all the ironworks in this neighbourhood are at a complete stand, and this very populous district may be considered in a most disturbed state . . . (H.O.40/16/9).

(368). *The Magistrates of Wellington to the Earl of Powis*[1]

Wellington, 4 February, 1821. (Copy).

. . . On Friday morning last . . . we received information that the colliers were assembled in a very large body and were proceeding successively to all the ironworks in this part of the country for the purpose of intimidating those men who were disposed to work at the reduced rate of wages and compelling them to stop the Works and join the body of rioters. About 70 men of Colonel Cludde's yeomanry cavalry having been assembled, we proceeded in search of the rioters to the ironworks at the Horse Way between this place and Coalbrookdale. Upon our arrival there, we found that having effected their purpose and completely stopped those Works, they had proceeded to the Works of Messrs. Botfields at the Old Park, to which place we immediately followed them. As we advanced we saw them retreating before us till they came to some large mounds formed of the refuse cinders from the furnaces where it clearly

---

[1] Communicated by Lord Powis to the Home Office on 12 February.

appeared that it had previously been concerted among them to make a stand ; and as soon as they had occupied them in formidable numbers, to the amount, we should apprehend of 3,000, they gave three cheers in token of defiance. The cavalry being halted at a distance, the magistrates rode up to the rioters, and after vainly endeavouring to reason with them and to persuade them to disperse, proceeded to read the Riot Act . . .[1]

As we are informed by the ironmasters that many of their workmen would return to work if they could be protected against the ill-disposed, it is hoped that with the reinforcements of troops which have since arrived, we may be enabled tomorrow by stationing troops in different parts of the docks, to afford them effectual protection. *Ibid. to Ibid., Wellington, 10 February, 1821.*[2] *(Copy)* .— . . . Everything has remained quiet since our last report. At the Works in the immediate neighbourhood of Wellington where the ironmasters have adopted the more moderate reduction of 4d. per day, the men have in general returned to their work, but as the notice for the reduction of wages in the vicinity of Coalbrookdale where the iron masters still insist upon the reduction of 6d. per day only expires this day, we are by no means free from uneasiness in that quarter. (H.O.40/16/15 and 33).

(369). *Henry Hobhouse to H. Enfield*

Whitehall, 31 *March,* 1821.

I am directed by Lord Sidmouth to acknowledge the receipt of your letter of the 29th inst. announcing the circumstance of the workmen in one branch of the stocking manufactory having struck with a view to obtain an advance in wages, and enclosing a handbill which has been put forth by the magistrates of Nottingham on this occasion. His Lordship regrets that the workmen should have recourse to this illegal mode of obtaining an advantage which, whether they were justly entitled to it or not, can not with prudence to them by the manufacturers in the present circumstances [*sic*]. His Lordship hopes that the employers will bring some of the leaders of this illegal measure to justice. But he quite agrees with the magistrates of Nottingham that it is not fit for them to interfere

---

[1] One rioter was killed in the skirmish that followed ; another died of his injuries. Six prisoners were taken, and they were committed for trial at the next Assizes.

[2] Communicated by Lord Powis to the Home Office on 12 February.

until there is danger of the peace being broken. The cautionary handbill appears to his Lordship to have been very judiciously issued. (H.O.43/30/218).

(370). *L. Rolleston, J.P., to Viscount Sidmouth*

Watnall, 8 April [1821].

I have hitherto forborne troubling your Lordship respecting the combination of the framework-knitters of this county against their employers chiefly from a hope that the workmen would before this have seen the futility of their measures, or at least have acted so cautiously as to have avoided all grounds for the interference of the magistrates. But from the various Resolutions and documents entered into and published by the committee during the last six months, your Lordship will not be surprised to find the reverse has been the case, and that poverty and distress has attended those who complied with the Resolutions, whilst outrage and violence has compelled the industrious and contented to abandon their frames. I am fully aware a more prompt interference on the part of the magistrates has been warranted, and perhaps called for, but the desire of a strict adherence to the principle of non-interference between the master and workman, has for a time induced a relaxation, which present circumstances will no longer admit. By the operations of the committee, the whole community of stocking-makers are, with very little exception, out of employ and without any visible means of subsistence. Some of the men, it is true, obtain a trifling assistance from delegates, but their wives and families are reduced to the utmost wretchedness, and some serious result must occur if measures of counteraction are not speedily adopted. Depredations on the person and property of those who are willing to work have become very general, where threats and intimidation have failed in the desired effect ; indeed, so completely organised are the different plans of these men, that it is with the greatest difficulty even the most industrious can work a few hours in the day without interruption. I think your Lordship will agree with me that a combination so extensive and powerful required an adequate and decided check ; with this view I yesterday issued warrants, conjointly with Mr. Edge, for apprehending the whole of the committee, having received sufficient information and evidence, I hope, for convicting them under the third section of the Combination Act 39 and 40 George III. Should we succeed in this, I have little doubt it will go far towards restoring tranquillity to the County, and reconciling the workmen to their masters. The case will be heard on Wednesday next, when if anything occurs worthy your Lordship's notice, I will not fail to write . . . (H.O.40/16/25).

(371). *J. Lloyd to Henry Hobhouse*

Chester, 12 *April*, 1821.

Another serious conspiracy had taken place amongst the hatters, which was to be general. They tried the experiment at Stockport of controlling the masters there, and met in conclave, calling before them witnesses [?] and honest workmen who had refused to confederate with them, levying fines on the refractory. The masters waited upon me. I encouraged them to firmness, and have prevailed over their fears, have brought three houses and four workmen here, have this day preferred an indictment against ten, which has been returned a true bill, and Bench warrants are now in my hands to be executed against persons at Oldham, other parts of Lancashire and Stockport and other parts of Cheshire, and a *salutary* sensation will be excited very soon amongst them.

I think it right to apprise you although I have been acting for the *masters only* . . . (H.O.44/7/37).

(372). *J. Langlands (Secretary) to Henry Hobhouse*

West India Dock House, 20 *August*, 1821.

I am desired by the Directors of the West India Dock Company to acquaint you that a most serious impediment to the dispatch of business at the Docks has arisen from a combination among the coopers, and to request the aid of his Majesty's Secretary of State.

The journeymen-coopers employed as extra men have struck as it is termed, for an advance of wages. The Directors, under a sense of public duty, feel that they must resist any demand thus made, but that they must at the same time provide for the due execution of the business. They, therefore, relying upon their permanent coopers, have tried the effect of working extra hours, and have engaged to make good such compensation to the officers of the Customs and Excise for their extra attendance, as the Boards may be pleased to direct.

These exertions having proved insufficient to meet the pressure of the moment, and the discharge of a great number of vessels being impeded, the Directors dispatched proper officers to Bristol and

Liverpool to engage any cooper who might be out of employ. They, however, find that the extent of the combination is so great, and such a system of intimidation exists, that no men in the metropolis or its environs will venture to return to their work, however well disposed, and that the men who have arrived from the outports have been seduced and broken their engagements.

It has been suggested that a measure which was adopted under similar circumstances some time ago at Bristol by the General commanding his Majesty's Forces, would be of material assistance, viz., granting furloughs to such men in the regiments quartered in the neighbourhood as were at all competent to work as coopers.

The Directors of this Company therefore request that you will confer with His Royal Highness the Commander-in-Chief,[1] and suggest the expediency of acceding to their wishes in this respect. The pay allowed to coopers in the Docks, and which would be given to such men, is five shillings per day of eight hours, viz., from 8 a.m. to 4 p.m. Those employed are at present from 6 in the morning to 6 in the evening earn 7s. 6d. a day.

You will not fail to observe that the inconvenience experienced by this Company is comparatively of little moment compared with that which is sustained by the West Indian planters and merchants, shipowners and others, and that the public revenue is suffering materially from the draining of sugars on ship-board and on the quay before passing the King's beam.

Ibid. to Ibid., 27 August, 1821 :—I am to acknowledge the receipt of your letter of the 21st instant, and am desired by the Directors of the West India Dock Company to request that you will convey to Lord Bathurst[2] their thanks for the prompt attention paid to their communication, although circumstances did not admit of its being acceded to.

I am further directed to acquaint you for his Lordship's inform-ation that, formidable as the combination was by which the business of this establishment has been impeded, the measures adopted by the Directors in conjunction with the honourable Boards of Customs and Excise have proved entirely successful, and that the refractory coopers have returned to their work unconditionally. The knowledge that the application which I had the honour to address to you had been made, may probably have accelerated this desirable result. (H.O.40/16/65, 98).

---

[1] The Duke of York, George IV's brother (1763–1827).
[2] Secretary of State for War and the Colonies, 1812–27. (1762–1834).

(373). *The Marquess of Bath to Robert Peel*[1]

Longleat, 20 January, 1822.

. . . The cloth weavers in this neighbourhood have assembled in considerable numbers (as many, it is said, as seven or eight hundred) in the town of Frome in consequence of some weavers working at 12d. per yard whilst others had received 15d. They go to the weavers' houses who work at the low prices, and take the cloth from the looms, returning it to the clothier to whom it belongs. In two instances they have broken into houses to take the cloth, and a week or ten days ago the Earl [of] Cork and the magistrates committed several to prison, who have been sentenced at the Quarter Sessions, one to twelve months' imprisonment, one to two years, one to eighteen months, two to six months' imprisonment. But I apprehend this has not checked their proceedings, as a large body of weavers were at Warminster yesterday, and took the cloths from the weavers' houses . . .

Ibid. to Ibid., Longleat, 24 January, 1822 :—. . . The town of Frome is now quiet and some of the weavers in the neighbourhood are returning to their work, but at Frome the clothiers and the weavers have not yet agreed upon the rate of wages and I understand no work is as yet given out to them. (H.O.40/17/30, 37).

(374). *The Rev. W. Powell to Henry Hobhouse*

Abergavenny, 30 March [1822], 10 o'clock p.m.
[The colliers employed by Messrs. Bailey at Nant-y-Glo had struck work] . . . The ironmasters all seem to think that the bad spirit of Mr. Bailey's colliers may be spread by evil communications tomorrow and require a greater force effectually to put it down . . . Last night there appeared a number of men from other works among the misled colliers, who were doing everything in their power to prevent their acceding to their employer's terms — but I have just now received a letter from Mr. Bailey to inform me that from two to three hundred of his miners have promised to stand by him and assist in protecting the lives and property of those who are in danger . . .

Ibid. to Ibid., 4 April, 1822 :— I beg leave to communicate to you the intelligence I this morning received from Mr. Bailey, that the

---

[1] Peel had just succeeded Sidmouth as Home Secretary.

differences with his workmen have been adjusted, and that most of the men have returned to their employment. But I should have felt more satisfaction in this communication had I not to announce also that this desirable result had been produced by Mr. Bailey having acceded to all the demands of the men. This circumstance may, I fear, offer a temptation to the men, employed in the neighbouring works to adopt similar measures for enforcing any claim they may hereafter be induced to make upon their employers, and may be productive of most extensive mischief in case of any future disagreement. I understand that a sudden increase in the demand for iron rendered it almost absolutely imperative on Mr. Bailey to give way in this instance . . . (H.O.40/17/14, 101).

(375). *J. Clare, J.P., to Robert Peel*

Bilston, near Wolverhampton. 17 April, 1822.
In consequence of information from some of the principal coalmasters in the neighbourhood of Wednesbury and Tipton in this county, stating that the colliers had refused to work, and prevented others from working also, and that very serious disturbances were likely to arise, and calling upon the Rev. Wm. Leigh and self as magistrates for protection, I take the liberty to inform you that we are now sitting at this place for that purpose . . .

Up to the present moment nothing more serious has happened than refusing to work and preventing others, stopping loads of coals in transitu to the furnaces, shouting at and hissing the master colliers, and in one instance pelting with stones one person, an agent of Lord Dudley . . .　　　(H.O.40/17/48).

(376). *L. Rolleston to the Duke of Grafton*

Watnall, 20 April, [1822].
The disorderly spirit alluded to in my former letter to your Grace, as existing in this county, is solely confined to the frameworkknitters, and I have no reason to believe these people are connected politically or otherwise with anyone out of their own trade. The unwise support afforded them last year under similar circumstances by persons of high consideration, has been mainly the cause of the present turn-out, but as that assistance has not on the present occasion been so liberally afforded them, a great majority appear now anxious to return to their frames, and I have every reason to

hope by the end of the week all will be quiet, at least as far as concerns Nottinghamshire, for the Derbyshire people still hold out, and say they will come and forcibly compel our hands to do the same. But this threat I look upon as quite idle ; they are too well aware of the reception they would meet with, should they venture on so imprudent a step.

The outrages have chiefly been confined to the parishes of Lambley, Basford, Burton, and parts of the parish of Greasley bordering on Derbyshire ; the plan has been to ascertain by delegates what persons were at work during the day, then to return in the night, and make a grand attack on their houses with all kinds of missiles . . . (H.O.40/17/58).

(377). *L. Rolleston to Robert Peel*

Watnall, 20 April, 1822.

. . . A turn-out . . . of most of the framework-knitters of this county and Derbyshire took place a few weeks since, for the purpose of compelling their employers to an advance of wages, but as this demand at the present time could be sustained on no just principle, many of the hands refused to cease from working, and the consequence, as is always the case with us, was the adoption towards them of compulsory measures . . . (H.O.40/17/57).

(378). *The Rev. John H. Moggridge to Robert Peel*

Woodfield Lodge, 21 April, 1822.

. . . Finding on my return from the Quarter Sessions that symptoms of the spirit which has been and continues to be so alarming in the neighbouring ironworks had infected our collieries, I sent to several of my brother magistrates to meet me at Pontypool on Friday. The measures adopted there you will have been informed of, as well as of the previous mutiny of the colliers at the Rock Colliery and the inefficacy of my endeavours aided by some of their masters to induce them to return to their duty . . . (H.O.40/17/60).

(379). *The following handbill, dated Bilston, 23 April, 1822, was published by A. B. Haden, J. Clare and W. Leigh, magistrates :*—
'At a meeting of the principal coal and iron-masters, held at the King's Arms, Bilston, on Tuesday the 23rd day of April, 1822, at

the request of the magistrates, for the purpose of investigating the causes of the present disturbances in the mining districts of this neighbourhood, which meeting was most numerously and respectably attended, it appeared that the colliers are getting from 2s. 6d. to 3s. per day, with the advantages of three pints of pit drink and firing for their families, and can, at the present moment, generally have full employment.

That the practice of paying miners otherwise than in money (which has been so industriously propagated) is by no means the general practice, for it appeared that not one of this numerous meeting paid in any other way than in cash and cash notes.

These facts being fully established to our satisfaction, we feel it our duty to declare that it is our determination to protect and support those men who are willing to return and follow their usual employments, and to put the Vagrant Act in force immediately against "all persons going about from door to door, or placing themselves in streets, highways or passages, to beg or gather alms".' (H.O.40/17/69).

(380). *J. Curtis, Jun., to Edward Grove*

Walsall, 5 May, 1822.

The origin of the colliers' complaint was the circumstance of the Hocker Hill and Moat Colliery Company at Tipton (two individual firms) having some time ago reduced the wages of their men in consequence of the depression of the iron trade. This for some time was by no means a general measure, nor is it yet entirely so, but the dissatisfaction of the workmen at such an attempt, and the same measures having been since partially adopted throughout the iron and coal districts, have caused the stoppage of most of the iron furnaces, works and collieries. The present price of iron will not permit the makers even to save themselves from loss, and the alternative of stopping their works is so disastrous that they are anxious by any expedient to avoid it, which has given rise to the system of truck (better known by the local phrase of *tommy shops*) of which the men have now availed themselves as a plausible and (I may safely add) a real cause of complaint. By this practice the coal and iron masters compel their workmen to accept of two-thirds of their wages in goods, such as sugar, soap, candles, meat, bacon, flour, &c., instead of money, at an unreasonable large profit. This appears the real cause of complaint more than the reduction of wages, and is really very hard upon them, and as the masters contrive to evade the Act of Parliament,[1] the men seem to have no relief but ceasing to work. On the other hand, there being still a demand for iron, the workmen think it a paradox that the trade should be bad. They therefore refuse to work and by cutting the ropes and by ducking and half drowning those who are disposed to work, they endeavour to compel the masters into their measures, and in consequence of their riotous proceedings, the Scots Greys, the Staffordshire Yeomanry and Militia have been called out . . .

Many of the colliers are in the custody of the civil power,[2] but there seems no present appearance of their returning to work, and in the meantime they are systematically living upon their Club funds and by begging from the neighbouring towns, &c. A general meeting of the coal masters will be held on Tuesday next, when it is hoped some comprehensive and uniform measures will be agreed upon. There are no collieries now open at Pelsall. Mr. Hanbury at Brownhills pays part in goods but on as good terms as the colliers can buy elsewhere, and his workmen are all satisfied and at work.

[P.S.] It is a well known fact that the ironmasters throughout this district are men almost without capital. The trade must eventually get into the hands of men of capital, and till this happens, difficulties of one kind or other will constantly arise . . . Heavy failures are now announced almost every week in the Birmingham newspapers . . . J.C. Senr. (H.O.40/17/16).

(381). *Resolutions passed at a meeting of Ironmasters held at Walsall, 7 May,* 1822.
At a meeting of the coal and iron masters held at the George Inn at Walsall, on Tuesday the 7th of May, 1822, to investigate the causes of the present disturbances in the mining district of this neighbourhood, and of the most effectual means of suppressing them, Thomas Price, Esq. in the chair it was unanimously resolved :—

That the sole and entire cause of the disturbances has been a refusal of the workmen to work at the rates of wages which have been offered them (which exceed those given in other mining dis-

[1] The Act 57 George III, c. 122, extended to coalminers the provisions of the Act 12 George I, c. 34, which declared illegal the practice of paying wages other than in the lawful coin of the realm to persons employed in the woollen industry.
[2] On charges of rioting.

tricts) and not, as hath been industriously propagated, the payment of wages otherwise than in money.

That the present low prices of all the necessaries of life, the reduced prices of coal and iron render such refusal on the part of the workmen highly injudicious, unreasonable and unwarrantable, tending to prolong the disturbance of the public peace, to drive the iron and coal trades to other parts of the kingdom, and eventually to produce the ruin and starvation of the workmen and their families, and therefore

That this meeting will neither agree to or sanction any other rate of wages than those which the workmen now refuse to accept . . . (H.O.40/17/19).

(382). *The Rev. William Powell to Henry Hobhouse*

April [May] 18, ½ *past* 5 *p.m.*
. . . A deputation of his [Mr. Hill's, of Blaenavon] colliers have just waited upon him to tender their unqualified submission, and to state that to a man they are ready to return to their work on Monday without conditions. I have reason to believe that this most desirable result was produced in a great measure by the determined tone which I was fortunate enough to prevail upon my brother magistrates to adopt on Wednesday last at Pontypool . . .

I have also just seen Mr. Homfray of Tredegar, whose master colliers have resumed their work, and I have little doubt that the rest will speedily follow the example of the Blaenavon men, as I have this day convicted and committed their chief speaker.

This triumph of the law is at this moment of unspeakable consequence, because if the men had been able to hold out for another month or six weeks, I fear the masters would have felt obliged to give way, the trade being certainly in an improving state, with the almost certain prospect of a rise in price next quarter day, which will enable the masters to give an advance of wages . . . (H.O. 40/17/43).

(383). *The Rev. W. Leigh to Robert Peel*

Bilston 18 *May*, 1822. 10 *o'clock p.m.*
. . . At the beginning of the disturbances in this neighbourhood, I felt most anxious to ascertain the true state of the case between the masters and their men, and I have spared neither time nor pains

to get at the truth. I first examined the alleged ground of their complaint, which was, not so much the reduction of their wages as the circumstance of their not having been paid in money. I found however, upon inquiry that not more than one-fifth of the whole of the workmen in this mining district were paid otherwise than in cash or cash notes ; and I have observed throughout, those who have been paid in cash [are] just as discontented and as riotously disposed as those who have been in part paid in provisions.

. . . With respect to the wages of colliers, and to their having constant employment, there has been and still is offered by the proprietors of eight coal works, the greater part of them the most extensive in this neighbourhood, the sum of 3s. per day to each man, for six days in each week, together with two quarts of good drink per day, and coal for his family. With the ironstone getter the pay is certainly not so good, being only 2s. 6d. per day ; no coal and not so much drink allowed, and without such constant employment ; but I do think almost all of them may have five days work, and very many six, if they choose it . . .

Ibid. to Ibid., Bilston, 24 *May*, 1822. *Noon* :— . . . The men who are peaceably inclined follow their employments with increasing confidence ; the evil disposed are afraid to shew themselves, and numbers return to their work daily at the reduced wages . . . (H.O.40/17/42 and 59).

(384). *The Rev. W. Powell to Henry Hobhouse*

Abergavenny, 29 *May*, 1822.
. . . Another important member [Ebbw Vale] is cut off from the confederacy . . . A very strong impression has been made upon the minds of the Tredegar workmen by my having committed six of the leaders on Monday to the House of Correction for *three months* under 6 George III, c. 25, for I found that they laughed at the commitment for one month . . .

Ibid. to Ibid., 8 *June*, 1822 :—I was in very great hope of being able by this time to congratulate Mr. Peel on the return of *all* the workmen on our hills to their employment. But I regret to say that only nine colliers have yet gone to work at Tredegar, though near fifty promised to do so yesterday. They were prevented by some sinister influence, of which I have not yet been able to obtain sufficient evidence to enable me to lay hold upon the parties concerned. But I have again sent six of the most obstinate of the men to prison, and trust that the good effects of these unrelaxing measures of severity will have their effect by Monday . . .

Ibid. to Ibid., 15 *June*, 1822 :—. . . Our firmness has at last produced the desired effect — for . . . thirty of his [Mr. Homfray's] colliers went in yesterday to their work, and . . . these were among the most respectable of his men. They would have been followed by many more today, but for a circumstance which will shew you the determined spirit with which they struck two months ago. When they came to fetch their tools to go in, the greater part were found to have had the helves or handles burnt to a cinder . . .

When I committed seven men to Monmouth on Tuesday, their obstinacy appeared so invincible that I had almost given up all hopes of making any further impression upon them. But the result has most agreeably belied my expectations. (H.O.40/17/13, 36, 67).

(385). *Samuel Homfray to the Rev. W. Powell*

Tredegar Iron Works, 17 *June*, 1822.

I am happy to be able to confirm what I wrote you on Friday last respecting out colliers. I believe all those that are here are either at work or getting their tools, so that you may now consider the contest as completely at an end, and I hope by the end of the week that we shall have most of the coal work in pretty good order.

There were several meetings near Dowlais last week between our men and the Merthyr men, but not to much purpose. I trust the men have now had a sufficient lesson and that they will not be so ready to take upon themselves to dictate what a master is to do.

I believe today finishes the imprisonment of *the commander*, Josiah Evans. As soon as he returns he shall have his discharge, as I shall not employ him upon any account . . . (H.O.40/17/39a).

(386). *Major Eckersley to Sir John Byng*

Manchester, 1 *August*, 1822.

There has been a partial 'turning out' of the cotton spinners at Stockport, owing to an attempt to lower the wages of the work-people. They however returned to their work on Monday last, the master spinners having consented to give them their old prices . . . (H.O.40/17/8a).

(387). *R. Bell (Mayor) to Robert Peel*

Newcastle-upon-Tyne, 5 October, 1822.
I feel it my duty to inform you that since Monday last the public peace has been disturbed, and the navigation of the river interrupted by a riotous body of keelmen, who navigate the lighters or keels, which convey the coals from the repositaries or staiths upon the river to the ships at the mouth of the harbour, and that I have been obliged to call on a part of the military force stationed here and in the neighbourhood, in aid of the civil power . . .

Ibid. to Ibid., 25 *October*, 1822 :— . . . The great body of them [the keelmen] still continue obstinate and have withdrawn themselves entirely from the service of their masters, so that no coals can be shipped except from the spouts below the Bridge which deliver their coals immediately into ships of small burthen without the intervention of keels or lighters.

Having strong hopes that some of the keelmen were willing to return to their duty and to navigate their keels, if they were protected from the violence of the ill-disposed, strong measures were yesterday adopted to afford that protection . . . but so far from any part of the keelmen availing themselves of the arrangement and performing their duty, a large and riotous body of sailors belonging to the ships at Shields, in concert probably with the keelmen, assembled in boats on the river, and by violence compelled several of the sailors on board the ships loaded at the spouts, to quit their ships . . .[1] (H.O.40/17/6, 47).

(388). *The Duke of Northumberland to Robert Peel*

Alnwick Castle, 29 October, 1822.
. . . The keelmen have as yet abstained from any acts of general violence or aggression, although they obstruct the passage of any craft down the river which their late employers have endeavoured to navigate by persons unconnected with themselves. The magistrates and Lieut. Col. Brandling have both endeavoured to secure the transit of coals, so conveyed but hitherto, I grieve to say, with only partial success. The windings of the river, the difficulty of access, and a variety of other causes, present many impediments to their exertions . . .

[1] With military assistance the magistrates arrested 28 rioters.

I think, Sir, I may venture to assure you that there is no bad disposition amongst the seamen, but they who are not serving on board vessels of large tonnage are totally dependent upon the craft for freight, and they see with some degree of jealousy the smaller ships loaded by the spouts from the staiths to which their small draught of water allows them to approach.

They are now, however, peaceable and have acknowledged their error to some of the magistrates who have been amongst them, although I must fear that a continued withholding of their loadings by the obstructed navigation of the Tyne may be a severe trial of their temper.

It is right also to add that the keelmen, however improperly they may have acted upon this occasion, are, generally speaking, a decent body of men ; that, misguided as they are, it is by no political delusion, and that their present ill behaviour is mainly to be accounted for by the constant hostility of unenlightened manual labourers to the improvement and facilities of machinery.[1] (H.O.40/17/54).

(389). *The Mayor of Newcastle to Robert Peel*

Newcastle-upon-Tyne, 25 November, 1822.
. . . The magistrates have had no information, nor have I any ground to suppose that the keelmen have received pecuniary assistance from the Friendly Societies.

They are much dispersed throughout the country and chiefly support themselves by begging and perhaps enforcing their requests by the terror of their numbers. In some cases I have been told that they have been assisted by small subscriptions from other bodies of men, employed in the coal trade.

I regret to add that they still continue in a state of insubordination.

Ibid. to Ibid., Newcastle-upon-Tyne, 10 *December,* 1822 : —. . . The

---

[1] The authorities published the following handbill on 22 November : 'The civil authorities regret to find the deluded keelmen still continue to insult his Majesty's boats by throwing stones when protecting those that are willing to work ; and finding forbearance any longer will endanger the lives of those so employed, this is to caution the peaceable inhabitants, and women and children, to keep within their houses during the time the keels are passing from the staiths to Shields, as the marines have orders *to fire on the first man that shall dare to throw a stone at them*' (H.O.40/17/52b).

keelmen of the river Tyne, after persisting for nearly ten weeks in a system of combination amongst themselves and intimidation towards others have at length yielded to the power of the laws and returned to their duty . . . (H.O.40/17/19, 52).

(390). *The Duke of Northumberland to Robert Peel*

Alnwick Castle, 13 *December*, 1822.
. . . It is but justice, Sir, to the keelmen to say that they have conducted themselves with more moderation than could have been expected, and have abstained from committing acts of violence except in preventing others from performing that labour which they were unwilling to do themselves.

They have at length voluntarily returned to their duty without any concessions on the part of the coalowners, and seem aware that they have been the dupes of mischievous and designing individuals. (H.O.40/17/23).

(391). *Major Eckersley to Major-General Sir John Byng*

Manchester, 16 *February*, 1823.
The working spinners of Bolton and its neighbourhood have lately formed themselves into an 'Union Club' for regulating the rates of their wages, by which arrangement, it is stated, they have obtained from 15 to as much as 50% more for their labour than is paid elsewhere ; and they now demand from 6 to 11% more. This the master spinners refuse to accede to, and a 'turning-out' of the workpeople has been the consequence.

At the rates of wages offered, a man can earn from 30s. to 40s. per week.

No disposition to disturbance has shown itself, and it seems likely that the master spinners will in the end find themselves obliged to comply with the demands of their workpeople.

Ibid. to Ibid., 17 *February*, 1823.[1] It is estimated that 5,000 persons are idle in consequence of the 'turnout' at Bolton and in its vicinity which I reported to you yesterday. It commenced with a demand made upon certain masters for an advance of wages, which was complied with by one or two of them. This emboldened the committee of the 'Union Club' to make similar demands upon other

[1] In Sir John Byng's letter to Peel, 20 February 1823.

masters. One of them resisted it, and his workpeople turned out about three weeks ago. This led to a resolution on the part of many of the masters to endeavour to prevent their workpeople from influencing other 'turnings-out' in particular mills, to which end they published a new list of prices, lower than those demanded, and giving it to be understood that unless the new rates were accepted, their mills would be stopped on the 8th inst. The latter took place, in most instances.

It would be difficult to say which party may first recede, as that must depend, in a great measure, on the quantum and duration of the contributions from the working spinners in other towns. But even were these aids continued, a very large proportion of those now out of work must soon be in a state of starvation, because those monies are distributed among the *wheel-men* and a few others, leaving probably two-thirds of the whole number without any means of subsistence whatever.

No immediate disturbance is apprehended, but it is impossible to say that it may not lead to something to disturb the public peace. (H.O.40/18).

(392). *Henry Houldsworth to Robert Peel*

Glasgow, 19 *April*, 1823.

Having a large capital at stake in the cotton manufactures of this city and also as a magistrate of the county, I beg to call your attention to the insubordination of the working classes in the district, and particularly of those employed in cotton factories. The secret and perfect organisation by which this insubordination is rendered effectual have [*sic*] now reached such a point that unless speedily and effectually checked [it] threatens the total loss of the immense capital which has been embarked in the business of cotton spinning, and a complete revolution in the relations of society. By combined resistance and private intimidation, the servants are rendering themselves absolute masters of the will and the property of their employers as well as of the labour of their own more prudent companions. I do not refer to the combinations merely for raising wages ; that unfortunately is no new evil, although it was the first occasion which called the destructive spirit of which I have to complain, into existence, and the spirit itself, finding in this country no law of sufficient energy, however well administered, to curb its excesses, has naturally extended to other objects. It has now assumed the power of dictating to the master what regulations he shall be allowed to establish for the internal economy of his works, and what not ; what workmen he shall be allowed to employ and what he shall dismiss ; even his upper servants, the very overseers, to whose vigilance and fidelity so much is necessarily entrusted, are not to be selected at his own pleasure but continued or dismissed according to the mandates of the combined workmen. Several of the masters in Glasgow and the neighbourhood have been obliged to give up in part the management of their own business and leave it in the hands of these united rulers. Every person to whom they may object, even foremen and superintendents, whose vigilance or honesty stands in their way, the master must instantly dismiss ; only those who are agreeable to themselves are allowed to be employed. However good a reason the master may have to be dissatisfied with a workman, he must retain him if those who are combined think fit, for if dismissed against their wish, no one is to be found bold enough to take his place. The consequences of a refusal to obey the orders of these powers are, that the whole body instantly desert their work, and neither person nor property are any longer secure. The effects of the desertion itself, independently of the violence which almost invariably accompanies it, may be judged of from the fact that on Monday the 7th April, 65 male workmen employed in one establishment turned out, as it is termed — that they thereby immediately threw upwards of 600 persons idle, and deprived nearly 2,000 of their regular means of support. That you may understand the sort of control which is thus exercised, and the boldness of the socii in avowing their systematic combination, I take the liberty of enclosing a copy of part of their written demands and statement of their grievances which led to the very occurrence which has been mentioned.

The organisation by which the associated act is most perfect. The order of a single man in any factory is sufficient to induce every workman in it to desert his work or contribute any portion of his wages that may be called for, to purposes of which he is perfectly ignorant. The management of the whole system is vested in persons whose turbulent spirits have excluded them from regular employment, while their dispositions qualify them for the most illegal and diabolical acts. This secret and sovereign junto have divided the manufacturing parts of the country into sub-divisions, in each of which they have a confidential agent. These agents receive from their superiors and transmit to one individual in every shop in their several districts, the necessary instructions for raising contributions, for confirming the wavering, coercing the reluctant, and rewarding the devoted among their companions. The directing committee hold regular meetings, but seldom twice in the same place. The district agents receive instructions to be at a given place on a given day ; there they generally find a stranger who conducts them to the rendezvous of the directors. To these they pay over the contributions and give in reports of the state of the different shops ; from these they receive instructions to be communicated to the shop agents, and the allotted aliment for such as are thought to have established a good claim to it by a proper degree of insubordination ; and so well are all these measures concerted, that no vigilance has hitherto been able to detect them.

The means which are used by this destructive combination are just as atrocious as the object. Not only the masters but the industrious workmen must obey its orders circulated by this gradation of agents, if they wish to avoid being murdered or excoriated with vitriol. One or other of these punishments does not fail to be inflicted on the workman who refuses to obey their commands or is suspected of having divulged their secrets. The frequency of the latter diabolical mode of violence has become frightful. Many living and melancholy proofs of it are now lingering in their beds or pining through the streets blind and disfigured, rendered for life equally burdensome to themselves and to the community . . .

No blame can be attached to our local authorities for any want of vigilance. The difficulty of procuring conviction, and the total inefficacy of the punishment after conviction, have enabled the system to set law and police at defiance . . .

The punishment of simple combination by the common law of Scotland, and in this matter Scotland has no Statute Law — is imprisonment for a longer or a shorter period according to the extent or continuance of the conspiracy. Were it accompanied with very aggravated assaults it is no doubt in the power of the Court of Justiciary to inflict transportation, but the highest punishment inflicted on the most active of the criminals in 1813 (on the trial of McKimmie and others) where the conviction was not merely of combination but of combination 'aggravated by various acts of violence, intimidation and extortion,' was imprisonment for eighteen months. Imprisonment however has no effect, especially as it is inflicted in the same neighbourhood where the offence was committed. The criminal considers it as an honour ; he and his family live better than when he was at liberty, for the purses of the whole workmen of the district are opened by compulsion for their support. If imprisonment is to be the punishment, ought it not to be imprisonment in the severest form of prison discipline and prison privation, and above all at a distance from the spot where the criminal is surrounded by his equally criminal comrades, and perhaps it would not be contrary either to public utility or the principles of law in a crime which goes to the root of the commercial prosperity of the country, that a second conviction should in every case be followed by transportation?

Another difficulty arises from the circumstance that those who direct the combination employ to execute the actual violence, persons who either are no members of the general conspiracy, or whose connection with it is impossible to establish. If it were declared therefore that the fact of having used threats or violence or attempted to intimidate should be held by presumption of law until the contrary were proved to have been done in connection with and to forward the objects of the combination, this difficulty would likewise be diminished, and it does not appear that the presumption could in any case be erroneous.

Above all, considering the frequency, the object, the melancholy effects of the practice of maiming by throwing vitriol on workmen because he dares to be honest and industrious, it would be well if the benefit of Lord Ellenborough's Act[1] against cutting and maiming were extended to Scotland, and this case expressly comprehended in it . . .

[Enclosure.]

1. We have too many masters, therefore we insist that you give the power to one man, and we will abide by him if reasonable.

2. We entreat you to take these two men back to their wheels, as you see no other man will take them, and we hope it will prove better for you and us both.

2. Two men who had been discharged for drunkenness and making bad work, but who were offered a fortnight's warning.

---

[1] This Act, passed in 1803, subjected to capital punishment persons found guilty of stabbing, cutting or wounding, even if they had not lain in wait for that purpose, provided the offence was committed under such circumstances that if death had ensued it would have been murder. See *Cobbett's Parliamentary History*, xxxvi. 1245.

3. We consider Mr. — and Mr. — too vigilant in their office by imposing on the general part of the men, therefore we wish you to give them a reprimand before us.

3. Two foremen, one a spinning master, the other the person who weighs and books the spinners' and other workers' work. This reprimand of the two foremen was immediately followed by another written communication stating that 'they had unanimously agreed and determined that they shall go out of your employment, as we shall never turn a wheel till these requests are accomplished.'

4. We consider Mr. — no judge of his business. We therefore insist upon you to turn him off and get a man that's a judge of his business.

4. A reeling master.

5. We insist that you will make no examples on this occasion, as we are all involved alike and will stick to each other if done.

6. The fines for drunkenness and neglect of attendance is given to support the operatives' sick fund ; those for bad work and damaging machinery amounts to 63s. since 1st October.

6. We wish all fines to be done away with entirely.

7. And lastly, we insist that you will not admit any indifferent characters to work among us, and that — may not be admitted among us in future.

7. A spinner who has been six weeks confined to bed in consequence of vitriol being thrown in his face in going from his work towards his own house. He is deprived of the sight of one eye, his face, head and one hand burnt to the bone.[1]

These demands were presented to the proprietor of the cotton mill by a deputation of six of the turn-outs. The blanks in this extract contains in the original the names of the overseers and spinner referred to. (H.O.40/18).

[1] Cases of vitriol throwing seem to have been confined to Scotland, apart from one which had nothing to do with trade unionism. On 9 July, 1824, William Hampson, overseer of the poor of the township of Barton-on-Irwell, near Manchester, whilst discharging the duties of his office, was attacked by a mob. A pan of boiling water was thrown at his face, and also a quantity of sulphuric acid, which luckily burnt only his clothes ; these were torn off him before the acid came into contact with his skin. See H.O.40/18. J. Watkins to Peel, 10 July, 1824.

(393). *Colonel Fletcher to Henry Hobhouse*

Bolton-le-Moors, 26 April, 1823.

. . . The journey[men] spinners not acceding to the terms offered by their masters, and hindering by various means all fresh hands from entering into the service, a warrant was granted on the 29th ult., under the powers of the Combination Act, to apprehend certain spinners who were known to be leaders, and connected with, if not forming part of a Combination Committee. In pursuance of this warrant, seven persons were arrested and a sum of money exceeding £24, and various books, papers and correspondence were seized, and after a hearing (before two magistrates) of the charge made by the masters, and a defence set up by these seven journeymen (having counsel on each side) the whole seven were convicted and sentenced to two months hard labour in the House of Correction. From this conviction they appealed to the Salford Quarter Sessions, where, after a full hearing, six of the seven convictions were confirmed, and their sentences carried into execution.

The books and papers seized, together with the evidence given before the Court, afforded such irrefragable proof of the existence of a combination, or union of journeymen cotton spinners, and that for several years past, that the counsel for the defence could say little, excepting by way of recrimination, charging the masters with combination on their parts.

The subscription books commence in the year 1811 and are regularly continued to the present time. On each page is a number, and under the number is a list of names corresponding with the names of the journeymen spinners employed at each of the mills in the neighbourhood, and opposite the names are columns in which are inserted the weekly contribution of each man. A card was found amongst the papers, which is an index to the subscription book, containing the same number, and opposite the number the name of the master spinners of the different mills, a list of whose journeymen is entered in the subscription book.

The cash books found commence only in 1821. The contributions received from 30th November last amount [to] £1,090 8s. 3d., and the payments from the same date, to £1,090 15s. 0d.; about £24 being found on the table, there must of course have been received some sums which at the seizure had not been entered.

In 1821 the said cash books shews money paid for the support of Mr. *Makinson's* spinners who had struck, and in February, 1822, the same books shew the same sort of support given for several months together to Mr. Wylde's spinners when they struck.

On the 18th November last, the spinners at Messrs. Bolling's Coronation Mill struck work, and several who had so struck were apprehended under warrants for quitting their employment without having given the requisite notice, of whom some were committed to prison but were liberated on promise to return to their employment. In a few days after this indulgence *all* the spinners at three of the cotton mills of [the] said Messrs. Bollings gave a fortnight's notice to quit, unless their wages were advanced from 5 to 15%, demanding that the number of apprentices should be limited, and that a certain overlooker should be discharged.

With these demands, as far as the $7\frac{1}{2}$% advance on the wages, Messrs. Bolling (being at the time under very extensive contracts for yarns) were under the necessity of complying. During the fortnight's time these men were out, the cash books shew payments at 12s. per man per week, amounting to £40 4s. od. The success of Messrs. Bolling's men led to similar demands on the part of Mr. Wingfield's men — and as he stated in evidence, not being able to stand against his men *single-handed*, he was obliged to comply.

In December last, Messrs. Jones's spinners, by their delegates at their factory in Tyldesley (about six miles distant) made similar demands for an advance, with which he, not complying, they gave him in a few days afterwards simultaneous notice to quit, and did accordingly quit, and still remain out. The cash books shew that there had been paid to these men (about 28 in number) in ten weeks to the amount of £319 9s. 6d., being for the first four weeks about £1 per head per week, and for the last six weeks about seven shillings per week, it being understood that the deficiency below 12 shillings per week is to be made good to each person when, from the accomplishment of their advance, and from return to their work on such advance, their funds shall be replenished. The appeal against a conviction of these men is yet to be heard at Kirkdale (Liverpool) Sessions, Tyldesley being in Derby Hundred.

Hitherto the journeymen spinners had been the assailants, and many of the masters finding the evil likely to spread, did agree to use their endeavours to free themselves from the control of their journeymen — and accordingly on the 18th January, gave their respective spinners notice that they should discharge them in three weeks, and if they then wanted their services they should be paid according to a new rate of wages, which was hung up in their mills for inspection. The spinners were accordingly discharged, and have not returned to their employ, but use every means to annoy such fresh hands as had entered ; and in consequence of this state of things the masters obtained a warrant under which the convictions above-mentioned took place.

In consequence of these disputes there may have been 500 spinners out of work, and of various other descriptions of persons employed at cotton mills, dependent on such spinners, to the number of 3,000 men, of which the latter description, receiving no benefit from the Union Fund, were reduced to great distress.

The extent of the district from which contributions flowed and correspondence was kept up either in writing or by delegates, will appear from the enclosed printed list. Among the items of expenditure is the following curious one — 'September 8, 1819. Given to Mr. Naisby, Treasurer of Peterloo Battle, £4.'

. . . In them [the books and papers] I have not found any direct contribution for regulating cotton factories, nor has it appeared to me that among the journeymen cotton spinners of this town and neighbourhood, any very lively interest is felt on that subject. Indeed, many of them, I fear, would prefer working at those mills where they work the greatest number of hours, and have the opportunity of earning the most money. There may be, however, and doubtless are, many exceptions in this respect — but were there none at all, it would seem very desirable that, as far as regards children of tender age, the number of hours of labour in cotton factories should be lessened, and particularly on the afternoon of Saturdays, that they might have some leisure for recreation and healthy exercise.

In these disputes between the masters and their journeymen, which I am sorry to say, still continue, I do not perceive any immediate connection, either of favour or opposition, to any meditated amendment of the law of the regulation of cotton factories. The dispute, in my view, has arisen from a combination of the journeymen to control their masters, which has led to an agreement among many of the masters to free themselves from such control.

With respect to the difference of the rate of wages which the men were receiving before they struck in November last, as compared with those they compelled the masters to give and with those which their masters offered in what is called the new list, Mr. Wingfield, one of the masters examined in court, swears that the additional wages he was compelled to advance was about 4s. per week, and that the wages he offered in his new list, even a reduction of 3s. out of the 4s., leaving his spinners' wages 1s. more per week than before they first struck.

The masters call their new list a regulation of wages, which from the best information I can obtain, is an advance on some of the numbers and a reduction in others — probably averaging all the cotton mills in this town and neighbourhood, together — not much different to what was given in the early part of November last. Taking an average from the books seized, as to Messrs. Jones and from Messrs. Bolling's account of the wages paid by them, the weekly earnings of their respective spinners will probably be from 26s. to 36s. per week.

[Printed Enclosure.]

Sir — We are requested to inform you that this day a number of journeymen cotton spinners have been convicted under the Combination Act, and that upon their apprehension, various books and papers were taken possession of by the constables, from which it appears that contributions in money have been sent to the journeymen spinners' committee by the different trades, and from the different places mentioned below.

We are, Sir,

Your obedient servants,

Ravald & Watkins }
Robert Kay } Solicitors for the prosecutions.

Sessions Room, Bolton,
    31 March, 1823.

From the cotton spinners at Rochdale, Know Mill, Burnley, Colne, Heywood, Glossop, Dindsdell Mill, Warrington, Preston, Stockport, Ashton-under-Lyne, Manchester, Chorley, Westleigh, Wigan, Horwich, Dickenson Mill, Blackburn, Stirrup Brook, Skelmersdale, Patricroft Mill, Pendleton Mill, Tyldesley Banks, Douglas Green, Chowbent, Stayleybridge, Ashton-in-Willows, Oldham.

From the paper makers at Prestolee, Mr. Openshaw's men, Mr. Hughes' men, Mr. Seddon's men.

From the coalminers at Tong, Mr. Fletcher's colliers, colliers at 7 Stars.

From the bleachers at Breightmet, Lever Banks, Messrs. Cockers' men, Bradshaw Hall, Firwood, Mr. Fell's crofters, crofters at Gravel Hole.

From the calico printers at Turton, Edgeworth, Darwen, Cross Hall, Sunnyside, Manchester, Stubbins, Didsley, Houghton Bottoms.

From the pin-makers at Warrington.

And from the reed makers, the mechanics, the journeymen sawyers, the journeymen tailors, the foundrymen, the millwrights, the stonemasons, the slaters, the butchers. (H.O.40/18).

(394). *The Memorial to the Home Secretary of the Subscribers, Proprietors and Occupiers of Spinning Mills, and Managers and Agents for Fire Insurance Companies in Dundee and its neighbourhood.*[1] [*April* 1823]:

Sheweth, that the spinning of yarn from flax, hemp and tow, and the manufacturing of that yarn into cloth, is the staple trade of this district.

That this trade is carried on to such an extent at Dundee and its immediate neighbourhood, taht the imports of flax and hemp at Dundee last season were above 10,000 tons . . .

That there is a great body of men employed in heckling or dressing the flax and hemp preparatory to its being spun, not fewer, it is believed, than about 1,500 in Dundee and its immediate neighbourhood . . .

That the hecklers in Dundee and in other places have long been in the practice of forming combinations for the purpose of keeping up the rate of wages, and by means of suddenly striking work at particular mills, and collecting funds and mutually supporting one another, they have been frequently enabled to compel their employers to grant what they demanded.

That the masters have hitherto submitted to these proceedings without attempting to resist otherwise than by endeavouring, although generally without success, to obtain relief by applying for servants in other towns. But the matter has now assumed another shape, and the memorialists consider it to be proper and indeed necessary to represent the circumstances to his Majesty's Government.

That about 18 months ago the demand for yarn in this district was so great that the hecklers were enabled to compel their masters to raise their wages to what was considerably beyond the rates

---

[1] This memorial was sent to the Home Office by the Sheriff Depute of Forfarshire and the Provost of Dundee on 30 April, 1823.

previously in use. Since then the demand for yarn has declined, and owing to the rise in the price of the raw material and other causes, the trade has become unprofitable. In consequence, several masters have individually endeavoured to reduce the rate of wages, but those who have made the attempt or proposed to resort to it, have been met by opposition of a kind which until now was unknown in this district. In particular, threats have been used against those hecklers who were willing to work to deter them from working ; and letters have been sent anonymously to several mill masters threatening to use violence to their persons and to burn their spinning mills if the demands of their servants were not complied with . . .

The Sheriff Substitute of Forfarshire has with much promptitude instituted an investigation into the nature of the Association among the hecklers and as to their conduct on this occasion, and the result has been such that four of them have been committed to prison for trial. But no information has yet been obtained with regard to the persons who wrote and sent the threatening letters to the mill masters, and it is not likely that the punishment ordinarily awarded in Scotland for the minor offence of an illegal combination will have much effect in preventing crime.

. . . These letters have actually had the effect of seriously disturbing the minds of individuals and putting them in fear for their families, persons and property, and have induced mill masters to comply with the demands thus illegally made. One extensive establishment has been altogether stopped, and a great number of poor persons have been thrown idle, and if means be not used for the protection of the masters and the workmen willing to work, the example will in all likelihood be followed . . .[1] (H.O.102/35/36).

(395). *The Rev. J. H. Moggridge to Robert Peel*

Woodfield Lodge, near Newport, Mon., 18 *May,* 1823.
I have good reason to know that the workmen in the collieries of this neighbourhood are at present in a state of great irritation and discontent owing to that abuse which has been the real though sometimes latent cause of all the disturbances which have taken place

---

[1] The suggestion that a reward should be offered for the discovery of the offenders, follows.

amongst them, namely, the pernicious practice of paying workmen in shop goods instead of money, which now prevails here to a degree unknown since the riots of 1816 . . .

I some time since received a deputation from the workmen, and succeeded in persuading them to use their influence to prevent the workmen from executing their declared intention of suddenly and simultaneously leaving their work. The rapid rise in the prices of provisions since, and the unrestrained manner in which the men are compelled for the most part to receive their wages in shop goods instead of money at prices 20%, 30% and 40% higher than in the markets and open shops, have been of late laying the sure foundations of future, it may not be very distant, disturbances — and the great rise which took place in the price of wheat at Pontypool market on Saturday last, with the representations made to me yesterday by another deputation of the workmen, induce me to lose no time in communicating to you, Sir, my apprehensions on the subject . . .

I believe the practice and danger are both confined *to the collieries*, and that the masters of iron works who agreed to put down their shops last year have faithfully adhered to their engagements with the magistrates, and that to the best of my knowledge *their* colliers are contented. (H.O.44/13).

(396). *The Rev. Henry Sainsbury, J.P., to Robert Peel*

Beckington, near Frome, Somerset, 12 June, 1823.

. . . A very considerable agitation exists in the town and neighbourhood of Frome, in consequence of the weavers employed in the clothing manufacture having simultaneously struck for advanced wages, and refused to work without additional prices. The proceedings of these men have as yet chiefly consisted in persuading each other not to take out any work, and not to finish that already begun. I have been engaged in investigating some charges brought before me, which I thought at the time might be of sufficient importance to justify me in committing the offenders for robbery for entering some of the weavers' houses, who were working at the present prices, and compelling them to deliver it up to them, and to carry it back to their masters, attended by them in regular rank-and-file, offering however no violence to anyone in their march. I had some doubts whether the capital part of the charge could be sub-

THE WEAVERS OF FROME

stantiated, and as I thought also rigorous measures at first might be dispensed with, I felt justified, with the concurrence of the clothiers, to hold some of the parties to bail for their appearance at the next Assizes, if called on. Many of the weavers were present during this investigation, and showed me a petition recently presented to his Majesty, and Mr. Hobhouse's answer. I was in hopes that they would have duly appreciated my forbearance towards their companions and have returned to their work. I regret, however, to say that these expectations have been disappointed, and that the men are daily parading the streets and country in large parties of two and three hundred, carefully avoiding all appearance of a breach of the peace and behaving with the utmost civility, but equally determined not to resume their work. Their proceedings seem to be founded on system, as they assemble daily in the open fields under orders, and have sentinels to prevent intruders of every description. If a weaver be known to take out work *now* at any price, he is in a few hours compelled to take it back, from an avowed resolution 'that they will all hold together.' Great management appears in this point also, as the working weavers positively declare they do not know by name the persons who compel them to return their work, and that if they ventured to identify them, they are in fear of their lives ; but I think they understand each other very well.

As other branches of the clothing trade depend on the labour of the weavers, those persons (men, women and children) must soon lose their employment, unless the weavers return to work. From information given me, I have ascertained that the causes of complaint are of considerable standing, the wages of the weavers having been reduced about eighteen months ago, and they want to have their old price, viz., 1s. 3d. paid at the double loom, which is now reduced to 1s. per yard at the spring loom ; saying also that one person has lost thus his employment entirely. I anticipate that as soon as the other branches lose employment, there will be a general *turn-out*, as it is called.

. . . Although there be not an immediate prospect of riot, yet I think it very likely that on the least show of the law being put in force, a tumult would instantly appear, and formidable numbers soon collected from this populous neighbourhood (containing in this Division at the last Census, 20,000 souls) and which would be greatly augmented by the junction of the weavers from the neighbouring parts of Wiltshire, with whom, I am informed, the Somerset weavers are in correspondence . . . (H.O.40/18).

(397). *Henry Hobhouse to Henry E. Edgell and the Rev. Henry Sainsbury*

Whitehall, 6 *July,* 1823.

I am directed by Mr. Secretary Peel to acknowledge the receipt of your letter of the 4th inst. from which he collects that you have convicted eight weavers for neglect of their work, and committed them to gaol in addition to those who were committed on the 1st inst.

You likewise state that at the instance of some of the masters you had been induced to issue warrants authorising the Peace Officers to take measures for the preservation of the masters' property which was in the looms of the weavers, although such warrants were not authorised by law ; that this process being resisted, the constables opened the houses by force and executed the warrants, from whence some riots ensued, which were not terminated without the interference of the yeomanry cavalry.

Upon this statement Mr. Peel directs me to remark that, however desirable it may be to preserve the property from deterioration, it is vastly more important that the magistrates should act strictly within the line of their authority ; and without meaning to cast any reflection on the motives which induced you to act as you have done, he thinks the tendency of the measure you adopted is rather to foment than to allay the existing discontents.

To one of the reasons adduced by the clothiers for requiring your interference in regard to the restoration of their yarn, namely, that if it were withheld, the weavers would in some degree triumph, Mr. Peel can attach no weight. The propriety of such interference must depend upon other considerations, and the triumph of the weavers will be most certain if, at the instance of their employers an authority is assumed with regard to them, which the law does not warrant. (H.O.41/7/91-2).

(398). *The Rev. Henry Sainsbury, J.P., and Henry H. Edgell, J.P., to Robert Peel*

Frome, 7 *July,* 1823.

We have to acknowledge receipt of Mr. Hobhouse's letter of yesterday's date, and regret to find that our proceedings which originated in the best intentions do not appear to have met with your approbation. The clothiers were reduced to the alternative of obtaining by force a restitution of their property, or suffering the materials to be spoilt for want of use. One house alone has £5,000 worth of property in this predicament, and we are confident that, although the law may not strictly sanction what we have done, our acting on the emergency of the case and under its peculiar circumstances was the means of preventing any outrages on the second list of commitments which took place, and we have the satisfaction of knowing that no personal injury was inflicted.

The state of the town, Sir, is far from being tranquil. The weavers are daily compelled or persuaded to take their work home unfinished, and they have in no instance discovered the person using the persuasions or threats. The clothiers have applied for other warrants to obtain a restitution of their property which is daily getting worse, but we consider ourselves restricted from interfering in consequence of Mr. Hobhouse's letter. They have therefore resolved to send a deputation to London and have requested us to give them this introduction.

Ibid. to Ibid., Frome, 15 *July*, 1823 :— ... The clothiers now report to us that the weavers are daily bringing home work finished, and soliciting more, and the town at present is perfectly quiet. This restoration of tranquillity may in our opinion be attributed to various causes. First, to the arrival of a troop of regular cavalry, which tends to convince the disaffected persons that the magistrates, supported by Government, are determined to put a stop to their practices ; secondly, to the starving state of the weavers and their families, owing to their having been so long out of work and with so little support ; and thirdly, to the circumstance of eighteen weavers being sent off to gaol to hard labour, and of those remaining at liberty feeling conscious that a similar fate may await them ; and also to the weavers finding that they could not satiate the vindictive feeling of leaving the work to rot on the loom while they went to gaol, as the clothiers in all cases have recovered the possession of their property, where the wives or friends of the weavers refused to complete the work ...

We hope, Sir, you will give us credit when we assure you that our duties have been far from enviable on this occasion. We had a very delicate as well as painful part to act. It was not our province to give an opinion on the question of prices in favour either of master or servant, and in fact we are not yet able to get at the truth ; but in cases where the law was violated, we had a straightforward path to pursue, and with the assistance of the other magistrates (who were occasionally in attendance) we awarded the sentence in each case according to its peculiar circumstances. We have from the beginning thought that the practice of paying wages in truck or goods instead of money was alike injurious to the fair trader and the weaver ; and to convince the latter that we were as ready to render justice to him as to his master we repeatedly and publicly declared that if any cases of this description were established before us, we were resolved to enforce the strictest penalty of the law. One conviction in £20 penalty has accordingly taken place, and we entertain very sanguine hopes that the weavers, on finding they will have money for their labour, will cheerfully resume their work, and that no further disturbance will take place. (H.O.40/18).

(399). *Sanuel Powell* (*Borough Bailiff*) *to Henry Hobhouse*

Knaresborough, 16 *July*, 1823.

In answer to a letter received from you this morning addressed to the Mayor of Knaresborough, I beg to state that there is a dispute between the weavers and several of the master manufacturers of Knaresborough, in consequence of a reduction in wages, and that the weavers paraded the town for two or three evenings in a very orderly manner, and meetings have been and are held every evening by the weavers, but there does not seem to be any appearance or disposition on their part to disturb the peace. A great many of the weavers have left the town to seek for work elsewhere. so that the meetings are not near so numerous as they were about ten days ago.

The magistrates have been applied to, but they did not see any necessity for their interference. (H.O.40/18).

(400). *Henry Hobhouse to the Rev. Henry Sainsbury and Henry H. Edgell*

Whitehall, 26 *July*, 1823.

. . . Mr. Peel is well aware that your duties have been arduous, but he is convinced that they would have been much more so if you had not taken the determination to pursue the strait path of administering the law equally to all parties without entering into the question of prices or wages, which are matters of contract between individuals and not to be adjusted by the hand of power . . (H.O.41/7/94-5).

(401). *The Rev. H. Sainsbury and H. H. Edgell to Robert Peel*

Frome, 29 July, 1823.

. . . We have now the honour of informing you that the weavers in general have returned to their work, and that tranquillity appears to be completely restored. In our opinion the spirit of tumult and discontent which prevailed among the weavers was in a great degree subdued before the arrival of the troop of the 14th Light Dragoons, but their appearance had the full effect of quieting persons in their work who had formerly been disturbed, and of inducing others to take out work who had been so obstinate before as to refuse it . . . (H.O.40/18).

(402). *The Shipbuilders of the River Wear to the Acting Magistrates of Sunderland*

Jowsey's Bridge Inn, 6 April, 1824.

We take the liberty of informing you that it is not our intention to bring before you any more cases at present ; but we have thought it absolutely necessary, should the resident shipwrights not immediately shew a disposition to return generally to work, to endeavour to procure men from other places, as it is totally impossible that the trade of the port can remain in this inactive state.

From all we can learn we have reason to believe that the introduction of strangers will be resisted by the resident shipwrights, unless we can shew to them that they (the strangers) can be protected from acts of violence.

Under these circumstances we respectfully beg leave to suggest the propriety of some military force being ordered into the town prior to our bringing strangers here, for it appears to us that the appearance of a few military will operate as a check upon any mischievous attempts either against those we may employ or our property.[1] (H.O.40/18).

(403). *The Acting Magistrates for Sunderland to Sir John Byng*

Justice Room, Sunderland, 7 April, 1824.

. . . There have for several weeks past differences existed between the shipbuilders and their workmen which have led to the conviction and commitment to prison of several of the shipwrights.

These measures however do not appear to be likely to induce the shipwrights to return to their work, in consequence of which the shipbuilding business on the Wear is almost at a stand.

The shipbuilders are anxious to introduce into this port workmen from other places, which step they fear may lead to acts of violence on the part of the old shipwrights . . .

The shipwrights we estimate to amount to about five hundred, and we beg leave, Sir, to request you will have the goodness to order to Sunderland a competent number of military to assist the civil power in case of emergency.[1] (H.O.40/18).

(404). *The Earl of Stamford and Warrington (Lord Lieutenant of the County) to Robert Peel*

Dunham-Massey, 8 April, 1824.

. . . I understand an arrangement has taken place between the silk weavers and their masters, and as the men are chiefly returned to their work, I hope the disturbances are at an end.

[Enclosure.]

Thomas Parker to the Earl of Stamford and Warrington

Astle, 7 April, 1824. *(Copy)*.

I was on Monday sent for to Macclesfield on account of the operative silk weavers having struck work and shewing a disposition to riot by breaking the windows, &c. of several factories, and assembling in great numbers and insulting the proprietors. The Mayor had sent to Manchester for troops, and to Stockport for the Stockport Yeomanry. I found the town in so disordered a state that I gave an order for the calling out of the Macclesfield, Adlington and Stockport troops of yeomanry, which I hope your Lordship will approve.

I understand the men had not returned to their work yesterday. I have had no report this morning. (H.O.40/18).

(405). *Brigade-Major Eckersley to Major-General Sir John Byng*

Manchester, 8 April, 1824. *(Copy.)*

The master silk-manufacturers of Macclesfield having given up the point for which they contended with their workpeople, good order has been restored in that town . . . [2] (H.O.40/18).

[1] Enclosed in Sir John Byng's letter to Peel, 9 April.
[2] In Sir John Byng's letter to Hobhouse, 9 April.

(406). *The Marquess of Bath to Robert Peel*

Grosvenor Square, 17 *April*, 1824.

. . . It appears that the town [Frome] and neighbourhood are tranquil, and that the weavers are at work, but some of the manufacturers have expressed an apprehension that the weavers are still dissatisfied, and might avail themselves of the absence of the military to make fresh disturbances.

[*Enclosure.*]

Henry H. Edgell, J.P. and George Rous, J.P., to the Marquess of Bath
. . . We have this day received an intimation from some of the principal manufacturers in Frome that the weavers are still acting in secret concert with each other, in hopes of getting an advance of wages, and that their quiet appearance at present is chiefly to be attributed to the circumstance of the military being stationed in Frome, and although of our own knowledge we are not aware of anything to justify us in anticipating further disturbances, we are not prepared to say whether riotous attempts may not again take place in case the troops were removed. (H.O.40/18).

(407). *Sir Cuthbert Sharp to Francis Freeling*

[*Sunderland*, 17 *April*, 1824].

We have 600 carpenters here who won't work. They are peaceable yet — but how long they may continue so is another matter. (H.O.40/18).

(408). *Sir Charles Palmer to Robert Peel*

Wanlip, 20 *June*, 1824.

I am just informed that our manufacturers have determined to assemble tomorrow for the purpose of compelling those who remain in employ (some on improved prices and others for what they can get) to leave off work. This if put in execution will create a tumult, and I should be glad to know your sentiments on the subject . . . (H.O.40/18).

(409). *George Perry to Robert Peel*

Hinckley, 24 June, 1824.

Knowing your wish to be acquainted with what is going on here relative to the stocking-makers' turn-out, I would introduce what I have to say by stating an opinion that the causes of the low rate of their wages are various and deep-rooted, and that some if not all of them will remain very long, perhaps for ever, in operation.

Competition, local and individual advantages and disadvantages in making, purchasing and selling goods ; the employment of manufacturing agents or undertakers, and the practice of paying workpeople in provisions and clothing instead of money, have an evident and an irresistible power in forcing down wages whenever supply goes beyond demand.

You are aware how very unfairly and imprudently the operatives here began the struggle, and you may have heard that the 'Statement' of 1817 for which they are contending, has ever been complained of by all parties as defective and bad. It is indeed so framed that marketable goods cannot be made by it in 18 and 20 gages, which abound in this town and neighbourhood . . .

Nearly the whole of P.P. and A.'s hands had gone to work at the 'Statement,' but they have been stopped again under the pretence that all the hosiers' workmen must go in together . . .

Yesterday from one to two hundred came in from Barwell and Shelton to 'strike' the hands who had gone in here. Basset, the workhouse master, informs me that a party of these unwelcome visitors went to his daughter's shop, pulled her frame off the level, cut the slur strings and carried off a truck . . . (H.O.40/18).

(410). *The Rev. J. H. Spry to Robert Peel*

West Grove, near Birmingham, 17 August, 1824.

. . . Combinations exist here at present among the workmen in every branch of our manufactures, and several symptoms of a riotous spirit have shown themselves, which have excited great alarm in the minds of the inhabitants. I have reason to believe that the old disturbers of the public peace are endeavouring to take advantage of this state of things, and to give the discontents of the men a political bias, but in this I think they will not succeed. (H.O. 40/18).

(411). *Brigade-Major Eckersley to Major-General Sir John Byng*

Manchester, 27 January, 1825.
Although the newspapers make mention of combinations amongst the operative spinners and others here and in the neighbourhood, it does not appear there is anything very likely to disturb the public peace, at least, not for the present. The master manufacturers, who have large capitals embarked in this business, are naturally a good deal alarmed, and a wish for the re-enactment of the Act against combinations is often expressed. Were I allowed an opinion on the subject, I should certainly say it might be well to pause for a while upon such a measure, sufficient time not having yet been allowed to see its effects fairly tried. It has at any rate the salutary one of making the masters bestir themselves, and to look a little to their workpeople, which in most cases was before almost entirely neglected.

The wages of the spinners are ample — not so the weavers, as is generally said. Associations of the latter have consequently been formed at Bolton, Stockport and elsewhere, in conjunction with those of Glasgow, to obtain an advance of prices.

At Hyde, near to Ashton-under-Lyne, where the power-loom weaving has been very generally introduced, there has been a turning-out of the workpeople in considerable numbers, but peaceably.

The colliers (particularly those of the mines belonging to the Countess Grosvenor) have turned out for higher wages. They have sunk a loaded boat in the canal to stop up the navigation of it, but nothing more. The minor trades of dyers, farriers, shoemakers, &c. have successively turned out, and having obtained their objects, respectively, have returned to work.[1] (H.O.40/18).

(412). *John H. Richardson to Robert Peel*

North Shields, 28 January, 1825.
... I now forward you some account relating to the very alarming height combination (under the cloak of a charitable institution) has attained amongst the seamen of this and the Port of Sunderland. They hold meetings daily, enter into covenants for the support and defence of what they call their rights and have a committee of management to issue tickets or passports to those who have joined or contributed to the support of their association, for which they pay

[1] In Sir John Byng's letter to Henry Hobhouse, 29 January, 1825.

2s. 6d., and without the same they will not allow any seaman to be employed, inasmuch as they all, immediately on such a man being shipped by the owner, refuse to proceed with the vessel until that man *'joins the Union.'*

As I have no hesitation in asserting they are in communication with other ports, and reason to believe, in correspondence with some of the manufacturing towns, it is evident they have other purposes in view than that of *regulating* their own employment and wages, and this combination is now to be feared from its secrecy and correctness of management, which is similar to the Rules observed at Glasgow, &c. . . .[1] (H.O.40/18).

(413). *Robert Marflitt and E. H. Hebden (Bailiffs of Scarborough) to Robert Peel*

Scarborough, 9 *March*, 1825.

. . . On Saturday the 26th ult., Mr. Henry, the owner of a vessel chartered for the Baltic, and his captain, waited upon us to state that after repeated, fruitless attempts to obtain seamen here, they had procured two men from Whitby, who had arrived and were placed in lodgings : that the Union seamen were aware of their arrival and appeared on the alert. They therefore suspected an attack and wished to know whether we would give them our support. We told them that every exertion should be used on our parts to afford protection ; at the same time recommended their concealing the two men till Monday morning, when they might proceed on board.

We heard nothing more till Monday, when Mr. Henry informed us, the Union men had gained access to them and prevailed on them to return home on receiving 7s. each.

On Tuesday morning we learnt from Mr. B. Walker (owner and master of a ship in the coal trade) that six men had arrived the preceding evening from Bridlington to go in his vessel — that they had been dragged from their inn by a mob and forced to return home during the night, having been conducted by a crowd some distance on the road. We requested he would collect the best evidence he could of the outrage, and we immediately summoned the

[1] A printed copy is enclosed of the 'Articles of Agreement between the members of the Seamen's Loyal Standard Association for the Tyne and the Wear, resident in and near South Shields' (5 October, 1824).

inhabitants to support us in preserving the public peace, and have since sworn in 220 special constables . . .

On Friday evening we received a note from Mr. Walker stating that his six men would come again from Bridlington the following morning, accompanied by seamen for two other vessels at this place, and that they would arrive about 9 o'clock.

We instantly summoned the special constables to meet us at a quarter before 9 o'clock, and in consequence upwards of 150 attended. We proceeded nearly two miles on the road to meet them, suspecting that the Union men, who were seen hovering about in small groups, might proceed on the road and endeavour to intercept them. The seamen met us in a covered cart, in which they were completely secured from public view. We proceeded with them to their respective ships, where they were safely deposited.

The Union men and their adherents were very angry, but durst not proceed further than indulging in invectives. The masters of these three vessels were requested by us to proceed to sea the following tide, and they instantly set about preparing to do so, when the six Bridlington seamen on board Mr. Walker's vessel became alarmed at the idea of going to Shields where they understood they were sure of being maltreated and turned ashore by the Union men of that Port, and in consequence they left the ship. Their companions on board the other vessels did the same — when they were all taken out under the protection of the Union men, who regaled them previous to returning home.

Since, the shipowners (many of them having their vessels under charter) have acceded reluctantly to the terms of the Union men, and a considerable portion of the ships have gone to sea.

The seamen's Union here consists of 240 members, and no doubt this Club is in regular correspondence with Shields and other places.

The shipwrights have been off *new* work the last fortnight for an advance of wages. A similar demand was made for old work by them, which the shipowners, having vessels under repair, were reluctantly compelled to submit to : a considerable number of them are consequently remaining in idleness.

There is little doubt that combinations will be formed in every branch of trade, for the shoemakers in this place (consisting of only about 9,000 inhabitants) are in union, and last week one of that craft was so maltreated for not joining the Society that he summoned the offenders to appear before us, but they had the address to get him to compromise before we had a hearing . . . (H.O.40/18)

(414). *Memorial of the Master Cotton Spinners of Glasgow and Neighbourhood, to Robert Peel*

April, 1825.

Sheweth . . . That the period since the passing of this Act [repealing the Act of 1800] has been marked by a constant succession of intimidation, insult and outrage on the part of the operatives, and of alarm, anxiety and disturbance to the public peace of this populous manufacturing district. For the information of his Majesty's Government the memorialists consider it their duty to narrate as briefly as possible, in an Appendix, some of the outrages which have been committed . . .

Appendix

Mr. Harry Houldsworth was willing to have employed an operative cotton spinner who came from Belfast to Glasgow in February, 1824, but though well recommended, Mr. Houldsworth's men would not allow him to enter the mill. He applied to several other masters, with the same result, till at length he was employed by Mr. Humphreys. In a few days he was told that some shillings had been collected for him, and advised to leave his work, as he endangered not only himself but the family with whom he lodged. He then moved his lodgings but was told soon afterwards by the same person that unless he left the work by the following Saturday it would be the last day of his life, it having been determined that no Renfrewshire or Belfast spinner should ever be allowed to work in Glasgow. His spirit sunk under this persevering cruelty, and he quitted the country, and is now working at Belfast.

Another operative having been paid off at Crofthead Hill in Renfrewshire in April, 1824, was employed in a mill in Glasgow as an occasional spinner. He was desired by some spinners to 'take himself off,' and warned to take care of himself, and his brother, who also spun in Glasgow at that time, advised him to go back to Crofthead (which he did accordingly) as he was persuaded that the operatives would put their threat into execution.

On the 3rd of September last, the operatives in the employment of Messrs. Dunlop and Sons . . . struck work, and accompanied this step by delivering to Messrs. Dunlop the following paper :

'The Grievances of Broomward Cotton Spinners.

1. Sir — Our determination is that we will not work so long as

Robert Craig has the power of changing our pinions or abusing our piecers or any person whatever over us.

2. We are further determined not to pay for any tear or wear of machinery.

3. We are further determined to have wholesome water to drink and refreshment in the afternoon if need require. For all these grievances we have given you ample reasons already, and we wish an answer yea or nay.'

To the above paper, Messrs. Dunlop and Sons, on the same day returned the following answer :—

'Broomward Mill, 3 September, 1824.

To the operative cotton spinners at Broomward Mill.

We have received your letter addressed to Mr. William Dunlop . . .

In reply to your first determination that you will not allow Mr. Craig to change your pinions or have any power whatever over you, we think you are wrong in this, but we will submit to the determination of the master cotton spinners in Glasgow and the neighbourhood on Monday next, and shall be guided by their advice and instructions. As to his "abusing your piecers" he has neither the right nor the power to do so, nor are we aware that he ever attempted it.

As to your second grievance, you have never had to pay for the tear and wear of machinery, nor do we intend to charge you for anything of the kind, but only for breakage and abuse of the machinery arising from carelessness or wilful mischief on your part.

As to your complaint about the water you have had to drink, it has been supplied for some months past by the Anderston Water Company, and this grievance shall be redressed as speedily as possible by procuring water either from the Glasgow Water Company or from the pump in our own premises.

As to your having refreshments carried into the mill for you in the afternoons, we have no objection to this whatever. It [is] only the abuse of this liberty which we complain of, that of your carrying spirituous liquors in such quantities as to unfit you for work — James Dunlop & Sons.'

The associated proprietors of cotton works had by this time become satisfied by painful experience that the encroachments of their workers were the result, not of differences between a particular master and his men, but of a regularly organised combination, acted upon at the mere mandate of a secret committee of delegates from all the mills, which, while it aimed at usurping a constant control over the masters, kept the sober, quiet and industrious workmen in a state both of ignorance and intimidation, without any alternative but yielding to the demands of the ringleaders, or being deprived of employment. It was evident therefore that if the masters kept aloof from one another as they had too long done, and left one individual after another to resist, unaided, the mandates of a confederacy as formidable in point of numbers, union and secrecy of operation, the spinners would soon obtain any terms and conditions which they might choose to dictate. It was solely with a view to resist this most galling interference on the part of the combined operatives, with the memorialists' authority over their own servants, that their Association was formed.

A meeting of the Association having been held on the 6th of September, the foregoing statement of grievances and the answer thereto were laid before them, when they were of opinion that the demand made by the operatives 'that Robert Craig should have no power whatever over them' was an unwarrantable and dangerous interference with Messrs. Dunlop's prerogatives as masters. They were further of opinion that the concessions stated in Messrs. Dunlop's letter in reference to the other alleged grievances, removed every pretext for complaint. The question therefore came plainly to this, whether it was expedient for the memorialists to leave Messrs. Dunlop under the necessity of discharging a superior servant with whose conduct they were entirely satisfied, and whose dismission was imperiously demanded, for no other reason than that he was not connected with the combination of operatives.

This was a question on which there could be but one opinion, and the memorialists were satisfied that their own safety, comfort and independence were involved in the resolution which they might adopt upon the subject. Acting under this conviction, the meeting resolved that the whole mills belonging to them should be shut on the 10th of September unless Messrs. Dunlop's spinners returned to their work on or before the morning of that day. They further resolved, in terms of a previous resolution adopted on the 21st of July, 1823, and then intimated to the operatives by their respective masters, 'that in case the mills shut up in consequence of the present strike, or at any future time, the spinners shall bear the loss thereby occasioned to their respective masters by throwing their capital idle, to the extent and at the rate of 20s. per 1,000 spindles weekly, which shall be kept off their gross wages by the masters, at the rate of 20%, or one-fifth part thereof, each pay, until the amount be paid up ; and that Messrs. Dunlop's men who are now out, be assessed at this rate from the date of the strike'. This Resolution your memorialists never intended to act upon to its full extent. They rather held it out *in terrorem*, and with a view to impress the spinners with a conviction that the memorialists had at length seriously taken the alarm, and were resolved to submit no longer to unmeasured and interminable encroachments. The proposed rate of compensation for the memorialists did not amount to more than $3\frac{1}{2}\%$ per annum on the cost of the buildings and machinery ; and had Messrs. Dunlop's men (whose clear earnings averaged 28s. per week) returned by the day specified in the Resolution, the whole percentage would not have exceeded 5s. each man. The Resolution was intimated to all the operatives, and as Messrs. Dunlop's men continued their strike, all the mills were shut up accordingly.

Mr. Neil Snodgrass, after his mill had been shut for four weeks, ventured to try a few weavers. That very day his mill was surrounded by a multitude of women, piecer-boys and operative spinners, who, after huzzas and opprobrious language, proceeded to break the windows. This riot continued for several hours until the civil power was called in, and with all their exertions did not succeed in dispersing the mob till late in the evening. After this it became necessary to arm the new workers and guard them to their lodgings by an escort. For two succeeding weeks there were partial riots and insults ; directed sometimes against Mr. Snodgrass, but more seriously against his workers. On the 25th October, his spinning master was knocked down in Saltmarket Street and dreadfully cut in the face by six operative spinners, one of whom being identified was committed to jail. On the 20th November, Mr. Snodgrass's female spinners were insulted in going home from their work ; one of them was knocked down by an unemployed spinner, and would probably have been much abused if a piecer-boy who was along with her had not called to him by name, which made him and an accomplice run off, and in consequence of subsequent threats, several men and women left the mill . . .

About the 18th or 19th of October last, Messrs. James and Andrew Monach sent notice to the piecers lately employed by them, that they would be employed at spinning until the spinners returned to their work. But though they had been six weeks out of employment, and subscriptions had been raised to supply their wants, only two came forward. Some declared that they durst not for fear of violence. Others rejected the offer with scorn, and the two who began to spin, discontinued at the end of a single day, in consequence of being insulted or intimidated.

On the 15th of November six women of respectable character began to spin in the mill of Mr. William Kelly, jun. Before two days had elapsed three male spinners called upon them at their lodgings, and informed them that if they desisted from work they would be allowed 'maintenance,' but if they persisted they would expose themselves to the most frightful consequences. The result was that the girls declared they would rather be reduced to beggary than work another hour under such terror, and they left the mill accordingly.

On the 14th December, Messrs. Dunlop ventured to engage a few new hands as piecers and spinners. Many weavers likewise requested to be engaged and taught to spin ; and as many of them were employed as could be conveniently instructed. For safety they were all accommodated within the premises, and none of them ventured abroad without being well armed. The spinners who had been formerly employed at this mill planted spies in different places to watch those who might appear to be applying for employment, and their whole carriage having indicated some hostile purpose, the Sheriff Depute, on the 15th of December, issued a Proclamation forbidding assemblages near the gates of cotton mills. The old spinners then endeavoured, by threats or persuasion, to induce the carders and stretchers to leave the work, that what is termed the 'preparation,' being stopped, the new spinners might be thrown idle for want of roving. Disappointed in these attempts, they began to illtreat these inoffensive persons by hooting, shouting and throwing stones at them, when going to and from their work. By the 1st of February, nearly a third of the mill had been occupied by new hands. The former spinners then offered to return to their work and Messrs. Dunlop agreed to take back as many of them as would fill up the unoccupied wheels, previously to which the operatives, through their delegates, had promised that they would not interfere with or molest any hands whom their masters might choose to employ. Messrs. Dunlop next ventured to bring a few of the new hands down to the ground floor of the mill, where the coarser numbers of yarn are spun ; when the piecers, under the old spinners, and in their pay, immediately began to annoy the new hands and to interrupt them in their work. Every effort was made to put a stop to this persecution, and by way of greater protection, all the new hands were placed in the ground flat. Crowds then assembled every day at meal hours around the mill, and endeavoured to intimidate the new workers by hooting, huzza-ing, throwing stones and occasionally breaking the windows of their dwelling houses, till Saturday the 12th of March, when, just before the mill was shut, two shots were fired, one of which entered a window of the ground floor where the new hands were working, and left a mark on the opposite wall.

The same insults, throwing of stones and occasional assaults upon the new hands continued . . . till Wednesday the 30th of March, when, at the usual hour in the evening, the new spinners left the mill by themselves, at which time a considerable crowd was collected at the gate. They had proceeded about 70 or 80 yards on their way homeward when two or three ruffians started from the crowd and discharged two pistols at a weaver of the name of John Graham, who had for some time been employed as a spinner, and ten or eleven slugs were lodged in his back. Surgical aid was immediately procured, two of the slugs were extracted, and though it was not expected that he would have survived till the morning, he still lives. A person was instantly seized on suspicion, and the case is presently under judicial investigation . . .

It would be endless to enumerate all the instances of assault and maltreatment which have been committed at Messrs. Dunlop's mill since it was re-opened, and of which several persons have been convicted before the Justices of the Peace.

. . . It is a part of the system organised by the spinners in employment, that they seldom commit acts of violence *themselves*. The unemployed spinners, who are constantly prowling about the streets, are ready for every species of mischief which may be resolved upon by the others, and it is notorious that many of them receive regularly, from those employed, a weekly allowance of ten or twelve shillings. The piecers, who are a numerous class, from 10 to 20 years of age, are likewise useful tools in the hands of the spinners, being engaged and paid by them, and under their exclusive control. Now the crowds by which the new hands have been so grievously molested are found to consist chiefly of these piecers, backed by the idle spinners, but evidently encouraged by the spinners at work . . .
(H.O.102/36).

(415). *Robert Peel to the Attorney and Solicitor-General*

Whitehall, 2 April, 1825.
I transmit to you herewith the whole of the evidence taken before
the Select Committee of the House of Commons appointed last
Session to inquire into the state of the law with regard to artisans
and machinery, and, in calling your particular attention to that part
of it which has reference to the combination of workmen, I am to
desire that you will lose no time in preparing and submitting to
Parliament a Bill to amend the provisions of the Act of the last
Session, cap. 95. (H.O.49/7/267-68).

(416). *London Tavern*

27 April, 1825. (*Copy*).
At a meeting of the shipbuilders of the Port of London held this
day, Resolved unanimously :
 That it having been represented that the shipwrights in several of
the dock establishments have communicated to their respective
employers their refusal to comply with the printed Regulations,
except on condition of certain alterations being made therein,
 The shipbuilders having formed those Regulations on mature
deliberation, will not consent to any alteration whatever being
made in them ; and that unless the shipwrights on or before Friday
morning next, the 29th inst., return to their work in every yard
from which they have withdrawn, and express individually and
unequivocally their full consent to the Regulations in their present
form,
 No shipwright will be thenceforward employed while he continues
a member of the Shipwrights' Provident Union. (H.O.40/18).

(417). *George Whieldon to Robert Peel*

Cotton Hall, near Cheadle. 21 *May* [1825].
. . . I was lately sent for by Mr. Heathcote and several gentlemen
and manufacturers in the Potteries to check the disorderly proceedings of the colliers throughout that district, who had combined
for the purpose of raising their wages ; and accordingly I went to
Lane End where I issued warrants against two of the ringleaders,

who were soon after brought before me, one of whom I committed to Stafford till the Sessions for want of sureties, to answer to an indictment for his assault and disorderly conduct, and the other I admitted to bail for similar misconduct. Having thus deprived the combination of two of its most active and violent members, the remainder shortly after dispersed and returned to their work. There was no disposition to rescue the prisoners, nor to resist the civil power — and it appeared to me that the men had been misled by an idea that the Act of the last Session allowed of their combining and acting in the way complained of. They were, however, easily undeceived on this point, and their conduct was such as to require or justify no violent measures for coercing or restraining them, beyond what the common law provides.

I am induced to trouble you with these observations on this subject, because I learnt with regret a short time ago that an alarming statement had been forwarded to you, and an application made for the extraordinary interference and protection of Government, for which there certainly was not an adequate necessity. I took the opportunity of inquiring of the colliers whether they had any real grievances that ought to be redressed, but I could hear of none. The most discontented amongst them admitted their wages were paid in *money, not in truck*, and that they had *constant work at* 3/11 per day! But they required 4/6! Had that been granted they would very soon have '*turned out*' again for 5s. or perhaps more.

I have not the least doubt but they were in communication with other discontented districts in the country, and that the alteration of the laws effected by the last Act on this subject (as above observed), originated the disturbances in general, more than any real grievances they sought to redress . . . (H.O.40/18).

(418). *George Robert Dawson*[1] *to the Magistrates of Sunderland*

Whitehall, 31 August, 1825.

I am directed by Mr. Secretary Peel to acknowledge the receipt of your letter of the 27th August, enclosing a representation from the shipowners on the conduct of the refractory seamen, and stating the necessity which exists for stationing a ship of war in the Wear.

Mr. Peel desires to be informed what measures have been taken

[1] Under-Secretary of State in the Home Department since January, 1822.

with the view of bringing to justice the parties concerned in the shameful outrage committed on board the ship *Harmony*.

It appears to Mr. Peel that the parties who committed that outrage must be known. It is stated that a number of men came on board the vessel on the morning of the 24th, demanding to know whether the Captain intended to discharge two of his crew who were strangers, that during the day several men came on board making similar inquiries, and that in the evening a great number of seamen came on board the vessel and beat the crew, went below, cut down the hammocks and forcibly drove them on shore.

It cannot be difficult to trace out the perpetrators of such acts as these. Mr. Peel presumes that the utmost efforts have been made to secure the apprehension of and to bring to punishment all those who were concerned in a violation of the law so daring that the hope of escaping detection seems to be precluded.

He requests to be informed what those efforts have been, and what has been the result of them, being perfectly satisfied that unless the law be steadily and vigorously enforced against all those by whom such acts of violence are committed, no other measures, such as the detachment of military or the stationing of ships of war in the Port, will be efficacious. (H.O.41/7/109-10).

LIST OF HOME SECRETARIES
AND UNDER-SECRETARIES OF STATE
1790-1825

Ministry	Home Secretary	Under-Secretary of State[1]
Pitt (1783-1801)	Lord Grenville (since 5 June, 1789) Henry Dundas (8 June, 1791) The Duke of Portland (11 July, 1794)	Hon. John Thomas Townshend (since 10 Feb., 1784)
		Charles Greville (1796) William Wickham (1798) Edward Finch Hatton (1800) Sir George Shee (1800)
Addington (1801-4)	Thomas Pelham [cr. Lord Pelham, 1801] (30 July, 1801) Charles Philip Yorke (17 Aug., 1803)	Reginald Pole Carew (1803)
Pitt (1804-6)	Lord Hawkesbury (12 May, 1804)	John Henry Smyth
Lord Grenville (1806-7)	Earl Spencer (5 Feb., 1806)	Charles Watkin Williams Wynn (19 Feb., 1806)
Duke of Portland (1807-9)	Lord Hawkesbury [Earl of Liverpool, 1808] (25 March, 1807)	Hon. Chas. Cecil Cope Jenkinson (10 October, 1807)
Perceval (1809-12)	Richard Ryder (1 Nov., 1809)	Henry Goulburn (Feb. 27, 1810)
Liverpool (1812-27)	Viscount Sidmouth (11 June, 1812)	John Hiley Addington (21 Aug., 1812) Henry Clive (21 April, 1818)
	Robert Peel (17 Jan., 1822)	George Robert Dawson (17 Jan., 1822)

[1] There were other Under-Secretaries of State whose position was still anomalous. Just as there was as yet no clear-cut distinction between the two Secretaries of the Treasury, the one with financial duties and the other the Parliamentary Secretary (the Chief Whip), so there was no sharp dividing line between the Under-Secretary (whether in the Home Department or in the Foreign Office) who was a politician with a seat in the House of Commons and the Under-Secretary who was a civil servant holding a permanent appointment. The dates of appointment of the following Under-Secretaries of State for the Home Department (it would be inaccurate to describe them as Permanent Under-Secretaries) are given in brackets :
Evan Nepean (1782) [transferred to the War Office in 1794.]
Scrope Bernard (1789).
John King (1792).
John Beckett (1806) [succeeded by Hobhouse in 1817.]
Henry Hobhouse (28 June, 1817) [resigned, July, 1827.]
No rule was laid down as to whether they should be in Parliament. Scrope Bernard was the only one to have a seat in the House of Commons whilst Under-Secretary of State.

APPENDIX

THE LAW OFFICERS OF THE CROWN
1790–1825

Date of appointment	The Attorney-General	The Solicitor-General
1788, 28 June	Sir Archibald Macdonald	Sir John Scott
1793, 13 February	Sir John Scott	Sir John Mitford
1799	Sir John Mitford	Sir William Grant
1801, 21 February	Sir Edward Law	Spencer Perceval[1]
1802, April	Spencer Perceval	Thomas Manners-Sutton
1805, 20 February		Sir Vicary Gibbs
1806, 12 February	Sir Arthur Pigott	Sir Samuel Romilly
1807, 7 April	Sir Vicary Gibbs	Sir Thomas Plumer
1812, 26 June	Sir Thomas Plumer	Sir William Garrow
1813, 4 May	Sir William Garrow	Sir Robert Dallas
1813, 22 December		Sir Samuel Shepherd[2]
1817, 7 May	Sir Samuel Shepherd	Sir Robert Gifford
1819, 24 July	Sir Robert Gifford	Sir John Copley
1824, 9 January	Sir John Copley	Sir Charles Wetherell

[1] Perceval, as an Earl's son, was permitted to decline the customary knighthood.
[2] He was not knighted until May, 1814.

GENERAL INDEX

[The numbers refer to the letter not the page]

A

Aberdeen, 20

Abergavenny, 189n., 220, 374, 384

Ackworth, 150, 245, 248

Adlington, 404

Alert, the (warship), 341

Alkrington Colliery, 272

Alnwick Castle, 342, 354, 388, 390

American War (1812–14), economic consequences of, 133

Amiens, Peace of, 230

Ancoats, Manchester, 275

Anderston, 138, 164n.

Anderston Water Company, 414

Arnold (Notts.), 330

Ashover (Derbyshire), 116

Ashton (Somerset), 7

Ashton, 121

Ashton-in-Willows, 393

Ashton-under-Lyne, 94, 200, 224, 260, 272, 278, 283, 289, 293, 327–8, 393, 411

Astle, 404

Atherstone, 212

Ayrshire, 123

B

Bagillt, 360

Bakers, combination of London master (1816), 202

—, combination of journeymen

—, (1799), 30–1

Baltic, the, 170, 413

Banbury, 22

Barton, 121

Barwell, 409

Basford (Notts.), 376

Bath, 58, 61, 70, 75, 80, 210

Batley, 43

Beckington, 396

Bedminster (Somerset), 7

Belfast, 414

Belper, 219

Benefit Societies. *See* Friendly Societies

Berwick, 39

Bewicke and Craisters Colliery (Wallsend), 355, 357

Bilston, 207, 375, 379, 383

Birmingham, 1, 301, 308, 380, 410

Birstall, 56

Bishop Wearmouth, 175, 179, 183, 349

Blackburn, 25n., 96, 110, 164n., 165, 280, 297–8, 300, 302–4, 308, 394

Blackmen [*i.e.*, blacklegs], 361

Blacksmiths of Lancashire, 260

Blaenavon, 382

Blanket manufacture, 361

Bleachers, the Lancashire, 312, 393

Boatmen of Deal, 211

Bolton, 23, 28, 96n., 99, 140, 146, 185, 201, 232, 243, 271–2, 285, 288, 291, 297, 300, 303–4, 308, 312, 362, 391, 393, 411

Boot and shoe makers, the, 7, 42, 74 sqq., 193, 210, 260, 308, 411, 413

—, Rules of their Society, 82

Bowbridge, nr. Derby, 216

Bradford (Wilts.), 45–6, 55, 59, 61–2, 64, 67–8

Bradshaw Hall, 393

Brecon, 189n., 206, 220

Breightmet, 393

Bricklayers, the, 159, 159n., 234, 260

Bridlington, 413

Bristol, 7, 72, 80, 372

Broomward, 414

Brownhills (Staffs.), 380

Burnley, 135, 298, 300, 302–4, 393

Burton, 215, 376

Burton-on-Trent, 223

Bury, 25n., 27, 94, 121, 224, 260, 291, 297–8, 300, 303, 308, 319

Butchers, the, 393

C

Calico printers, 147, 149, 151, 164–8, 172, 185, 260, 308, 393

Cannell coal, 11n.

Cantreff, 206

Cape of Good Hope, 336

Cardiff, 220

Carlisle, 63, 119, 165

Carpenters, of Liverpool, 2–5

—, of Yarmouth, 13

—, of London, 205

—, of Manchester, 234

—, of Sunderland, 407

Castle Eden, 14

Caulkers, the, 51, 53, 57, 69

Charters Moss, nr. Bolton, 96n.

Chatham, 53

Cheadle, 417

Cheadle Hulme, 121

Cheshire, 102, 147, 233, 268, 291, 306, 371

Chester, 204, 282, 315, 360, 371

Chorley (Lancs.), 25n., 393

397

CC

[The numbers refer to the letter, not the page.]

[The numbers refer to the letter, not the page.]

INDEX OF PERSONS

[The numbers refer to the letter, not the page].